WIRTSCHAFTSREGION OLDENBURGER LAND

BUSINESS LOCATION OLDENBURGER LAND

Herausgegeben in Zusammenarbeit mit
Published in cooperation with

Industrie- und Handelskammer Oldenburg
Oldenburg Chamber of Commerce and Industry

Autoren / Authors:
Thorsten Bruns, Lisa Knoll, Mareike Lange, Thorsten Lange, Peter Ringel,
Torben Rosenbohm, Claus Spitzer-Ewersmann, Alke zur Mühler

Sechste, völlig neue Ausgabe 2021
Sixth, completely new edition 2021

Kommunikation & Wirtschaft GmbH
Oldenburg (Oldb)

Bibliografische Information der Deutschen Bibliothek
Die Deutsche Bibliothek verzeichnet diese Publikation
in der Deutschen Nationalbibliografie; detaillierte bibliografische
Daten sind im Internet unter www.dnb.de abrufbar.

Das Buch erscheint im Verlagsbereich Regionalmedien.
Alle Rechte bei Kommunikation & Wirtschaft GmbH,
Oldenburg (Oldb)

Printed in Germany 2021

Das Manuskript ist Eigentum des Verlages. Alle Rechte vorbehalten.
Auswahl und Zusammenstellung sind urheberrechtlich geschützt.
Für die Richtigkeit der im Inhaltsverzeichnis aufgeführten Autoren-
beiträge und der PR-Texte übernehmen Verlag und Redaktion keine
Haftung.

Redaktion/Editorial:
Olaf Burblys, Kommunikation & Wirtschaft GmbH, Oldenburg
MEDIAVANTI GmbH, Oldenburg

Übersetzungen/Translations:
KERN AG, Sprachendienste, Bremen

Bildbearbeitung/Image processing:
Kommunikation & Wirtschaft GmbH, Oldenburg (Oldb)

Druck/Printing:
Gutenberg Beuys Feindruckerei GmbH, Langenhagen

ISBN 978-3-88363-427-2

Bibliographic information of the German National Library
The German National Library records this publication in the
German National Bibliography. Detailed bibliographic data can
be called up on the internet via www.dnb.de.

This book is published in the division Regionalmedien.
All rights reserved by Kommunikation & Wirtschaft GmbH,
Oldenburg (Oldb)

Printed in Germany 2021

The manuscript is the property of the publisher. All rights reserved.
The selection and compilation are protected by copyright. The
publisher and editor accept no liability for the accuracy of the author
contributions and PR-texts detailed in the contents.

Kommunikation
& Wirtschaft GmbH

INHALT
CONTENT

DER ENERGIEWENDER

The Energy Transitioner

AUTOR:
PETER RINGEL

Auf See ist ein klarer Kurs gefragt. Auf der Kommandobrücke eines Unternehmens ebenfalls. Und so gibt der gelernte Seemann Stefan Dohler nach seinem Antritt als EWE-Chef bald die Richtung vor: Der Regionalversorger soll in Zukunftsfeldern wie Wasserstoff, Elektromobilität und digitalen Dienstleistungen Fahrt aufnehmen – und den Klimaschutz als Kompass nutzen.

Bei der Neuausrichtung geht einiger Ballast über Bord. Der Konzern trennt sich von seiner Offshorewindtochter. Das Geschäft in der Türkei wird verkauft. Und beim Kohleausstieg zählte ein Bremer Kraftwerk des Unternehmens zu den ersten, die vom Netz gingen. „Was wir machen, machen wir richtig", bestimmt Dohler. Und zwar überall dort, wo man eine relevante Marktposition einnehmen kann. Die sieht er beim Offshoregeschäft in weiter Ferne, obwohl der Versorger mit Deutschlands erstem kommerziellem Windpark Alpha Ventus ein Pionier war. Um auf See vorne mitzuspielen, müsse man jedes Jahr bis zu 2 Mrd. Euro investieren. Weder Summe noch Risiko passen zur Bilanz der EWE, die im Jahr knapp das Dreifache umsetzt. Dohler zieht die Reißleine.

You need a clear course when you're at sea. And also if you're a captain of industry. And so the trained seaman Stefan Dohler is soon setting the course after taking over at EWE: the regional utility company should go full steam ahead in key future fields such as hydrogen, electromobility and digital services, with climate protection serving as the compass.

A certain amount of ballast is going overboard in the process. The company is shedding its offshore wind subsidiary. It is selling its business in Turkey. And the fossil fuel phase-out means that one of the company's power stations in Bremen was among the first that went off the grid. "When we do something, we do it properly", says Dohler. Particularly when a relevant market appears to be viable. As far as the offshore business is concerned for instance, he sees this as only a very remote possibility, despite the pioneering EWE played role here with Germany's first commercial wind farm Alpha Ventus. To keep ahead of the offshore game, they would have to invest up to 2 billion Euro every year. Neither the amount nor the risk have a place on the company's balance sheet, with annual sales of roughly three times that amount. Dohler pulls the ripcord.

Stärken kombinieren, Risiken teilen

Stattdessen setzt der Versorger auf Windturbinen an Land. Zusammen mit der Aloys Wobben Stiftung, die den Auricher Hersteller Enercon kontrolliert, will man aus der Flaute bei der Windkraft herauskommen. Mit der Telekom wird ein weiterer namhafter Partner gewonnen. Ein gemeinsames Unternehmen für Glasfaser-Infrastruktur soll in zehn Jahren eineinhalb Millionen Haushalte im Nordwesten mit schnellem Internet versorgen. Beim grünen Wasserstoff kooperiert EWE sogar mit rund 90 Unternehmen. Die Idee, alles alleine zu stemmen, hält der CEO für ein Relikt der alten Energiewelt. Gerade bei neuen Themen heißt Dohlers Devise: Stärken kombinieren und Risiken teilen.

Am EWE-Verwaltungssitz in Oldenburg – dort gibt es immerhin einen kleinen Seehafen – schnuppert der an der Mosel aufgewachsene Dohler nicht zum ersten Mal Küstenluft. Nach seiner Ausbildung zum Schiffsmechaniker, die ihn auch aufs Schulschiff „Deutschland" in Bremen verschlägt, will er eigentlich Kapitän werden. Auf den Containerfrachtern von Hapag Lloyd stellt er aber bald fest, dass die spannende Arbeit von der Landcrew oder elektronisch erledigt wird. Dohler entscheidet sich gegen ein nautisches Studium und wechselt das Element. Als Ingenieur für Luft- und Raumfahrttechnik verkauft er Kraftwerke in Asien und beherrscht nach einem berufsbegleitenden MBA auch Bankerjargon und Projektfinanzierung. Dann heuert er beim Hamburger Versorger HEW an, der später in Vattenfall aufgeht. Bei den Schweden, den fünftgrößten Stromerzeugern in Europa, steigt der Vater zweier Kinder bis zum Finanzvorstand auf.

Möglichst vor der Welle sein

Die Zuständigkeit fürs Zahlenwerk beim Staatskonzern tauscht Dohler mit der Verantwortung fürs Ganze bei der vergleichsweise kleinen EWE AG. Seit Anfang 2018 im Amt, sorgt der Vorstandsvorsitzende mit seinem Team in drei Jahren für eine neue Strategie, räumt das Portfolio auf und gewinnt mit Ardian einen Ankerinvestor für die Wachstumspläne. Die Mannschaft, knapp 9.000 Beschäftigte, wird neu organisiert und auf Performance getrimmt: „Wir dürfen den Veränderungen im Markt nicht hinterherlaufen", betont der Konzernkapitän, „sondern müssen vor der Welle sein." Prozesse sollen sich nicht länger an der internen Struktur orientieren, sondern am Kunden. Der wolle von Deutschlands fünftgrößtem Versorger nicht nur Gas und Strom, sondern auch Mobilfunk, Internet und Mobilität. Als gewerblicher Kunde außerdem Licht, Wärme oder IT-Dienstleistungen.

Mit seinem Kurs reagiert der CEO auf den fundamentalen Umbruch der Energiebranche. Beim Vertrieb von Strom und Gas sinken die Margen, die Erträge aus dem Netzbetrieb sind staatlich reguliert. Dohler will die konzerneigenen Netze für Energie und Telekommunikation weiter ausbauen, vor allem aber mit Energiewende und Digitalisierung Geld verdienen. Dazu gehört eine Plattform, die Verbrauchsdaten aus elektronischen Zählern sammelt. EWE und Dritte können den Informationspool auswerten und daraufhin Dienstleistungen oder Produkte anbieten. Eine Voraussetzung für das Geschäftsmodell: Kunden müssen darauf vertrauen, dass sorgsam mit ihren Daten umgegangen wird. Hier sieht sich der regional verankerte Versorger gegenüber anonymen Datengiganten wie Google oder Amazon im Vorteil.

Spektakuläre Aussicht von einem Windrad in Hatten.

Spectacular view from a wind turbine in Hatten.

Energiebranche im Umbruch

Biogas, Sonne und Wind ersetzen Atomkraft und Kohle. Rund die Hälfte unseres Stroms stammt bereits aus regenerativen Quellen. Im Nordwesten wird wegen der vielen Windkraftanlagen sogar mehr erneuerbare Energie erzeugt als verbraucht. Dieser Wandel wirbelt die Energiewirtschaft durcheinander – zahlreiche neue Unternehmen entstehen und die etablierten Konzerne bauen ihre Strukturen um.

Damit erlebt die Branche innerhalb weniger Jahre bereits den zweiten tiefgreifenden Strukturwandel. Mit der Liberalisierung waren Ende der 1990er-Jahre die Energielieferung und der Netzbetrieb getrennt worden. Durch die Marktöffnung kamen bei Strom und Gas viele neue Versorger hinzu. Beim Netzbetrieb ist dagegen weiterhin für jedes Gebiet ein Unternehmen zuständig. Wegen dieser Monopolstruktur unterliegen die Leitungsnetze der staatlichen Regulierung. Bei der Stromversorgung gibt es bundesweit vier Übertragungsnetzbetreiber und rund 900 Verteilnetzbetreiber wie EWE Netz.

Viele Versorger sind ganz oder zum Teil im Besitz der öffentlichen Hand. Das gilt auch für die EWE AG, die zu den größten kommunalen Unternehmen Deutschlands zählt. An der nicht börsennotierten Aktiengesellschaft hält ein Zweckverband, in dem 21 Städte und Landkreise aus dem Bereich Ems-Weser-Elbe vertreten sind, 74 Prozent der Anteile. Die Wurzeln des Unternehmens liegen in der Versorgung des Nordwestens mit Strom und Gas. Als Geschäftsregion kommt Ostdeutschland und über die swb auch Bremen hinzu.

Upheaval in the energy sector

Biogas, solar energy and wind are replacing nuclear power and coal. Regenerative sources already account for around half of our electricity. The many wind farms in the North West actually generate more renewable energy than is consumed. This transition is causing upheaval in the energy sector with the emergence of many new companies, while established corporations are having to reorganise their structures.

The sector is thus going through the second far-reaching structural transformation within a short period of time. Liberalisation of the sector in the late 1990s separated the supply of energy from corresponding grid operations. Once the market was opened, many new providers started supplying electricity and gas. On the other hand, each region still has just one company responsible for grid operation. The power grids are thus under state regulation due to the monopoly structure. Germany has four transmission grid operators and around 900 distribution grid operators such as EWE Netz. Together they are responsible for the country's power supply.

Many utility companies are wholly or partly publicly owned. This also applies to EWE AG, which is one of Germany's largest municipal companies. An administration union consisting of 21 towns and rural districts from the Ems-Weser-Elbe region holds 74 percent of the shares in the non-listed stock corporation. The company's origins are rooted in supplying electricity and gas in the North West. Another business region for the company is East Germany, together with Bremen through swb.

Combining strengths, sharing risks

Instead, the energy company advocates wind turbines on land. The aim is to get the wind power business out of the doldrums in cooperation with the Aloys Wobben foundation, which is the organisation behind the wind turbine manufacturer Enercon in Aurich. Another big-name partner to come on board is Telekom. Over the next ten years, a joint venture for fibreglass infrastructure is to provide high-speed internet to one and a half million households in the North West. There are even 90 companies cooperating with EWE when it comes to green hydrogen. The CEO sees the concept of one firm doing everything on its own as a relic of the old energy world. Particularly where new topics are concerned, Dohler's motto consists in combining strengths and sharing risks.

EWE's headquarters are in Oldenburg, which actually has a small harbour. It's not the first taste of coastal air for Dohler, who grew up on the river Mosel in central Germany. After an apprenticeship as a ship mechanic on the training ship "Deutschland" in Bremen, he actually wants to be a captain. But life on Hapag Lloyd's container ships soon shows him that the really exciting work is done by the crew on land or by the electronic systems. So he decides not to study nautical science and changes the element. His engineering degree in aerospace technology soon sees him selling power stations in Asia; while working, he also studies part-time for an MBA to acquire banking jargon and project finance skills. He takes a job with the Hamburg utility firm HEW which is subsequently taken over by Vattenfall. As the father of two children, Dohler's career with the Swedish company which is the fifth largest electricity producer in Europe takes him to the position of CFO.

Best to be ahead of the wave

Dohler then swaps his financial responsibility at the big player from Sweden with responsibility for everything at the comparatively small EWE AG. As CEO since 2018, Dohler and his team have spent three years implementing a new strategy, streamlining the portfolio and acquiring Ardian as an anchor investor for their growth plans. The workforce of about 9,000 employees has been reorganised and primed for optimum performance. "It would be fatal to lag behind the changes that are going on in the market," the boss emphasises. "Instead, we must keep ahead of the wave." Processes should be geared to the customers rather than internal structures. Customers expect Germany's fifth largest utility to provide not just gas and electricity but also mobile communications, internet and mobility. Corporate customers also want light, warmth or IT services.

The course chosen by EWE's captain is his response to fundamental transformations in the energy sector. Margins on electricity and gas sales are sinking, and grid operation revenues are state-regulated. While aiming to expand the company's own energy and telecommunication networks, Dohler sees the energy transition and digitisation as the main money earners. This also includes a platform for collecting consumption data from electronic meters. The information pool can be evaluated by EWE and third parties so that they can then offer corres-

Klimaschutz ist kluges Unternehmertum

„Digitale Teilhabe und Klimaschutz sind die großen Themen unserer Generation", ist Dohler überzeugt. Um EWE bis 2035 in eigenen Bereichen wie Energieerzeugung und Netze klimaneutral zu machen, sollen 10 Mrd. Euro in zehn Jahren investiert werden. Wer im Unternehmen Geld bekommen will, müsse den Beitrag für das Klimaziel nachweisen, im Vertrieb wie im Kraftwerksbau. „Wenn wir nicht jetzt handeln, werden wir unserer Verantwortung nicht gerecht", betont der Firmenchef. Das gelte auch aus kaufmännischer Sicht: „Klimaschutz ist kluges Unternehmertum." Wenn Nachhaltigkeit für Finanzmärkte, Verbraucher und staatliche Regulierer eine immer größere Rolle spielt, könne man sich dem Thema nicht verweigern.

Dohler führt als Beispiel das Bremer Stahlwerk an, das bislang mit Koks produziert. Würde stattdessen grüner Wasserstoff eingesetzt, ließen sich E-Autos mit klimaneutral erzeugtem Stahl bauen. Dabei ist ein langer Atem gefragt, mit Wasserstoff lässt sich wohl erst in einigen Jahren Geld verdienen. Dann aber sieht sich EWE gut gerüstet. Per Schiff importiertes oder in den eigenen Windparks erzeugtes Elektrolysegas lässt sich durch die Netze leiten und in den Salzkavernen des Unternehmens speichern. Beim Dienstwagen setzt Dohler schon heute auf Wasserstoff und tauscht den Hybrid-Volvo gegen ein Brennstoffzellenauto. Sein Motorrad ist weiterhin ein Benziner, kommt allerdings nur auf wenige tausend Kilometer im Jahr – der CEO findet selten Zeit fürs Zweirad.

Stellt er irgendwann auf elektrischen Antrieb um, kann Dohler die Ladestationen und Mobilitätsdienstleistungen seiner Firma nutzen. In dieser Sparte ist der Versorger überregional aktiv, weil es wie bei der Erzeugung erneuerbarer Energie eine gewisse Größe und Anzahl von Projekten braucht, um im Wettbewerb zu bestehen. Das Stammgebiet im Nordwesten allein ist dafür nicht groß genug. Gleichwohl versichert der Vorstandsvorsitzende: „Das Herz der EWE schlägt heute und morgen in der Region." Dort werden Breitband, Gas- und Stromnetze sowie die Erzeugung grüner Energie ausgebaut. Arbeitsplätze, Wertschöpfung und Dividende bleiben so im Nordwesten. Über einen Zweckverband halten 21 Städte und Landkreise aus der Region knapp drei Viertel der Unternehmensanteile.

Verzicht auf Limousine und Taschenträger

Durch die kommunale Struktur wird das Unternehmen als Gesprächspartner mit gesellschaftlicher Verantwortung wahrgenommen, wenn es etwa in Berlin gilt, Botschaften in die Politik zu tragen. In die Hauptstadt oder zu anderen Terminen fährt der Konzernchef meist mit dem Zug. Er verzichtet auf eine Oberklasselimousine und einen „Taschenträger", wie Dohler es nennt, der alles für ihn mitschreibt. Dass er wenig Wert auf Status legt, mag auch mit seiner Zeit bei Vattenfall zu tun haben. Geprägt habe ihn dort auf jeden Fall der hohe Stellenwert von Diversity. Skandinavische Belegschaften seien vielfältiger, Eltern führen auch in Teilzeit. Dadurch sind mehr Frauen in Spitzenpositionen zu finden, erklärt der 1966 Geborene mit dem blanken Schädel, „und

ponding services or products. One prerequisite for the business model is that customers must be able to depend on their data being handled with all due care and attention. Here the regionally based utility offers considerable advantages compared to anonymous data giants such as Google or Amazon.

Climate protection is clever business strategy

"Digital participation and climate protection are the major issues of our generation", says Dohler with conviction. Over the next ten years, 10 billion Euro are to be invested to give EWE a neutral climate footprint with its energy generating and grid operating activities by 2035. Whether in sales or power station construction, whenever anyone in the company applies for funding, they have to verify their contribution towards the climate objective. "We'll never live up to our responsibility if we don't act now", emphasises the company boss. This also applies in commercial terms: "Climate protection is clever business strategy". There's no getting away from sustainability with its ever increasing significance for the financial markets, consumers and state regulators.

Dohler illustrates this with Bremen's steel works, which ran on coke up to now. If green hydrogen were used instead, the resulting climate-neutral steel could be used to make electric cars. Staying power will be needed here: after all, it's going to take a few years before there's any profit in hydrogen. But then EWE sees good chances. Electrolysis gas imported by ship or generated in the company's own wind farms can be transmitted through the grid and stored in EWE's salt caverns. Dohler has already changed over to hydrogen for his company car, replacing his hybrid Volvo for a fuel cell car. His motorcycle still runs on petrol, but that's only for limited mileage each year: the CEO rarely finds time for his bike.

If he were to change to an electric drive, he could use his company's charging stations and mobility services. Here the utility company operates on a far wider scale. Projects need to reach a certain size and number to be competitive, as with the generation of renewable energy. But the company's established catchment in the North West is simply not big enough. Even so, the CEO gives firm assurance that "EWE's heart beats firmly in and for the region, today and in future." Here the company is expanding its broadband, gas and electricity networks, together with its activities for generating green energy. In this way, jobs, value creation and dividends stay in the North West. Just about three quarters of the company's shares are held by an administrative union of 21 towns and rural districts in the region.

No luxury limousine, no bag carrier

The municipal structure gives the company social responsibility as an ambassador and interlocutor for political negotiations in Berlin, for example. The train is Dohler's preferred means of getting to meetings in the German capital and elsewhere. He has no need for a luxury limousine or a "bag carrier", as Dohler puts it, to write everything

Die EWE arbeitet verstärkt daran, mehr Frauen in Führungspositionen zu bringen.

EWE is working harder to get more women into management positions..

nicht nur mittelalte weiße Männer mit Glatze." Die Unternehmenskultur lasse sich allerdings nicht von heute auf morgen umkrempeln, das brauche Zeit. Dass sich bereits etwas tut, zeigt eine Studie von Financial Times und Statista, die EWE als einem von 850 europäischen Unternehmen bescheinigt, bei Diversity Fortschritte zu machen.

„Wir können auf die vielen Talente nicht verzichten", argumentiert Dohler beim Thema personelle Vielfalt. Diese sei auch ein Faktor für den geschäftlichen Erfolg. Auch in anderen Bereichen will der Firmenchef mit Argumenten überzeugen. Als Ingenieur und Kaufmann benennt er Risiken und Chancen, wenn es etwa um Investitionen in neue Technologien geht. Er macht eindeutige Ansagen, zugleich ist ihm Feedback wichtig. Wenn Führungskräfte in Intranet-Blogs die neue Organisationsstruktur erläutern, können Beschäftigte das anonym oder mit Klarnamen kommentieren. Dohlers offene Art, sein Zuhören und transparente Entscheidungen kommen im Unternehmen und außerhalb an. Um einen klaren Kurs vorzugeben, braucht es offenbar kein nautisches Patent.

down for him. His indifference to status symbols may come from his time at Vattenfall. He was certainly impressed by the way they handled diversity. Scandinavian workforces are far more varied, and parents working in leading positions can even opt for a part-time basis. As a result, there are more women in top positions, explains the bald-headed 55-year old, "and not just middle-aged white men with no hair." On the other hand, he knows full well that corporate culture cannot be turned inside out overnight: that's something that takes time. The fact that things are already changing has been verified in a study by the Financial Times and Statista, confirming that EWE is one of 850 European companies to make progress in terms of diversity.

"We simply can't manage without all the many talents", is the argument Dohler gives for workforce diversity. This is also a factor in business success. The CEO wants to use the force of his arguments in other areas too. As an engineer and businessman, he is well aware of the risks and chances involved in investing in new technologies. He makes clear statements but also appreciates feedback at the same time. When senior executives explain the new organisation structure in intranet blogs, employees can add their comments either stating their names or remaining anonymous. Dohler's open approach, his ability to listen and his transparent decisions are well received both inside and outside the company. It seems you don't need to be a licensed mariner to steer a clear course.

Die Zukunft der E-Mobilität schon heute

Für eine lebenswerte Welt von morgen wollen wir heute die Fragen der Mobilität neu beantworten. Egal, ob Sie privat ein Elektroauto fahren und eine Ladelösung suchen oder ob Sie Mobilitätslösungen für Ihr Business einführen möchten: Unser Portfolio reicht von einer einfachen Wallbox für Privathaushalte bis hin zu komplexen innovativen Mobilitätslösungen für Unternehmen.

Seit 2017 sind wir der marktführende Betreiber von Ladeinfrastruktur im Nordwesten Deutschlands. Unsere 900 Ladepunkte werden dabei mit 100 Prozent Ökostrom versorgt. Da eine gut ausgebaute Ladeinfrastruktur die Basis für einen noch stärker wachsenden Elektromobilitätsmarkt ist, erweitern wir unser Ladenetz stetig. Damit liefern wir unseren Kunden die perfekte Basis, ihre individuellen Mobilitätslösungen umzusetzen.

Mit der EWE Go Mobility Card können Privat- und Geschäftskunden an diesen Ladepunkten grenzenlos Ökostrom laden. Außerdem haben sie Zugriff auf ein europaweites Netzwerk von rund 88.000 Partnerladepunkten.

Future of e-mobility begins today

We want to provide a new answer to e-mobility today, for the sake of having a world worth living in tomorrow. Regardless whether you need a charging solution for your private electric car or want to introduce mobility solutions for your business, our range extends from a simple wall box for private households, to complex innovative mobility solutions for companies.

We have been leading the market for the operation of charging infrastructure in North West Germany since 2017. Our 900 charging points are supplied with 100 percent green electricity. We are constantly expanding our charging network, given that a well-developed charging infrastructure is the foundation for further growth in the electromobility market. This gives our customers the perfect basis for implementing their individual mobility solutions.

With the EWE Go Mobility Card, both private and corporate customers can recharge their vehicles with unlimited green electricity at these charging points. It also gives them access to a network of around 88,000 partner charging points throughout Europe.

EWE Go GmbH

Information
Gründungsjahr: 2018
Leistungsspektrum:
Entwicklung und Bereitstellung von Mobilitätslösungen für Privatleute und Unternehmen wie z. B. billing@home, Wallboxen (Smart/Basic), Mobility Card, Schnellladestationen (Hypercharger), Ladeinfrastrukturservices Standort- und Fuhrparkanalyse, bauliche Vorbereitungen, Grundlagenschulungen zur E-Mobilität

Year founded: 2018
Range of services:
Development and provision of mobility solutions for private and corporate customers, such as billing@home, wall boxes (smart/basic), Mobility Card, fast charging stations (hyper-chargers), charging infrastructure services, site and fleet analysis, structural preparations, basic e-mobility training

www.ewe-go.de

Fidenti Personal GmbH

Fidenti Personal GmbH wurde 2015 gegründet. Die zwei Gesellschafter des inhabergeführten Unternehmens blicken auf langjährige Erfahrung und vertrauensvolle Zusammenarbeit in der Personalgestellung für Unternehmen in ganz Deutschland zurück. Mit der Fidenti Personal GmbH haben sie eine neue Plattform geschaffen, um Kunden mit ihrem Verständnis einer verlässlichen Partnerschaft und mit ihrem Netzwerk den bestmöglichen Service anzubieten. Erweiternd zur Arbeitnehmerüberlassung sowie der direkten Personalvermittlung, betreibt und unterhält die Fidenti Personal GmbH im Rahmen von Werkverträgen auch eigene Produktionsstätten und produziert dort im Auftrag von namhaften Windenergieherstellern den Formbau sowie GFK Verkleidungsbauteile für Windenergieanlagen. Spezialisiert auf gewerbliche Berufe, verfügt die Fidenti Personal GmbH über einen großen Mitarbeiter- und Bewerberpool, um den Anforderungen ihrer Kunden jederzeit gerecht zu werden.

Fidenti Personal GmbH was founded in 2015. The two partners at the helm of this owner-operated company look back on many years of experience and reliable co-operation in the field of personnel provision for other companies located in Germany. With Fidenti Personal GmbH, they have created a new platform to offer customers the best possible service with their understanding of reliable partnership and with their network. In addition to employee placement and direct personnel recruitment, Fidenti Personal GmbH also operates its own production facilities in the framework of contracts for work and labour, producing moulds and GRP cladding parts for wind turbines on behalf of renowned wind energy manufacturers. As a specialist for industrial occupations, Fidenti Personal GmbH has a large pool of employees and applicants to meet the customers' demands at any time.

Information

Gründungsjahr: 2015	**Year founded:** 2015
Leistungsspektrum:	**Range of services:**
– Personalberatung	– personnel consulting
– Personalvermittlung	– personnel placement
– Personalüberlassung	– personnel secondment
– eigene Produktion	– own production
Branchenschwerpunkte:	**Industrial focus:**
industrieller Form- und Kunststoffbau, Windenergie, Industriewerften im Schiffs- und Bootsbau, Lager und Logistik, Lebensmittel, Metall usw.	industrial mould and plastic production, wind energy, industrial shipyards and boatyards, warehousing and logistics, food products, metal etc.

www.fidenti-personal.de

ExxonMobil

Die Erdgasaufbereitungsanlage Großenkneten während der großen Inspektion 2020
The natural gas processing facility in Großenkneten during the major inspection in 2020

Versorgungssicherheit beginnt bei uns vor Ort

Erdgas ist nicht nur flexibel einsetzbar, sondern auch ein wichtiger Baustein für den modernen Energiemix von morgen. Deswegen suchen und fördern wir Erdgas in Niedersachsen. Dabei setzen wir auf eine verantwortungsvolle Produktion mit hohen Sicherheits- und Umweltstandards. Diese gelten auch in unserer Erdgasaufbereitungsanlage in Großenkneten. Seit fast 50 Jahren reinigt die Anlage das zuvor geförderte Erdgas, damit es von Haushalten und Unternehmen als zuverlässige Energiequelle genutzt werden kann. In den letzten Jahren konnten wir unseren Energieverbrauch für die Aufbereitung des Gases pro Kubikmeter um fast 30 Prozent senken. Eine von vielen Maßnahmen, mit denen wir die Energieeffizienz im gesamten Unternehmen laufend optimieren und die auf unsere Nachhaltigkeitsstrategie einzahlen.

Reliability of supply starts here

Natural gas is not only flexible to use but also an important component in the modern energy mix of tomorrow. That is why we explore for and produce natural gas here in Lower Saxony in a responsible manner, including high safety and environmental standards. These also apply to our natural gas processing facility in Großenkneten. For nearly 50 years, the facility has been treating the previously produced natural gas to make it suitable as a reliable source of energy for households and companies. In recent years, the energy consumption per cubic meter for processing the gas has been reduced by nearly 30 percent. This is just one of many measures that we are implementing for ongoing improvements in energy efficiency throughout the company, thus making a contribution towards our sustainability strategy.

Information

Seit der Inbetriebnahme unserer Erdgasaufbereitungsanlage wurden circa 200 Mrd. Kubikmeter Erdgas gereinigt – eine Menge, mit der man alle niedersächsischen Haushalte für mehr als 40 Jahre mit Energie versorgen könnte.	Since it started operating, our gas processing facility has treated approximately 200 billion cubic meters of natural gas – a quantity that could keep all households in Lower Saxony supplied with energy for more than 40 years.
Inbetriebnahme: 1972	**Commissioned:** 1972
Mitarbeiter: etwa 150	**Employees:** approx. 150

www.exxonmobil.de

KEHAG
Unternehmensgruppe

ERFOLG = ENERGIE + ERFAHRUNG

Als unabhängiger und zuverlässiger Energiepartner beliefert die KEHAG Unternehmensgruppe Geschäftskunden, Institutionen und Kommunen bundesweit mit Strom und Erdgas. Neben individuellen Energieversorgungslösungen bieten wir innovative Messkonzepte sowie die komplette Umsetzung kundeneigener Stromerzeugungsanlagen an. Seit vielen Jahren verbindet KEHAG erfolgreiches Wirtschaften mit sozialer und ökologischer Verantwortung. Dazu zählt eine umweltverträgliche Energieerzeugung ebenso wie soziales Engagement auf lokaler Ebene.

Information

Gründungsjahr: 2011
Mitarbeiter: 75
Geschäftsfelder:
– Energieversorgung
  (Strom und Erdgas)
– Messstellenbetrieb
– Energielösungen in den
  Bereichen dezentrale Versorgungskonzepte, erneuerbare
  Energien und Ladeinfrastruktur
  für Elektromobilität
Unternehmensstandorte:
Oldenburg (Hauptsitz), Kassel
und Wien (Österreich)
Umsatz: rund 297 Mio. Euro
jährlich
www.kehag.de

Year founded: 2011
Employees: 75
Business areas:
– Energy supply
  (gas and electricity)
– Metering operations
– Energy solutions for decentralised supply concepts,
  renewable energies and
  charging infrastructure for
  electromobility.
Company sites:
Oldenburg (headquarter), Kassel
and Vienna (Austria)
Turnover: around 297 million
Euro annually

ENERGIE WEITERDENKEN

Wie gestalten wir künftig die Energieversorgung? Durch unsere Beteiligung an einer Vielzahl von Forschungsprojekten, wie beispielsweise einem lokalen Leuchtturmprojekt, sammeln wir Erfahrungen und setzen diese in praktische Lösungen um. Dadurch können wir unseren Beitrag zur Energiewende leisten und entwickeln uns daher konstant weiter. Nur so können wir eine individuelle und innovative Lösung anbieten, die uns auch in Zukunft eine stabile, bezahlbare und ökologisch vertretbare Energieversorgung garantiert.

IHR ENERGIEPARTNER

Entdecken Sie mit uns die Möglichkeiten von zukunftsorientierten und modernen Energieversorgungskonzepten. Wir bieten Ihnen verschiedenste Produkte in den Bereichen dezentraler Energieversorgung, erneuerbare Energien und Elektromobilität an. Von der Konzepterstellung bis zu fertigen Lösungen. Wir unterstützen Sie dabei, Kosten zu sparen und gleichzeitig die Umwelt zu schonen. Sie möchten autark sein und den benötigten Strom direkt vor Ort dank Blockheizkraftwerk oder Photovoltaikanlagen erzeugen? Dann stehen wir Ihnen als Energiepartner zur Seite. Sie denken darüber nach, Ihre Wärmeversorgung zu erneuern? Abhängig von Ihren Standortbedingungen entwickeln unsere Experten für Sie eine effiziente und individuell zugeschnittene Lösung. Mit einer KEHAG-Lösung zur E-Mobilität tragen Sie dazu bei, die Elektromobilität in Deutschland weiter voranzutreiben. Ob für Ihre Firmenflotte oder als öffentlich zugängliche Ladesäule: Wir finden gemeinsam die passende Lösung. Wie sieht die Energieversorgung von morgen aus? Um Ihnen als KEHAG-Kunden langfristig erfolgreiche und innovative Energiedienstleistungen bieten zu können, investieren wir in unsere gemeinsame Zukunft.

SUCCESS = ENERGY + EXPERIENCE

KEHAG is an independent, reliable energy partner, supplying gas and electricity to corporate customers, institutions and municipalities nationwide. Besides individual energy supply solutions, we offer innovative metering concepts together with a complete implementation of customers' own power generating plans. For many years, KEHAG has been combining successful business with social and ecological responsibility, including both environmentally compatible energy generation and social commitment on a local scale.

ENERGY OF TOMORROW

What will the energy supply look like in the future? Our involvement in many research projects, such as a local light-house project, brings us valuable experience which we implement in practical solutions. We thereby contribute to the energy transition which contributes to a further development of our company. This is the only way for us to offer an individual, innovative solution for guaranteeing robust, affordable and ecologically sound energy supplies in the future.

YOUR ENERGY PARTNER

Join us to discover the possibilities of future-oriented, modern energy supply concepts. We offer a wide range of different products for decentralised energy supply, renewable energies and electromobility. From the initial concept to ready-made solutions. We help you save costs while protecting the environment at the same time. You want to be self-sufficient and generate the electricity you need on site with cogeneration units or photovoltaic systems? Then we are the energy partner at your side. Thinking about replacing your heat supply? Concerning your local conditions, our experts work with you to develop an efficient, individually tailored solution. With a KEHAG E-mobility solution, you help to advance electromobility in Germany. Whether for your company fleet or as a public charging station. Together we find the right solution. What will energy supply look like in the future? We are investing in our joint future to offer KEHAG customers innovative energy services that are successful in the long term.

So geht Licht heute

Unser innovatives Geschäftsmodell ist so einfach wie nachhaltig: Mit Light as a Service (LaaS) bieten wir eine Komplettlösung für moderne, umweltfreundliche Beleuchtung für Unternehmen und Kommunen. Unsere Kunden mieten ihre neue Beleuchtungsanlage, anstatt sie zu kaufen. Alle Leistungen, die im Rahmen einer Beleuchtungsmodernisierung und laufenden Wartung anfallen, sind in der Miete enthalten. Investition, Aufwand und Gewährleistung übernehmen wir. Unsere Vision: „Wir verändern die Welt der Beleuchtung – zum Nutzen von Unternehmen, Menschen und Umwelt."
Unsere Kunden profitieren von besserem Licht, geringeren Kosten und einer deutlichen Verbesserung ihrer Ökobilanz. Die Elektro- und Vertriebspartner unseres Partnernetzwerks schöpfen aus neuen Möglichkeiten und unsere Investoren profitieren von einem ökologisch sinnvollen Geschäftsmodell in einem stark wachsenden Markt.

Light as a Service – wenn aus Beleuchtung Dienstleistung wird

Light as a Service ist eine Innovation im Bereich Dienstleistung. Licht zu vermieten liegt besonders nahe, denn bei der Lichtplanung in Unternehmen geht es schon lange nicht mehr nur allein um die Beleuchtung an sich, Aspekte wie Sicherheit und Gesundheit am Arbeitsplatz, Umweltfreundlichkeit, Energieverbrauch und die Lebensdauer der Produkte werden zunehmend bedeutsamer. Als Dienstleister für LED-Beleuchtung übernehmen wir alles: Die Lichtplanung, die Auswahl der Leuchten aus einem breiten LED-Portfolio, die Projektsteuerung, Umrüstung sowie Wartung, Reparatur und Austausch im Rahmen unserer Produktgarantie. Und das alles für eine fixe monatliche Mietrate. Unsere Kunden erhalten die Lichtlösung aus einer Hand mit genau den Parametern, die sie benötigen.

Deutsche Lichtmiete
Unternehmensgruppe

Maximale LED-Beleuchtungsqualität für Unternehmen und Mitarbeiter

Viele Faktoren bestimmen die optimale Beleuchtung. Unsere Beleuchtungsprofis beziehen jedes noch so kleine Detail und jeden Wunsch in die Lichtplanung ein. Ergebnis ist ein technisch einwandfreies, für den Kunden wirtschaftlich rentables und umsetzbares Lichtkonzept – mit maximaler LED-Beleuchtungsqualität.
Die Qualität der Beleuchtung ist essenziell. Ermüdungserscheinungen und Unfälle werden reduziert; Arbeitssicherheit und Wohlbefinden steigen. Das richtige Licht fördert die Konzentration zu jeder Tages- und Nachtzeit. Mit der Erfahrung aus über 600 Umrüstungsprojekten und unserem umfangreichen Leuchtenportfolio haben wir für jede Anforderung die richtige Lösung. Unser ganzheitliches Premiumsortiment umfasst sowohl Leuchten aus der eigenen Produktion in Sandkrug (made in Germany) als auch Leuchten renommierter europäischer Hersteller wie BEGA, Zumtobel, Waldmann oder Regent.
Und schließlich ist auch die effiziente Lichtsteuerung aus wirtschaftlichen und energetischen Gründen heute ein wichtiges Kriterium. Von Bewegungsmeldern bis Tageslichtsteuerung – intelligente Sensorik ist wesentlicher Bestandteil einer optimalen Beleuchtungslösung, die wir für unsere Kunden planen und umsetzen.

Lighting today

Our innovative business model is as simple as sustainable: with Light as a Service (LaaS), we offer a complete solution for modern, environmentally friendly lighting in companies and municipalities. Our customers rent their new lighting system instead of buying it. The rent includes all services involved in modernisation and any necessary maintenance of the lighting system. We take charge of investment, expenditure and warranty. Our vision: "We change the world of lighting, to the benefit of companies, people and the environment."

Our customers benefit from better light, lower costs and a clearly improved carbon footprint. The electrical and sales partners in our partner network make full use of all new possibilities and our investors profit from an ecologically meaningful business model in a strongly growing market.

Light as a Service: turning lighting into a service

Light as a Service is a service innovation. It makes real sense to rent lighting, because planning the lighting systems in companies meanwhile goes way beyond the lighting itself. Increasing significance is also being attributed to safety and health in the workplace, eco-friendliness, energy consumption and product lifecycle. As service provider for LED lighting, we take charge of the following: light planning, selection of the lamps from an extensive LED portfolio, project management, modification and maintenance, repairs and replacements in the framework of our product guarantee. All for a fixed monthly rental instalment. In turn, our clients receive your lighting solution from a single source with exactly the parameters they need.

Maximum LED lighting quality for companies and employees

Many factors contribute towards optimum lighting. Our lighting professionals consider every tiniest detail and every request in their light planning. The result is a technically perfect, feasible lighting concept that is economically viable for the customer while offering maximum LED lighting quality.

Information

Gründungsjahr:
2008 in Oldenburg
Mitarbeiter: über 120 an acht Standorten in ganz Deutschland
Fakten:
– Nummer Eins im Wachstums-markt Light as a Service
– Geschäftsmodell vielfach ausgezeichnet
– bis heute über 600 Modernisie-rungsprojekte in den Bereichen Industrie, öffentliche Hand, Gewerbe und Dienstleistung

Year founded:
2008 in Oldenburg
Employees: more than 120 at eight sites throughout Germany
Facts:
– number One in the Light as a Service growth market
– multiple award-winning business model
– up to now more than 600 modernisation projects for industry, the public sector, commerce and the services

www.lichtmiete.de

The quality of a lighting system is essential. It helps reduce signs of fatigue and accidents with an improvement in occupational safety and well-being. The right light enhances concentration at any time of day and night. With experience from more than 600 modification projects and our extensive portfolio of lamps, we offer the right solution for every requirement. Our holistic premium range includes lamps from our own production in Sandkrug (made in Germany) as well as lamps from renowned European manufacturers such as BEGA, Zumtobel, Waldmann or Regent.

And finally, economic and energetic reasons make efficient light management important today. From movement detectors to daylight control, smart sensors are essential elements in the optimum lighting solution that we plan and implement for our clients.

DIE FAMILIEN-UNTERNEHMERIN

The Family Entrepreneur

AUTORIN:
LISA KNOLL

Nur wenige Geschäfte in der Oldenburger Innenstadt blicken auf eine so lange Tradition zurück wie Lederwaren Hallerstede. Das lebensgroße Pferd im Erker schaut seit 170 Jahren auf die Lange Straße. Dass „Die mit dem Pferd" ihrem Qualitätsanspruch auch in den letzten Jahrzehnten treu geblieben sind, sich dabei aber stetig weiterentwickelten und mit der Zeit gingen, ist das Verdienst von Annette Hallerstede. Schon als sie 1983 ins Familienunternehmen einheiratete, wusste sie: „Es ist mein Lebensplan, alles für diese Firma zu tun." Mit ihrem Sohn Maximilian ist inzwischen die sechste Generation am Zug. Zeit für einen Rückblick.

Ihren Mann Heiner lernte Annette Hallerstede Ende der 1970er-Jahre beim Reiten kennen. Es folgten gemeinsame Studienjahre in Offenbach und Münster. Doch mit dem großen Namen kam auch schnell große Verantwortung: „Eines wurde mir früh unmissverständlich von der Familie deutlich gemacht: entweder Mann und Geschäft – oder nichts von beidem." Bedenken, das Abenteuer Familienunternehmen zu wagen, hatte sie aber als junge Frau nie, wohl wissend, dass das Leben und Arbeiten mit drei Generationen unter einem Dach eine große Herausforderung werden würde.

Few businesses in Oldenburg city centre look back on quite such a long tradition as Lederwaren Hallerstede. The life-size horse has been peering down on Lange Straße from the bay window above the entrance for 170 years. It is thanks to Annette Hallerstede that in recent decades, "the shop with the horse" has remained true to its quality claim while continuing to develop and go with the times. Already back in 1983 when she married into the family company, she knew that "My life plan is to do everything for this business". Meanwhile her son Maximilian has taken over the reins in the sixth generation. Time for a retrospective.

Annette Hallerstede met her husband Heiner when horse riding at the end of the 1970s. They then studied together in Offenbach and Münster. But the big name soon brought great responsibility: "Right from the start the family made it clear to me: either the man and the business, or neither at all." But as a young woman she had no qualms about venturing into the family firm, although she was well aware of the fact that living and working with three generations under one roof would be a great challenge.

Nach der Geburt ihrer Söhne ging das Paar 1986 zurück nach Oldenburg. Dort absolvierte sie nach dem Jurastudium eine Ausbildung zur Einzelhandelskauffrau. Gemeinsam mit ihrem Mann reiste sie in den Folgejahren durch ganz Europa, schaute sich an, wie der Handel andernorts aufgestellt ist. Als Heiner Hallerstede 1990 die Firma übernahm, hatten sie jede Menge Ideen für einen großen Umbau im Gepäck, denn die Oldenburger sollten merken, dass nun eine neue Generation am Zug war.

Rationalität trifft Kreativität

Annette Hallerstede war von Anfang an in alle Abläufe im Unternehmen involviert. Auch in vorigen Generationen hätten die Frauen immer ihren Anteil am Erfolg des Unternehmens gehabt, erzählt sie. Die größten Veränderungen in der Firmengeschichte seien häufig von ihnen ausgegangen. „Es heißt nicht umsonst: ‚Der Mann ist der Kopf und die Frau ist der Hals, der den Kopf dreht.‘ Das war in dieser Familie immer so", sagt die erfahrene Unternehmerin mit einem Lächeln. Mit ihrem Mann habe sie immer eng zusammengearbeitet. Dabei ergänzten sie einander gut, denn er war der zahlenaffine Betriebswirt, sie die Kreative. Ihr gemeinsames Motto „Tradition verpflichtet zu immer neuen Anfängen" verlor sie dabei nie aus den Augen.

Durchsetzen musste sie sich damals dennoch. „Natürlich war es am Anfang schwer, als branchenfremder Newcomer allen zu beweisen, dass auch ich meinen Teil zum Familienunternehmen beitragen wollte", erinnert sich die 62-Jährige. So richtig verstanden habe ihr Umfeld das jedoch erst, als ihr Mann sich 1996 krankheitsbedingt aus dem Geschäftsalltag zurückziehen musste. Fortan führte sie den Betrieb allein. Drei Monate nach seinem Tod 1999 später erkrankte sie selbst schwer, die Ärzte machten ihr wenig Hoffnung auf eine Genesung. Doch sie ließ sich nicht unterkriegen und stürzte sich noch während der Behandlung in einen großen Umbau, um den Fortbestand des Unternehmens zu sichern. Rückblickend betrachtet sei das eine Art Therapie gewesen, erzählt sie heute.

Langfristiger Erfolg durch Kopf und Bauch

Dass das Familienunternehmen mit 170-jähriger Geschichte sich bis heute erfolgreich am Markt behauptet, ist zu einem großen Teil Annette Hallerstedes Durchhaltevermögen zu verdanken. Und auch Bedacht spielte seit jeher eine wichtige Rolle. „Bei uns ist jede Veränderung mit Augenmaß und Vorsicht passiert. Kopf und Bauch sind immer gleichzeitig gewachsen, deshalb haben wir uns nie verkalkuliert." Diesem steten, aber nie übereilten Wachstum der letzten Jahrzehnte sei es auch zu verdanken, dass das Unternehmen heute trotz Pandemie auf stabilen Füßen steht.

Zu den vorausschauenden Entscheidungen der letzten Jahre zählt unter anderem die bewusste Abkehr von schnelllebiger Billigware. „Als verantwortungsvolle Kaufleute müssen wir zukunftsorientiert handeln. Das geht nur, wenn wir auf hochwertige und nachhaltige Ware setzen. Denn unsere Stammkunden von heute geben ihr Qualitätsbewusstsein an ihre Kinder und Enkel weiter."

Annette Hallerstede war immer viel in Großstädten wie München, Hamburg, Düsseldorf und Berlin unterwegs und kaufte persönlich die Ware der nächsten Saisons ein. Hinzu kamen Aufenthalte in Ita-

Das Einzelhandelsgeschäft der Familie Hallerstede prägt seit mehr als 170 Jahren die Kaufmannschaft in Oldenburgs Innenstadt.

The shop belonging to the Hallerstede family has shaped the retail sector in Oldenburg town centre for more than 170 years.

Miteinander statt Gegeneinander

Der Onlinehandel ist einer der großen Gewinner der Corona Krise, der stationäre Einzelhandel einer der großen Verlierer – auch im Nordwesten. Während Amazon und Co. satte Gewinne einstreichen konnten, geriet ein großer Teil der Händler vor Ort in existenzielle Schwierigkeiten. Der Handelsverband Deutschland (HDE) sah bis zu 120.000 Geschäfte in Gefahr. So gab etwa die Hälfte der in einer Studie befragten Bekleidungshändler an, ohne weitere staatliche Unterstützung das Jahr 2021 wirtschaftlich nicht überleben zu können. Auch Versuche wie „Click and Meet" böten häufig keine neue Perspektive. 13 Prozent schätzten es mit Blick auf die Personal- und Gebäudekosten als Verlustgeschäft ein.

Bei aller Skepsis wird aber auch deutlich, dass viele Händler die Zeit des Lockdowns genutzt haben, um sich im Internet ein zweites Standbein zu schaffen. Insbesondere Händler in der Größenklasse zwischen zwei und fünf Millionen Umsatz im Jahr haben seit Beginn der Krise digitale Vertriebswege auf- und ausgebaut. Für knapp 40 Prozent der Befragten gab sie den entscheidenden Anstoß, um auf anderen Kanälen als im stationären Geschäft aktiv zu werden. 46 Prozent der Händler waren bereits vor der Corona-Krise auf digitalen Vertriebswegen wie Onlinemarktplätzen, mit Lieferservices, per Click & Collect oder über Social Media für ihre Kunden da.

Die Vertriebskanäle im Handel verzahnen sich zunehmend miteinander. Kein Einzelhändler kommt heute mehr ohne eine Präsenz im Web und in den Social Media-Kanälen aus. Corona hat deutlich gemacht, wie bedeutsam die digitale Verfügbarkeit und die einfache Bestellung von Waren für die Verbraucher ist. Deshalb ist es umso wichtiger, die Voraussetzungen für ein Miteinander der verschiedenen Vertriebsplattformen zu sorgen – auch wenn das manch alteingesessenem Einzelhändler nicht ganz leicht fallen dürfte.

After their sons were born, the couple returned to Oldenburg in 1986 where the law graduate did retail training. During the next few years, she and her husband travelled throughout Europe to see how the retail trade works in other places. When Heiner Hallerstede took charge in 1990, they had plenty of ideas for introducing radical changes because they wanted the people of Oldenburg to notice that a new generation had taken up the reins.

Rational meets creative

Annette Hallerstede was involved in all the company's processes from the very beginning. The women had always been involved in the success of the business in previous generations too, she tells. They were often the driving force behind major changes in the company's business. "After all, they say 'The man is the head and the woman is the neck that turns the head.' At least it's always been like that in this family", says the experienced entrepreneur with a smile. She always worked closely with her husband. They were a good match, with him being the businessman with a head for numbers while she had the creative ideas. They never lost sight of their shared motto, which says "Tradition is the obligation to keep starting anew".

Even so, in the early stages she had to assert herself. "Of course it was hard at the beginning: I was completely new to the business and had to show that I wanted to play my part in the family company", the 62-year-old recalls. But they didn't really understand what she meant until ill health forced her husband to withdraw from everyday business in 1996. From then on, she ran things on her own. Three months after he died in 1999, she herself was taken seriously ill and the doctors had little hope that she would recover. But she wouldn't be defeated and, while still undergoing treatment, threw herself headlong into major restructuring to safeguard the continued existence of the company. Looking back, she says she sees it as a kind of therapy.

Lasting success with mind and body

The continued success of the family company with its 170 years of history is due to a great extent to Annette Hallerstede's perseverance and staying power. Prudence has also always been an important factor. "Every change that we have made has been based on sound judgement and caution. Mind and body have always grown at the same time, so we have never miscalculated." This constant but never hasty growth of recent decades also means that the company stands on a secure footing today, even despite the pandemic.

One of the far-sighted decisions taken in recent years was the deliberate departure from short-lived cheap goods. "As responsible entrepreneurs, we must take a future-oriented approach. We can only do that by advocating top quality, sustainable goods. After all, our quality-conscious regular customers of today influence the mindset of their children and grandchildren."

Annette Hallerstede often went to cities like Munich, Hamburg, Düsseldorf and Berlin, personally purchasing the next season's goods. She also spent time in Italy to work on her own collections. "I always enjoyed being away on business, but that also made me all the happier to come back to my lovely city of Oldenburg", she emphasises.

With each other, not against each other

Online trading is one of the big winners of the corona crisis, while stationary retail is one of the big losers – and that also applies here in North West Germany. While Amazon & Co. have seen escalating profits, most local retailers have seen themselves being confronted with existential problems. According to the German Retail Federation (HDE), up to 120,000 businesses are at risk. About half of the clothing stores interviewed in a study said they wouldn't survive 2021 financially without support from the state. Attempts at solutions such as "Click and Meet" frequently failed to offer any change in perspective, with 13 percent seeing it as a loss-making venture in terms of staff and building costs.

But despite all scepticism, many retailers have clearly also used the time during lockdown to establish a second (online) mainstay. Since the crisis began, digital sales channels have been set up and developed particularly by retailers generating turnover between two and five million Euro a year. About 40 percent of the study respondents said that the crisis had given the crucial impetus to expand their stationary business along other channels. 46 percent of the retailers had already established digital sales channels such as online market places, delivery services or Click & Collect and used social media to communicate with their customers.

Retail sales channels are growing increasingly integrated. No retailer can survive today without a presence on the internet and in the social media channels. Corona has clearly revealed the significance that consumers give to digital availability and simple ordering procedures. That makes it all the more important to create the prerequisites for working together on the various sales platforms, even if some venerable old-established retailers might not find that so easy.

lien, um an eigenen Kollektionen zu arbeiten. „Ich habe die beruflichen Reisen immer genossen, aber wenn ich zurück in mein schönes Oldenburg kam, war ich umso glücklicher", betont sie. „Unsere Stadt hat inzwischen alles, was auch Metropolen bieten, ist dabei aber nicht protzig geworden, sondern geerdet und heimelig geblieben."

Nicht zuletzt deshalb liegt ihr die Förderung der Oldenburger Kulturlandschaft am Herzen. Bei jeder größeren Familien- oder Firmenfeier, zuletzt zur Eröffnung des großen Umbaus im Jahr 2019, sammelt die Familie Spenden für einen guten Zweck. Die Unterstützung der Erna-Schlüter-Operngesellschaft und der Erwerb des „Eiderland"-Radierzyklus für das Horst-Janssen-Museum sind nur zwei Beispiele für ihr kulturelles Engagement. „Warum sollen wir uns Materielles wünschen, wenn wir doch alles haben?", fragt die engagierte Geschäftsfrau.

Auf zu neuen Ufern

Damit ein Familienunternehmen auch nach mehr als anderthalb Jahrhunderten konkurrenzfähig bleibt, müssen zwangsläufig Neuerungen her. Für Annette Hallerstede war das nie ein Problem. Als Anfang der 1990er-Jahre das Internet zum großen Thema unserer Zeit wurde, sah sie sofort das Potenzial für einen weiteren Geschäftszweig: den Onlinehandel. Wenig später gingen schon mehrere Artikel pro Woche über den digitalen Ladentisch – in einer Zeit, in der Internetanschlüsse in Privathaushalten noch in weiter Ferne lagen, eine Sensation.

Nach der Erkrankung ihres Mannes musste sie sich allerdings für das stationäre Ladengeschäft und gegen den Onlineshop entscheiden. „Beides konnte ich nicht parallel bewältigen. Aber die Idee, unsere Ware auch online zu vertreiben, spukte weiter in meinem Kopf herum." 2008 wagte sie deshalb einen neuen Anlauf und gründete **Kofferworld.de**. Noch immer war sie eine der ersten in Oldenburg, die sich ins Onlinegeschäft wagten. Ein immenser Vorteil, denn: „Es geht oft nicht darum, besser zu sein als die anderen, sondern schneller." Der Erfolg sollte ihr Recht geben. Heute sorgt Kofferworld.de mit Kunden in ganz Europa für einen Großteil des Firmenumsatzes. „Ich war überzeugt, dass das ein Erfolg wird. Die Zeiten ändern sich, deshalb darf man nicht nur an alten Zöpfen festhalten."

Dass der Onlineverkauf nicht das Aus für den stationären Handel bedeuten muss, war für Annette Hallerstede selbstverständlich. „Es wird immer Kunden geben, die lieber vor Ort einkaufen möchten, und auch immer solche, die lieber online shoppen. Da ist es doch perfekt, wenn man beides anbieten kann und so zwei Welten Hand in Hand gehen lässt." Der Servicegedanke spielt bei Kofferworld.de deshalb eine ebenso große Rolle wie im Ladengeschäft in der Langen Straße. Wer einen Termin zur Videoberatung vereinbart, kann sich in Echtzeit verschiedene Taschen-, Rucksack- oder Schulranzenmodelle vorführen lassen.

"Oldenburg meanwhile has everything the big cities have to offer, without getting too ostentatious about it: instead, it remains well-grounded and homely."

That's just one of the reasons why she is so passionate about promoting Oldenburg's cultural landscape. Donations for charity are collected at every larger family or company celebration, including the recent inauguration of the major modifications in 2019. Supporting the Erna Schlüter Opera Company and the acquisition of the "Eiderland" etchings for the Horst Janssen Museum are just two examples of their cultural involvement. "Why should we want material things when we've got everything we need?", asks the committed businesswoman.

New ways of doing business

For a family company to remain competitive even after more than one and a half centuries, it will inevitably have to accept new things. That was never a problem for Annette Hallerstede. When in the early 1990s the internet emerged as one of the big new issues of our time, she immediately recognised the business potential of online trading. It wasn't long before several items per week were being sold across the digital counter – a sensation back in those days, long before every private household had its own internet connection.

However, when her husband was taken ill she had to opt for stationary retailing and give up the online shop. "I couldn't cope with both at once. But the idea of selling our goods online as well was ever-present in the back of my mind." In 2008 she had another go and founded **Kofferworld.de**. This still made her one of the first in Oldenburg to venture into online business, a move that brought huge benefits: "Often enough, what counts is being quicker than the others, not better." Her success soon proved her right. Today, a large share of the company's turnover is generated by Kofferworld.de with its customers all over Europe. "I was convinced it would be a success. Times change and there's no point in getting stuck in the past."

For Annette Hallerstede it was a matter of course that online sales wouldn't mean the end of stationary retailing for the company. "You'll always have customers who'd rather come into the shop and others who prefer to do it all online. So ideally, the best thing is to offer both and let the two worlds continue side by side." Service is therefore just as important at Kofferworld.de as in the shop on Lange Straße. Customers can make an appointment for a video consulting session where they can see a real-time presentation of various bags, rucksacks and school satchels.

Setting the points for the future

The company's highly committed workforce of 30 and more employees is one of the reasons why things go smoothly. Many of them have been here all their working life. It is no rarity for people to celebrate 40 years

Neben dem Ladengeschäft betreibt das Familienunternehmen mit Kofferworld.de eine europaweit erfolgreiches Onlineportal.

In addition to the shop itself, the family company also runs a successful online portal called Kofferworld.de.

Die Weichen für die Zukunft stellen

Dass das reibungslos funktioniert, liegt nicht zuletzt am großen Engagement der mehr als 30 Mitarbeiterinnen und Mitarbeiter. Viele von ihnen haben ihr gesamtes Berufsleben hier verbracht. 40-jährige Dienstjubiläen sind im Hause Hallerstede keine Seltenheit. Das Wort „Personal" sei dabei schon lange nicht mehr das richtige, sagt die Chefin. Es brauche heute „Mitstreiter", um das Geschäft im richtigen Geiste fortzuführen.

Sie selbst will künftig kürzertreten. Mit Sohn Maximilian und Schwiegertochter Katja leitet inzwischen die sechste Generation die Geschicke des Hauses. Den jungen Leuten überlässt sie gern das Zepter. „Die beiden arbeiten paritätisch zusammen – so, wie mein Mann und ich es getan haben. Trotzdem schätzen sie in vielen Angelegenheiten weiterhin meinen Rat und meine jahrzehntelange Erfahrung", sagt sie. „Es ist ein Miteinander auf Augenhöhe. Und das ist gut so."

Wenn sie abschalten möchte, zieht es die Seniorchefin ins Wochenendhaus am Zwischenahner Meer. Das war schon immer so. „Die besten Ideen hatte ich tatsächlich dort. Wenn gar nichts mehr ging, dann setzte ich mich auf den Steg, schaute aufs Wasser und dachte: Was sind deine kleinen Sorgen im Laufe der Welt?" So bescheiden, wie Annette Hallerstede durchs Leben geht, sind auch ihre Ziele, die sie sich für die nächsten Jahre gesteckt hat: Ein besseres Handicap beim Golfen wäre schön, und noch einmal an ihr liebstes Reiseziel Mauritius zurückkehren. Bei so viel Power wird ihr das sicher gelingen.

at Hallerstede. "Staff" is certainly no longer the right word for them, says the boss. Today it takes "co-workers" to move business on in the right spirit.

She herself wants to slow down a bit in future. Her son Maximilian and daughter-in-law Katja are meanwhile in charge of the company in the sixth generation. She is more than happy to pass on the sceptre. "The two of them work together on an equal footing, just like my husband and I did. Even so, there are many aspects where they still appreciate my advice and my decades of experience", she says. "It's a joint effort on eye level. And that's good the way it is."

When she wants to switch off, the senior company boss retreats to the weekend home on Zwischenahner Meer. It's something she's always done. "Actually, that's where I had my best ideas. When things came to a halt, I'd sit on the jetty, stare out at the water and think how insignificant my worries were in the bigger picture of things!" Modest is one way to describe how Annette Hallerstede has gone through life. And modest also describes her aims for the next few years: it would be nice to improve her golf handicap, and to return one more time to her favourite holiday destination Mauritius. That surely won't be a problem for someone with so much power.

DER PRAGMATIKER

The Pragmatist

AUTOR:
CLAUS SPITZER-
EWERSMANN

Handel ist Wandel. Suchte man nach einem Leitmotiv für den Kaufmann Erhard Flocke, es wäre hiermit gefunden. Dabei lief der Delmenhorster nie Trends hinterher. Vielmehr war und ist es für ihn wichtig, Veränderungen zielgerichtet anzugehen. Genau das fordert er auch für seine Heimatstadt: die Gestaltung der Zukunft.

Sänger Sven Regener, selbst aus Bremen stammend, hat der Stadt an der Delme einst ein musikalisches Denkmal errichtet: „Ich bin jetzt da, wo ich mich haben will – Und das ist immer Delmenhorst" schrieb er in seiner lakonischen Hymne an die Tristesse der vermeintlichen Provinz. Der Frontmann und Gründer der Band „Element of Crime" führte das Flüsschen Ochtum in die Pophistorie ein, arbeitete sich am örtlichen Nahversorger „Getränke Hoffmann" ab und schloss mit den Worten „Sag Bescheid, wenn du mich liebst". Ironischer Spottgesang, wütende Abrechnung oder verzweifelte Liebeserklärung? Von allem etwas.

Delmenhorst. Für Erhard Flocke ist das Vieles. Nicht gleich der Nabel der Welt, aber zumindest der Mittelpunkt seines Lebens. „Ich wollte hier nie weg", sagt er, „hier bin ich schon als kleiner Junge durch die Gärten getobt". Und hier – im Geschäft der Eltern – nahm auch seine berufliche Karriere ihren Lauf. Mehrere Jahrzehnte hat Flocke eines der wohl bedeutendsten Lederwarenfachgeschäfte im norddeutschen Raum geleitet.

Trade is constantly changing. If you wanted a leitmotif for the businessman Erhard Flocke, you wouldn't have to look any further. And yet the man from Delmenhorst was never one to run after trends. On the contrary, he felt and still feels it is important to take a purposeful approach to change. That is also exactly what he demands for his home town: to shape the future.

Singer Sven Regener, himself from Bremen, once composed a musical memorial for the town on the river Delme: "I'm there where I want to be – And that is always Delmenhorst", he wrote in his laconic hymn to the alleged provincial dreariness of the place. The lead singer and founder of the band "Element of Crime" put the little river Ochtum into pop history, venting his frustration on the local supplier "Getränke Hoffmann" and finishing with the words "Let me know when you love me". An ironical, satirical song? An angry reckoning? Or perhaps a desperate profession of love? Probably a bit of each.

Delmenhorst. For Erhard Flocke, the town is lots of things. Perhaps not necessarily the heart of the universe, but at least the centre of his life. "I never wanted to go away", he says. "This is where I raced around the gardens as a little boy." And here, in his parents' shop, is also where his career began. For several decades, Flocke has been running what must be one of North Germany's most famous leather shops.

Die Suche nach dem Wir-Gefühl

Die Stadt sei sein Hafen, seine Heimat, sagt der 74-Jährige. Mit ihr fühlt er eine tiefe Verbundenheit, auch wenn – wie er freimütig einräumt – „hier schon seit langem nicht mehr alles rund läuft". Oder liegt gerade darin der Grund für die Zuneigung? Delmenhorst ist rau und schroff, voller Risse und Bruchstellen. Sicher nichts für die Liebe auf den ersten Blick. Weder glattgebügelt noch feingeschliffen oder gar künstlich aufgehübscht.

Sind das womöglich alles Vorurteile? Vermutlich oft. Aber manche Ansichten basieren auch auf realen Ereignissen. Fest steht: Der Ruf der Stadt ist ausbaufähig. Was fehlt zum Aufbruch in bessere Zeiten? Das Wir-Gefühl, meint Flocke. Und Selbstbewusstsein. Man war immer Vorstadt Bremens. Nicht wirklich etwas Eigenes. Das prägt und hinterlässt Spuren. In vielerlei Hinsicht.

Andererseits: Man kennt sich an der Delme und weiß, was man aneinander hat. „Hier bin ich in Netzwerke eingebunden und verfüge über Kontakte in alle Bereiche des gesellschaftlichen Lebens", betont Erhard Flocke. Und das ist wichtig für jemanden, der lange Zeit im Herzen der Stadt ein Unternehmen führte, das die Delmenhorster seit Generationen schätzen.

Von der Aushilfe zum Chef

Die Geschichte nimmt ihren Lauf 1906. Sattlermeister Georg Strudthoff und seine Frau Elise gründen in Delmenhorst ein Lederwarengeschäft mit Polsterei, Sattlerei und Dekorationsartikeln. Sechs Jahre später verlegen sie den Betrieb in die Lange Straße – eine Entscheidung mit Weitblick von der man bis heute profitiert.

Nach dem Zweiten Weltkrieg übernehmen Ernst und Ilse Flocke die Geschäftsführung. Mit dem nötigen Fingerspitzengefühl steuern sie das Unternehmen durch die Jahre des Wiederaufbaus. Sie erweitern das Angebot an modischen Lederwaren und etablieren einen zusätzlichen Sortimentsbereich: Sport und Camping. Der Erfolg macht es darüber hinaus unumgänglich, weitere Geschäftsräume anzumieten. Was bleibt, ist der Name „Strudthoff", er entwickelt sich zur Marke.

Erhard Flockes Zeit beginnt 1971. Nach seiner Ausbildung steigt der 24-Jährige ins elterliche Geschäft ein und sichert damit den Fortbestand des Familienbetriebs. Lange habe er nicht überlegen müssen, erinnert er sich, denn „Interesse meinerseits bestand schon eine Weile". Schließlich hatte er schon mit 16 Jahren regelmäßig im Laden ausgeholfen und Feuer gefangen.

Rückblickend gesteht er allerdings ein, dass Übergänge von einer Generation zur nächsten immer auch eine gefährliche Gratwanderung sein und schiefgehen können: „Die Kunst bestand damals darin, unsere Stammkunden zu halten und gleichzeitig neue für uns zu gewinnen." Verlässlich bleiben, zugleich für frische Impulse sorgen – eine Herausforderung, die sich bei Betriebsnachfolgen häufiger stellt. „Wir haben den Spagat aber recht gut hinbekommen."

Was vor mehr als 100 Jahren als Handwerksbetrieb mit Ladenverkauf begann, prägt heute nachhaltig die Delmenhorster Innenstadt.

One of the lasting characteristic features of Delmenhorst's town centre today began life more than 100 years ago as a skilled craft business with a shop at the front.

Frische Ideen für die Mode von morgen

Mit mehr als 30 Milliarden Euro Umsatz im Jahr zählt die Textil- und Modebranche zu den wichtigsten Wirtschaftsbranchen in Deutschland. In rund 1.400 Unternehmen sind etwa 135.000 Mitarbeiterinnen und Mitarbeiter tätig. Als stärkster Wachstumstreiber gilt der Bereich der technischen Textilien, die in einer Vielzahl von Hightech-Produkten zu finden sind. Ein gutes Drittel ihrer Umsätze erwirtschaftet die Branche im klassischen Feld Mode und Bekleidung. Mode aus Deutschland genießt weltweit einen hervorragenden Ruf.

Die Bekleidungswirtschaft verfügt auch im Nordwesten über einige interessante Standorte. Zu den Unternehmen mit einem guten Namen im Oldenburger Land gehört etwa die Popken Fashion Group mit Sitz in Rastede, deren Wurzeln bis ins Jahr 1880 zurückreichen. Der Hosenspezialist Atelier Gardeur, beheimatet in Mönchengladbach, betreibt in Augustfehn einen Outlet-Store. In Wilhelmshaven hat Melvin Lamberty mit „BornOriginals" ein Label für individuell gestaltete Turnschuhe geschaffen, das auch international Aufmerksamkeit erregt. Und junge Designer, wie etwa die von „Bauernkind" in Lohne, zeigen, dass frische Ideen auf positive Resonanz stoßen können.

Ein zentrales Thema für die neue Generation an Modemachern ist die Nachhaltigkeit. Textile Produkte sollen heute verstärkt aus nachwachsenden Rohstoffen und zudem klimaneutral gefertigt werden. Den insgesamt 16 Textilforschungsinstituten in Deutschland, darunter das Faserinstitut Bremen e. V., kommt dabei eine wichtige Rolle zu. Die Palette der Forschung reicht vom Textilmaschinenbau bis zur Entwicklung moderner Fasern mit integrierter Sensorfunktion oder Hochleistungs-Textilien aus nachwachsenden Rohstoffen wie etwa Polymilchsäure.

Looking for togetherness

The town is his harbour, his home, says the 74-year old. He feels deeply attached to it, even though he frankly admits "things haven't been running smoothly here for a long time now". Or is that exactly the reason for his affection? Delmenhorst is rough and rugged, full of cracks and fractures. It is not a place to fall in love with at first sight. Neither smoothed out nor honed and polished or even artificially spruced up.

Could it all be prejudice? Probably, for the most part. But sometimes, opinions are also based on real events. One thing is for sure: the town's reputation has room for improvement. What will it take for things to get better? A feeling of togetherness, says Flocke. And self-confidence. Delmenhorst always has been Bremen's doorstep. Not really a place in its own right. This goes deep and leaves traces. In many respects.

On the other hand: people know and appreciate each other here. "Here I am part of the networks and have contacts to all parts of social life", emphasises Erhard Flocke. And that's important for someone who for a long time ran a business at the heart of town, and one that the people of Delmenhorst have appreciated for generations.

From helper to boss

The story begins in 1906. Master saddler Georg Strudthoff and his wife Elise found a leather business in Delmenhorst with upholstery, saddlery and decorative items. Six years later they move the business to Lange Straße – a far-sighted decision that continues to be beneficial today.

After the Second World War, Ernst and Ilse Flocke take over the running of the business and steer it with the necessary flair and instinct through Germany's years of reconstruction. They add fashionable leather goods to the range and establish an additional line of business with sport and camping. Furthermore, they are so successful that they have to find additional premises for rent. What remains is the name "Strudthoff" which becomes a brand of its own.

Erhard Flocke's time begins in 1971. On completing his training, the 24-year-old joins his parents' business, thus ensuring the continued existence of the family firm. He didn't have to think about it much, he remembers, as "I'd already been interested in the business for a while". After all, he had helped out regularly in the shop already as a 16-year-old teenager, which sparked his interest.

However, in retrospect he has to admit that the transition from one generation to the next always seemed like walking the tightrope: a dangerous undertaking that could always go wrong: "The art in those days was to make sure we kept our regular customers while acquiring new ones at the same time." Remaining reliable while also creating new momentum: a challenge frequently encountered when firms are handed down to their successors. "But we managed the balancing act quite well."

Fresh ideas for tomorrow's fashion

With annual sales in excess of 30 billion Euro, the textile and fashion industry is one of Germany's key economic sectors. About 135,000 employees work here in around 1,400 companies. The technical textiles found in a great many high-tech products are seen as the strongest growth motor. Classic fashion and clothing generate a good third of the sector's sales. German fashion enjoys an outstanding global reputation.

The clothing industry also has some interesting locations here in the North West. Companies with a good name in Oldenburger Land include the Popken Fashion Group with its headquarters in Rastede and roots reaching back to 1880. The trousers specialist Atelier Gardeur, based in Mönchengladbach, runs an outlet store in Augustfehn. In Wilhelmshaven, Melvin Lamberty has created a label for individually designed trainers with "BornOriginals" that are attracting attention on an international scale. And young designers, such as those working for "Bauernkind" in Lohne, show that fresh ideas can meet with a positive echo.

One key issue for the new generation of fashion designers is sustainability. Today, textile products should be made to a greater extent from renewable raw materials and also with a neutral carbon footprint. An important role in this context is played by Germany's altogether 16 textile research institutes, including the FIBRE Faserinstitut Bremen e.V. The range of research extends from textile mechanical engineering through to the development of modern fibres with integrated sensor function or high-performance textiles from renewable raw materials. For example, textiles such as polylactic acid.

Zuerst misstrauisch beäugt

In der Folge setzt Flocke Zeichen. Er gibt dem Thema Ledermode mehr Raum, auch in einem eigenen Fachgeschäft. Er stärkt den Bereich Sport. Und er wagt 1989 den Sprung über die Weser. Durch die Übernahme des 1931 gegründeten Traditionshauses Dittfeld bekommt Leder Strudthoff eine Bremer Adresse in 1-A-Lage: auf der Sögestraße. Das Geschäft wird bis heute unter dem Namen Dittfeld geführt und ist auf Kleinlederwaren und Reisegepäck spezialisiert.

Natürlich habe es Vorbehalte gegen den für Delmenhorster Einzelhändler bis dahin ungewöhnlichen Schritt in die benachbarte Hansestadt gegeben, weiß Erhard Flocke zu berichten. Normalerweise gehe es eher in die umgekehrte Richtung. Bremer Inhaber eröffnen Filialen in den umliegenden Städten und Gemeinden. Auch am neuen Standort sei er zunächst misstrauisch beäugt worden. „Aber ich bin dann einfach zu den Nachbarn und den Mitbewerbern gegangen und habe mich freundlich vorgestellt. Das kam gut an und hat das Eis in den meisten Fällen gebrochen." Viele hätten sich am Ende sogar erfreut gezeigt, dass der Betrieb inhabergeführt blieb und nicht von einem der großen Konzerne übernommen wurde.

Das Beispiel zeigt: Kaufmann Flocke macht das, was gut fürs Unternehmen ist. Notfalls – wie in diesem Fall – auch entgegen der Erwartungshaltung. „Bremen war zum einen ein wichtiges Signal an unsere Geschäftspartner und bot uns zum anderen die wunderbare Möglichkeit, uns noch einmal ganz neu aufzustellen."

Raus aus dem Tagesgeschäft

Ein Pragmatiker also; aber einer mit klaren Wertvorstellungen. Verlässlichkeit ist ihm wichtig. Berechenbarkeit. Glaubwürdigkeit. Ein Wort ist ein Wort. Man dürfe den Zeitgeist nicht ignorieren, aber man müsse auch nicht jedem Trend hinterherlaufen. „Ich kann und will mich nicht verbiegen." Im Übrigen seien die Werte, die im Geschäftsleben eine Rolle spielen, identisch mit denen, die im Privaten gelten.

Auch Kontinuität gehört zu Flockes Wertekanon. Und so passt es ins Bild, dass mit Sohn Julian 2005 bereits die vierte Generation in die Unternehmensführung eingetreten ist. Wieder gab es neue Ideen und Veränderungen. 2015 nahm die Familie für die bis dato größte Umbaumaßnahme der Firmengeschichte noch einmal richtig Geld in die Hand. In einer Zeit, in der die Konkurrenz aus dem Internet längst von Erfolg zu Erfolg eilte, investierten die Delmenhorster in den stationären Handel. Erhard Flocke sieht darin keinen Widerspruch. „Wenn wir unseren Stellenwert behalten wollen, dürfen wir nicht abwarten, sondern müssen etwas dafür tun."

Mittlerweile hat sich der Seniorchef aus dem Tagesgeschäft zurückgezogen. Bei seinem Sohn und seiner Schwiegertochter sieht er das Familienerbe in guten Händen. Dennoch hat Erhard Flocke nach wie vor ein kleines Büro über dem Ladenlokal, in dem er täglich einige Stunden verbringt – „als eine Art Hausmeister", wie er schmunzelnd

As time moved on, Flocke makes his own mark on the business. He gives more space to leather fashion, also in a separate shop. He puts more emphasis on sport. And in 1989 he dares to cross the river Weser. By taking over the traditional business Dittfeld founded in 1931, Leder Strudthoff acquires a prime address in Bremen's Sögestraße. To this day, the shop is still run under the name of Dittfeld and has specialised in small leather goods and luggage.

Of course the retailer from Delmenhorst met with reservations on taking the hitherto unusual step into the neighbouring Hanseatic city, reports Erhard Flocke. Normally things tend to move in the opposite direction: Bremen's proprietors open branches in the surrounding towns and villages. In the early stages, he was viewed with suspicion in the new location too: "But I simply went over to the neighbours and competitors and introduced myself in a friendly manner. This was well received and broke the ice in most cases." In the end, many were glad that the shop remained in the hands of the new proprietor and had not been taken over by one of the big chains.

The example shows that Erhard Flocke does what's good for companies. If necessary, as in this case, contrary to expectations. "While sending an important signal to our business partners, Bremen also offered us a wonderful opportunity to reorganise ourselves completely."

No longer part of everyday business

So yes, Flocke is a pragmatist; but one with clear-cut values. He sets great store by reliability. Predictability. Credibility. A word is a word. One shouldn't ignore the zeitgeist, but nor should one run after every new trend. "I've always tried to be true to myself." What's more, the values that are important in business are identical to those that apply to private live.

Continuity is another of Flocke's values. So it fits in with the overall pattern that his son Julian joined the company's management team in 2005, representing the fourth generation. Once more this triggered new ideas and changes. In 2015, the family once more invested a vast sum in the hitherto largest modernisation project in the history of the company. At a time when online competition was already racing from one success to the next, the Delmenhorst company invested in its brick-and-mortar business. That is not a contradiction for Erhard Flocke. "If we want to maintain our standing, we can't just sit back and wait, we have to do something about it."

Meanwhile, the senior boss has retired from daily business. He knows the family legacy is in good hands with his son and daughter-in-law. Even so, Erhard Flocke still has a small office over the shop where he spends a few hours each day – "like a kind of caretaker", he admits with a grin. But it can't be compared with the times when it was quite normal for him to work a 60-hour week.

In Delmenhorst tritt Strudthoff seit 2015 als Dachmarke der Filialen Leder Strudthoff, Jeans Strudthoff und Intersport Strudthoff auf.

Since 2015, Strudthoff has become the umbrella brand in Delmenhorst for the branches Leder Strudthoff (for leather goods), Jeans Strudthoff and Intersport Strudthoff.

gesteht. Aber das ist natürlich kein Vergleich zu den Zeiten, als eine 60-Stunden-Woche der Normalfall war.

Hier schlägt das Herz der Kommune

Gedanken macht er sich weiterhin über die Zukunft Delmenhorsts. Sein größtes Sorgenkind ist – wen wundert's – die Innenstadt. Viele Ladenlokale stehen leer, der Branchenmix stimmt nicht mehr. Attraktiv sieht anders aus. Und das liegt nicht nur an Corona und den Folgen der Pandemie. „In der Innenstadt muss das Herz der Kommune schlagen", bekräftigt Flocke. „Wir brauchen eine Mischung aus Handel und Gastronomie, die die Leute anzieht. Außerdem Menschen, die in der Innenstadt wohnen und sie wieder lebendig machen." So wie bisher könne es jedenfalls nicht weitergehen: „Die Politik muss handeln!"

Zurück zu Sven Regener. Der Musiker und Schriftsteller („Herr Lehmann", „Neue Vahr-Süd") und Erhard Flocke würden sich vermutlich gut verstehen. Beide stimmen eine Ode an den so gern unterschätzten Charme der Provinz an, an die kleinen Orte voller ungehobelter, krachender Poesie. „Sag Bescheid, wenn du mich liebst": Hiermit geschehen.

The heart of the community

He is still concerned about the future of Delmenhorst. He worries most about the town centre – which is no great surprise. Many shops are vacant, the mixture of businesses has got out of balance. No-one could call it attractive. And that is not just because of corona and the results of the pandemic. "The town centre must be the heart of the community", emphasises Flocke. "We need a mixture of retail and hospitality that will attract people. And we need people who live in the town centre and bring it back to life again." Things certainly cannot carry on as they have been: "Something has to be done, on the political level!"

Back to Sven Regener. The musician and German author ("Herr Lehmann", "Neue Vahr-Süd") would probably get on really well with Erhard Flocke. Both sing an ode to the frequently underestimated provincial charm of the little places full of unpolished, fulminating poetry. "Let me know when you love me": done!

KISS
Deutschland GmbH

Information

Gründungsdatum: 1. März 2016	**Year founded:** 1 March 2016
Mitarbeiter: 80	**Employees:** 80
Leistungsspektrum:	**Range of services:**
Einzelhandel mit Schwerpunkt Tabakwaren, Zeitungen, Back- und Süßwaren sowie Lottoannahmestellen und Postagenturen	retailing with a focus on tobacco products, newspapers, bakery products and confectionery together with lottery counters and postal agencies.
Standorte: 13 Shops	**Sites:** 13 shops

happyshop. Der Kiosk, der alles hat!

Die KISS Deutschland GmbH mit Gesellschafter Ömer Kalender und Geschäftsführer Manfred Klawitter führt seit dem 1. März 2016 die unter dem Namen happyshop firmierenden Kioske in Oldenburg und Umgebung. Täglich wird jeder Shop von 400 bis 600 Kunden besucht. Das Sortiment umfasst nahezu alle Artikel des täglichen Bedarfs. Der absolute Renner ist unsere bunte Stückartikeltüte. Es gibt elf Lottoannahmestellen, in zehn Shops befindet sich eine Postagentur, eine davon mit integrierter Postbank. Auch Bus- und Bahnfahrkarten sind in den Shops erhältlich, die an 365 Tagen im Jahr geöffnet haben. Derzeit gibt es 13 happyshops in Oldenburg, Rostrup, Varel und Rastede. 2022 wird ein neuer Standort dazukommen.

happyshop. The kiosk that has it all!

KISS Deutschland GmbH with partner Ömer Kalender and managing director Manfred Klawitter has been running kiosks under the name of happyshop in Oldenburg and the surroundings since 1 March 2016. Between 400 and 600 customers visit each shop every day. The range covers practically the full scope of everyday convenience goods. Our colourful single-item bag is an absolute hit. Eleven sites have a lottery counter and ten have a postal agency, one with an integrated post bank. Bus and train tickets can also be bought in the shops, which are open every day of the year. At the moment there are 13 happyshops in Oldenburg, Rostrup, Varel and Rastede. A new site will be opened in 2022.

Wilhelmhavener Str. 202
26180 Rastede • Hahn-Lehmden
Telefon: 04402-972060 • Fax 04402-972062

Wolke Back & Snack GmbH

Wir backen Glücksmomente

Wir legen größten Wert auf die Qualität unserer Produkte. Und das schmeckt man! Wir backen täglich – oder besser Nacht für Nacht – in echter Handarbeit und nach erprobten Rezepten, damit unsere Backwaren in perfekter Frische ihren Weg zu unseren Kunden finden.

Wolke ist ein Familienbetrieb aus Dinklage und fest mit der Region verwurzelt. Unsere Rohstoffe beziehen wir bei kompetenten Partnern. Dort bekommen wir alles, was wir zum Backen brauchen – streng kontrolliert und sorgfältig ausgewählt. Mit unserem Team aus professionellen Bäckern, zuverlässigen Fahrern, freundlichen Verkaufskräften, Zahlenvirtuosen und Organisationstalenten in unserer Verwaltung sichern wir zahlreiche Arbeitsplätze.

Die Wolke-Familie besteht aktuell aus mehr als 200 Mitarbeiterinnen und Mitarbeitern. Wir sind stets auf der Suche nach neuen Talenten mit Biss, die mit ihrer offenen, engagierten Art zu unserer Wolke-Familie passen. Talente werden bei uns gesucht und gefunden, gefördert und gefordert.

We bake happiness

The quality of our products matters a great deal to us. And you can really taste it! We bake every day, or rather every night, with real craftsmanship and use proven recipes to make sure that our customers receive perfectly fresh baked goods.

Wolke is a family company from Dinklage and deeply rooted in the region. Our raw materials come from expert partners who supply us with all the things we need for baking, with strict quality controls and meticulous selection. Our team consists of professional bakers, reliable drivers, friendly sales staff, number crunchers and organisation talents taking care of administration, thus safeguarding numerous jobs.

There are currently more than 200 employees in the Wolke family. We are always on the look-out for new edgy talents with an open, committed approach that fits in well with our Wolke family. We recruit, foster and promote talent.

Information

Gründungsjahr: 1961

Mitarbeiter: etwa 200

Angebotsspektrum:
Brote, Brötchen, süße Naschereien wie Kuchen und Torten sowie eine große Auswahl an GenussWerken – Snacks, kalte und warme Gerichte, perfekt für unterwegs und zwischendurch

Standorte:
26 Fachgeschäfte im gesamten Oldenburger Münsterland und Artland

www.baeckerei-wolke.de

Year founded: 1961

Employees: about 200

Range:
bread, rolls, sweet delights such as cakes and gateaux as well as a great range of tasty goodies: snacks, hot and cold meals, perfect for out and about and in between

Sites:
26 bakeries throughout the Oldenburger Münsterland and Artland

Die Cetex-Rheinfaser GmbH aus Ganderkesee ist Spezialist für den Handel mit Viscose- und Polyester-Stapelfasern. Traditionell importieren wir aus West- und Osteuropa, Asien und Afrika. Die Verwendungen für die gehandelten Fasern sind extrem vielfältig: Vom Babypflegetuch bis zum Putzlappen, von der Kissenfüllung bis zum Dämmmaterial (vor allem in der Automobilindustrie) – überall wird das Material eingesetzt. Seit einigen Jahren gibt es einen starken Trend zu Fasern aus recyceltem Material, etwa aus aufgearbeiteten PET-Flaschen oder Sekundärprodukten der Polyesterindustrie. Europaweit sind wir das einzige Unternehmen, das sowohl das „EU-Ecolabel" der Europäischen Union als auch das Umweltzeichen „Blauer Engel" vorweisen kann. Seit 2020 führen wir außerdem die internationalen Zertifizierungen „Ocean Cycle" und „Global Recycle Standard". Unsere 15 Mitarbeiter handeln jährlich mit rund 35.000 Tonnen Fasern und erzielen dabei einen Umsatz von 40 Mio. Euro.

Cetex-Rheinfaser GmbH

Cetex-Rheinfaser GmbH from Ganderkesee is a specialist company trading in viscose and polyester staple fibres which are traditionally imported from West and East Europe, Asia and Africa. The traded fibres are put to many different uses. From baby wipes to cleaning cloths, from pillow stuffing to insulation material (primarily in the automotive industry), the material is in use everywhere. For some years now there has been a strong trend to make fibres from recycled material, such as processed PET bottles or secondary products produced by the polyester industry. We are the only company in Europe to hold both the "EU Ecolabel" and the "Blue Angel" environmental label. We have also held the international "Ocean Cycle" and "Global Recycle Standard" certificates since 2020. Every year, our 15 employees trade with around 35,000 tonnes of fibres, generating turnover of 40 million Euro.

Information

Produkte:
– PreCoFILL® und PreCoPET®
– Polyester-Fasern
– Viscose-Fasern
– Spezialfasern und Garne
Branchen: Haushalt, Betten und Polster, technische Textilien, Automobil, Hygiene, Bau
www.cetex-rheinfaser.de

Produkte:
– PreCoFILL® and PreCoPET®
– polyester fibres
– viscose fibres
– special fibres and yarns
Markets: household products, bedding and upholstery, technical textiles, automotive, hygiene and construction

GOLDBECK GmbH

Information

Gründungsjahr:
1969 in Bielefeld
2008 in Bremen
2021 in Oldenburg
Mitarbeitende: mehr als 8.500
europaweit, 70 in Bremen,
7 in Oldenburg
Schlüsselfertiger Neubau:
Planung und Bau von Logistik-
und Industriehallen, Büro- und
Schulgebäuden, Parkhäusern
und Wohngebäuden
Serviceleistungen:
Property Services, Facility
Services, Parking Services
und Öffentlich-Private
Partnerschaften
www.goldbeck.de

Year founded:
1969 in Bielefeld
2008 in Bremen
2021 in Oldenburg
Employees: more than 8,500
Europe-wide, 70 in Bremen,
7 in Oldenburg
Turnkey construction:
design and construction of
warehouses and factories,
office and school buildings,
multi-storey car parks and
residential buildings
Services:
Property Services, Facility
Services, Parking Services and
Public-Private Partnerships

GOLDBECK im Nordwesten: In der Region zu Hause

Das Bau- und Dienstleistungsunternehmen GOLDBECK realisiert Gewerbeimmobilien in systematisierter Bauweise. Das sorgt für hohe Qualität, Wirtschaftlichkeit und Termintreue, schont Ressourcen und hat einen positiven Effekt auf den CO_2-Fußabdruck.

Auch das Medienhaus der Nordwest Zeitung hat GOLDBECK nach diesem Prinzip realisiert – ein Bürogebäude, das durch seine offene Architektur, flexible Raumkonzepte, modernste Gebäudetechnik und eine nachhaltige Bauweise alle Ansprüche an zeitgemäße Arbeitswelten erfüllt. Harold Grönke, Geschäftsführer der NWZ: „Steine verändern Köpfe – so könnte man stark verkürzt den Wandel unseres Unternehmens beschreiben, der durch den Umzug in das neue Gebäude möglich wurde. Das neue Gebäudekonzept macht uns beweglicher und schneller. Und auch die öffentliche Wahrnehmung des Unternehmens hat sich spürbar geändert."

GOLDBECK in the North West: at home in the region

GOLDBECK is a construction and services company that produces commercial properties with a systematic construction process. This ensures high quality, economic efficiency and punctual completion while saving resources, as well as having a positive effect on the carbon footprint.

GOLDBECK also used this principle in constructing the "Medienhaus" building for the "Nordwest Zeitung" newspaper: this is an office complex with open architecture, flexible room concepts, state-of the art-building technology and sustainable construction methods that fulfills all demands for modern working world. Harold Grönke, Managing Director of NWZ: "Bricks change brains: that's one way of describing what has happened to our company since we moved into the new building. The new concept makes us faster and more agile. And there has been a noticeable change in the public perception of our company."

Robert C. Spies

#WirklichMacher seit 1919 – nun auch in Oldenburg.

Seit über 100 Jahren gehört die Robert C. Spies Gruppe zu den führenden Immobilienunternehmen in Norddeutschland und ist seit 2019 auch auf dem Oldenburger Immobilienmarkt aktiv. Mittlerweile sind rund 100 Mitarbeiter beratend und vermittelnd in den Bereichen privatwirtschaftliche Wohnimmobilien, Anlageimmobilien, Industrie- und Logistikflächen, Büro- und Handelsflächen, Hotelimmobilien sowie Investment tätig. Unser inhabergeführtes und unabhängiges Beratungshaus mit Standorten in Oldenburg, Bremen, Bremen-Nord, Hamburg und Frankfurt begleitet Family Offices, institutionelle Anleger, Stiftungen und Privatkunden bei der Suche nach Wohn- und Gewerbeimmobilien. Dabei unterstützt unser Team aus qualifizierten Spezialisten unsere Kunden stets mit tiefgehender Marktkenntnis, aktuellem Branchenwissen und kreativen Ideen im Rahmen eines ganzheitlichen Beratungsansatzes.

#WirklichMacher (Makers and doers) since 1919 – now also in Oldenburg. The Robert C. Spies Group has been one of Northern Germany's leading property companies for more than 100 years and has bee n operating on the Oldenburg property market since 2019. Meanwhile around 100 employees act as consultants and estate agents for private housing, investment properties, industrial and logistics premises, offices and retail premises, hotel properties and investment. Our proprietor-run independent consulting firm with offices in Oldenburg, Bremen, Bremen-North, Hamburg and Frankfurt assists family offices, institutional investors, foundations and private clients in their search for residential and commercial property. Our team of qualified specialists always supports customers with in-depth knowledge of the market, the latest sector expertise and creative ideas in the framework of a holistic consulting approach.

Information

Gründungsjahr: 1919
Mitarbeiter: rund 100
Leistungsspektrum:
– Wohnimmobilien
– Anlageimmobilien
– Industrie- und Logistikflächen
– Büro- und Handelsflächen
– Hotelimmobilien
– Investment

Year founded: 1919
Employees: around 100
Range of services:
– residential properties
– investment properties
– industrial and logistics premises
– offices and retail premises
– hotel properties
– investment

www.robertcspies.de

Promondis GmbH

Die Firma Promondis GmbH ist ein inhabergeführtes Unternehmen in Lohne (Oldenburg), in dem sich alles um den Verkauf von Radladern, Teleskopstaplern, Hebebühnen und anderen Baumaschinen dreht. Das Unternehmen wurde im Jahr 2008 von Klaus-Ulrich Pöppelmann gegründet. Das herstellerunabhängige Unternehmen bietet außerdem einen Mietpark mit derzeit 100 Mietfahrzeugen, die kurz- und langfristig angemietet werden können. Ein Drittel der Fahrzeuge ist bereits elektrisch unterwegs.

Neben der Maschinenvermietung ist der Großhandel mit Gabelstaplern ein weiteres wichtiges Standbein des Unternehmens. Hierfür werden Fahrzeuge aus Flottenrücknahmen und Leasingrückläufer aufgekauft und sowohl an regionale Endkunden und Wiederverkäufer in aller Welt wieder verkauft.

Promondis GmbH is a proprietor-run company in Lohne (Oldenburg) where everything is about wheeled loaders, telescopic forklifts, lifting platforms and other construction machinery. The company was founded in 2008 by Klaus-Ulrich Pöppelmann. The company is not tied to any specific manufacturer and also offers a rental park with currently 100 vehicles for hire in the short and long term. One third of the vehicles already have an electric drive.

Besides hiring out machinery, wholesale trading with forklift trucks is another important mainstay for the company. This entails purchasing vehicles from fleet and leasing returns and selling them to both regional end users and resellers all over the world.

Information

Gründungsjahr: 2008
Mitarbeiter: 5
Leistungsspektrum:
Verkauf, Vermietung und Serviceleistungen für Gabelstapler, Radlader, Teleskopstapler, Hebebühnen und viele andere Baumaschinen

Year founded: 2008
Employees: 5
Range of services:
sales, hiring and servicing of forklift trucks, wheeled loaders, telescopic forklifts, lifting platforms and many other types of construction machinery

www.promondis-stapler.de

ray facility management group

Ganzheitliches Facility Management ist unsere Profession. Aus den einzelnen Bausteinen des klassischen Facility Managements, dem infrastrukturellen, dem technischen und dem kaufmännischen Gebäudemanagement, schnüren wir maßgeschneiderte FM-Konzepte für Immobiliennutzer, Immobilienbewirtschafter oder Immobilieneigentümer. Von der Gebäudereinigung über Industriewartung und Maschinenreinigung bis hin zu Wachschutz, Hausverwaltung oder Arbeitnehmerüberlassung – unser Dienstleistungsangebot deckt alle Bedürfnisse an bereichsübergreifendem Facility Management ab.

Die Unternehmensgruppe geht zurück auf das Jahr 1996. Seither wird das Leistungsangebot kontinuierlich erweitert. Ab 2007 etablierte sich die Dachmarke ray. Hier bündeln wir die Kompetenzen von mehreren spezialisierten Unternehmen, damit Sie umfassendes Know-how aus einer Hand bekommen.

Die ray facility management group ist ein familiengeführtes Unternehmen, das viel Wert auf Nachhaltigkeit und soziale Unternehmensführung legt. Unsere Mitarbeiter werden seit über 10 Jahren in unserem eigenen Schulungszentrum fortgebildet und die Führungskräfte in diversen Coaching-Maßnahmen weiterentwickelt.

Information

Gründungsjahr: 1996 unter dem Namen Nils Bogdol GmbH

Mitarbeiter: rund 3.000 in sieben Tochterunternehmen

Leistungsspektrum:
– Gebäudereinigung
– Industriereinigung
– Sicherheitsdienstleistungen
– Wartung und Gebäudetechnik
– kaufmännisches Gebäudemanagement
– Personalüberlassung

www.ray.de

Year founded: 1996 under the name of Nils Bogdol GmbH

Employees: around 3,000 in seven subsidiaries

Range of services:
– facility cleaning
– industrial cleaning
– security services
– maintenance and building technology
– commercial facility management
– placement services

Holistic facility management is our profession. We take the individual components of classic facility management, infrastructure, technical and commercial facility management, and put them together into tailor-made FM concepts for property users, property managers or property owners. From facility cleaning via industrial maintenance and machine cleaning through to security service, building management or employee placement, our range of services covers all the needs of cross-functional facility management.

The company group goes back to 1996. Since then, the range of services has been extended continuously. Ray was established as the umbrella brand in 2007, pooling the expertise of several specialist companies to provide comprehensive service from a single source.

The ray facility management group is a family business that sets great store by sustainability and social company management. For more than 10 years, our own training centre has provided further training for our employees, and the senior executives attend various coaching measures for their ongoing development.

DER WEITBLICKER

The Visionary

AUTOR:
CLAUS SPITZER-
EWERSMANN

Global erfolgreich, heimisch im Oldenburger Land: Kaum ein Unternehmen verkörpert diese Mentalität so sehr wie Big Dutchman in Vechta-Calveslage. Seit über einem Vierteljahrhundert gibt Bernd Meerpohl bei dem auf fünf Kontinenten vertretenen Weltmarktführer für moderne Stall- und Fütterungstechnik den Ton an.

Bestimmt 30 Mal sei er schon in Peking gewesen, sagt Bernd Meerpohl. Aber die Verbotene Stadt, eine der bedeutendsten Sehenswürdigkeiten der chinesischen Hauptstadt, habe er noch nicht besucht. Warum nicht? „Weil ich meine Sekretärin nach beruflichen Terminen immer beauftrage, den nächstmöglichen Rückflug nach Deutschland zu buchen." Länger vor Ort zu bleiben, hieße unnötig Zeit zu verschwenden.

Heimatverbundenheit und Arbeitseifer – diese beiden Eigenschaften kennzeichnen den Unternehmer aus Vechta-Calveslage sehr treffend. Meerpohl ist hier aufgewachsen, verwurzelt und im besten Wortsinne: zu Hause. Von der Wohnung ins Büro ist es nur ein Katzensprung. Der Vorstandsvorsitzende von Big Dutchman legt den kurzen Weg in der Regel mit dem Fahrrad zurück. Was er am Oldenburger Münsterland schätzt? „Die Leute reden Klartext. Und man kann sich auf sie verlassen." Beides sei wichtig in einer Welt, die sich permanent verändert. „Der Mensch braucht Konstanten." Und was fehlt ihm in der Region? „Ein paar Hügel vielleicht", meint er. Die Dammer Berge seien schon zu weit weg.

Successful global player at home in the Oldenburger Land: scarcely any other company epitomises this mentality as well as Big Dutchman in Vechta-Calveslage. For more than twenty five years, Bernd Meerpohl has set the tone at Big Dutchman, the world market leader across five continents for modern housing equipment and feeding systems.

He must have been in Peking at least 30 times, says Bernd Meerpohl. But he still hasn't been to the Forbidden City, one of the major tourist attractions in the Chinese capital. Why not? "Because I always ask my secretary to book the very next flight back to Germany once business has been done." To stay there for any longer would be an unnecessary waste of time.

Home-loving and passionate about his work: that's a fairly accurate way of describing the entrepreneur from Vechta-Calveslage. Meerpohl grew up here, it's where his roots are, and, in the best sense of the word, it's home. The office is just a stone's throw from where he lives. The chairman of Big Dutchman usually cycles the short distance. What does he like best about the Oldenburger Münsterland? "People say exactly what they mean. And they're totally reliable." Both so important in a constantly changing world. "People need constancy". And what doesn't the region have? "Well, a few hills perhaps", he says. He reckons the Damme Hills are already too far away.

Von der Handelsvertretung zum Welt-Champion

Bernd Meerpohl ist seit 1992 für Big Dutchman verantwortlich. Die Ursprünge des Unternehmens gehen auf seinen Vater Josef zurück. Der Geflügelbauer hatte sich 1958 überreden lassen, in Calveslage die Handelsvertretung für eine aus den USA stammende Firma zu eröffnen, die auf die Herstellung von automatischen Tierfütterungsanlagen spezialisiert war. Die Sache lief so gut, dass Meerpohl schon 1963 Geschäftsführer der Tochtergesellschaft Big Dutchman Deutschland wurde und schließlich 1985 durch ein Management-Buy-out das komplette Unternehmen übernahm. Der Firmensitz wurde von Pennsylvania in den Landkreis Vechta verlegt.

Es folgte ein beispielloser Siegeszug zum Weltmarktführer bei Entwicklung und Vertrieb von Stalleinrichtungen und Fütterungsanlagen zur modernen Geflügel- und Schweinehaltung – mit einem Umsatzrekord in Höhe von 986 Mio. Euro im Jahr 2019. Heute ist Big Dutchman mit Niederlassungen rund um den Globus vertreten. Standorte finden sich im brasilianischen Araraquara, im indischen Hyderabad, in China und den USA, in Russland, Malaysia und Südafrika.

Ist der Chef da nicht – Stichwort Heimattreue – viel zu oft unterwegs? Bernd Meerpohl schmunzelt. „Das war schon mal schlimmer." Da sei er sicherlich das halbe Jahr auf Achse gewesen. Zwischenzeitlich habe er das Pensum aber bewusst reduziert. „Ich bin inzwischen verheiratet und habe zwei kleine Kinder." Noch ein guter Grund, nach getaner Arbeit schnell wieder zurückzukehren.

Ihm selbst, erinnert sich der Mittfünfziger, habe der Vater schon früh Verantwortung übertragen, zum Beispiel beim Umgang mit Tieren. So war es nur folgerichtig, nach der Ausbildung zum Bankkaufmann und Wirtschaftsprüfer ins Familienunternehmen einzusteigen. Bis zu seinem Tod im Alter von 85 Jahren stand Josef Meerpohl dem Junior unterstützend zur Seite – als Aufsichtsratsvorsitzender der Big Dutchman AG ebenso wie als väterlicher Freund. „Wir waren selten unterschiedlicher Meinung, einen besseren Berater hätte ich mir nicht wünschen können."

Bauchmensch auf der Suche nach Antworten

Meerpohl bezeichnet sich selbst als Mann des Bauchgefühls. Und im Bauch grummelt es durchaus gelegentlich. Dann spricht der Zweimeterhüne – Stichwort Klartext – die Probleme offen an. Als im Frühjahr 2017 nahe der malaysischen Hauptstadt Kuala Lumpur ein neues Logistikzentrum für den asiatisch-pazifischen Raum feierlich eröffnet wurde, fragte er in seiner Rede: „Wie und von wem wird die Weltbevölkerung im Jahr 2050 ernährt werden?" Er machte deutlich, dass auch seine Branche eine Antwort geben müsse und dabei das Gleichgewicht von Wirtschaftlichkeit und Nachhaltigkeit nicht aus den Augen verlieren dürfe. Und fügte hinzu: „Ich bin mir sicher, dass viele Ideen zur Lösung dieser Frage hier entwickelt werden."

Dass dem Bereich Forschung und Entwicklung eine große Bedeutung zukommt, versteht sich angesichts dieser Worte von selbst. Rund 450 hoch qualifizierte Mitarbeiterinnen und Mitarbeiter sind in der entsprechenden Abteilung beschäftigt. 2016 wurde direkt an der B 69 eine nicht mehr benötigte Lagerhalle in ein modernes Testcenter umgebaut.

Markante Architektur an der B 69: Die Big Dutchman-Unternehmenszentrale in Vechta-Calveslage"

Striking architecture on the main road B69: company headquarters of Big Dutchman in Vechta-Calveslage

Landwirtschaft 4.0 auf dem Vormarsch

Niedersachsen ist ein Agrarland mit langer Tradition. Dabei geht es nicht nur um Anbau und Ernte, sondern auch um die Entwicklung und Produktion der dafür nötigen Technik. Eine zentrale Rolle spielen dabei Unternehmen im alten Oldenburger Land, insbesondere die beiden Landkreise Cloppenburg und Vechta sind hier involviert. So entwickeln Maschinenbauer und Stallausrüster vielfältige Innovationen für die Tierhaltung, den Landbau und die Verarbeitung von Lebensmitteln. Dank der zunehmenden Automatisierung werden Produktionsabläufe sicherer und ressourcenschonender.

Die Qualität der Maschinen und Geräte aus dem Nordwesten zeigt sich auch auf internationalem Terrain. Einen Großteil ihres Umsatzes machen die Unternehmen längst im Ausland. Namen wie Grimme, Prüllage oder Vogelsang verfügen auch international über einen mehr als guten Klang. Folge: Die Exportquote steigt kontinuierlich. Kontakte werden unter anderem auf der Agritechnica in Hannover geknüpft, der Weltleitmesse für Landtechnik. Die Region ist hier Jahr für Jahr stark vertreten.

Ein großes Thema war hier in den letzten Jahren die Digitalisierung der Landwirtschaft. Sie habe, sagt Professor Dr. Joachim Hertzberg von der Universität Osnabrück, „das Potenzial, den gesamten agrarischen Prozess im Pflanzenbau und in der Tierhaltung ökologischer und ökonomischer zu gestalten". Dazu rückt das komplette, hochkomplexe Wertschöpfungsnetz der Agrar- und Ernährungswirtschaft ins Blickfeld – gerade unter dem Gesichtspunkt, dass der Einsatz digitaler Technologie sowohl ökonomisch als auch ökologisch sinnvoll sein kann.

Fest steht: Die Agrarwirtschaft ist so zukunftsorientiert wie kaum eine andere Branche. Sie lässt sich mit Fug und Recht als Vorreiter der digitalen Transformation bezeichnen. Dennoch sind nicht alle damit zusammenhängenden Fragen beantwortet. So weist etwa das Zukunftslabor Agrar darauf hin, dass der Konflikt zwischen der Datentransparenz im Wertschöpfungsnetz und dem Schutz der Datenhoheit der Akteure bislang nicht gelöst ist.

From commercial representative to world champion

Bernd Meerpohl has been responsible for Big Dutchman since 1992. The company's origins go back to his father Josef. In 1958, the poultry farmer was persuaded to become the commercial representative for an American company specialising in automatic animal feeding systems. Business went so well that in 1963 Meerpohl was made managing director of the subsidiary Big Dutchman Germany; eventually in 1985 he took over the whole company with a management buy-out. The headquarters were relocated from Pennsylvania to the rural district of Vechta.

The company then blazed an unprecedented trail of success to become world market leader in the development and sales of modern pig and poultry housing equipment and feeding systems, generating record sales amounting to 986 million Euro in 2019. Today Big Dutchman has branches all around the world. It maintains sites in Araraquara/Brazil, Hyderabad/India, in China and the USA, Russia, Malaysia and South Africa.

If he loves his home so much, doesn't this mean he's away too much? Bernd Meerpohl grins. "It used to be worse than it is now." There were times when he was away for six months without a break, but he has now deliberately reduced his workload. "Meanwhile I'm a married man with two small children", says the businessman who is in his mid-fifties. Another good reason to hurry home after work.

His father taught him to take responsibility already at an early age, for example in dealing with animals. It was therefore the right thing for him to join the family business after training as a bank clerk and auditor. Right through to his death at the age of 85, Josef Meerpohl was always at his son's side to offer support and assistance, both as Supervisory Board Chairman at Big Dutchman AG and as a fatherly friend. "We rarely differed in opinion. I couldn't have wished for a better advisor."

Guided by gut feeling and searching for the answers

Meerpohl says he Is very much guided by his gut feeling. And sometimes the emotions can get the better of him. Then the six-foot-six giant calls the problems by their real name. No beating about the bush. During his speech at the official opening ceremony of a new logistics centre for the Asian-Pacific region near the Malaysian capital Kuala Lumpur in 2017, he asked: "Who is going to feed the world's population in 2050 and how?" He made it quite clear that an answer will also have to come from his own industry, while still keeping a balance between profitability and sustainability. He added: "I am sure that many ideas are being developed to solve this question."

These words explain the huge significance given to research and development at Big Dutchman, with around 450 highly qualified employees working in the corresponding department. In 2016, a disused warehouse right on the main road B 69 was converted into a modern test centre.

Agriculture 4.0 on the advance

Lower Saxony has a long tradition as an agricultural state. The focus is not just on cultivation and harvesting but also on developing and manufacturing the necessary technical systems. Companies in the old Oldenburger Land play a major role here, particularly in the two rural districts of Cloppenburg and Vechta. Here mechanical engineers and animal shed specialists develop a wide range of innovations for husbandry, land cultivation and food processing. Increasing automation makes production safer with less consumption of precious resources.

The quality of machinery and equipment from the North West also sets standards on the international stage. Companies have been generating most of their sales abroad for a long time now. Names such as Grimme, Prüllage or Vogelsang have acquired more than a good reputation also in an international setting. As a result, the export quota is constantly on the increase. Among others, contacts are made at the Agritechnica in Hanover, the world's leading trade fair for agricultural machinery. The region has a strong presence at this event year for year.

The digitisation of agriculture has been one of the key topics in recent years. According to Professor Dr Joachim Hertzberg from Osnabrück University, it has „the potential of making the whole agrarian process in plant cultivation and animal husbandry more ecological and more economical". This turns the focus to the whole, highly complex value network of the agri-food sector: after all, digital technology makes both economic and ecological sense.

One thing is for sure: scarcely any other branch is as future-oriented as agriculture. It rightly claims to be a pioneer of digital transformation. Even so, not all related questions have been answered. The Agricultural Lab of the Future for example draws attention to the fact that there is still no answer to the conflict between data transparency in the value network and protecting the data sovereignty of the players.

Nebenbei: Innovationen sind bei Big Dutchman nichts Neues. Schon vor rund 60 Jahren wurden erste Patente angemeldet. In den weltweit geführten Datenbanken finden sich heute über 700 Patent- und Gebrauchsmusteranmeldungen „made in Calveslage". Sie gehen auf etwa 300 Erfindungen zurück, die Hälfte stammt aus dem neuen Jahrtausend.

Und das Tierwohl? Meerpohl wirkt nachdenklich. Die Frage, ob man wirklich so viel Fleisch essen müsse wie etwa in Deutschland oder den USA, sei „legitim", sagt er und gibt sich überzeugt, „dass die Tiere in den meisten Teilen der Welt heute sehr ordentlich gehalten werden". Es gebe einen Umdenkprozess, dieser sei aber noch lange nicht beendet. Dabei blicke die Welt besonders Richtung Deutschland. „Wir haben eine Vorbildfunktion, auch wenn wir auf keinen Fall glauben sollten, dass sich alles, was bei uns funktioniert, problemlos auf andere Länder übertragen lässt."

Kein Mann für halbe Sachen

Eine zeitgemäße Landwirtschaft ist für den 56-Jährigen ohne Computerisierung und Digitalisierung schon lange nicht mehr denkbar. Und er weiß: Die Erkenntnisse der Informationstechnologie kommen auch dem Tierwohl zugute. So lassen sich etwa Stallklima, Fütterungsrhythmen und Beleuchtung über Sensoren steuern. Feuchte und Ammoniakgehalt werden automatisch erfasst. Reicht das Trinkwasser beispielsweise für die Legehennen nicht aus, signalisiert das Kontrollsystem dies sofort auf dem Bildschirm. Auch die Zahl gelegter Eier, das Gewicht des Geflügels und der Verbrauch von Futter werden digital dokumentiert und in der Cloud gespeichert. Simulieren lassen sich sogar Sonnenauf- und -untergänge. Licht gilt als wesentlicher Bestandteil einer artgerechten Tierhaltung und beeinflusst die Produktion positiv.

Das Potenzial der Automatisierung sei bei weitem noch nicht ausgeschöpft, die Entwicklung werde weitergehen, betont Meerpohl. „Es muss uns aber gelingen, unseren Kunden immer wieder den Nutzen der Digitalisierung zu verdeutlichen", bekräftigt er. Die Technik sei schließlich kein Selbstzweck, sondern solle dazu beitragen, die Ernährung der Weltbevölkerung langfristig zu sichern. Er selbst möchte seinen Teil beisteuern und Einfluss nehmen. „Wenn ich mich mit etwas beschäftige, dann engagiere ich mich voll und ganz." Halbe Sachen? Nicht mit Bernd Meerpohl.

Seine Arbeitszeiten hat er dennoch reduziert. Statt um 6 Uhr früh kommt er jetzt erst um 7 Uhr ins Büro. „Die Kinder möchte ich morgens noch sehen." Zum Arbeitsbeginn kümmert er sich um das Asiengeschäft, beendet wird der Tag mit Telefonaten nach Amerika. Um 18 Uhr macht er gern Feierabend, häufig wird es 20 Uhr. „Ich würde mich als Perfektionisten sehen, da kann ich nicht einfach etwas liegen lassen, nur weil die Uhr das vorgibt."

Incidentally, innovations are nothing new at Big Dutchman. They started registering patents already 60 years ago. Today there are more than 700 patent and utility model registrations "made in Calveslage" in the worldwide databases, resulting from about 300 inventions, half of them since the turn of the millennium.

And animal welfare? Meerpohl looks thoughtful. It's legitimate to ask whether we really have to eat as much meat as we do in Germany or the USA, he says, while being convinced that "today, animals are kept in very good conditions in most parts of the world". A lot of rethinking is going on, but this is still a work in progress. Here the world is looking particularly to Germany. "We are role models in this context, although we should be no means believe that things that work here are always going to work perfectly in other countries too."

Doesn't do things by halves

Contemporary agriculture without computers and digitisation is meanwhile simply inconceivable for the 56-year old. He knows that animals also benefit from information technology, with sensors to control housing climate, feeding rhythms and the lighting. Humidity and ammonia levels are registered automatically. If there is no longer enough drinking water for the layer breeders for example, this is immediately shown on the screen by the control system. Digital records document the number of eggs laid, the weight of the animals and their feed consumption and are saved in the cloud. It is even possible to simulate sunrise and sunset. Light is an important aspect of appropriate animal husbandry with positive impacts on production.

There is still huge scope for further automation, this is an ongoing development, says Meerpohl. "But we have to get our customers to understand the benefits of digitisation", he emphasises. After all, technology is not an end itself but just one contribution to feeding the world population in the long term. He would like to make his own contribution and play a part in developments. "When I get involved with something, then I give it my full commitment." Doing things by halves? Not Bernd Meerpohl.

Even so, he has reduced his working hours. Instead of starting at 6 am, he now doesn't get to the office until 7 am. "I want to see the children in the morning before I leave home." First thing in the office, he's dealing with Asia; at the end of the day, he's on the phone to America. He likes to finish work at 6 pm, but often he keeps going to 8 pm. "I'd say I'm a perfectionist. I can't just stop doing something because the clock tells me to."

He also deals with the bad news

What makes him a good boss? He sets great store by justice, says Meerpohl. That's why he found it so very difficult to make altogether 125 employees redundant in summer 2020. "But we had to take urgent action otherwise even more jobs would have been at risk." The sales figures for certain regions had failed to reach the targets set in 2016. For a long time they kept putting off the decision to make people redundant, also in view of the corona crisis. "But the point came when

Auch schlechte Nachrichten sind Chefsache

Was zeichnet ihn noch als Chef aus? Gerechtigkeit sehe er als hohes Gut an, sagt Meerpohl. Deshalb sei es ihm persönlich sehr schwergefallen, im Sommer 2020 insgesamt 125 Beschäftigten zu kündigen. „Aber wir mussten die Notbremse ziehen, sonst wären noch mehr Arbeitsplätze gefährdet gewesen." Grund für die Entlassungen waren Umsatzzahlen in einzelnen Regionen, die hinter den 2016 gesteckten Zielen zurückgeblieben waren. Man habe – auch wegen der Corona-Krise – lange überlegt, zu welchem Zeitpunkt man die Kündigungen aussprechen sollte. „Aber dann konnten wir nicht mehr warten." Und: „So etwas gehört leider auch zu meinen Aufgaben."

Am Ende bleibt das Bild eines Unternehmers, der sehr genau auf die Welt um sich herum achtet. Der Entwicklungen wahrnimmt und stetig versucht, sie mit Verantwortung und Weitblick zu steuern. Der mit sich und seinem Leben im Reinen zu sein scheint. Und der im Oldenburger Münsterland bestens aufgehoben ist – auch wenn das von ihm geführte Unternehmen längst in aller Welt Maßstäbe setzt.

Wenn es um tierfreundliche Stalleinrichtungen und Fütterungsanlagen für die moderne Schweine- und Geflügelhaltung geht, gilt Big Dutchman als Marktführer der internationalen Branche.

Big Dutchman is the international market leader when it comes to animal-friendly housing equipment and feeding systems for modern pig and poultry production.

we couldn't wait any longer." And: "Unfortunately, this is also one of the tasks incumbent on me."

All in all, we see the picture of an entrepreneur who sees exactly what is going on around him. A man who is aware of developments and tries to steer them with responsibility and a vision. A man who seems to be at peace with himself and his life. And a man who fits in well here in the Oldenburger Münsterland even though the company he runs meanwhile sets standards all over the world.

Ruhe Agrar GmbH

Als landwirtschaftlich geprägtes Familienunternehmen verwaltet die Ruhe Agrar vom Hauptsitz in Lüsche mehrere landwirtschaftliche Betriebe in Niedersachsen, Mecklenburg-Vorpommern und Brandenburg. Das Bestreben des Unternehmens ist es, Regionen mit innovativen, nachhaltigen und in sich geschlossenen Konzepten zu stärken und einen positiven Beitrag zur Energiewende zu leisten. Mit viel Erfahrung und Leidenschaft sowie einem modernen Maschinenpark arbeitet das Unternehmen im Bereich der Veredelung landwirtschaftlicher Erzeugnisse durch Biogasproduktion, Fernwärmeversorgung und Rindermast. Während Wind- und Solarenergie wetterabhängig sind, steht Biogas als Energieträger jederzeit zur Verfügung. In einem geschlossenen System kann Energie besonders effizient und ressourcenschonend produziert werden. Diesen Sachverhalt macht Ruhe Agrar sich zunutze. Als moderner, nachhaltiger Energieversorger der Region.

As an agricultural family business, Ruhe Agrar manages several agricultural operations in Lower Saxony, Mecklenburg-Western Pomerania and Brandenburg from its headquarters in Lüsche. The aim of the company is to strengthen the region with an innovative, sustainable and self-contained concept and to make a positive contribution to the energy transition. With a lot of experience and passion as well as modern machinery, the company works in the refinement of agricultural products through biogas production, district heating supply and cattle fattening. While wind and solar energy are weather-dependent, biogas is always available as an energy source. In a closed system, energy can be produced particularly efficiently and in a way that conserves resources. Ruhe Agrar takes advantage of this fact as a modern, sustainable energy supplier in the region.

Information

Gründungsjahr: 2010	**Year founded:** 2010
Mitarbeiter: 130 (Unternehmensgruppe)	**Employees:** 130 (group of companies)
Leistungsspektrum:	**Range of services:**
– Landwirtschaft	– agriculture
– Biogas	– biogas
– Fernwärme	– district heating
– Rindermast	– bull fattening
www.ruhe-agrar.de	

Ruhe Biogas Service GmbH

Als Unternehmen der Ruhe-Gruppe hat die Ruhe Biogas Service ihren Ursprung in der Betreuung der Biogasanlagen und Blockheizkraftwerke der Ruhe Agrar. Zum Tagesgeschäft gehörte bisher die Montage sowie das Instandsetzen und Instandhalten von Blockheizkraftwerken und von technischen Komponenten für Biogasanlagen.
Die Ruhe Biogas Service bietet heute Technologien an, um aus Biogas die alternativen und nachhaltigen Kraftstoffe Biomethan und Bio-LNG („Liquefied Natural Gas") zu erzeugen. Eine produzierte Tonne Bio-LNG bedeutet 3.750 Kilometer Reise ohne Emissionen. Ruhe Biogas Service hilft damit den wirtschaftlichen Betrieb von Biogasanlagen nach dem EEG sicherzustellen und einen Beitrag zur CO_2-Einsparung im Verkehrssektor zu leisten.

As a company of the Ruhe Group, Ruhe Biogas Service has its origins in the service of the biogas plants and combined heat and power plants of the Ruhe Agrar. Up to now, day-to-day business has included the assembly, repair and maintenance of combined heat and power plants as well as technical components for biogas plants.
The Ruhe Biogas Service offers technologies to produce the alternative and sustainable fuels biomethane and bio-LNG („Liquefied Natural Gas") from biogas. One ton of bio-LNG produced means 3,750 km of travel without emissions. Ruhe Biogas Service helps to ensure the economic operation of biogas plants according to the EEG and to make a contribution to CO_2 savings in the transport sector.

Information

Gründungsjahr: 2017	**Year founded:** 2017
Mitarbeiter: 9	**Employees:** 9
Leistungsspektrum:	**Range of services:**
– Technischer BHKW- und Anlagenservice	– technical CHP and system service
– Biomethan und Bio-LNG	– biomethane and bio-LNG
– Fachbetrieb nach Wasserhaushaltsgesetz	– specialist company according to the Water Resources Act
www.ruhe-biogas-service.de	

Weltweit die Nr. 1

1938 haben die Big Dutchman-Firmengründer in den USA die erste automatische Fütterungsanlage der Welt erfunden. Heute befindet sich die Zentrale des lupenreinen Familienunternehmens in Vechta-Calveslage.

Geht es um die Entwicklung und den Vertrieb von tierfreundlichen Stalleinrichtungen und Fütterungsanlagen für die moderne Schweine- und Geflügelhaltung, gilt Big Dutchman als Marktführer der internationalen Branche. Auf fünf Kontinenten in mehr als 100 Ländern der Erde steht das Big Dutchman-Markenzeichen für dauerhafte Qualität, schnellen Service und großes Know-how.

Das lückenlose Big Dutchman-Produktprogramm umfasst einfache Anlagen, computergesteuerte Fütterungseinrichtungen mit Ausrüstungen für die Klimaregelung, Abluftreinigung und Reststoffverwertung sowie Computer-Hard- und Software für das Management. Der Leistungsumfang reicht vom Aufbau kleiner Landwirtschaftsbetriebe bis hin zu voll integrierten Farmkomplexen – vom ersten Konzept bis zur Inbetriebnahme.

Information

Gründungsjahr: 1938

Mitarbeiter: mehr als 3.400 weltweit, davon rund 900 in Vechta-Calveslage

Leistungsspektrum: Entwicklung und Vertrieb von tierfreundlichen Stalleinrichtungen und Fütterungsanlagen für die moderne Schweine- und Geflügelhaltung

weltweit: Die Produkte werden über sieben regionale Hauptniederlassungen und Logistikzentren, mehr als zwei Dutzend Niederlassungen und etwa 200 unabhängige Agenturen weltweit vertrieben.

Founding year: 1938

Employees: more than 3,400 worldwide, with approx. 900 in Vechta-Calveslage

Range of services: development and distribution of animal-friendly housing and feeding equipment for modern pig and poultry production

Worldwide: The products are distributed worldwide via seven regional head offices and logistics centres, more than two dozen offices and about 200 independent agencies.

www.bigdutchman.de

Big Dutchman AG

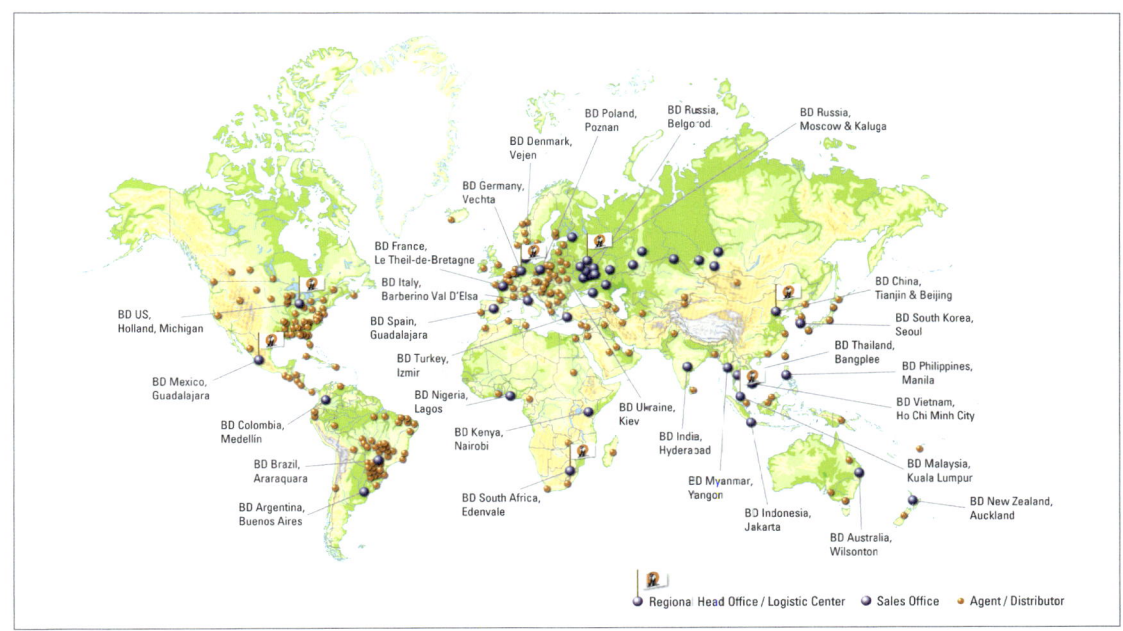

Mit mehr als 30 Tochterfirmen in allen wichtigen internationalen Märkten ist Big Dutchman weltweiter Marktführer in seinem Branchensegment.

With more than 30 subsidiaries in all key international markets, Big Dutchman is the global market leader in its industry segment.

The World's No. 1

In 1938, the Big Dutchman founders invented the world's first automatic chain feeder in the USA. Today, the headquarters of the true family business are located in Vechta-Calveslage, Germany. With regard to the development and distribution of animal-friendly housing and feeding equipment for modern pig and poultry management, Big Dutchman is considered to be the international market leader. Across five continents and in more than 100 countries around the world, Big Dutchman is a trademark for lasting quality, reliable service and extensive know-how.

The complete Big Dutchman product line comprises simple installations, computer-controlled feeding equipment with devices for climate control, exhaust air and residue treatment as well as computer hardware and software for management. The scope of services includes fitting small farms as well as fully-integrated farm complexes – from the first concept all the way to commissioning.

DER NIMMERMÜDE

The Indefatigable

AUTOR:
CLAUS SPITZER-
EWERSMANN

HELMUT URBAN

Auf einem eher kleinen Bauernhof in Wüsting entsteht die Idee zu einem weltweit agierenden Agrartechnik-Unternehmen. Doch Gründer Helmut Urban reicht das nicht. Mit der „LandTageNord" etabliert er eine höchst erfolgreiche Landwirtschaftsmesse, die Jahr für Jahr Zehntausende in die Region lockt. Und er hat noch mehr vor.

Anknüpfungspunkte für ein Gespräch mit Helmut Urban finden sich einige. Der 70-Jährige aus Wüsting führt schließlich seit Jahrzehnten ein mehr oder minder öffentliches Leben. Und will davon auch im Alter nicht lassen. Im Gegenteil, es mangelt ihm nicht an Ideen. Gerade erst hat er mit den „Urban ClassX" – Corona zum Trotz – ein Reitturnier auf die Beine gestellt. Wenige Monate zuvor gehörte er zu den Initiatoren des örtlichen Autokinos. Ein kulturelles Highlight inmitten der Pandemie-Tristesse. „Man kann doch das Leben deshalb nicht einstellen", sagt er. Und man sieht ihm an, dass sich da schon wieder etwas Neues im Kopf zusammenbraut.

Aber gehen wir es chronologisch an.

A rather small farm in Wüsting gives rise to the idea for a global agricultural engineering firm. But that on its own is not enough for founder Helmut Urban. He establishes the "LandTageNord" (Country Days North) as a highly successful agricultural show that brings tens of thousands of visitors to the region. And he has lots more up his sleeve.

There is always plenty to talk about with Helmut Urban. After all, the 70-year-old from Wüsting has been living more or less in the public eye for decades. And has no intention of stopping just yet. On the contrary, he still has more than enough ideas. Despite Corona, he has just organised "Urban ClassX", which is a horse show. A few months previously, he was one of the initiators behind the local drive-in cinema. A cultural highlight amid the gloom of the pandemic. "You can't just stop living", he says. And it's plain to see that he's already working on new ideas.

But let's take things chronologically.

Die Innovation aus der elterlichen Garage

Gründermythen haben ihren Ursprung häufig in Garagen. Das ist bei Helmut Urban nicht anders als etwa bei Apple-Erfinder Steve Jobs, Microsoft-Chef Bill Gates oder den Kumpels William Harley und Arthur Davidson, die in der Holzgarage eines Freundes ihr erstes Motorrad zusammenschraubten. Urbans Garage stand auf dem elterlichen Bauernhof in Wüsting. Hier tüftelte der junge Landwirt Anfang der 1980er-Jahre an einem technischen System zur Kälberfütterung.

Wie es dazu kam? „Wir hatten damals 15 Kühe und 25 Hektar Fläche", erinnert sich Urban, „und mein Vater war ein wirklich harter Arbeiter." Der Sohn, der eine Landwirtschaftslehre absolviert und seinen Meister gemacht hatte, denkt größer, will es aber auch leichter haben. Ihm ist klar: Ohne die entsprechende Technik und ohne Automatisierung geht es nicht. „Vadder, ich will hier richtig Gas geben", lässt er den Senior wissen.

Wenig später ist es so weit. Helmut Urban hat in der Garage ganze Arbeit geleistet. Der Prototyp seines Kälbertränkemixers ist fertig. Milchpulver und Wasser werden darin zu einem wohldosierten und -temperierten Kälbertrunk zusammengemischt. Urban ist vom Erfolg des Geräts so überzeugt, dass er 1984 seine Firma gründet. Die Vermarktung nimmt er erstmal selbst in die Hand – immer die Worte seines Vaters im Ohr: „Jung, du musst dir die Menschen ankieken." Die Geschäfte besiegelt er am liebsten klassisch per Handschlag. Und seine Devise „Aus der Praxis für die Praxis" kommt an. Wer mit ihm verhandelt, merkt gleich: Da kennt sich einer wirklich aus.

Auf allen Kontinenten vertreten

Eine der ersten Großbestellungen kommt aus Wuppertal. Fünfzig Maschinen sollen ins Bergische Land gehen. „Wir haben Tag und Nacht daran gearbeitet, um die Lieferung rechtzeitig abzuwickeln." Stück für Stück baut Urban ein Netz regionaler Vertriebspartner auf, die seine Produkte in ihr Sortiment aufnehmen. Und die Palette wächst. Vor allem die 1987 auf den Markt kommende computergestützte Kälberfütterung sorgt für eine Hightech-Revolution in den Ställen.

Heute gilt die Marke Urban als Standard der modernen Kälberaufzucht. Und das nicht nur in Deutschland und bei den europäischen Nachbarn. Das Unternehmen exportiert auf alle fünf Kontinente und ist inzwischen in rund 60 Ländern vertreten, viele davon in Übersee. Rund zwei Drittel des Umsatzes werden im Ausland gemacht. „Anfangs war unsere Internationalisierung für mich noch schwierig", räumt der Firmengründer ein und fügt selbstkritisch hinzu: „Einer meiner größten Fehler war es, dass ich den Englischunterricht in der Schule immer boykottiert habe." Vielleicht liegt es auch daran, dass er die Software für die Urban-Produkte in mehr als 30 Sprachen programmieren ließ.

2018 wird die Urban GmbH & Co. KG mit dem Niedersächsischen Außenwirtschaftspreis für ihre Exporterfolge ausgezeichnet. Ein schöner Abschluss für Helmut Urban, der sich im gleichen Jahr aus dem

Helmut Urban gründete seine Firma im Jahr 1984 auf seinem landwirtschaftlichen Hof in Wüsting.

Landwirtschaft zum Erleben

Schon seit einigen Jahren beklagen Kenner der Agrarbranche eine erschreckende Entwicklung: Immer weniger Kinder und Jugendliche haben einen direkten Bezug zur Landwirtschaft. Dass die Milch von der Kuh stammt und die Kartoffel aus dem Boden, das überrascht viele. Und was den Beruf des Landwirts ausmacht, wissen sie häufig ebenso wenig. Vielerorts wird deshalb versucht, Bauernhöfe als schulische Lernorte zu etablieren. Auch im Nordwesten gibt es solche Ansätze, sie beispielsweise zum Ziel von Projekt- und Wandertagen oder Klassenfahrten zu machen.

Einen ähnlichen Weg gehen die „LandTageNord" in Wüsting. Schon der Untertitel „Erlebwas-Messe" verrät, worum es hier geht: ums Anfassen, ums Bestaunen, ums Erleben. Da gibt es tatsächlich lebendige Schafe, Gänse oder Kühe. Für viele Stadt-Kids ist das ein echtes Aha-Erlebnis, das sie so schnell nicht vergessen. Dass bei dieser Gelegenheit auch die Technikfans auf ihre Kosten kommen, versteht sich von selbst. Einmal auf dem Trecker oder dem Mähdrescher zu sitzen, lässt bei vielen Kindern das Herz für die Landwirtschaft um einiges höher schlagen. Mitunter werden bei dieser Gelegenheit sogar erste Wünsche für das spätere berufliche Leben geweckt.

Im norddeutschen Messekalender haben auch die „Mein Tier" in Oldenburg sowie die „EuroTier" und die „Agritechnica" in Hannover ihren festen Platz. Ob und wann welche dieser normalerweise mehrtägigen Veranstaltungen tatsächlich stattfinden, hängt ganz entscheidend vom weiteren Verlauf der Corona-Pandemie ab. Ob die 2018 in den Oldenburger Weser-Ems-Hallen gestartete „RegioAgrar Weser-Ems" als regionale Fachmesse für landwirtschaftliche Produktion, Handel und Management wieder an die Hunte zurückkehren wird, ist zurzeit nicht bekannt.

Helmut Urban founded his business in 1934 at his farm in Wüsting.

Innovation from his parent's garage

Founder myths often begin in the garage. In this respect, Helmut Urban is just the same as Apple inventor Steve Jobs, Microsoft boss Bill Gates or pals William Harley and Arthur Davidson, who assembled their first motorcycle tinkering away together in a friend's wooden garage. Urban's garage was on his parent's farm in Wüsting. Here the young farmer tinkered away at a technical system for feeding calves in the early 1980s.

How did this come about? "In those days, we had 15 cows and 25 acres of land", Urban recalls, "and my father worked really hard." Young Helmut, who did a farming apprenticeship and gained his master's qualifications, thinks on a bigger scale but also wants an easier life. He is well aware that technology and automation is the way forward. "Dad, I really want to make progress here", he tells his father.

It doesn't take long. Helmut Urban has done a good job in the garage. His prototype liquid calf feed mixer is ready. It mixes milk powder and water together to produce carefully measured liquid calf feed at just the right temperature. Convinced that his machine will be a success, Urban he sets up his own company in 1984. He does his own marketing, always remembering his father's words: "Son, you have to see who you're dealing with." He prefers doing business the traditional way with a handshake. And his motto "Practical solutions for practical use" goes down well. Right from the start, those involved in negotiations with him can see that he really knows what he's doing.

On all continents

One his first big orders comes from Wuppertal: fifty machines for the "Bergisches Land". "We worked day and night to get the delivery out on time." Bit by bit, Urban builds up a network of regional sales partners include his products in their assortment. And the range grows. It is above all the computerised calf feeding systems launched in 1987 that revolutionise the cowsheds.

Today, the Urban brand is the benchmark for modern calf rearing, in Germany and in neighbouring European countries, and with exports to all five continents. The company is meanwhile represented in around 60 countries, including many overseas. Around two thirds of its turnover is generated abroad. "In the early days, I still struggled a bit with going international", admits the company founder, adding with a touch of self-criticism: "One of my biggest mistakes was to boycott English lessons at school." Perhaps that's just one of the reasons why he made sure the software for Urban products is programmed in more than 30 languages.

In 2018, Urban GmbH & Co. KG is awarded the Lower Saxony Foreign Trade Prize for its successful exports. A fitting conclusion for Helmut Urban, who retired from operative business in the same year. "This wasn't a sudden decision; we'd been planning it for some time. Even so, it still wasn't easy for me to let go." From now on, his daughter Nicole Urban-Sprock runs the SME company with her husband Thomas Sprock.

Hands-on agriculture

For some years know, agricultural experts have been lamenting an alarming development: fewer and fewer children and youth can relate directly to farming. Many are astonished to discover that milk comes from cows and potatoes from the ground. They often simply don't have a clue what a farmer does. And so many attempts are being made all on a wide scale to establish farms as places where school children can come and learn. Corresponding efforts are also being made in the North West, with project days, days-out and school trips on the farm.

The approach is similar with the "LandTageNord" in Wüsting. The subtitle "hands-on show" indicates what it's all about: farming as an amazing hands-on experience. With real live sheep, geese or cows: an absolute eye-opener for many city kids, and one they won't forget in a hurry. Needless to say that there's also plenty on display for technology fans as well. Sitting on a tractor or combine harvester is all it takes to make some children passionate about farming. They might even decide it's what they want to do with their lives later on.

Other established items in Northern Germany's trade-fair calendar also includes "Mein Tier" (My Animal) in Oldenburg, and also the "EuroTier" (EuroAnimal) and "Agritechnica" in Hanover. To what extent these usually multi-day events can still take place depends to a great extent on what happens with the Corona pandemic. It is currently not known whether the "RegioAgrar Weser-Ems" that began in 2018 as a regional trade-fair for agricultural production, retail and management in the Weser-Ems-Hallen in Oldenburg, will actually come back to the town on the river Hunte.

operativen Bereich zurückzieht. „Das war kein plötzlicher Entschluss, wir haben das lange geplant. Dennoch war das Loslassen für mich dann doch nicht leicht." Fortan führen seine Tochter Nicole Urban-Sprock und ihr Mann Thomas Sprock den Mittelständler.

Landwirtschaft zum Anfassen und Staunen

Aufs Altenteil zurückziehen und den Ruhestand genießen? Das kommt für Helmut Urban selbstverständlich nicht infrage. Schon einige Jahre zuvor hat er sich mit „LandTageNord" ein zweites Standbein geschaffen. Auslöser sei das Aus für die Messe „Tier und Technik" in Oldenburg gewesen. „Ich war mir sicher, dass es einen Ersatz dafür braucht." Gesagt, getan. Im Sommer 2004 werben erstmals rund 3.000 Plakate mit der fröhlichen Kuh Agrathe in ganz Norddeutschland für die neue Veranstaltung.

Und das Konzept „Landwirtschaft zum Anfassen, Staunen und Kennenlernen" geht trotz zuvor geäußerter Bedenken auf. Zehntausende Besucherinnen und Besucher tummeln sich bei der Premiere auf dem Messegelände, rund 350 Aussteller sind vor Ort. „Die ersten habe ich noch persönlich akquiriert", berichtet Helmut Urban schmunzelnd. Mittlerweile läuft der Anmeldeprozess von selbst, die meisten Aussteller kommen jedes Jahr.

Die Messe bleibt keine Eintagsfliege, sie kann sich binnen kürzester Zeit etablieren. Schon im zweiten Jahr spricht der damalige Bürgermeister Axel Jahnz euphorisch von einem „Lichtstrahl in der Gemeinde" und lobt den Initiator sowie sein Team für ihr Engagement. Bleibt die Frage nach dem Erfolgsgeheimnis. „Wir sind eine Businessmesse, bieten aber ein attraktives Programm für die ganze Familie", antwortet Urban.

Eisprinzessin und Lindenberg

Dass er die LandTage im Corona Jahr 2020 erst verschieben und dann absagen muss, macht dem Unternehmer Monate später noch immer zu schaffen. Großveranstaltungen bleiben auch zum neuen Termin im September verboten. Letztlich wolle man kein Risiko eingehen und die Gesundheit der rund 600 Aussteller und der 70.000 erwarteten Besucherinnen und Besucher schützen. Und die Messe ins Internet verlegen? „Nein, das würde überhaupt nicht funktionieren."

Also die Hände in den Schoß legen? Nichts tun und abwarten? Das wäre nicht Urban-like. Gemeinsam mit seinem Team greift er einen Trend auf, den es wohl ohne die große Krise nicht gegeben hätte. Er organisiert ein frühsommerliches Autokino auf dem Messegelände. Als Programmmacher ist Tobias Roßmann, der Geschäftsführer des Casablanca-Kinos in Oldenburg, mit an Bord. Und so kommen über mehrere Wochen Tag für Tag Filmfreunde nach Wüsting, um sich an Streifen wie „Die Eisprinzessin" oder „Lindenberg – Mach dein Ding!" zu erfreuen. Zweimal gibt es zusätzlich Autokonzerte mit Musikern aus der Region.

Beruflich über lange Jahre höchst erfolgreich, privat von einigen Schicksalsschlägen getroffen – was treibt einen solchen Mann zu immer neuen

So what does he do now? Slow down and enjoy his retirement? That of course is out of the question for Helmut Urban. A few years previously he had already established a second foothold with the "LandTageNord", following the end of the "Tier und Technik" (Animals and Technology) show in Oldenburg. "I was sure we needed something else to put in its place." No sooner said than done. In summer 2004, 3,000 posters with the happy cow Agrathe can be seen throughout Northern Germany, advertising for the new event for the first time.

And the concept "Amazing hands-on agriculture" works, despite concerns raised beforehand. The show ground bustles with tens of thousands of visitors, with around 350 exhibitors taking part. "I personally acquired the first ones", reports Helmut Urban with a grin. Meanwhile, registration for the show takes care of itself with most exhibitors coming every year.

The event is not a flash-in-the-pan and swiftly becomes a permanent feature. Already in the second year, the then mayor Axel Jahnz euphorically talks of a "ray of light in the village", praising the commitment showed by the initiator and his team. So why is the show a success? "It's a trade show that also offers an attractive programme for the whole family", replies Urban.

Ice Princess and Lindenberg

The fact that Corona forced him to initially postpone and then cancel the LandTage in 2020 continues to niggle the entrepreneur months later. Major events are still banned through to the new date in September. After all, nobody wants to take a risk and priority must be given to protecting the health of the roughly 600 exhibitors and anticipated 70,000 visitors. Putting the show online? "No, that wouldn't work at all."

So just sit back and twiddle thumbs? Do nothing but wait and see? Not the Urban way. Together with his team he picks up a trend that wouldn't have emerged without the major crisis. He organises an early-summer drive-in cinema on the show ground, together with Tobias Roßmann, managing director of the Casablanca cinema in Oldenburg, who is responsible for the programme. And so for several weeks, movie lovers come to Wüsting every day to enjoy films such as "The Ice Princess" or the German biopic "Lindenberg – Mach dein Ding!". In addition, two drive-in concerts are organised with musicians from the region.

Professionally successful for many years, a man whose private life had its own fair share of misfortune – what makes him keep going all the time? "I can't sit still", says Helmut Urban, "and I'd like to give something back to this community that means so much to me." In fact, he has always remained true to his village and never had the ambition to move away. The North Sea is where the avid swimmer's favourite place for a holiday. Even so, travelling overseas is also something he might like to do, possibly to South Africa.

Aktivitäten an? „Ich kann nicht stillsitzen", sagt Helmut Urban, „und ich möchte auch dieser Gemeinde, die viel für mich bedeutet, etwas zurückgeben." Tatsächlich ist er Wüsting immer treu geblieben, hatte nie Ambitionen, wegzuziehen. Urlaub macht der passionierte Schwimmer am liebsten an der Nordsee. Dennoch: Mal wieder eine weite Reise, etwa nach Südafrika, das könnte ihm gefallen.

Weitere Veranstaltungen und eine neue Halle

Bis dahin werden aber wohl noch einige Tage ins Land gehen. Dabei wird es dem 70-Jährigen ganz sicher nicht langweilig. „Ich möchte mich gern um weitere Veranstaltungen kümmern und extra dafür eine neue Halle errichten", verrät er. Zuletzt gab er mit den „Urban ClassX" bereits einen Vorgeschmack darauf, was ihm dabei vorschwebt. Die Turnierserie für Spring- und Dressurreiter bot auch während der Corona-Zeit exzellenten Sport – wenn auch ohne Publikum.

Dass die Serie im März 2021 abgebrochen werden musste, lag allerdings nicht an der Pandemie. Alle Hygiene- und Abstandsregeln waren penibel eingehalten worden. Der Ausbruch des Equinen Herpesvirus (EHV-1) beim spanischen Reitturnier in Valencia machte hingegen eine Fortführung unmöglich.

„Sehr bedauerlich für den Sport, aber nicht zu ändern", fasst Urban zusammen. Rückschläge werfen den nimmermüden Macher nicht aus der Bahn. Vermutlich hat er sowieso schon die nächsten Ideen und Pläne im Kopf.

Die Firma Urban ist heute ein familiengeführtes und international agierendes Unternehmen, das auf Produkte und Fütterungstechnik für die Kälber- und Lämmeraufzucht spezialisiert ist.

Today, Urban is a family-run company and an international player specialised in products and systems for feeding calves and lambs.

More events and a new building

However, that probably won't happen for a while yet. But the 70-year-old certainly won't get bored. "I'd like to organise more events and have a new building constructed specially", he says. His recent "Urban ClassX" already gave a foretaste of what he has in mind. The show jumping and dressage event offered excellent sport even under Corona conditions, all-be-it without spectators.

The fact that the series then had to be cancelled in March 2021 had nothing to do with the pandemic. All hygiene and social spacing rules were followed meticulously. But the outbreak of equine herpes virus (EHV-1) at the Spanish equestrian event in Valencia made it impossible to continue.

"A great pity for the sport, but there was nothing we could do about it", summarises Urban. Setbacks don't divert the indefatigable man of action from his course. He's probably already busy with his next ideas and plans.

Information

Gründungsjahr: 1964
Mitarbeiter: 450 weltweit, mehr als 10 Ausbildungsberufe
Produkte:
– Premixe für die Futtermittelindustrie
– Zusatzstoffe
– Mineralstoffe
– Vitamine
– Pulver, Pasten und Liquids
MIAVIT international:
weltweit drei Produktionsstandorte und zwei weitere Vertriebsniederlassungen; Exportquote von mehr als 50 Prozent in über 85 Länder der Welt

Year founded: 1964
Employees: 450 worldwide, more than 10 occupational training schemes
Products:
– pre-mixtures for the feed industry
– supplements
– minerals
– vitamins
– powders, pastes and liquids
MIAVIT international:
three production sites worldwide and two additional sales branches; export quota of more than 50 percent to more than 85 countries around the world

www.miavit.com

MIAVIT GmbH

Die MIAVIT GmbH mit Hauptsitz in Essen (Oldb.) ist ein erfolgreiches Familienunternehmen, das heute bereits in dritter Generation geführt wird. Der Leitgedanke „Prävention statt Medikation" ist dabei von Beginn an unser Antrieb, qualitativ hochwertige Vormischungen sowie Zusatzstoffe für Wiederkäuer und Nutztiere wie Schweine, Rinder und Geflügel herzustellen. Abgerundet wird das Sortiment um Produkte für den Heimtierbedarf.

Der Name MIAVIT steht als Kürzel für alle wichtigen **Mi**neralstoffe, **A**minosäuren und **Vit**amine, die in unseren Vormischungen/Premixen enthalten sind. Unsere Produkte werden in modernen Produktionsanlagen mit absoluter Präzision gefertigt und zudem ständig von zertifizierten Laboren untersucht. Als deutscher Marktführer im Bereich Vormischung haben wir die moderne und umweltgerechte Tierernährung stets im Blick. Darüber hinaus arbeiten wir ausschließlich mit zuverlässigen und zertifizierten Lieferanten.

MIAVIT umfasst die Unternehmensbereiche Nutztierernährung, PetFood, Food und Biogas. Das letztgenannte Geschäftsfeld ist bei CAM Energy angesiedelt.

MIAVIT GmbH based in Essen (Oldb.) is a successful family company that is currently being run by the third generation. The guiding principle of our family business then as now consists of "prevention instead of medication", motivating us to produce top quality pre-mixtures and supplements for ruminants and livestock such as pigs, cattle and poultry. Pet supplies round off the range. The name MIAVIT is an abbreviation for all important **Mi**nerals, **A**mino acids and **Vit**amins that are contained in our pre-mixtures. All our products are made with absolute precision in our modern manufacturing plants and are also constantly examined by certified laboratories. As the German market leader in the field of pre-mixing, our focus is constantly on modern, environmentally compatible animal nutrition. Furthermore, we work exclusively with reliable, certified suppliers.

MIAVIT consists of the animal nutrition, pet food, food and biogas business units, with the latter hived off to CAM Energy.

Daten & Fakten:

- umfassendes Know-how über Biologische Additive für Biogasanlagen seit 2004
- optimale Biologie im Bereich der Biogasanlagen mit einer Produktpalette aus effektiven Spurenelementen, Enzymprodukten, Makroelementen, Siliermitteln und Dosierstationen
- effiziente Technologie für Separatoren, Pumpen und Rührwerke
- individuelle und modular aufgebaute Servicekonzepte
- Standorte: Essen (Oldb.) und Mittenwalde

Facts & figures:

- comprehensive know-how about biological additives for biogas plants since 2004
- optimum biology in biogas plants with a product range of effective trace elements, enzyme products, macro elements, silage additives and dosing systems
- efficient technology for separators, pumps and mixers
- individual, modular service concepts
- sites: Essen (Oldb.) and Mittenwalde

www.cam-energy.de

CAM Energy GmbH

CAM Energy ist ein junges Start-up im Bereich Agri-Business und bietet seinen Kunden innovative Komplettlösungen rund um die Biologie, die Technologie und den Service von Biogasanlagen sowie Konzepte für die Gülle- und Gärresteaufbereitung im Agri-Business. Als 100-prozentige Tochter der MIAVIT GmbH profitieren wir von deren langjähriger Erfahrung und Expertise in der Agrarwirtschaft.

Von unseren zwei Standorten in Essen (Oldb.) und Mittenwalde (Brandenburg) aus unterstützen wir Sie dabei, Ihre Biogasanlage oder den Nährstoffkreislauf auf Ihrem Hof zu optimieren. Denn als Tierhalter oder Biogasanlagenbetreiber stehen Sie vor einer gewaltigen Herausforderung: Sie müssen trotz immer schärferer Auflagen den wirtschaftlichen Betrieb Ihres Hofes sicherstellen. Deswegen haben wir ein modulares System zur Gülle- und Gärresteaufbereitung entwickelt, das alle wichtigen Faktoren wie Wasser, Nährstoffe, Energie und Wirtschaftlichkeit berücksichtigt und Ihnen ein nachhaltiges Wirtschaften ermöglicht. Zu unserem Portfolio gehören biologische Additive sowie praxisnahe und technisch umfangreiche Lösungen, um Ihre Biogasanlage optimal auszurüsten.

CAM Energy is a young start-up in the agribusiness sector that offers innovative all-in-one solutions associated with the biology, technology and servicing of biogas plants, as well as the related areas of slurry and digestate processing. As a fully-owned subsidiary of MIAVIT GmbH, we benefit from their extensive experience and expertise in the agricultural sector.

From our two locations in Essen (Oldb.) and Mittenwalde (Brandenburg), we can help to optimise your biogas plant or the nutrient cycle on your farm. As livestock farmers or biogas plant operators, you face the huge challenge of keeping your farm operating at a profit despite the ever stricter regulations. We have therefore developed a modular system for slurry and digestate processing that gives equal consideration to all key factors such as water, nutrients, trace elements, energy and profitability, while making sustainable agriculture possible. Our range includes immediate remedies, permanent solutions and extensive machinery as the ideal equipment for your biogas plant.

Genossenschaftsverband Weser-Ems e. V.

Der Genossenschaftsverband Weser-Ems ist Prüfungs- und Beratungsverband für die Genossenschaften und genossenschaftlichen Unternehmen in Weser-Ems. Nach dem Leitbild „In der Region für die Region" steht der Verband seit über 130 Jahren als moderner und unternehmerisch ausgerichteter Dienstleister an der Seite seiner rund 300 Mitgliedsunternehmen.

Die 200 Mitarbeitenden fördern die Leistungsfähigkeit der Mitglieder, indem sie prüfen, beraten, bilden und ihre Interessen vertreten. Die Mitglieder sind ein stabiler Kern der mittelständischen Wirtschaft in Weser-Ems. Zu ihnen gehören u. a. die Volksbanken Raiffeisenbanken, die Waren-, Vermarktungs- und Dienstleistungsgenossenschaften, die Energiegenossenschaften und weitere Unternehmen mit Rechtsform der eingetragenen Genossenschaft (eG). Sie zählen annähernd 555 000 Mitglieder und beschäftigen fast 10 000 Mitarbeitende. Als bedeutender Wirtschaftsfaktor in der Region vereinen sie wirtschaftlichen Geschäftsbetrieb und soziale Verantwortung.

Information

Gründungsjahr: 1890

Daten und Fakten:
– Prüfung der Genossenschaften
– breites Beratungsspektrum: Steuer-, Rechts- und Unternehmensberatung
– Bildungsangebote über die Genossenschaftsakademie Weser-Ems in Rastede
– Sitz in Oldenburg

www.gvweser-ems.de

Year founded: 1890

Facts and figures:
– auditing the cooperatives
– broad advisory range: tax, legal and management consultancy
– training courses offered by the Genossenschaftsakademie Weser-Ems (Cooperative Academy) in Rastede
– headquarters in Oldenburg

Genossenschaftsverband Weser-Ems (Weser-Ems Cooperative Association) is the auditing and advisory association for cooperatives and cooperative companies in Weser-Ems. According to the motto "In the region for the region", the association has been working as a modern, business-oriented service provider on behalf of its roughly 300 member companies for more than 130 years. The 200 employees promote the members' performance and efficiency by auditing, advising, training and representing their interests. The members comprise a robust core for the SME sector in Weser-Ems. They include among others the Volksbanken Raiffeisenbanken (banks), the merchandise, marketing and service cooperatives, the energy cooperatives and other companies operating as registered cooperatives (eG). Altogether, they have approximately 555,000 members and have a workforce of nearly 10,000 employees. As a significant economic factor in the region, they combine economic business operations and social responsibility.

Landkreise Vechta und Cloppenburg

www.lkclp.de
www.landkreis-vechta.de
www.oldenburger-
muensterland.de

„Viel grün. Viel drauf."

Dieses Motto des Verbundes Oldenburger Münsterland ist in den Landkreisen Cloppenburg und Vechta Programm. Um über 60 Prozent ist das Brutto-inlandsprodukt der Boom-Region seit 2000 gewachsen. Mittelständische Traditionsbetriebe sind hier genauso zu Hause wie Global Player und junge Start-ups.

Zu den Schwerpunktbranchen gehören die Agrar- und Ernährungswirtschaft, die Kunststofftechnik, der Maschinen- und Anlagenbau sowie die Bauwirt-schaft. Neben dem attraktiven Arbeitsmarkt ziehen die vielfältige Natur, ein abwechslungsreiches Kulturprogramm und zahlreiche Volksfeste immer mehr Menschen in die insgesamt 23 Städte und Gemeinden und 5 Erholungsgebiete zwischen den Dammer Bergen im Süden und dem maritimen Fehngebiet im Norden.

"Lots of green. Lots on."

This motto of the Oldenburger Münsterland Business Association says it all for the districts of Cloppenburg and Vechta. Since 2000, the gross domestic product of the boom region has grown by more than 60 percent. Medium-sized traditional firms are just as much at home here as global players and young start-ups.

Key sectors include the agro-food sector, plastics technology, machine and plant construction together with the building trade. Besides the attractive job market, more and more people are being attracted to the 23 towns and municipalities with 5 recreational areas in the region between the Damme Hills in the south and the maritime fens in the North.

DER WEINKENNER

The Wine Expert

AUTORIN:
LISA KNOLL

James Wright gehört zu den klügsten Köpfen der Weinbranche. Der Australier berät Kunden in aller Welt, ist Betreiber einer renommierten Forschungsdatenbank und hört trotz allem Erfolg niemals auf, neue Pläne zu schmieden. Mit einem verschmitzten Lächeln und viel Humor erzählt der Wahl-Lastruper von einer großen Leidenschaft, die er vor 20 Jahren zu seinem Beruf machte.

Aufgewachsen ist James Wright in einer 2.000-Seelen-Gemeinde westlich der australischen Hauptstadt Canberra. Sein Vater war Ackerbauberater für die Landwirtschaft. „Das hat mich sehr geprägt, in den Ferien habe ich mir auf den umliegenden Farmen gern etwas dazuverdient", erinnert er sich. Später selbst einmal als Landwirt zu arbeiten kam jedoch nie infrage. Etwas Eigenes, Neues sollte es stattdessen sein. Zunächst arbeitete Wright daher einige Jahre als Unternehmensberater, bevor er sich entschied, noch einmal alles auf null zu setzen. „Dass die Weinbranche vor der Jahrtausendwende in Australien so geboomt hat, hat mich einfach neugierig gemacht. Sie war voller junger Leute, die coole neue Ideen hatten. Und da dachte ich, da passe ich ganz gut rein." Nach seinem Studium arbeitete Wright einige Jahre als Weinbergmanager im Süden des Landes, bevor er sich mehr und mehr der Beratung zuwandte und fortan Kunden in aller Welt unterstützte – von der Wahl der richtigen Rebsorte bis hin zur ausgefeilten Vermarktungsstrategie für die erste Ernte.

James Wright has one of smartest minds in the wine industry. The Australian advises customers from all over the world, operates a renowned research database and despite, all his success, he never stops making new plans. With a charming grin and lots of humour, he tells how he turned his passion into a career, before making his home in Lastrup.

James grew up in a village of 2,000 souls to the west of Canberra, Australia's capital city. His father worked as an agricultural consultant. "This shaped my life and gave me an opportunity to work on neighbouring farms during the holidays", he remembers. But he never wanted to end up as a farmer. He wanted to do his own thing, begin something new. So to start with, James worked for a few years as a business consultant before deciding to do a complete reset. "I was simply curious about the boom in Australia's wine industry during the 1990s. It was an industry full of young people with cool new ideas. And I thought I'd fit in quite well." After his degree, he worked as vineyard manager for a few years in the south of the country before turning more and more to the consultancy side of the business. From then on, he provided advice and support for customers all over the world, from selecting the right type of grape through to ideal marketing strategies for the first harvest.

Dass der 50-Jährige heute nicht in Down Under, sondern im Oldenburger Münsterland lebt und arbeitet, hat einen einfachen Grund: seine Frau Alexandra. Die Lastruperin reise 1992 durch Australien und traf dort auf Wright. „Das war zunächst nur eine Urlaubsbekanntschaft. Nach ihrer Abreise blieben wir über Postkarten in Kontakt", erinnert er sich. Zwei Jahre später folgte der Gegenbesuch in Deutschland und beiden wurde klar: Das hier ist was Ernstes. Alexandra ging mit nach Australien.

Etwas Neues wagen

16 Jahre verbrachte das Paar gemeinsam am anderen Ende der Welt. 2011 folgte dann der Umzug nach Deutschland. „Meine Frau wollte zurück in ihre Heimat. Es war natürlich keine einfache Entscheidung für mich, aber rückblickend die richtige", findet Wright. Seine Töchter gewöhnten sich schnell an ihr neues Zuhause, und auch er selbst wurde von den Lastrupern gut aufgenommen. „Es hat schon Vorteile, Australier zu sein", lacht er, „denn hier wollte mich jeder sofort kennenlernen, weil ich ein Novum war." Das habe es ihm am Anfang sehr leicht gemacht, mit den Leuten ins Gespräch zu kommen. Nach und nach entwickelte sich ein enger Freundeskreis, und auch die große Familie seiner Frau nahm ihn herzlich auf und half ihm bei der Eingewöhnung. Natürlich vermisse er seine Freunde und Familie in Australien. Komplett dorthin zurückkehren wolle er aber nicht. „Ich fühle mich wohl hier und schätze es, mitten in Europa zu wohnen. Da ist die nächste Weinregion nie weit", sagt er mit einem Augenzwinkern.

Ein paar Eigenheiten hätten ihn an der deutschen Lebensart am Anfang aber schon sehr gewundert, das gibt der gut gelaunte Australier zu. Dass Leute hier gern allen ihre Meinung mitteilen, obwohl man sie gar nicht danach gefragt hat, zum Beispiel. In seiner Heimat mache man das nur bei sehr guten Freunden. Das ist ihm vor allem in seinem Job aufgefallen. „Weil Australien ein vergleichsweise junges Land ist, gibt es dort keine großen Traditionen wie in Europa. Das ist auch beim Thema Weinbau so", erzählt er. Deshalb gebe es im gesamten Land viele unterschiedliche Ansätze, Weinberge zu managen. In Deutschland habe er jedoch überall ein ähnliches System entdeckt. „Für jeden Boden und jede Rebsorte gibt es hier einen festen Fahrplan. Wie wäre es aber, wenn man einfach mal vom Altbewährten abweicht und etwas Neues probiert?" Bei einem Kunden in Bad Iburg tat James Wright genau das – und erntete viele Ratschläge von verwunderten Kollegen aus der Branche. Natürlich ungefragt. Das nimmt er aber niemandem übel. „Ich weiß ja, dass die Leute es nur gut meinen und sehr an ihren Traditionen hängen. Aber ich bleibe dann auch standhaft und verfolge meinen eigenen Plan." Dass er damit genau richtig liegt, zeigt sich in Bad Iburg. Dort konnte 2020 bereits die zweite Ernte eingefahren werden.

Eine Datenbank für alle

In den ersten Jahren nach dem Umzug flog James Wright mehrmals pro Jahr für berufliche Termine zurück nach Australien. Inzwischen läuft das meiste in seinem Job online. Denn Weinbau findet nicht nur draußen auf dem Weinberg statt – im Gegenteil: Über 100 branchenrelevante Forschungsberichte werden pro Woche veröffentlicht. Hier den Überblick zu behalten, scheint selbst für Fachleute schier unmöglich. Wright zaubert sogleich sein Ass aus dem Ärmel: die offene

Ernte in Bad Iburg am „Teutoburger Südhang" auf dem Weinhof Brinkmann

Harvest in Bad Iburg on the "Teutoburger Südhang" at the Brinkmann wine yard

Tradition und Innovation

Im Oldenburger Land nimmt die Grüne Branche einen hohen Stellenwert ein. Vor allem die Landwirtschaft im Oldenburger Münsterland und der Garten- und Landschaftsbau im Ammerland zählen als gewichtige Teilbereiche. Eine der drei niedersächsischen Lehr- und Versuchsanstalten für Gartenbau findet sich im Herzen des Ammerlands. In Rostrup ist auf 90.000 Quadratmetern Fläche eine weltweit einmalige Sammlung an Rhododendren, Azaleen, Nadelgehölzen und Heidearten untergebracht. Im Jahr 2019 erzielte der Garten- und Landschaftsbau in Niedersachsen und Bremen erstmals einen Umsatz von mehr als eine Mrd. Euro. Der bundesweite Jahresumsatz konnte seit 2005 auf nunmehr 8,9 Mrd. Euro verdoppelt werden.

Nur etwas mehr als ein Prozent der landwirtschaftlich genutzten Fläche in Deutschland entfällt auf Dauerkulturen wie etwa den Weinanbau. Mit einem Exportwert von rund einer Mrd. Euro zählt Deutschland zwar zu den Top Ten der Weinproduzenten weltweit, landet aber mit bescheidenen 3,2 Prozent Weltmarktanteil nur auf dem achten Platz. Als größte Player der Branche sorgen Frankreich und Italien für rund die Hälfte des weltweiten Umsatzes.

Während die größten deutschen Anbaugebiete vorrangig im Süden des Landes liegen, will seit einigen Jahren auch der Nordwesten mitmischen. Die Bundesanstalt für Landwirtschaft und Ernährung (BLE) genehmigte den Weinanbau in Niedersachsen bisher auf etwa 24,5 Hektar Fläche. Zum Vergleich: In Rheinland-Pfalz sind es über 64.000 Hektar. Der Niedersächsische Weinbauverband möchte das Bundesland nicht nur als ernstzunehmendes Anbaugebiet etablieren, sondern auch eine Vermarktungserlaubnis mit regionaler Kennzeichnung erwirken. Zurzeit darf Wein aus Niedersachsen nämlich lediglich als „Deutscher Wein" ausgezeichnet werden.

Tradition and innovation

The green industry plays a significant role in the Oldenburger Land, including in particular agriculture in the Oldenburger Münsterland and horticulture and landscaping in the Ammerland. The Ammerland is home to one of Lower Saxony's three horticulture teaching and research facilities. A globally unique collection of rhododendrons, azaleas, conifers and species of heather can be found here on an area covering 90,000 square metres in Rostrup. In 2019 for the first time, horticulture and landscaping in Lower Saxony and Bremen generated turnover exceeding one billion Euro. Since 2005, annual nationwide sales have doubled to what is now more than 8.9 billion Euro.

Only just over one percent of agricultural land in Germany is taken up with permanent crops such as wine-growing. Although Germany is one of the top ten wine producers in the world with an export value of around one billion Euro, it has a modest 3.2 percent of the global market share, ranking only in eighth place. France and Italy are the biggest players in the industry, accounting for around half of global sales.

While Germany's main wine-growing areas are in the south of the country, the North West has also been on the scene for a few years now. Hitherto, the Federal Office for Agriculture and Food (BLE) has issued wine-growing permits for about 24.5 hectares in Lower Saxony. This contrasts with more than 64,000 hectares in the Rhineland-Palatinate. The Lower Saxony Viticulture Association wants not only to establish the state as a serious wine-growing region but also to obtain a marketing permit with regional declaration. At the moment, wine from Lower Saxony may only be declared as "German Wine".

There's one simple reason why the meanwhile 50-year old lives and works in the Oldenburger Münsterland rather than Down Under: his wife Alexandra, from Lastrup. In 1992 she travelled to Australia where she met James. "To start with it was just a holiday romance. After she'd left, we kept in touch with postcards", he recalls. Two years later, he paid a return visit to Germany and they both realised that this was something serious. Alexandra went back to Australia with him.

Trying something new

The couple spent 16 years together on the other side of the world. In 2011, they moved back to Germany. "My wife wanted to come home. It wasn't an easy decision for me of course, but looking back it was the right thing to do", he thinks. His daughters soon settled into their new home and he too was welcomed by the people of Lastrup. "There's a certain advantage in being Australian", he laughs. "Everyone wanted to meet me straight away, it was the novelty factor!" Right from the start, that made it easy for him to get talking to people and a close group of friends gradually emerged. James was also warmly received by his wife's family who helped him to settle in. Of course he misses his friends and family in Australia. But he doesn't want to go back for good. "I feel happy here and like living at the heart of Europe. The next wine region is never far away", he says with a grin.

But the good-natured Australian admits there were a few things about the German way of life that he struggled with in the early days. The fact that people like to tell you what they think even if you haven't asked them, for example. Back home in Australia, you only do that with very good friends. He sees this particularly in his job. "Australia is a comparatively young country and doesn't have such great traditions as in Europe. It's the same in the wine industry too", he says. That's why there are so many different approaches to vineyard management throughout the country. But in Germany you find a similar system is being used everywhere. "Here there's a fixed schedule for every type of soil and every type of grape. But how about doing something different and trying something new?" James did exactly that with a customer in Bad Iburg – and received lots of advice from astonished colleagues in the industry. Unsolicited, of course. But he doesn't blame them for it. "I know they mean well and are really attached to their traditions. But I stick to my guns and follow my own plan." And the fact that he's doing the right thing can be seen in Bad Iburg, where they brought in the second harvest already in 2020.

A database for all

During his first few years in Germany, James used to fly home to Australia on business several times a year. Meanwhile he can do most of his job online. After all, viticulture doesn't just happen in the vineyard. On the contrary, more than 100 relevant research reports are published every week. Even experts find it impossible to keep a clear overview of what's happening. And so he conjures the ace out of his sleeve with the open database VitiSynth. He uploads research papers into the database, sorts the individual datasets according to headings and regularly selects the most important results from the publications.

Datenbank VitiSynth. Hier lädt er Forschungspapiere hoch, sortiert die einzelnen Datensätze nach Rubriken und wählt regelmäßig die wichtigsten Ergebnisse aus den Veröffentlichungen aus.

Sogar internationale Verbände und namhafte Weinfirmen aus dem In- und Ausland nutzen die Datenbank. Für Wright ist sie inzwischen zu einer Visitenkarte geworden. Sein Vertrag mit einem großen internationalen Weinhersteller und Kooperationen mit Verbänden in Frankreich und Großbritannien kamen nicht zuletzt deshalb zustande. „Ich habe mit VitiSynth ein klares Ziel vor Augen", sagt er. „Es ist nicht immer einfach und natürlich sehr zeitintensiv, aber der große Zuspruch aus der Fachwelt motiviert mich, weiterzumachen."

Etwa 9.500 Weinprofis aus aller Welt hält Wright per wöchentlichem Newsletter auf dem Laufenden. „Der Trend geht ohnehin weg vom persönlichen Berater, denn heute kann man sich online alle Informationen selbst besorgen", weiß Wright. „Meine Arbeit trägt dazu bei, dass die Fachwelt schnell und einfach alle Forschungsergebnisse an der Hand hat. Letztlich kann die Weinbranche durch meine Datenbank innovativer arbeiten."

Wein aus Norddeutschland

Die Weinbranche voranbringen – das möchte James Wright nicht nur digital, sondern auch direkt vor der eigenen Haustür. Denn dank einer neuen EU-Verordnung gilt Niedersachsen seit 2016 offiziell als Weinbaugebiet. Inzwischen haben mehr als 20 Winzer hier eine Anbaugenehmigung erhalten und sich zum Niedersächsischen Weinbauverband zusammengeschlossen. Wright ist natürlich ebenfalls Mitglied. „Der Weinbau steht hier noch am Anfang", weiß der Experte. „Aber es werden mehr und mehr Winzer hinzukommen, sodass wir die Region in der Branche etablieren können."

Dass Weinbau nur im warmen Klima möglich ist, sei nämlich ein Irrglaube. „Im Grunde kann man überall Wein anbauen, solange die Rebfläche etwas höher gelegen ist und sich keine Staunässe bildet. Alles andere ist eine Sache der richtigen Rebsorte." Chardonnay und Grauburgunder made in Niedersachsen sind also alles andere als fixe Ideen, sondern bereits Realität. Und auch in Lastrup soll es bald ein paar edle Tropfen geben. James Wright plant in Absprache mit der Gemeinde den Anbau mehrerer Rebsorten. Der Wein soll dann in den Feinkostläden der Region verkauft werden. Auf lange Sicht hofft er, sogar ein jährliches Weinfest etablieren zu können.

Ein Wiki für Weinprofis

Und auch für VitiSynth hat Wright ambitionierte Zukunftspläne. „Bei jeder Forschungsarbeit wird nur ein kleiner Teil des Gesamten untersucht, zum Beispiel die Auswirkungen bestimmter pH-Werte im Boden", erklärt er. „Die Zusammenhänge zwischen all diesen einzelnen, separat gefundenen Ergebnissen gehen jedoch durch die Fülle an Material schnell verloren." Deshalb will er seine Forschungsdatenbank in den nächsten Jahren um eine interaktive Wissensplattform

Even international associations and renowned wine companies at home and abroad use the database. For James, it has meanwhile become his business card. Among others, it played a role in his contract with a major international wine manufacturer and cooperation with associations in France and the United Kingdom. "I have a clear vision with VitiSynth", he says. "It isn't always easy and of course it takes a lot of time. But the echo from the experts is my motivation to carry on."

He sends weekly newsletters to about 9,500 wine professionals all over the world to keep them up to date: "The trend is moving away from personal consultants: after all, today anyone can get all the information they need online", James knows. "My work helps to ensure that the experts have all the research results at their disposal quickly and easily. In the end, my database makes the wine industry more innovative in its work."

Wine from North Germany

Helping the wine industry make progress: that's something James wants to do not just digitally but also directly on his doorstep. Thanks to a new EU Regulation, since 2016 Lower Saxony has officially become a winegrowing region. Meanwhile more than 20 vintners have received a cultivation permit and joined forces in the Lower Saxony Viticulture Association. He is also a member, naturally. "Wine-growing is still in the early stages here", says the expert. "But the number of vintners will continue to grow so we can get the region established in the industry."

It's wrong to think that wine only grows in a warm climate. "Basically you can cultivate vines anywhere, as long as the vineyard is on slightly raised land with no waterlogging. Everything else is simply a case of choosing the right type of grape." Chardonnay and Pinot Gris made in Lower Saxony are now already reality and not just an idea. Lastrup should also soon be home to a few fine wines. James is currently talking to the local authority about cultivating several types of grape. The wine will then be sold in the region's speciality delicatessens. In the long term, he even hopes to establish an annual wine festival.

Wikipedia for the wine industry

James is also ambitious for VitiSynth's future. "Every research project only looks at a small part of the overall picture, for example the impacts of certain pH levels in the soil", he explains. "But the sheer volume of material makes it easy to lose sight of the relationships between all these individual, separately elaborated results." And so his aim over the next few years is to turn his research database into an interactive knowledge platform. In future, users should be able to see at a glance which factors influence growth, yield and flavour, and to which extent. With about 2,000 different aromatics and hundreds of types of soil, that's surely a massive undertaking.

But not for him. "I think it can be done", is his simple but typically laid-back Australian opinion. He hopes that big international wine organisations will support him with this project, which is a bit like a

Niedersachsen gilt seit 2016 als Weinbaugebiet, mehr als 20 Winzer haben sich bereits zu einem Verband zusammengeschlossen.

Lower Saxony has been a wine-growing region since 2016, and more than 20 winegrowers have already formed an association.

erweitern. Nutzer sollen künftig auf einen Blick nachverfolgen können, welche Faktoren Wachstum, Ertrag und Geschmack in welchem Maße beeinflussen. Bei etwa 2.000 verschiedenen Aromastoffen und Hunderten Bodenarten eine wahre Mammutaufgabe.

Nicht für James Wright. „Ich glaube, dass man das schaffen kann", ist seine schlichte, aber eben typisch australisch-entspannte Einschätzung. Verwirklichen will er dieses Projekt, das in seiner Grundidee an eine Art Wikipedia für Weinprofis erinnert, mit der Unterstützung großer internationaler Weinorganisationen. „Es hat bereits Gespräche gegeben, und ich bin guter Dinge", verrät er. Das wäre wohl jeder, der ihn kennt. Denn wer könnte ein solches Vorhaben besser in die Tat umsetzen als James Wright, der Australier aus Lastrup.

Wikipedia for the wine industry. "We've already had some talks and I'm quite optimistic", he says. Anyone who knows him would agree. After all, who else could be better at this kind of project than James Wright, the Australian from Lastrup?

Weinkontor Pollmann in Oldenburg

Information

Gründungsjahr: 1968	**Year founded:** 1968
Mitarbeiter: 3	**Employees:** 3
Angebotsspektrum:	**Range:**

Angebotsspektrum:
– Oldenburg Wein aus Südafrika sowie Weißweine, Roséweine und Rotweine aus allen Weinanbaugebieten der Welt
– edle Spirituosen und Weinzubehör
– Fachberatung und Verkostung

Range:
– Oldenburg wine from South Africa together with white wine, rosé and red wine from all wine-growing regions of the world
– fine spirits and wine accessories
– expert advice and wine tasting sessions

www.weinkontor-pollmann.de

Weinkontor Pollmann – Kompetenz trifft Qualität

Wer zum ersten Mal das Weinkontor Pollmann betritt, spürt sofort: Hier ist der gute Geschmack zu Hause! Gründer und Inhaber Egon Pollmann ist bekennender Weinliebhaber. Und wenn er über sein Lieblingsthema spricht, dann spiegelt sich in seinen Worten nicht nur eine große Leidenschaft, sondern auch eine besondere Kompetenz für die edlen Tropfen wider. Bei einer Weinverkostung präsentiert der Inhaber seinen Gästen höchstpersönlich ausgesuchte Weine, die dazugehörigen Geschichten der Weingüter und der Menschen, bei denen er die Weine einkauft. Ein besonderes Highlight sind die „Oldenburg Weine". Diese werden in den berühmten Oldenburg Vineyards in Südafrika angebaut.

Im Weinkontor Pollmann wird Wein als ein lebendiges und unglaublich vielfältiges Produkt präsentiert, das einzigartig schön sein kann und das man am besten mit einem Lächeln auf dem Gesicht genießt.

Ein Newsletter namens „Der Weinschwärmer" ist eine weitere Innovation des umtriebigen Unternehmers, für den Stillstand ein Fremdwort ist: „Fange nie an aufzuhören, höre nie auf anzufangen", lautet das Lebensmotto von Egon Pollmann.

Weinkontor Pollmann – expertise meets quality

Anyone entering Weinkontor Pollmann for the first time realises immediately that this is where good taste is as at home! Founder and proprietor Egon Pollmann is an avowed wine connoisseur. And when he talks about his favourite subject, his words reflect both great passion and also special expertise for fine wine. During wine tasting sessions, the proprietor takes delight in personally presenting his guests with exquisite wines accompanied by stories about the vineyards where they are produced and the people who sell them. One particular highlight is the Oldenburg Wine, cultivated in the famous Oldenburg Vineyards in South Africa.

Weinkontor Pollmann presents wine as an incredibly versatile living product that can be uniquely lovely and is best enjoyed with a smile on your face! A newsletter called "Der Weinschwärmer" (the wine lover) is another innovation by the bustling entrepreneur for whom standing still is simply not an option. Egon Pollmann's motto: "Never start stopping, never stop starting".

DER WEGBEREITER

The Pathfinder

AUTOR:
THORSTEN LANGE

Alles begann in Cincinnati, USA. Um das Jahr 1845 herum entstanden dort die ersten industriellen Schlachthöfe mit Fließbandproduktion. Danach ging es nur noch in eine Richtung: größer, schneller, billiger. Entscheidendes Kriterium war nicht mehr Herkunft oder Qualität, sondern der Preis. Genau das hält Niko Brand für falsch. Der Geschäftsführer des mittelständischen Schlachtbetriebs Brand Qualitätsfleisch GmbH & Co. KG aus Lohne geht bewusst einen anderen Weg: Der 32-Jährige setzt auf Tierwohl und Transparenz, stellt Qualität über Quantität, schafft Marken statt Masse. Damit mischt er die Branche gehörig auf.

Dabei ist Brand kein Revolutionär. Er ist niemand, der aus Prinzip alles anders macht. Allerdings orientiert er sich nicht an Gegebenheiten und Gewohnheiten, sondern bewertet Situationen selbst. Diese Haltung ist in seiner persönlichen Vergangenheit verankert. Schon früh lernte Niko Brand, dass auch ein Schlachthof eigene Wege gehen kann. Im heimischen Familienbetrieb wurde Tierwohl bereits mitgedacht, als es den Begriff noch gar nicht gab. Zudem war Leiharbeit in der 90-jährigen Unternehmensgeschichte kaum ein Thema. „Wir waren immer zu 100 Prozent Team Brand", berichtet der Geschäftsführer in vierter Generation nicht ohne Stolz. Eine Seltenheit in dieser Branche.

It all began in Cincinnati, USA, where the first industrial slaughterhouses started using assembly-line production methods around 1845. After that, developments went just one way: bigger, faster, cheaper. Price rather than origin or quality was now the key criterion. But that's exactly what Niko Brand thinks is wrong. The managing director of the medium-sized slaughterhouse Brand Qualitätsfleisch GmbH & Co. KG in Lohne has deliberately chosen another path: the 32-year-old advocates animal welfare and transparency, puts quality above quantity, creates brands, not bulk. In doing so, he's really stirring things up in the industry.

But Brand is not a revolutionary. He's not the sort of person who does things differently as a matter of principle. Instead, he assesses situations for their own value and not according to circumstances and habits. This mindset is anchored in his personal past. Niko Brand learnt early on that a slaughterhouse can choose its own path. The company run by his family already focused on animal welfare long before the phrase even existed. And the firm has rarely resorted to temporary staff in the 90 years of its existence. "We were always 100% Team Brand", reports the fourth generation managing director with a fair portion of pride. A rarity in this industry.

Vom Experiment zur Exzellenz

Eigene Wege gehen: Das wurde schnell zum Markenzeichen von Niko Brand. So war das Studienfach seiner Wahl nicht etwa Agrarwirtschaft, sondern Maschinenbau mit Schwerpunkt Produktionsinformatik. Beruflich tätig war er danach nicht in Vechta oder Oldenburg, sondern in den Niederlanden, Spanien, Belgien, Dänemark und sogar in Thailand. Der Blick über Fach- und Landesgrenzen hinweg hat Brand geprägt: „Mein Vater hat immer gesagt: Klau mit den Augen. Nimm mit, was du mitnehmen kannst." Genau das hat er getan und seine „Beute" schließlich mit zurück nach Lohne gebracht. Die Neugier auf Unbekanntes und Anderes wurde in Form von Reisen zum persönlichen Hobby. Sie prägte fortan aber auch den analytischen Blick auf Betrieb und Branche. Vermeintliche Gesetzmäßigkeiten stellte Brand in Frage. Statt alten Pfaden zu folgen, sucht er neue – eben: eigene – Wege.

Die Rolle des Spiritus Rector übernahm dabei der „Duke of Berkshire". Wer sich hinter diesem ehrwürdigen Namen verbirgt? Nicht etwa ein britischer Landadliger, sondern: eine altenglische Schweinerasse. Ein Händler kam vor einigen Jahren auf Brand zu und fragte, ob er das besonders hochwertige Fleisch liefern könne. Konnte er – nachdem er kurzerhand eine eigene Wertschöpfungskette aufgebaut hatte. „Mit dem Projekt haben wir Neuland betreten," erinnert sich Brand. „Haltung, Fütterung, Vermarktung – alles musste neu gedacht werden, denn alles war voll auf Qualität ausgelegt." Viel Arbeit, viel Veränderung – doch die Erfahrungen waren äußerst positiv. Das Projekt widerlegte etliche Regeln des Geschäfts: Betriebsgröße? Nicht entscheidend. Stroh- und Offenställe? Lassen sich wirtschaftlich betreiben. Kupieren? In Offenställen unnötig. Antibiotika? Es geht auch ohne. Diese wichtigen Erkenntnisse führten auch zur Gründung des Offenstallvereins, der sich seit einigen Jahren mit wachsendem Erfolg für artgerechte Schweinehaltung einsetzt.

Was einst als Experiment begann, ist heute fest etabliert. Mit „Brand Meat Excellence" existiert mittlerweile eine eigene Marke für das Premiumsegment. Gleichzeitig hat das Unternehmen seine Rolle am Markt neu definiert: vom reinen Schlachthof zum gefragten Projektentwickler und -vermittler. „Die meisten Betriebe versuchen, Komplexität aus ihren Prozessen rauszuhalten – wir holen sie rein", erklärt Niko Brand selbstbewusst. „Wir verkaufen heute mehr als ein Stück Fleisch. Es geht auch um die Story dahinter und um Mehrwerte jenseits des Produkts."

Lieblingskurs? Gegen den Wind

Zwei Eckpfeiler der neuen Philosophie sind Transparenz und Kommunikation. „In einem Schlachthof werden Lebewesen zu Lebensmitteln. Das wird so bleiben. Aber ich finde: Darüber kann man reden." Als der NDR für eine Fernsehdokumentation den „Weg des Schnitzels" nachzeichnen wollte, überzeugte Brand die Redaktion, auch die Schlachtung zu zeigen – zur besten Sendezeit. Zudem werden Kanäle wie Facebook, Instagram oder YouTube bespielt. „Klar gibt's da auch mal Kritik. Wir hatten auch schon einen Shitstorm mit einigen tausend Kommentaren. Aber für mich gehört Kommunikation einfach dazu." Und natürlich hat das Engagement auch positive Effekte: Der Familienbetrieb aus dem Oldenburger Münsterland gilt heute als Innovationstreiber. „Wir sind gut vernetzt, wir tummeln uns überall. Und mittlerweile ist bekannt, dass wir eine gute Anlaufstelle für alles Besondere sind."

Der Familienbetrieb aus dem Oldenburger Münsterland hat seine Marktposition neu definiert – vom Schlachthof zum gefragten Projektentwickler.

The family company from Oldenburger Münsterland has redefined its role in the market – from slaughterhouse to coveted project developer.

Aus Tradition modern

Der Mensch isst Fleisch, seitdem er das Feuer beherrscht; das ist seit etwa 1,7 Millionen Jahren der Fall. Diese Form der Ernährung ist tief in uns verwurzelt. Der Pro-Kopf-Verbrauch war zuletzt zwar leicht rückläufig, mit über 57 kg pro Person und Jahr steht Fleisch aber nach wie vor weit oben auf der Speisekarte. Insbesondere: Schweinefleisch, das mehr als die Hälfte des Verzehrs ausmacht.

Entsprechend hoch ist die Bedeutung der Fleischveredelung in der deutschen Nahrungsmittelindustrie. Einschließlich der Schlachthöfe erzielt sie jährlich Umsätze im Volumen von ca. 45 Mrd. Euro. Und eines ihrer aktivsten Zentren ist das Oldenburger Land. Die hohe Nutztierdichte dieser Region wurde in der Vergangenheit mitunter despektierlich kommentiert. Vom „Schweinegürtel" war die Rede, von Agrarintensivwirtschaft und Massentierhaltung. Unbestritten ist aber auch der enorme wirtschaftliche Erfolg. Namen wie Wesjohann, Lohmann oder Rauffus sind nicht jedem Konsumenten geläufig, sie stehen aber für international agierende Konzerne mit tausenden Beschäftigten und Umsätzen in Milliardenhöhe.

Zudem zeichnet sich die Region seit jeher durch Lösungsorientierung und Innovationskraft aus. Nicht umsonst gilt das Oldenburger Münsterland als Silicon Valley der Agrarindustrie. Betriebe der Fleischveredelung sind Schwergewichte ihrer Branche. Auch strategisch: Häufig besetzen ihre Führungskräfte Schlüsselpositionen in Gremien und Verbänden. Expertise aus Nordwest ist im ganzen Land gefragt.

In den kommenden Jahren dürfte das Know-how auch vor Ort gebraucht werden, um einen Veränderungsprozess zu gestalten. Überwog in den letzten Jahrzehnten der Wunsch der Verbraucher nach günstiger Ware, setzte zuletzt zunehmend ein Umdenken ein. Themen wie artgerechte Haltung und ökologische Folgen gewinnen an Bedeutung, zugleich wächst der Marktanteil von Ersatzprodukten. Dass inzwischen selbst Discounter ankündigen, mittelfristig auf Billigfleisch verzichten zu wollen, ist beides: Beleg und Beschleunigung dieser Entwicklung.

Mittelfristig steht die traditionsreiche und erfolgreiche Branche also vor Herausforderungen. Man muss sie jedoch nicht als Risiko oder Gefahr verstehen, sondern kann auch Chancen in ihnen erkennen. Die Betriebe im Oldenburger Land sind in der Lage – und es entspräche auch ihrem Selbstverständnis –, den Wandel aktiv mitzugestalten.

Auch wenn die Alternativen an Bedeutung gewinnen, bleibt der Fleischkonsum vorerst in uns verwurzelt. Ob das weitere 1,7 Millionen Jahre so sein wird? Sicher ist eines: Die fleischverarbeitenden Betriebe aus dem Nordwesten werden eine Führungsrolle übernehmen. Schließlich sind sie aus Tradition modern.

Modern by tradition

People have been eating meat ever since they learnt to control fire. In other words, for about 1.7 million years. This form of nutrition is deeply rooted in us. Despite a recent slight decline in per capita consumption, meat remains right at the top of our bill of fare with more than 57 kg per person and year. Especially pork, which accounts for more than half of all meat eaten.

Meat processing therefore plays a correspondingly significant role in the German food industry, with annual turnover including slaughterhouses of approx. 45 billion Euro in volume. And the Oldenburger Land is one of the most active regions in this respect. In the past, the high density of livestock in the area often generated disrespectful comments along the lines of "pig belt", intensive farming and mass animal husbandry. But there's also no disputing the huge economic success. Consumers may not necessarily be familiar with names such as Wesjohann, Lohmann or Rauffus, but they stand for international players with thousands of employees and turnover in the billions

Furthermore, this is a region that has always stood out with a solution-oriented mindset and innovative spirit. The Oldenburger Münsterland is not known as the Silicon Valley of Agriculture for nothing. Meat processing companies are heavyweights in their industry. In strategic terms too: frequently their senior executives take up key positions in boards, bodies and associations. Expertise from the North West is in demand throughout the country.

In the years ahead, this know-how is sure to be needed in the local setting too in order to shape a change process. While customer preferences in recent decades clearly focused on low-priced goods, recently there has been an increasing mind shift. Issues such as species-appropriate animal husbandry and ecological consequences are becoming more significant, as well as the growth in market share for substitute products – a development both verified and accelerated by the fact that even discount stores have announced their intention to dispense with cheap meat in the long run.

In other words, this traditional and successful industry is facing challenges in the future. But these can be seen as an opportunity rather than risk or danger. As a reflection of how they see themselves, the companies in the Oldenburger Land are well able to play an active role in helping to shape the transformation.

Even if the alternatives are gaining ground, eating meat remains deeply rooted in us for the time being. Will that continue for another 1.7 million years? One thing is certain: the meat processing companies in the North West will be playing a leading role. After all, they are modern by tradition.

From experiment to excellence

Choosing his own paths soon became Niko Brand's trademark. For example, instead of studying agriculture, he chose to do a degree in mechanical engineering with a focus on production informatics. And after graduating, his career took him to the Netherlands, Spain, Belgium, Denmark and even Thailand rather than Vechta or Oldenburg. Looking outside the professional and geographical box is what has shaped Brand: "My father always said: Steal with your eyes. Take what you can get." That's exactly what he did, eventually bringing his "booty" back to Lohne. Always curious about everything that is different and unknown, this became his personal hobby in the form of travelling while also shaping his analytical view of company and industry. He challenged alleged laws and tenets. Instead of following old routes, he looks for new paths of his own.

The Spiritus Rector in process was the "Duke of Berkshire". Who is behind this venerable name? Actually, the "Duke of Berkshire" is not a member of the British landed gentry, but an old English breed of pigs. A few years ago, a retailer approached Brand and asked whether he could supply particularly high-quality meat. He could – after establishing a separate supply chain, just like that. "This project took us onto new ground", Brand recalls. "Husbandry, feeding, marketing: we had to rethink everything along completely new lines, all geared to quality." Lots of work and lots of change – but it was an extremely positive experience. The project contradicted many rules of the business. Size of the company? Doesn't matter. Straw and open pens? Economically possible. Tail docking? Not necessary in open pens. Antibiotics? We can manage without. These important insights also resulted in the founding of the Open Stall Association, which for several years now has been increasingly successful in advocating species-appropriate animal husbandry.

What began as an experiment has become established practice. The company meanwhile even has its own brand for the premium segment, known as "Brand Meat Excellence". At the same time, the company has redefined its role in the market, changing from pure slaughterhouse to coveted project developer and mediator. "Most companies try to keep complexity out of their processes. We deliberately make them complex", explains Niko Brand confidently. "Today we sell more than just a piece of meat. It's about the story behind it and added value beyond the product itself."

Preferred course? Into the wind

Transparency and communication are two mainstays of the new philosophy. "In a slaughterhouse, living creatures become food products. That's not going to change. But I think we can talk about it". When North German Television wanted to make a documentary about "The Way to the Schnitzel", Brand convinced the team to include the slaughtering process, despite being scheduled for prime-time viewing. The firm is also active on channels such as Facebook, Instagram or YouTube. "Of course we get criticised. We've even faced a shitstorm with several thousand comments. But for me, communication is part

Niko Brand ist jemand, der sich an einem klaren inneren Kompass orientiert. Seine Koordinaten sind Fairness, Tatendrang und Optimismus. Diese Haltung verbindet er mit einer Affinität für technologische Innovationen und betriebswirtschaftlichem Gespür. Das macht seine Projekte so erfolgreich. Am wichtigsten ist aber vielleicht etwas anderes: Trotz des nordischen Understatements ist deutlich zu spüren, wie viel Spaß ihm all das macht. Besonders motiviert fühlte er sich dabei von Sätzen wie „Das geht nicht, weil . . .". Seine intuitive Reaktion auf solche Aussagen lautet: „Das wollen wir doch mal sehen." Und siehe da: Häufig ging es doch. Vorausgesetzt, man brachte Pioniergeist und Ausdauer mit. „Nicht alles funktioniert sofort", weiß Brand heute. „Manche Projekte haben anfangs tiefrote Zahlen geschrieben. Aber wir waren überzeugt, dass sie richtig waren. Deshalb haben wir daran festgehalten." Zu Recht: Die meisten Konzepte zahlen sich längst aus – und zwar für alle Beteiligten. Das ist das Besondere am „System Brand": Es geht nicht um die Ziele eines einzelnen Akteurs, es geht dabei um gemeinsame Vorhaben, die Vorteile für die gesamte Wertschöpfungskette bedeuten: vom Tier und Landwirt bis zum Händler und Konsument. Ganz anders als damals in Cincinnati.

Und wie waren die Reaktionen der Branche zu alledem? Zunächst verhalten. „Lass das mal, sonst müssen wir das auch machen" – diesen Satz hat Brand von Landwirten nicht nur einmal gehört. Gelassen hat er es trotzdem nicht. Und obwohl niemand musste, haben die anderen schließlich doch mitgemacht. Zu deutlich waren die Vorteile: für die Tiere, für die Betriebe, für die Konsumenten. Zudem lässt sich der Erfolg auch in Zahlen ausdrücken: In den letzten zehn Jahren hat sich die Mitarbeiterzahl der Firma Brand vervierfacht, der Umsatz wuchs von 14 Mio. Euro ins Dreistellige.

Heute im Angebot: die Zukunft

Niko Brand bereitet Wege, für sich selbst und für andere, doch am Ziel wähnt er sich noch nicht. Etwa zehn Prozent tragen die Premiumprodukte aktuell zum Umsatz bei, bis zu fünfzig Prozent sollen es werden. Ein Vorbild ist dabei auch die kulinarische Konkurrenz: „Beim Rindfleisch hat sich das Angebot ausdifferenziert. Es gibt Angus, Dry Age, US Beef. Da haben sich Marken herausgebildet." Und beim Schwein? „Da gab's nichts von alledem. Es war einfach: Schwein." Neben Produkt- und Markenentwicklung liegt Brands Fokus deshalb auch auf dem Verkauf. Gelungene Inszenierung und Beratung sind Schlüsselfaktoren für den Erfolg. Wie so etwas aussehen kann, lässt sich zum Beispiel am Rathausmarkt in Oldenburg erleben. „Bauer & Metzger" ist der Gegenentwurf zum Discounter: gediegene Atmosphäre, wertige Einrichtung, aufmerksame Bedienung. Manches erinnert an die Apotheke, die dort über Jahrhunderte ihren Sitz hatte. Der Metzger als Boutique? Ist das die Zukunft? „Nein", wehrt Brand ab. Um schmunzelnd hinzuzufügen: „Es ist die Gegenwart."

Aber was kommt danach? Fleischersatzprodukte sind auf dem Vormarsch, In-vitro-Fleisch soll bald marktreif sein. Wird das 100-jährige Jubiläum des Unternehmens im Jahr 2030 vielleicht schon die letzte große Party? „Auf keinen Fall", lacht Brand. „Für den Discountbereich ist die eine oder andere Entwicklung sicher ein Problem. Qualitätsfleisch wird aber nie aus dem 3-D-Drucker kommen." Sowieso

and parcel of the whole thing." And of course, there's a side effect to such commitment: today the family company from the Oldenburger Münsterland is seen as an innovation driver. "We're well connected, you'll find us bustling about all over the place. And we've meanwhile got a name for being good at all the special stuff."

Niko Brand is someone who works according to a clear inner compass. His coordinates are fairness, drive and optimism. He combines this approach with an affinity for technological innovation and a flair for business. That's what makes his projects so successful. But there's something else that's possibly even more important: despite all his Nordic understatement, it's clearly obvious that he loves doing it all. He has always been particularly motivated by sayings such as "That won't work because . . ." to which his instinctive reaction would be: "Well, let's see about that." And lo and behold, often enough it would work after all. As long as you've got a pioneering spirit and endurance. "It doesn't always work at once", is an insight Brand knows today. "Some projects started off firmly in the red. But we were convinced they were right. So we stuck with them." And rightly so: most of the concepts have long since paid off, for everyone involved. That's the special thing about the "Brand System". It's not about the goals of a single player: it's about joint projects with benefits along the whole supply chain, from the animal and farmer right through to the retailer and consumer. Totally different to the old days in Cincinnati.

And how has the industry reacted? Cautiously to start with. "Stop doing that, or we'll have to do it too" – those are words Brand has heard from more than just one farmer. Even so, he didn't stop doing it. And although no-one had to, in the end the others joined in as well. The advantages were just too apparent: for the animals, for the companies and for the consumers. What's more, the numbers reflect this success. Over the last ten years, Brand's workforce has quadrupled, with turnover growing from 14 million Euro to three-figure amounts.

On offer today: the future

Niko Brand is a pathfinder who finds paths for himself and others, but he still doesn't think he's reached the finishing line just yet. Premium products currently contribute about ten percent to turnover, but he's aiming for fifty percent. The culinary competition acts as role model: "The beef market has a differentiated offering that includes Angus, Dry Age, US Beef, leading to the emergence of certain brands." And what about pork? "There's none of that. Just pork." So Brand's focus is on sales as well as product and brand development. Successful staging and advice are key factors for success. One possibility can be seen at the Rathausmarkt in Oldenburg. "Bauer & Metzger" (Farmer & Butcher) is an alternative concept to discount stores: dignified atmosphere, first-rate fittings, attentive service. It's almost like the chemist's that used these premises for centuries. The butcher as a boutique? Is that the future? "No", parries Brand. And adds with a grin: "It's the present."

But then what? Meat substitute products are gaining ground an in-vitro meat will soon be ready for market. Will the company's 100th anniversary celebrations in 2030 possibly be the last big party? "Certainly not"; laughs Brand. "Some of these developments may certainly be a problem

Das Oldenburger Land ist eines der Zentren der deutschen Nahrungsmittelindustrie und bekannt für seine Schweinehaltung. Dass diese auch in Offenställen effektiv und artgerecht betrieben werden kann, beweist das Unternehmen von Niko Brand jeden Tag aufs Neue.

Oldenburger Land is one of the centres of Germany's food industry and is well-known as a pig farming region. Niko Brand's farm shows each and every day how this can be done effectively with a species-appropriate husbandry concept also in open pens.

hat Brand längst das nächste Projekt im Blick: „Ein eigener Hofladen wäre toll. Er könnte unser Showroom werden, in dem wir unsere Story erzählen. Außerdem würden wir gerne ausbilden; und dort könnten wir zeigen, wie vielfältig der Job in unserer Branche sein kann. Meiner ist es jedenfalls!" Noch stehen die Überlegungen ganz am Anfang. Aber das galt für alle Ideen von Niko Brand einmal – und dann werden sie schneller Realität, als man denkt. Der eigene Weg geht also weiter. Und wer weiß? Vielleicht heißt es irgendwann in einem anderen Text: „Alles begann in Lohne . . ."

for the discount sector. But quality meat will never come from the 3D printer." Brand meanwhile is focusing on his next project: "I'd love to have our own farm shop. It could be our showroom where we tell our story. Furthermore, we'd like to get involved in training apprentices. This would give us an opportunity to show how diverse jobs can be in this industry. Well, my job certainly is!" At the moment, things are very much in the initial stages. But that applied to all Niko Brand's ideas at one stage – and they became reality sooner than expected. So he's continuing along his own path. And who knows? Maybe one day you'll find another text that begins with the words "It all began in Lohne . . ."

HEIDEMARK

Unsere Stärken: Unsere Mitarbeitenden, Qualität und Kompetenz

HEIDEMARK ist ein mit der Region Oldenburger Münsterland verbundenes inhabergeführtes Unternehmen in der dritten Generation. Der Ursprung des Unternehmens liegt in Höltinghausen und startete mit einem Mischfutterwerk, das sich bald auf die Fütterung von Puten spezialisierte. Später kam die Verarbeitung der Pute dazu. Neben der Haltung von Puten ist die Verarbeitung zu hervorragenden Putenprodukten das, was das Unternehmen HEIDEMARK heute auszeichnet.

Als Unternehmen haben wir die Verantwortung für nahezu die gesamte Wertschöpfungskette. Da wir einen sehr großen Teil davon in unserem Unternehmen bündeln, haben wir präzise aufeinander abgestimmte Verarbeitungsschritte, höchste Flexibilität und maximale Zuverlässigkeit in Qualität. Daneben sind wir ein leistungsstarker Partner für den Handel. Das bildet die Basis für ein nachhaltiges, vertrauensvolles und partnerschaftliches Wirtschaften.

Information

Gründungsjahr: 1965	**Year founded:** 1965
Mitarbeiter: rund 1800	**Employees:** around 1,800
Umsatz: 660 Mio. Euro pro Jahr	**Turnover:** 660 million Euros p.a.
Leistungsspektrum:	**Range of services:**
Herstellung von Putenprodukten für den Lebensmitteleinzelhandel und die Industrie	manufacturing turkey products for food retailing and for the industry
www.heidemark.de	

Geschäftsführender Gesellschafter
Executive Manager
Christopher Kalvelage

Our strengths: our workforce, quality and expertise

HEIDEMARK is a proprietor-run company in the third generation with close ties to the Oldenburger Münsterland region. The company's origins are to be found in Höltinghausen, where business began with a compound feet plant before soon specialising in the feeding of turkeys, followed later by processing the turkeys. Besides turkey husbandry, today it is the subsequent processing into outstanding turkey products that makes HEIDEMARK stand out. As a company, we are responsible for practically the whole supply chain. As most of the value creation process is pooled in our company, we work with precisely coordinated processing steps, greatest flexibility and maximum reliability in quality. Furthermore, we are a highly efficient partner for the retail trade. This forms the basis for sustainable, trusting business management based on partnership.

Emsland Food GmbH

Using nature to create

Die Emsland Group ist ein international agierendes Unternehmen, das auf Basis pflanzlicher Rohstoffe innovative Produkte für die weiterverarbeitende Industrie herstellt. In unserem Cloppenburger Werk produzieren wir jährlich rund 82.000 Tonnen Kartoffelflocken und verarbeiten dabei etwa 415.000 Tonnen Kartoffeln überwiegend von Vertragslandwirten aus der Region. Rund 85 Prozent der hergestellten Kartoffelflocken werden exportiert und in der weltweiten Snack- und Backwarenindustrie sowie als Bindemittel für Suppen und Saucen eingesetzt.

Die Emsland Group setzt konsequent auf Innovationen. Im hochmodernen „Emsland Innovation Germany" treffen die jahrzehntelangen Erfahrungen unserer Mitarbeiter und die neuesten Anlagen der Lebensmitteltechnologie zusammen, um kundenspezifische Produktlösungen zu kreieren und die Zukunft der Ernährungswirtschaft aktiv mitzugestalten.

In Cloppenburg bilden wir unsere eigenen Nachwuchskräfte aus in den Berufen Elektroniker*in für Energie- und Gebäudetechnik, Elektroniker*in für Betriebstechnik, Metallbauer*in Fachrichtung Konstruktionstechnik, Industriemechaniker*in und Fachkraft für Lebensmitteltechnik.

Using nature to create

The Emsland Group is a company that operates internationally that manufactures innovative products for the processing industry based on raw materials from vegetables. In our Cloppenburg plant, we produce around 82,000 tonnes of potato flakes every year, processing about 415,000 tonnes of potatoes mainly from contract farmers in the region. We export around 85 percent of the potato flakes that we make, which are used in the global snack and baked goods industry and also as a thickening agent in soups and sauces.

The Emsland Group is committed to innovation above all else. The ultra-modern "Emsland Innovation Germany" combines the decades of experience accumulated by our employees with state-of-the-art food processing technology, creating customised product solutions for our customers. We thus play an active role in shaping the food industry of the future.

In Cloppenburg we train our talented young people to become electronic technicians for energy and building systems, electronic technicians for operations technology, metal workers for design technology, industrial mechanics and food processing technicians.

Information

Gründungsjahr:
1966 von der Pfanni Otto Eckart KG; seit April 2000 Teil der Emsland Group
Mitarbeiter: etwa 120
Leistungsspektrum:
Produktion von Kartoffelflocken

Year founded:
1966 by Pfanni Otto Eckart KG; part of the Emsland Group since April 2000
Employees: approx. 120
Range of services:
production of potato flakes

www.emsland-group.de

Mittmann – Catering & Konzepte

Seit Gründung unseres Familienunternehmens Mittmann in 1962 führen wir nun in dritter Generation unser „Handwerk" in der Verantwortung gegenüber unseren Kunden und Mitarbeitern mit größter Sorgfalt und Aufmerksamkeit aus. Mit viel Leidenschaft und ständigen Innovationen haben wir uns aus einem Tante-Emma-Laden zu einem der führenden Anbieter für Automatendienstleistungen und bis heute zu einem Fullservice-Dienstleister für die betriebliche Mitarbeiterversorgung entwickelt.

Wir stehen unseren Kunden von der Projektierung bis zur täglichen Rund-um-Versorgung kompetent zur Seite. Dieses Gesamtkonzept kann aus verschiedenen Modulen der Betriebsgastronomie, des Caterings sowie des Vendings zusammengestellt werden. Von der stationären Automatenstraße für die 24-Stunden-Verpflegung über Büro- und Konferenzservice bis zu komplexen Angeboten mit Live-Cooking, Well-Food und Foodtrucks haben wir über die Jahre zahlreiche Kombinationen erfolgreich umgesetzt – ob für 5 oder für 5.000 Mitarbeiter. Wir finden für jede Unternehmensgröße das passende Konzept, immer ausgerichtet auf Ihre individuellen Bedürfnisse.

Die Verbundenheit mit unserer Region – dem Nordwesten – ist für uns keine Worthülse, sondern Leitmotiv unserer nachhaltigen Strategie. Wir setzen auf regionale Bezugsquellen und saisonale Produktvielfalt. Gleichzeitig wissen wir, dass sich Erfahrung und Innovation durch nichts ersetzen lassen. Dank kontinuierlicher Weiterentwicklungen bieten wir unseren Kunden nicht nur modernste Automatentechnik mit smarten Telemetrie- und Zahlungsmöglichkeiten, sondern auch Ernährungs- und Gesundheitskonzepte nach höchsten Standards (Job & Fit der Deutschen Gesellschaft für Ernährung), damit Sie ein gesundheitsbewusstes Betriebsklima etablieren können.

Mittmann
Catering Service & Konzept GmbH

Information

Gründungsjahr: 1962	**Year founded:** 1962
Mitarbeiter: 95	**Employees:** 95
Leistungsspektrum:	**Range of services:**

Betriebsgastronomie & Catering
– Bewirtschaftung von Gemeinschaftsverpflegungseinrichtungen
– Service für Konferenzen, Gästebewirtung und betriebliche Events

Corporate hospitality & catering
– management of public canteens
– service for conferences, guest hospitality and corporate events

Automatenservice
– Vending
– Office Coffee Service
– leitungsgebundene Wasserspender

Machine service
– vending
– office coffee service
– plumbed-in water dispensers

Technischer Support
– Automatentechnik
– Telemetrie- und Zahlungssysteme

Technical support
– vending technology
– telemetry and payment systems

www.mittmann-ol.de

Mittmann – catering & concepts

Since 1962, our Oldenburg family company Mittmann has been plying its trade with all due care and attention, showing great responsibility towards customers and staff. Meanwhile, the third generation of the family is in charge. With passion and constant innovation we have progressed from our early beginnings as a corner shop and are now a leading provider of vending machine services, meanwhile with full-service solutions for corporate employee catering. We offer our customers expert advice and support from project planning through to daily all-inclusive catering. The total concept can be put together from various modules for corporate hospitality, catering and vending. We have successfully implemented numerous combinations in recent years, from stationary vending systems for 24h catering via office and conference service through to complex solutions with live cooking, wellness food and food trucks, for just 5 or even 5,000 employees. We find the ideal concept for every company size, always aligned to your individual requirements.

Faith in our region, the North West, is not just an empty phrase for us: indeed, it is the guiding principle behind our sustainable strategy. We use regional sources and seasonal product diversity. At the same time, we know that nothing can replace experience and innovation. Continuous further developments put us in a position to offer our customers not only state-of-the-art vending technology with smart telemetry and payment options, but also nutrition and health concepts on the very highest standards ("Job & Fit" by the Deutsche Gesellschaft für Ernährung – German Nutrition Association) so that you can establish a health-conscious environment in your company.

M FOOD GROUP® GmbH

Wir veredeln Lebensmittel. Auf natürliche Weise.

Zu den Schwerpunkten der M FOOD GROUP® zählt die Entwicklung, Produktion und der Vertrieb von Starter- und Schutzkulturen, funktionellen Additiven und Gewürzmischungen. Dabei ist die Unternehmensgruppe vollumfänglich auf maßgeschneiderte Lösungen für die Lebensmittelindustrie spezialisiert.

Neben Meat Cracks® gehört seit 2018 auch die damals neu gegründete MicroTec GmbH zur M FOOD GROUP®. Mit erfahrenen Experten und innovativen Speziallösungen verschafft das inzwischen übergeführte Unternehmen seit der Firmengründung im Jahr 2001 seinen Kunden weltweit einen echten Technologievorsprung.

CULTURES TASTE TECHNOLOGY – Made in Germany.

We process food products. In a natural way.

The M FOOD GROUP® focuses on the development, production and distribution of starter and protective cultures, functional additives and spice mixtures. The company group is fully specialized in solutions for the food industry.

In addition to Meat Cracks®, the then newly founded MicroTec GmbH has also been part of the M FOOD GROUP® since 2018. Since the company was founded in 2001, the owner-managed company has been providing its customers worldwide with a real technological advantage by providing experienced experts and innovative special solutions.

CULTURES TASTE TECHNOLOGY – Made in Germany.

Information
Gründungsjahr/Year founded: 2001
Mitarbeiter/Employees: 130
Mission:
CULTURES TASTE TECHNOLOGY for
/Meat /Milk & Cheese /Veggie & Fresh /Fish
www.m-foodgroup.de

TURM-Sahne GmbH

Information

Gründungsjahr: 1949	**Year founded:** 1949
Mitarbeiter: etwa 75	**Employees:** about 75
Leistungsspektrum:	**Range of services:**
– Herstellung und Vertrieb sterilisierter Milchprodukte	– production and distribution of sterilised milk products
– mehr als 200 Artikel im Sortiment	– range of more than 200 items
– Spezialist im Bereich Glasflaschen	– specialist on the glass bottle segment

www.turm-sahne.de

Wir, bei der TURM-Sahne GmbH sind nicht nur die Spezialisten für die Herstellung und den Vertrieb von Kaffeesahne in Glasflaschen, sondern bieten neben Tradition auch Innovation.
Seit seiner Gründung im Jahr 1949 hat sich das Unternehmen stetig weiterentwickelt. Mit dem Umzug im Jahr 1994 in den Westerender Weg wurde auf dem Gelände der Molkerei Ammerland eG ein nachhaltiger Standort geschaffen, von dem aus die Geschäftsaktivitäten in über 40 Länder koordiniert werden.
Mehr als 70 Jahre Erfahrung machen das Oldenburger Unternehmen zu einem zuverlässigen Lieferanten für ausgezeichnete Produktqualität. Die TURM-Sahne GmbH hat ihr Sortiment stetig ausgebaut und arbeitet mit einer eigenen Produktentwicklung nun sogar an pflanzlichen Alternativen zur Milch, um stets allen Kundenansprüchen gerecht werden zu können.

At TURM-Sahne GmbH, we are not only specialists for producing and distributing coffee cream in glass bottles: we also offer tradition in combination with innovation.
Since it was founded in 1949, the company has continued developing all the time. The move to Westerender Weg in 1994 created a sustainable site on the premises of Molkerei Ammerland eG that today acts as the basis for coordinating business activities in more than 40 countries.
More than 70 years of experience make the company from Oldenburg a reliable supplier of excellent product quality. TURM-Sahne GmbH is constantly expanding its range. The company's own product development experts are even working on a plant-based alternative to milk in order to ensure all customer demands are always met.

DER YACHTBAU-KÜNSTLER

The Yacht Building Artist

AUTOR:
PETER RINGEL

Mega yachts for the super-rich, minesweepers for the navy and special pilot vessels: now in its fourth generation, the family company Abeking & Rasmussen stands for the art of shipbuilding in the Wesermarsch. Shipyard owner Hans Schaedla is the driving force behind the yacht building business.

Megayachten für Superreiche, Minensucher für die Marine und Spezialschiffe für Lotsen – das in vierter Generation geführte Familienunternehmen Abeking & Rasmussen steht für Schiffbaukunst aus der Wesermarsch. Werfteigner Hans Schaedla hat den Yachtbau forciert.

Zwischen Gegenwart und Vergangenheit liegen im Büro von Hans Schaedla nur wenige Meter. An der Wand hängen Konstruktionszeichnungen einer geplanten Superyacht. Vor dem Schreibtisch des Werftchefs steht ein Modell der *Hetairos*, eine 42-Meter-Ketch mit eleganter Linienführung. Der Rumpf des Originals besteht aus sieben Zentimeter starkem Mahagoni, auch die Details unter Deck sind aus dunklem Holz. Damit steht der Zweimaster in der Tradition tausender klassischer Segler, die auf der 1907 gegründeten Werft Abeking & Rasmussen gefertigt wurden. Mit seiner mondänen Ausstattung voller Hightech steht das Schiff zugleich in einer Reihe mit den Luxusyachten, die heute am Weserufer entstehen.

Only a few metres separate the present and the past in Hans Schaedla's office. The wall is taken up with construction drawings for a planned super yacht. In front of the shipyard boss's desk there's a model of the *Hetairos*, a 42-metre sloop with elegant lines. The hull of the original vessel consists of mahogany, seven centimetres thick. Details under deck are also made of dark wood. The two-master thus continues the tradition of thousands of classic sailing ships made by the Abeking & Rasmussen shipyard that was founded in 1907. At the same time, the ship with its sophisticated high-tech fittings and features also holds its own with the luxury yachts built today on the banks of the river Weser.

Die 1992 abgelieferte Mahagoni-Ketch war das zweite große Schiffs-projekt, dass Schaedla nach seinem Einstieg im Familienbetrieb ver-antwortete. Während sich sein Vater Hermann Schaedla vor allem den Neubauten für Marine und Behörden widmete, trieb der Sohn das Geschäft mit luxuriösen Megayachten voran. Dabei profitierte der Schiffbauingenieur von seiner Zeit in Neuengland. Er arbeitete bei einem Yachtdesigner, nahm an Regatten teil, besuchte den America's Cup. So lernte er, worauf es ankommt beim Umgang mit finanzkräf-tigen Yachtbesitzern und solchen, die es werden wollen: „Es ist wichtig, die Mentalität der Eigner kennenzulernen."

Verhandlungen sind Chefsache

Ende 2020 wechselte Schaedla von der Geschäftsführung an die Auf-sichtsratsspitze der nicht börsennotierten Abeking & Rasmussen Schiffs- und Yachtwerft SE. Doch er ist weiter persönlich gefragt, wenn sich Scheichs, osteuropäische Oligarchen oder US-Tycoone für die Schiffbaukünste aus Lemwerder interessieren – die angehenden Yachteigner wollen gerne mit dem Werfteigner verhandeln. Details wie Pools und Padel-Tennisplätze, Hubschrauberlandeplätze, Fahrstühle und Entertainment klären die Projektteams von Werft und künftigem Besitzer.

Bei den meisten nach individuellen Wünschen gefertigten Mega-yachten darf Schaedla nichts vom luxuriösen Innenleben verraten: „Diskretion gehört zum Geschäft." Die fällt dem hanseatisch zurück-haltenden Mehrheitsgesellschafter nicht schwer. Zugleich tritt der 1962 geborene Urenkel des Firmengründers Henry Rasmussen äußerst bodenständig auf. Der Helm, der in seinem Büro mit Weserblick über dem Feuerlöscher hängt, dient nicht als Deko. Wenn Schaedla durch die Werfthallen geht, wird er respektvoll mit „Moin Chef" empfangen. Schiffbau hat er auf der gegenüberliegenden Seite des Stroms, beim einstigen Bremer Vulkan, von Grund auf gelernt: vom Modellbau bis zum Schweißen und Gießen.

Drei bis vier Jahre dauert es, bis eine Superyacht fertig am Pier neben der Fähre nach Bremen-Vegesack liegt, mindestens ein Jahr entfällt auf die Konstruktion. Baunummer 6506 war eine soeben abgelieferte Motoryacht, zumindest schon auf Papier existieren die Neubauten bis zur Nummer 6512. Und sie werden stetig länger. Seit einem Anbau können auf der Werft 125 Meter lange Schiffe gebaut werden. Damit ist für Schaedla Schluss: „Für noch größere Schiffe ist der Markt zu klein." So viele Superreiche gibt es dann doch nicht.

Gern weiter unterm Radar bleiben

Bei Megayachten konkurriert die in vierter Generation geführte Firma weltweit mit einem guten Dutzend Werften. Der größere Wettbe-werber Lürssen ist der direkte Nachbar. Um Kunden etwa auf Messen in Monaco oder Fort Lauderdale zu gewinnen, gilt es nicht nur bei Perfektion und Exklusivität zu punkten. Ebenso geht es um den Preis, auf den selbst Multimillionäre achten. Moderne Fertigungstechno-logien sparen Zeit und Geld. Beim 3-D-Laserschweißen etwa entsteht weniger Hitze und es gibt keine Beulen im Stahl, die später auszuspach-teln sind. Bei manchen Kunden lässt sich auch mit Tempo punkten, indem bereits gebaute Yachten abgewandelt werden. „Auf Basis der Motoryacht *Excellence III* haben wir sieben verschiedene Schiffe ge-

Rendering eines Mehrzweckschiffes der Küstenwache mit Landeplatt-form für Helikopter

Rendering of a multi-purpose Coast Guard ship with a landing platform for helicopters

Werften vorwiegend mittelständisch geprägt

Die rund 130 Werften in Deutschland sind meist hochspezialisiert. Der Serienbau von Standardschiffen wurde von Hightech-Einzelfertigungen abgelöst. Während große Frachter und Tanker inzwischen meist in Ostasien gebaut werden, dominiert die europäische Industrie die Nischenmärkte. Auf den Werften entstehen Spezialschiffe für Behörden und Marine, Yachten und Passagierschiffe. Neben Neubauten gehören auch Reparaturen und Umbauten zum Geschäft.

Ihre große wirtschaftliche Bedeutung gewinnt die Branche nicht nur durch die Wertschöpfung der Werften, sondern auch durch die vielen Zulieferbetriebe. Der Verband für Schiffbau und Meerestechnik beziffert den heimischen Beschäftigungs-effekt auf mindestens 200.000 überwiegend hoch qualifizierte Arbeitskräfte. Deutschland verfügt über die weltweit führende Zulieferindustrie für den Schiffbau.

Die deutschen Werften sind weitgehend mittelständisch geprägt. Neben wenigen Konzerngesellschaften gibt es viele Familien-unternehmen. Im Nordwesten konzentriert sich der Schiffbau auf traditionsreiche Standorte an Ems und Weser. Während sich die Meyer Werft in Papenburg auf Kreuzfahrtschiffe spezialisiert hat, entstehen in der Wesermarsch sowie in Bremen und Bremer-haven vor allem Megayachten, Spezial- und Marineschiffe.

The mahogany sloop delivered in 1992 was the second large ship-building project for which Schaedla was responsible after joining the family business. While his father Hermann Schaedla focused primarily on new-builds for the navy and authorities, his son forged ahead with the business of luxury mega yachts. Here the shipbuilding engineer profited from his time in New England, where he worked for a yacht designer, took part in regattas and visited the America's Cup. This taught him what matters when dealing with well-heeled yacht owners and those who want to become just that: "It's important to understand the owners' mindset".

Negotiations are for the boss

At the end of 2020, he retired from the Board of Directors of the non-listed company Abeking & Rasmussen Schiffs- und Yachtwerft SE to become Chairman of the Supervisory Board. But he is still personally very much in demand when sheikhs, East European oligarchs or US tycoons show an interest in the art of shipbuilding here in Lemwerder: the soon-to-be yacht owners are always seen to negotiate with the shipyard owner directly. The project teams working for the shipyard and for the future owner then clarify the details such as pools and paddle tennis courts, heliports, elevators and entertainment.

In most cases, Schaedla is not in a position to talk about any aspects of the luxurious interiors for the mega yachts that are built to individual customer specifications. "Discretion is part of the business". That's not a problem for the majority partner with his typical Hanseatic reserve. Born in 1962 as the great-grandson of company founder Henry Rasmussen, Hans Schaedla nevertheless comes across as being extremely down-to-earth. The safety helmet hanging from the fire extinguisher in his office with its view of the river Weser is not meant for decoration. When Schaedla goes through the shipyard hangars, he's greeted respectfully with "Mornin' Boss". He learnt shipbuilding from scratch on the other bank of the river at the former Bremer Vulkan shipyard, from modelling through to welding and casting.

It takes three to four years before a super yacht will be moored ready for delivery at the pier next to the ferry that crosses to Bremen-Vegesack. At least twelve months of this time is taken up with the design. Construction number 6506 was a motor yacht that has just been delivered. The shipyard already has new-builds on paper at least up to construction number 6512. And they are getting longer all the time. A new production hangar now allows the shipyard to build ships of up to 125 metres in length. That's the end for Schaedla: "The market is too small for even bigger ships." There aren't so many super rich people after all.

Happily below the radar

When it comes to mega yachts, the family firm competes with a good dozen shipyards worldwide. The greatest rival Lürssen is right next door. When vying for customers at trade-fairs in Monaco or Fort Lauderdale, it's not just a question of perfection and exclusivity. The price also matters, even for multi-millionaires. State-of-the-art production technology helps to save time and money. 3D laser welding for example generates less heat and produces fewer dents in the steel that have to be

Shipyards primarily in SME hand

Most of the roughly 130 shipyards in Germany are highly specialised. Individual high-tech designs have taken over from the mass production of standard vessels. Most large freighters and tankers are meanwhile built in East Asia, while European shipbuilding dominates the niche markets. The shipyards are busy with special ships for the authorities and navies, as well as yachts and passenger ships. Repairs and refits are just as much a part of business as new-builds.

The great economic significance of the industry results not just from value creation in the shipyards themselves but also from the many supplier companies. The German Shipbuilding and Ocean Industries Association puts the local employment effect at a figure of at least 200,000 many highly qualified jobs. Germany has the world's leading supplier industry for shipbuilding.

German shipyards are primarily SME-owned, with many family companies alongside a few large corporations. Shipbuilding in the North West is focused on sites with a long tradition on the rivers Ems and Weser. While Meyer Werft in Papenburg has specialised in cruise ships, shipyards in the Wesermarsch and in Bremen and Bremerhaven mainly build mega yachts, special ships and naval vessels.

baut", erklärt Schaedla. Rumpf und Maschine bleiben beim Plattform-konzept gleich.

Schiffbau ist bei A&R ein hoch arbeitsteiliges Geschäft. 30 Prozent der Wertschöpfung entfallen auf die Werft mit ihren knapp 500 Mitarbeitern, das Gros auf Zulieferer für Elektronik, Interieur oder Stahlrümpfe. Die Rohbauten werden oft von anderen Unternehmen gefertigt und über die Weser eingeschwommen. Trotz der Konkurrenz im Yachtsegment wird in anderen Bereichen eng kooperiert. „Im Marinegeschäft bauen wir Schiffe auch in Arbeitsgemeinschaften mit anderen Werften", berichtet Schaedla. Ansonsten hielt sich die Firma aus den Fusionen und Verbünden in der jüngeren deutschen Schiffbaugeschichte heraus. Das bringt auch weniger öffentliche Aufmerksamkeit mit sich, die Rolle unterm Radar behagt Schaedla.

Flexibilität macht den Erfolg

Neben Megayachten gibt es mit den Spezial- sowie Marineschiffen zwei weitere Standbeine, die auf lange Sicht je rund ein Drittel des Geschäfts ausmachen. Führt zum Beispiel ein Embargo dazu, dass Oligarchen aus dem Osten keine Schiffe mehr bestellen, hat A&R Platz für andere Aufträge. Zehn Prozent des Umsatzes kommt durch Reparaturen, Umbauten und Wartung herein. Mal ist von sechs Schiffen, die auf der Werft liegen, nur eines ein Neubau, im nächsten Jahr kann sich das Verhältnis wieder umkehren. Minensuchboote werden bereits seit der Vorkriegszeit gebaut, inzwischen sind sie aus antimagnetischem Stahl, extraleise und mit geringem „Infrarot-Fußabdruck". Auftraggeber sind Marinestreitkräfte etwa aus Südostasien oder der Türkei. Mehr als 360 dieser Spezialschiffe sind bei A&R bereits vom Stapel gelaufen.

Für Minensuchboote war eigentlich auch die spezielle Rumpfform des Small Waterplane Area Twin Hull (SWATH) gedacht. Zwei torpedoförmige Auftriebskörper tief unter der Wasseroberfläche sorgen auch bei rauer See dafür, dass die Schiffe kaum auf den Wellen schaukeln. Ein auf eigene Rechnung gebauter Prototyp stieß bei der Marine auf Wohlwollen, mündete aber nicht in einen Auftrag, erzählt Schaedla. „Wir haben das Schiff dann rot statt grau angemalt und den Lotsen vorgestellt." Mit Erfolg: Auf den schwimmenden Plattformen kommen heute Lotsen an Bord großer Pötte und Arbeiter zu Offshore-Windparks. SWATH-Schiffe wurden zwar nicht auf der Werft erfunden, dort aber im Computer optimiert. Weltweit sieht sich A&R bei dem Schiffstyp vorn.

Beim SWATH-Prototypen hat es sich gelohnt, ins Risiko zu gehen. Bei anderen Projekten ohne konkreten Auftrag bleibt es dagegen oft bei Studien. Das gilt bis auf Weiteres auch für das anthrazitfarbene Modell eines SWATH-Kreuzfahrtschiffs im Foyer der Werft. In der wegen der Pandemie kriselnden Branche ist gerade nichts zu holen, winkt Schaedla ab: „Der Markt ist erst einmal tot." Immerhin hat die Werft schon einmal eine SWATH-Yacht gebaut, die besonders ruhig im Wasser liegt – die Ehefrau des Eigners neigte zur Seekrankheit.

smoothed over later on. Some customers can be won over with speed by modifying the design of existing yachts. "We built seven different ships based on the motor yacht *Excellence III*", explains Schaedla. The hull and machine remain the same in this platform concept.

Shipbuilding at A&R entails a high degree of division of labour. The shipyard itself accounts for 30 percent of value creation with its roughly 500 employees. The rest is generated by suppliers for electronic systems, interior fittings or steel hulls. The shells are often produced by other companies and floated across to the yard on the river Weser. Despite the competition in the yacht segment, there is close cooperation in other areas. "When it comes to naval vessels, we work together with other shipyards on a consortium basis", reports Schaedla. Otherwise the company stands well back from all the mergers and alliances recently featured in Germany's shipbuilding history. This also attracts less public attention. Schaedla likes to keep below the radar.

Success through flexibility

Besides mega yachts, special ships and naval vessels are two other mainstays that each account for roughly a third of the company's business in the long term. If, for example oligarchs from East Europe stop ordering ships due to an embargo, A&R then has capacity for other orders. Ten percent of turnover is generated by repairs, refits and maintenance. Sometimes only one of six ships in the yard will be a new-build. Then again, next year the situation can be reversed again. Minesweepers have been built since before the war. Meanwhile they are made of non-magnetic steel and are designed to be extra-quiet with a minimum "infrared footprint". They are ordered by navies from South East Asia or Turkey, for example. A&R have already launched more than 360 of these special ships.

Minesweepers were actually also the intended vessels for the special hull design of the Small Waterplane Area Twin Hull (SWATH). Two torpedo-shaped floatation structures deep under the water surface ensure that ships remain calm on the waves even in rough seas. A prototype built at the yard's own cost met with the navy's approval but failed to produce an order, says Schaedla. "So we changed the paintwork from grey to red and presented it to the pilots." A successful move: today the floating platforms brings pilots to huge ships and workers to offshore wind farms. Although SWATH vessels were not invented by the shipyard, this is where computers optimised them. A&R claims to lead the global field with this type of vessel.

It was definitely worth taking the risk with the SWATH prototype. Other projects that fail to produce a specific order often get no further than the study stage. This also applies to the anthracite model of a SWATH cruise ship on display in the foyer of the shipyard. There's nothing to be gained from this sector at the moment due to the crisis caused by the pandemic. Schaedla gives a thumbs down: "That market is dead for the time being." But even so, the shipyard has already built a SWATH yacht designed for particular stability in the water: the owner's wife suffered from seasickness.

Die 2019 fertiggestellte 80-Meter-Superyacht *Excellence* mit dem auffallend gebogenen Bug erinnert mit ihrer schnittigen Form unwillkürlich an ein Raumschiff.

The 80-meter superyacht *Excellence*, completed in 2019 with its strikingly curved bow and its sleek shape, is involuntarily reminiscent of a spaceship.

Oldtimer mit eigenem Spirit

Eine Episode in der Firmengeschichte blieb auch das Kapitel Rotec. Das Tochterunternehmen nutzte das Know-how der Schiffbauer beim Glasfaserkunststoff, um Rotorblätter für Windturbinen herzustellen. Als der Zulieferer wegen der Krise der Windbranche seine Tore schließen musste, hatte A&R seine Anteile längst weitergegeben. Den Ableger des Schiffbaus hatten Schaedlas Vater und Bruder vorangetrieben, auch weitere Familienmitglieder sind in der Werft aktiv. Das Unternehmen dürfte in Zukunft inhabergeführt bleiben.

Das Elternhaus von Schaedla am Rand der Werft dient heute den Zusammenkünften der Eigner. In seiner Kindheit entdeckte er von dort aus das Firmengelände. Am liebsten strich Hans über den Platz, auf dem das Holz des Sägewerks lagerte, ehe daraus schnittige Regattaboote wurden. Auch das Schiff der Werfteigner war solch ein Holzboot, fiel aber vor einigen Jahren den Flammen zum Opfer. Seitdem segelt Schaedla bei Freunden als Gast mit oder chartert ein Schiff. Fest im Kalender stehen Veranstaltungen auf der Ostsee wie die Classic Week oder Kiel Classics. Viele der dort segelnden Boote sind A&R-Oldtimer und gelten in der Seglerszene als Rolls Royce zur See. Manche haben mehr als ein Jahrhundert auf dem Buckel, sehen aber aus wie neu. Schaedla sagt stolz: „Die Boote haben einen eigenen Spirit."

Das gilt auch für die *Hetairos*. Yachtdesigner Andrew Winch erinnert sich an die Feier zur Fertigstellung des Schiffs: An Bord spielte eine Brassband und für die Bootsbauer gab es Bier im Cockpit. Schaedla umrundete währenddessen in einem kleinen Ruderboot die edle Ketch, die jetzt als Modell vor seinem Schreibtisch steht.

Classic boats with a spirit of their own

The Rotec chapter was also no more than just an episode in the company's history. The subsidiary used the shipbuilders' expertise with fibreglass composites to make rotor blades for wind turbines. By the time the supplier went out of business due to the crisis in the wind branch, A&R had already disposed of its shares. Schaedla's father and brother had been the driving force behind the shipbuilding offshoot. Other members of the family are also actively involved in the shipyard. It looks as if the company will remain a proprietor-run business in future.

Schaedla's parental home on the edge of the shipyard is used today to for owners' meetings. As a child, he'd set off from here to discover the premises. Young Hans would love to roam around the yard that stored the timber from the shipyard before it was turned into sleek regatta boats. The shipyard owners also had a wooden boat, but it went up in flames a few years ago. Since then, Schaedla sails with friends as a guest on their yachts or he charters a ship. Various fixed points in his diary include events on the Baltic such as the Classic Week or Kiel Classics. Many of the boats sailing here are vintage A&R vessels, often called the Rolls Royce of the seas in the sailing scene. Some have seen more than a hundred years of service but still look as good as new. Schaedla says with pride: "The boats have a spirit of their own."

That also goes for the *Hetairos*. Yacht designer Andrew Winch remembers the celebrations that took place when the ship was completed, with a brass band on board and beer in the cockpit for the shipbuilders. Schaedla meanwhile manoeuvred a small rowing boat around the noble sloop, that now stands as a model in front of his desk.

Abeking & Rasmussen

Information
Gründungsjahr: 1907
Mitarbeiter: 475, davon
45 Auszubildende
Leistungsspektrum:
Yachten, Spezial- und
Marineschiffe

Year founded: 1907
Employees: 475, including
45 trainees
Range of services: yachts,
special ships and naval vessels

www.abeking.com

Im Jahr 1907 gründeten Georg Abeking und Henry Rasmussen eine auf Holzbau spezialisierte Boots- und Yachtwerft am Ufer der Weser. Im Laufe der Jahrzehnte entwickelte sich daraus eine hochmoderne Werft mit Hallen für Schiffe von bis zu 125 Metern Länge. Das Spezialgebiet der Werft ist die Entwicklung, Konstruktion und der Bau von hochwertigen Spezialschiffen und Megayachten. Heute liefert das familiengeführte Unternehmen nach wie vor Yachten, Spezial- und Marineschiffe an anspruchsvolle Kunden in aller Welt.
Seit ihrer Gründung war die zukunftsgerichtete Ausbildung junger Nachwuchskräfte ein Schwerpunkt der Werft. Sowohl in den klassischen Ausbildungsberufen als auch im Studium im Praxisverbund starten bei Abeking & Rasmussen viele junge Menschen Jahr für Jahr ins Berufsleben.

In 1907, Georg Abeking and Henry Rasmussen founded a shipyard that specialised in building wooden boats and yachts on the banks of the river Weser. Over the decades, this has turned into a state-of-the-art shipyard with production hangars for ships up to 125 metres in length. The shipyard has specialised in the development, design and building of top quality special ships and mega yachts. Today the family business continues to supply demanding customers all over the world with yachts, special ships and naval vessels. Since it was founded, the shipyard has focused particularly on offering forward-looking training to the next generation of young talents. Every year, many young people start their working lives at Abeking & Rasmussen either in traditional apprenticeships or on academic programmes with on-the-job training.

Jade-Dienst GmbH

In Wilhelmshaven am Jadebusen, einem der drei umschlagsstärksten deutschen Seehäfen, hat die Jade-Dienst GmbH seit 1958 ihren Firmensitz. Fachkompetenz durch zahlreiche Spezialisten garantieren den idealen Partner für maritime Dienstleistungen. Festmacherei, Bereederung, Umschlag, Entsorgung, Maschinenreparaturen, Hafen- und Logistikdienstleistungen gehören zum Repertoire in Häfen, Binnengewässern, im Watt und an der Küste. Mit einer 24/7 besetzten Einsatzzentrale sorgt eine Flotte von Flachwasserschleppern, Versorgungs- und Ölauffangschiffen, Pontons und unterschiedlichen Arbeitsschiffen für die optimale Umsetzung der in Auftrag gegebenen Dienste.
An der eigenen Kaianlage mit Bootsslip steht ein modernisierter Schwimmkran, der als Mehrzweck-Trägergerät vielfältig für Kran-, Bagger- und Rammarbeiten eingesetzt wird. Bewegt werden hier Lasten bis zu 100 Tonnen.

Information
Gründungsjahr: 1958
Mitarbeiter: etwa 140
Leistungsspektrum:
– Festmacherei und
  Hafendienste
– maritime Dienstleistungen
– Bergung, Schwergutladung
  und Mobilisierung
www.jade-dienst.de

Year founded: 1958
Employees: about 140
Range of services:
– mooring and port services
– maritime services
– salvage, heavy lift and
  mobilisation

Wilhelmshaven, one of the three busiest seaports in Germany, has been home to Jade-Dienst GmbH since 1958. The company is the ideal partner for maritime services, guaranteed by the expertise of numerous specialists. Mooring, ship management, handling, disposal, machine repairs, port and logistics services are part of the repertoire needed in ports, on inland waterways, in the mud flats and at the coast. The operations centre is staffed 24/7 to ensure optimum implementation of the ordered services with a fleet of shallow water tugs, supply and oil recovery vessels, pontoons and various working vessels.
The company operates its own quay with a slipway and an upgraded floating crane that is used as a multi-purpose unit for a wide range of crane, dredging and pile driving work, moving loads of up to 100 tonnes.

Fr. Lürssen Werft
GmbH & Co. KG

Information

Gründungsjahr: 1875	**Year founded:** 1875
Leistungsspektrum:	**Range of services:**

Leistungsspektrum:
– Neubau von zivilen
  Großyachten
– Refit & Service von zivilen
  Großyachten

Standorte:
Bremen-Vegesack (Hauptsitz),
Lemwerder, Bremen-Aumund,
Berne, Schacht-Audorf und
Hamburg; zur Firmengruppe
gehören außerdem Werften
in Hamburg, Wilhelmshaven,
Wolgast und Rendsburg

www.luerssen.de

Range of services:
– new builds of
  civil super yachts
– refit & service
  of civil super yachts

Sites:
Bremen-Vegesack (head-
quarters), Lemwerder,
Bremen-Aumund, Berne,
Schacht-Audorf and Hamburg;
the group also includes shipyards in Hamburg, Wilhelmshaven, Wolgast and Rendsburg

Vom weltweit ersten Motorboot bis zur Erprobung umweltschonender Brennstoffzellentechnologien: Seit mehr als 140 Jahren setzt das Bremer Familienunternehmen Lürssen technisch-innovative Impulse im modernen Schiffbau. Damals wie heute entwickeln Teams aus Mitarbeiterinnen und Mitarbeitern hoch spezialisierter Fachdisziplinen maßgeschneiderte Lösungen für Yachtkunden aus aller Welt. Jede Yacht ist ein Unikat, ausgerüstet zum Beispiel mit effizienten Bordsystemen, modernsten Antriebstechnologien und High-End-Entertainmentsystemen.

Am Bremer Standort konstruieren und fertigen rund 1.200 hochqualifizierte Mitarbeiterinnen und Mitarbeiter Yachten mit über 110 Meter Länge. Gemeinsam mit der zur ebenfalls zur Unternehmensgruppe gehörenden Lürssen-Kröger Werft in Schacht-Audorf bietet Lürssen Neubaukunden ein diversiziertes Produktportfolio, flankiert von umfassenden Refit & Service-Leistungen u. a. auch am Hamburger Standort Blohm+Voss. Als verantwortungsvolles Unternehmen legt Lürssen ein besonderes Augenmerk auf eine nachhaltige Materialauswahl, umweltschonende Technologien und eine überwiegend regionale Wertschöpfung.

From the world's first motorboat to trialling environmentally friendly fuel cell technology: for more than 140 years, the family company Lürssen in Bremen has been a technically innovative pacesetter in modern shipbuilding. Then as now, teams of specialists from various disciplines develop tailor-made solutions for yachting customers from all over the world. Every yacht is unique, fitted for example with efficient on-board systems, state-of-the-art propulsion technology and high-end entertainment concepts.

Around 1,200 highly qualified employees at the company's site in Bremen design and produce yachts of more than 110 metres in length. Together with the group's Lürssen-Kröger shipyard in Schacht-Audorf, Lürssen offers a diversified product range for new-build customers, accompanied by extensive refit and services, among others at the Blohm+Voss site in Hamburg. As a responsible company, Lürssen has a special focus on sustainable material selection, environmentally-friendly technologies and primarily regional value creation.

MTZW Maritimes Trainingszentrum Wesermarsch GmbH

Partner für die maritime Wirtschaft und Offshore-Industrie

Als Trainingszentrum bieten wir die gesamte Bandbreite an Sicherheitstrainings gemäß den international anerkannten Standards der Global Wind Organisation (GWO) und den analog relevanten nationalen Richtlinien (DGUV). Im Jahr 2021 feiern wir unser 10jähriges Bestehen als erfolgreicher Partner der maritimen Wirtschaft und Offshore-Industrie.

Ergänzend bieten wir technische Trainings aus den Bereichen der Elektrotechnik, Mechanik/Mechatronik, Faserverbundtechnik sowie querschnittliche Zusatzqualifikationen an, deren praktische Anteile wir unter Rückgriff auf verschiedene Windenergieanlagen praxisnah und auf Grundlage konkreter Kundenbedarfe konzipieren und umsetzen. Dabei vermitteln wir Grundkenntnisse der Anlagentechnik und Wirkprinzipien für Branchenneulinge genauso wie Expertenwissen für branchenerfahrene Servicetechniker in den Bereichen Wartung, Service und Troubleshooting an Windenergieanlagen der aktuellen Generation.

Information

Gründungsjahr: 2011

Mitarbeiter: 7

Leistungsspektrum:
– Sicherheitslehrgänge nach STCW 78 Abkommen wie Basic Safety, Rescue Boat und Fast Rescue Boat
– Refresher-Kurse
– Berufsschule und überbetriebliche Ausbildung für Auszubildende zum Schiffsmechaniker
– Basic Safety Offshore Training für nicht-nautisches Personal
– Helicopter Underwater Escape Training (HUET) zur Selbstrettung aus notgewasserten Helikoptern
– Kransimulation für Ladevorgänge an Bord eines Schiffes oder im Offshore-Bereich

Partner:
– Berufsbildende Schulen für den Landkreis Wesermarsch
– Maritimes Kompetenzzentrum Elsfleth gGmbH (MARIKOM)
– Deutsche Windguard GmbH
– Heinemann Projektberatung GmbH

www.mtzw.de

Year founded: 2011

Employees: 7

Range of services:
– safety training pursuant to the STCW 78 Agreement, such as Basic Safety, Rescue Boat and Fast Rescue Boat
– refresher courses
– vocational college and external courses for ship mechanic apprentices
– Basic Safety Offshore Training for non-nautical staff
– Helicopter Underwater Escape Training (HUET) for self-rescue from ditched helicopters
– crane simulation for loading procedures on board a ship or offshore

Partners:
– Vocational colleges for the Wesermarsch District
– Maritimes Kompetenzzentrum Elsfleth gGmbH (MARIKOM)
– Deutsche Windguard GmbH
– Heinemann Projektberatung GmbH

Partner for the maritime and offshore industries

As a training centre, we offer the full range of safety training according to the internationally accepted standards of the Global Wind Organisation (GWO) and the equivalent relevant national regulations (DGUV). In 2021 we are celebrating our 10th year successful partner for the maritime and offshore industries.

In addition, we also offer technical training in the fields of electrical engineering, mechanics/mechatronics, fibre composite technology and supplementary cross-sectional qualifications, with practical components devised and implemented in hands-on fashion with recourse to various wind turbines and geared to specific customer needs. In doing so, we impart basic knowledge about the technology behind the systems and how they work for newcomers to the sector, together with expert knowledge for service technicians with professional experience in maintenance, service and troubleshooting, working with state-of-the-art wind turbines.

Im Trainingsbecken können Sicherheitstrainings und Rettungsmaßnahmen unter extremen Wetterbedingungen simuliert werden.

The training basin is used to simulate safety training and rescue operations under extreme weather conditions.

DER STEUERMANN

The Coxswain

AUTOR:
CLAUS SPITZER-
EWERSMANN

Dr. Torsten Bremer

Sein Beruf hat ihn in die Welt hinausgeführt. Bis ins brasilianische Ponta Grossa verschlug es Dr. Torsten Bremer, bevor er den Weg zurück in heimische norddeutsche Gefilde fand. Vor 17 Jahren ist der Manager zu BOGE gekommen und führte bis zum Eintritt in den Ruhestand am 1. Juli 2021 mit BOGE Rubber & Plastics eines der wichtigsten Unternehmen im Oldenburger Münsterland.

1980. Kalter Krieg. Sowjetische Truppen sind Ende des vorigen Jahres in Afghanistan einmarschiert. Der Westen ruft deshalb zum Boykott der Olympischen Spiele in Moskau auf. Die deutsche Politik entscheidet: Wir sind bei der Strafaktion dabei. "Sie zerstörte damit die sportlichen Träume einer ganzen Athletengeneration" sagt Torsten Bremer. Man sieht, dass es noch immer in ihm brodelt, wenn er an die Zeit zurückdenkt. Eine schlichte Urkunde gab es am Ende. Und dazu ein paar warme Worte vom Bundesinnenminister. "Robuste Kräfte hätten den Start in Moskau leider verhindert …", hieß es da. Kein Trostpflaster von bleibendem Wert.

His job has taken him out into the world. Dr Torsten Bremer ventured as far as Ponta Grossa in Brazil before finding his way back home to North Germany. The manager came to BOGE 17 years ago and, until he retired on July 1st 2021, headed BOGE Rubber & Plastics, one of the most important companies in the Oldenburger Münsterland.

1980. The Cold War. The Soviet army has just marched into Afghanistan. The West calls for a boycott of the Olympic Games in Moscow. The German government decides to join the boycott. "In doing so, they destroyed the sporting dreams of a whole generation of athletes," says Torsten Bremer. You can see he's still simmering when he recollects what happened back then. In the end, all he got was a simple certificate. And a few kind words from the Federal Minister of the Interior. "Robust forces meant it was unfortunately not possible to take part in Moscow …" was all that was said. Not a lasting consolation.

Der Osnabrücker hätte seinen Startplatz für das nur alle vier Jahre stattfindende Großereignis sicher gehabt. Er saß im Deutschland-Achter, einem der Medaillenkandidaten auf der olympischen Ruderstrecke. Schon in jungen Jahren hatte er mit Schulfreunden den Rudersport für sich entdeckt. Um erfolgreich zu sein, kommt es hier auf Körpergröße und -kraft an. So landete der eher schmächtige Torsten auf dem Sitz des Steuermanns – und musste gelegentlich sogar zusätzlichen Ballast mit ins Boot nehmen, um das bei Rennen vorgeschriebene Mindestgewicht zu erreichen.

Der Steuermann ist der einzige im Boot, der die noch zu rudernde Strecke vor sich sieht. Und er ist der Chef an Bord. Alles hört auf sein Kommando. „Im Training ist man verlängerter Arm des Coaches, im Rennen muss man vor allem mit dem Schlagmann harmonieren." Das gelang Bremer auch weiterhin gut, 1984 gab es einen neuen Angriff auf Olympia. „Aber bei der internen Ausscheidung wurden wir nur Zweiter und damit nicht berücksichtigt." Erneut war die Enttäuschung groß, zumal die Nominierung auf Messers Schneide stand.

Devise: Nur keine Zeit verlieren

Torsten Bremers sportliche Laufbahn blieb unvollendet. Fortan konzentrierte er sich auf sein Studium. Dafür nahm er nach seiner WM-Teilnahme 1986 in letzter Konsequenz auch den Abschied aus dem Nationalkader in Kauf. „Man wollte mir nicht gestatten, an einem Tag pro Woche direkt nach der Uni nicht von Osnabrück ins Leistungszentrum nach Dortmund zum Training zu fahren." An der Uni lief es dagegen wie geschmiert. Bereits mit 28 Jahren promovierte Bremer in Physik.

Sein Motto, auch heute noch: Nicht unnötig Zeit verlieren. Wenn sich im durchgeplanten Tagesablauf irgendwo eine überraschende Lücke von vielleicht fünf Minuten auftut, kann man die schließlich produktiv nutzen. „Die 15-minütige Kaffeepause an der Uni dauerte bei mir genau eine Viertelstunde", sagt er und fügt leicht schmunzelnd hinzu: „Man kann mich auch ungeduldig nennen." Zumindest Freunde, die ihn länger kennen, machen das gelegentlich sogar.

Die Physik also. Warum? Was reizt ihn daran? Die Antwort kommt wie aus der Pistole geschossen: „Die Objektivität!" Daran richtet sich seine ganze berufliche Karriere aus. Führungskräfte mit Biss und dem richtigen Sinn für Präzision, Timing und Taktzahl sind in der Industrie gern gesehen. Bremer geht nach der Promotion als Manager Central Engineering zur Continental AG nach Hannover, ist dort bald für technische Innovationen in allen Reifenwerken verantwortlich. Und er kommt viel rum in der Welt, ist beispielsweise Ende der 1990er-Jahre in Südamerika tätig. „Insgesamt sind wir 13-mal umgezogen", rechnet er vor. Bei Continental bleibt er bis Ende 2003. Zuletzt gehört er als Executive Vice President dem Management Board einer Conttech-Gesellschaft an. Dann erreicht ihn ein Anruf, der sein Leben noch einmal in ganz neue Bahnen lenkt.

Neue Herausforderung in der alten Heimat

Im südoldenburgischen Damme sitzt mit der ZF Boge Elastmetall GmbH ein wichtiger Zulieferer der Automobilbranche. Die Firma ist 2003 aus der Fusion der ZF Lemförder Elastmetall GmbH und der Bad Godesberger ZF Boge GmbH hervorgegangen. Gesucht wird

Im südoldenburgischen Damme sitzt mit der ZF Boge Elastmetall GmbH ein wichtiger Zulieferer der Automobilbranche.

Based in Damme, South Oldenburg, ZF Boge Elastmetall GmbH is an important supplier for the car industry.

Dem Abwärtstrend trotzen

Autos als Computer auf Rädern, wie von vielen Experten vorhergesagt – sieht so die Zukunft auf unseren Straßen aus? Fest steht: Die Mobilität ist im Umbruch. Digitalisierung und Elektromobilität sind die entscheidenden Stichworte. Schaffen es die Hersteller, sich noch mehr als bislang darauf einzustellen und marktfähige Konzepte zu entwickeln? Glaubt man einer Studie des Schmiermittelherstellers Castrol, dürfte sich das lohnen. Danach würde die Mehrheit der Verbraucher in Deutschland bis 2025 den Umstieg auf ein Elektroauto in Erwägung ziehen. Ausschlaggebend ist der Faktor Preis, danach folgen Ladezeit und Reichweite.

In den letzten Jahren produzierte die Branche vorwiegend Negativschlagzeilen. Die weltweite Produktion geht bereits seit 2018 zurück, Corona brachte die nächsten Hiobsbotschaften. So lag die Zahl der Zulassungen in Deutschland im April 2020 bei nur noch 61 Prozent des Vorjahreswertes. Auch in der Folgezeit gab es teils heftige Einbrüche. Ein solches Nachfragetief sei „beispiellos", heißt es beim Verband der Automobilindustrie (VdA).

Rund 830.000 Menschen waren Anfang 2020 in der deutschen Autoindustrie beschäftigt. Viele Hersteller waren im Laufe des Jahres von Kurzarbeit betroffen, auch Streichlisten machten die Runde. Und ein Ende der Krise ist nicht in Sicht. Experte Ferdinand Dudenhöffer vom CAR-Forschungszentrum geht davon aus, dass es fünf bis zehn Jahre dauern wird, bis der Automarkt wieder das Niveau aus der Zeit vor der Corona-Krise erreicht.

Auch die Zulieferer, von denen es in Deutschland etwa 1.800 gibt, bei denen in den besten Tagen etwa 310.000 Menschen beschäftigt waren, trifft es hart. „Fast 100 Prozent unseres Umsatzes machen wir mit der Erstausstattung von Fahrzeugen", erläutert Dr. Torsten Bremer, Geschäftsführer von BOGE Rubber & Plastics in Damme. Und ein Auto, das nicht gebaut wird, braucht auch keine Inneneinrichtung und keine Reifen. Hoffnung gibt es dennoch – und die hat u.a. mit der E-Mobilität zu tun. Nach Angaben von VdA-Präsidentin Hildegard Müller stammen vier von zehn weltweit erteilten Patenten bei E-Antrieben und drei von zehn in der Batterietechnik von Zulieferern und Herstellern aus Deutschland.

The man from Osnabrück would have been a certain candidate for the major sporting event that only takes place every four years. He was a member of Germany's eight-oar team, with every chance of winning a medal on the Olympic rowing course. He discovered his love of rowing with school friends while still a child. Success in this sport depends on body size and strength. Torsten, rather slight of build, was therefore the coxswain. Sometimes they even needed additional ballast in the boat to reach the minimum weight stipulated for racing.

The coxswain is the only one in the boat who sees the course ahead. And he's the boss. They all respond to his commands. "In training, the coxswain is the extended arm of the coach. In a race, he has to harmonise above all with the strokeman." Bremer continued to do well and in 1984 had another chance at the Olympic Games. "But this time we were only runners up during the internal eliminations so we weren't included." Huge disappointment once more, with the team missing out on being nominated just by the skin of their teeth.

Motto: no time to lose

Torsten Bremer's sporting career failed to reach the desired conclusion. Instead, he turned his attention to studying. To do so properly, he decided to retire from the national team after the World Championships in 1986. "They didn't want to give me one day a week when I could go straight after uni from Osnabrück to the training centre in Dortmund." By contrast, at uni everything went well, and Bremer was still only 28 when he got a PhD in physics.

His motto is still the same today: no time to lose. After all, if a gap of just five minutes suddenly emerges in the course of a precisely planned day, this time can be put to good use. "My 15-minute coffee break at uni lasted exactly just a quarter of an hour", he says and continues with a grin: "You could also say I'm impatient". Some of the people who know him best even dare to say so.

So physics. Why physics? What is so special about that? The answer comes quick like a shot: "It's so objective!" That's the basis for his whole career. Industry loves senior executives with determination and the right sense of precision, timing and clock rate. With his PhD in his pocket, Bremer works as Manager Central Engineering for Continental AG in Hanover and is soon given responsibility for technical innovation in all the tire factories. And he gets to travel, working for example in South America at the end of the 1990s. "We moved altogether 13 times", he recalls. He stayed with Continental until the end of 2003. His last position was as Executive Vice President on the Management Board of a Conttech company. Then he received a phone call that totally changed the direction of his life.

New challenge back home

ZF Boge Elastmetall GmbH is an important supplier for the car industry and based in Damme, South Oldenburg. The company was the result of a merger between ZF Lemförder Elastmetall GmbH and ZF Boge GmbH from Bad Godesberg in 2003. They were now looking for an experienced, innovative manager who could bring the two companies together to make them fit for the future.

The right task for Torsten Bremer? "When the call came, I had just turned 40." He wasn't at all unhappy at Continental, he says firmly.

Defying the downturn

Many experts talk about cars being computers on wheels. Is that what the future is going to be like on our roads? One thing is for sure: the mobility sector is in upheaval. Digitisation and electromobility are the key catchphrases. Will manufacturers make a better effort at adapting and developing concepts fit for the market? A study by lubricant manufacturer Castrol indicates it could be worthwhile. Accordingly, the majority of consumers in Germany would consider charging over to an electric car by 2025. The crucial factor is the price, followed by charging time and range.

In the last few years, the sector has produced mainly negative headlines. Global production has been on the decline since 2018, while corona brought the next bad news. In April 2020, the number of new cars registered in Germany was only 61 percent compared to the previous year. Numbers continued to fall drastically as the year went on. Such a slump in demand is "unprecedented", according to the German Association of the Automotive Industry (VdA).

At the start of 2020 about 830,000 people worked for the German car industry. In the course of the year, many manufacturers had to put people on short-time schemes, while redundancies were also on the cards. And no end to the crisis is in sight. Expert Ferdinand Dudenhöffer from the CAR Research Centre presumes that it will take five to ten years before the car market recovers to the pre-corona level.

This is also having severe impacts on the supplier industry, with about 1,800 companies in Germany and a workforce of roughly 310,000 people in its best times. "Almost 100 percent of our sales are generated with original equipment for vehicles", explains Dr Torsten Bremer CEO at BOGE Rubber & Plastics in Damme. And there is no demand for interior fittings or tyres for cars that are not being made. But there is still hope, and it comes from e-mobility. According to VdA President Hildegard Müller, suppliers and manufacturers in Germany account for four out of ten global patents for E-drives and three out of ten global patents for battery technology.

nun ein sowohl erfahrener als auch innovationsfreudiger Manager, der die beiden Unternehmen so zu einem zusammenführt, dass es für die Herausforderungen der Zukunft gewappnet ist.

Die richtige Aufgabe für Torsten Bremer? „Als die Anfrage kam, war ich Anfang 40." Er sei bei Continental keineswegs unglücklich gewesen, betont er. „Doch das ist ja eine Lebensphase, in der viele Menschen durchaus offen für etwas Neues sind und eine berufliche Umorientierung erwägen." Es kommt, wie es kommen muss. Die ersten Gespräche verlaufen gut und bringen schnell Gewissheit. Die Chemie stimmt, die Vorstellungen über die weitere Entwicklung des Unternehmens liegen dicht beieinander. Alles passt. Bremer wird neuer BOGE-Geschäftsführer.

Zwischen Damme und seinem Geburtsort Osnabrück liegen lediglich knapp 40 Kilometer. Zufall? Hat sich da jemand bewusst entschieden, nach all den Wanderjahren in die alte Heimat zurückzukehren? „Ich hatte schon ein wenig das Leben aus dem Koffer satt – zumal das mit inzwischen zwei kleinen Kindern auch nicht mehr so einfach war", erinnert sich Bremer. „Aktiv gesucht habe ich allerdings nicht, und dass es dann Damme geworden ist, war tatsächlich nicht abzusehen." Aber auch kein ernsthafter Hinderungsgrund – genauso wenig wie der Umstand, dass Bremers Familie schon zuvor ein Ferienhaus am nahe gelegenen Dümmer besaß. Hier kann er entspannen, sagt der Mann, der sich in der Freizeit gern mit seinen Oldtimern beschäftigt. Daneben gewinnt er auch – wie er sagt – banaleren Tätigkeiten wie dem Zaunstreichen oder dem Laubharken zum Abschalten von der Bürotätigkeit etwas Positives ab und stürzt sich mit Begeisterung in die alljährlichen Dammer Karnevalsfeierlichkeiten.

Erst Befürchtungen, dann Zustimmung

Verlaufen die ersten Jahre für den neuen Steuermann am nach Firmengründer benannten Dr.-Jürgen-Ulderup-Platz 1 noch berechenbar, ändert sich die Lage 2013 schlagartig. Gerüchte machen die Runde. Nicht nur in Damme, sondern in der ganzen Region. Der Eigentümer, die ZF Friedrichshafen AG, wolle die Gummi- und Kunststoffsparte veräußern, heißt es. Nach China. Droht ein Ausverkauf? Gar eine Demontage? Unter den Beschäftigten in Damme wächst die Unruhe, der Standort wäre unmittelbar betroffen.

Torsten Bremer ist gefordert. Als erfahrener Steuermann. Als derjenige, der das Boot auf Kurs hält und die Mannschaft einschwört. Man habe ihn „schon früh" in die Überlegungen einbezogen, berichtet er heute, und so die anfänglichen Unsicherheiten vertrieben. „Zunächst wusste wirklich niemand, was die Chinesen genau vorhaben und was aus uns wird." Dann aber stellt sich heraus, dass die vielfach befürchtete Zerschlagung des Unternehmens nicht zur Debatte steht. Im Gegenteil. Zusagen werden gemacht und eingehalten, neue Projekte angeschoben und am Standort Damme wird strategisch investiert. „So konnte ich guten Gewissens behaupten, dass ich hinter der Sache stehe", bekräftigt Bremer. Das sichert neben dem Vertrauen der Kunden auch das der Mitarbeiter.

"But by the time you reach 40, you've got to a phase in your life when you're willing to try something new and to change the direction of your career." And so the inevitable happens. The first interviews go well and before long it is all signed and sealed. The "chemistry" is right and the ideas about the company's further development coincide. It all fits. Bremer becomes the new CEO at BOGE.

It's only about 40 kilometres between Damme and his home town of Osnabrück. Pure chance? Was this a deliberate decision to come home after so many years of travelling? "Well yes, I had got a bit fed up of living out a suitcase – which was no longer so easy now that I also had two little children to think about", recalls Bremer. "But I wasn't actively on the look-out, and in fact there was no way you could have predicted that I would end up in Damme." On the other hand, this wasn't a serious obstacle either – just like the fact that Bremer's family already had a holiday home by nearby Dümmer lake. This is where he comes to relax, says the man who likes to spend his old time tinkering with his vintage cars. He also enjoys what he calls more trivial jobs such as painting a fence or sweeping the leaves as a contrast to sitting in the office, and is a real fan of Damme's annual carnival events.

Apprehension and approval

While the first few years run smoothly for the new coxswain working at company headquarters, at the address Dr-Jürgen-Ulderup-Platz 1 named after the founder, things change abruptly in 2013. Rumours start flying around. Not just in Damme but throughout the region. Apparently, the owner ZF Friedrichshafen AG, intended to sell the rubber and plastics business. To China. Was this going to be a sell-out? Would the whole place be dismantled? The workforce in Damme starts getting restless, apprehensive that the site would be directly affected.

Torsten Bremer has to take control. As experienced coxswain. As the one to keep the boat on course and get the team on his side. Today he reports that he got involved in the discussions "early on" which enabled him to dispel the initial uncertainties. "Initially, nobody knew what the Chinese would do and what would happen to us." But in fact, it transpired that the company would not be broken up as feared. On the contrary, promises are made and new projects instigated, with strategic investment at the site in Damme. "So is was with a clear conscience that I declared my support for it all", emphasises Bremer. He wins the trust of both customers and employees.

In the end, 98 percent of them approve of the takeover by Zhuzhou Times New Material Technology Co. Ltd. (TMT) in Hunan, South East China. The deal is completed on 1 September 2014. Big sighs of relief in Damme, big sighs of relief throughout the Oldenburger Münsterland. On the international stage, the company is now called BOGE Rubber & Plastics, while in Germany it is still known as BOGE Elastmetall.

Am Ende stimmen 98 Prozent von ihnen für die Übernahme durch die Zhuzhou Times New Material Technology Co. Ltd. (TMT) in der südostchinesischen Provinz Hunan. Am 1. September 2014 geht der Deal über die Bühne. Aufatmen in Damme, Aufatmen im ganzen Oldenburger Münsterland. International firmiert man nun unter dem Namen BOGE Rubber & Plastics, in Deutschland bleibt es bei BOGE Elastmetall.

Überlegungen zur Zukunft der Branche

Als verantwortungsvollen Manager bereitet Torsten Bremer der Wandel der Mobilität natürlich Kopfzerbrechen. Corona hat die ganze Autobranche in eine tiefe Krise gestürzt. Aber auch schon vor Ausbruch der Pandemie hatte es Umsatzrückgänge gegeben. „Das Auto und der Individualverkehr sind ziemlich in Ungnade gefallen", weiß der BOGE-Chef. Zeit also, nach Alternativen Ausschau zu halten. Eine Möglichkeit sieht er jenseits der Straße zum Beispiel im Schiffbau sowie im Industrie- und Bahnbereich, die auf Teile angewiesen sind, die mit dem Know-how aus Damme und Bonn produziert werden könnten.

Darüber hinaus setzt Bremer auf das 2019 eröffnete Innovation Center in Osnabrück. Hier liegt der Fokus ausdrücklich nicht nur auf dem Automotivemarkt. „Wir wollen in alle Richtungen denken und Neues kreieren." Die Vernetzung mit der Universität und jungen Start-ups soll helfen, innovative und wettbewerbsfähige Produkte und Systemlösungen zu entwickeln.

Schwierigkeiten werfen Torsten Bremer nicht um. Er begreift sie als Herausforderungen und versucht an ihnen zu wachsen. „Man muss sich hohe, aber erreichbare Ziele setzen", sagt er. „Und dann müssen alle dafür arbeiten, diese Ziele zu erreichen." Wie damals beim Rudern zählt das Team. Wer nicht mitzieht, gefährdet den Erfolg. Und der Steuermann muss bestimmen, wo es langgeht. So funktioniert der Sport und so funktionieren Unternehmen.

Im internationalen firmiert das Unternehmen unter dem Namen BOGE Rubber & Plastics, in Deutschland bleibt es bei BOGE Elastmetall.

On the international stage, the company is called BOGE Rubber & Plastics, while in Germany it is still known as BOGE Elastmetall.

Thoughts about the future of the industry

As a responsible manager, Torsten Bremer naturally worries about all the changes in mobility. Corona has plunged the whole car industry into a deep crisis. But sales were already declining before the outbreak of the pandemic. "Cars and individual transport have fallen out of favour", says the BOGE boss. Time to look for alternatives. One possibility for example would be to move away from road transport towards shipbuilding, the railway sector and industry in general, where they need parts that could be produced with know-how from Damme and Bonn.

Bremer also has hopes of Osnabrück Innovation Centre that opened in 2019. Here the focus is specifically set wider than just the automotive market. "We want to think in all directions and create something new." Networking with the university and young start-ups should help to develop innovative, competitive products and system solutions.

Torsten Bremer doesn't let difficulties stop him. He sees them as a challenge and tries to grow with them. "You have to set high targets but they must be attainable", he says. "And then everyone has to do everything to achieve them." The whole team counts, as with rowing. You'll jeopardise the team's success if you don't pull your weight. And the coxswain says where it's all going. In sport, and in industry.

KRONOS TITAN GmbH
Werk Nordenham

Information

Gründungsjahr: 1969
Mitarbeiter: rund 350
Leistungsspektrum:
Herstellung von Titandioxid
(rund 60.000 Tonnen jährlich)
und Eisensulfat
(rund 350.000 Tonnen jährlich)

Year founded: 1969
Employees: about 350
Range of services:
manufacture of titanium dioxide
(around 60,000 tonnes p. a.)
and iron sulphate (around
350,000 tonnes p. a.)

www.kronostio2.com

Seit 1969 wird in Nordenham das „weißeste" Material der Welt produziert. KRONOS TITAN ist der deutschlandweit größte Hersteller für Titandioxid. Oder, ganz einfach gesagt, für Weißpigmente, die sich in fast allen weißen und bunten Lacken und Kunststoffen finden.

Im Werk Nordenham beschäftigt KRONOS TITAN 350 Mitarbeiter in der chemischen Industrie, darunter 20 Auszubildende. Auch die Wirtschaft vor Ort profitiert vom Standort. Denn KRONOS TITAN investiert jährlich etwa 20 Mio. Euro in Erneuerungen und Reparaturen. Die europaweite Auslieferung der Produkte übernehmen Logistiker aus Nordenham.

KRONOS TITAN produziert in Blexen aus einem schwarzen Erz (Ilmenit), das auf dem Seeweg aus einer Mine in Norwegen angeliefert wird, Titandioxid als Pulver. Mit der Werkserweiterung im Jahr 1974 ist die maximale Produktionsmenge von 40.000 auf 60.000 Tonnen erhöht worden. Zweites Produkt ist Eisensulfat. Das wird u. a. zur Reinigung von Abwasser in Kläranlagen verwendet sowie in der Futtermittelindustrie und bei der Zementherstellung eingesetzt.

The "whitest" material in the world has been produced in Nordenham since 1969. KRONOS TITAN is Germany's largest producer of titanium dioxide, or, to put it simply, the white pigments that are to be found in nearly all white and coloured paints and plastics.

At the Nordenham plant, KRONOS TITAN has a workforce of 350 employees in the chemical industry, including 20 trainees. The local economy also benefits from the site, with KRONOS TITAN investing roughly 20 million Euros in renewal work and repairs every year. Logistics specialists in Nordenham ensure the products are delivered throughout Europe.

In Blexen, KRONOS TITAN produces titanium dioxide as a powder from a black ore (ilmenite) which is shipped in from a mine in Norway. The plant was extended in 1974 to increase the maximum production quantity from 40,000 to 60,000 tonnes. Iron sulphate is a second product. It is used to treat wastewater in sewage plants as well as in the animal feed industry and also in the production of cement.

REHAU AG + Co
Werk Visbek

Information

Gründungsjahr: 1948
Mitarbeiter: rund 20.000 weltweit, etwa 600 in Visbek
Standorte: 170 in mehr als 50 Ländern
Geschäftsbereiche: Automotive, Building Solutions, Window Solutions, Furniture Solutions, Industrial Solutions

Year founded 1948
Employees: worldwide about 20,000, about 600 in Visbek
Locations: 170 in more than 50 countries
Business units: Automotive, Building Solutions, Window Solutions, Furniture Solutions, Industrial Solutions

www.rehau.de/visbek

REHAU ist eine der führenden Premium-Marken für polymerbasierte Lösungen im Bau-, Automobil- und Industriebereich mit weltweit mehr als 20.000 Mitarbeitenden. Die Leidenschaft, jeden Tag die Grenzen des Möglichen zu verschieben, um eine nachhaltige Zukunft zu fördern, verbindet uns. Gleichzeitig prägen starke Unternehmenswerte unsere Arbeit, Kultur und Verhaltensweisen. Unser Ziel ist „Engineering progress. Enhancing lives." – das Leben durch den Einsatz innovativer Technologien nachhaltig zu verbessern.

In unserem REHAU Leitwerk für die Möbelbranche am Standort Visbek sorgen über 600 Mitarbeitende dafür, dass unsere Möbelkomponenten genau zum richtigen Zeitpunkt, in der richtigen Ausführung bei unseren Kunden aus der Möbelindustrie in ganz Europa eintreffen. Und das in über 30.000 Dekoren und Farben. Eine logistische Meisterleistung, denn sowohl der industrielle Möbelbau als auch der Innenausbauer oder Schreiner werden just-in-time und passgenau beliefert. In Visbek sind alle Fachbereiche unter einem Dach effizient versammelt: Rohwarendisposition, Materialaufbereitung, Qualitätssicherung inklusive Auditmanagement und hauseigene Laborprüfungen sowie Ausbildungswerkstatt und Werkzeugbau.

REHAU is a leading premium brand for polymer-based solutions in areas such as construction, automotive and industry, with more than 20,000 employees worldwide. We are all passionate about pushing back the boundaries of what is possible every day in order to create a sustainable future. At the same time, strong corporate values shape our work, culture and behaviour. Our goal is "Engineering progress. Enhancing lives." to make life better in the long term with innovative technologies.

With its workforce of more than 600 employees, our primary REHAU plant for the furniture branch in Visbek ensures that furniture components are delivered according to the individual specifications and on time to our customers in the furniture industry throughout Europe, and from more than 30,000 designs and colours. This is a true feat of logistics, with just-in-time, custom-fit deliveries to the industrial furniture manufacturers as well as interior fitters or carpenters. Visbek efficiently brings all departments together under one roof: raw material scheduling, material processing, quality assurance including audit management and internal laboratory tests, as well as training shop and toolmaking.

HIT Hafen- und Industrietechnik GmbH

Die HIT Hafen- und Industrietechnik GmbH ist seit über 20 Jahren ein international arbeitender, renommierter Anbieter für Automatisierungs- und Antriebstechnik sowie im Bereich Leitsysteme. Zusätzlich gibt es ein umfassendes Produktportfolio von selbstfahrenden Transportern (FTS) „Move-e-Star" für schwere Lasten von 3 bis zu 200 Tonnen.

Für die Regelung physikalischer Größen wie Drücke, Temperaturen, Drehzahlen, Kräfte oder Momente bietet HIT individuell projektierte Steuerungs- und Regelungstechnik an. In der mehr als 2500 Quadratmeter großen betriebseigenen Fertigungshalle werden elektrische und mechanische Komponenten gefertigt und getestet. Vor Ort erfolgt die Implementierung der getesteten Anlagen und Fahrzeuge durch unser erfahrenes Montage- und Ingenieurteam. Zusammen mit seinen Partnern erstellt die HIT als erfahrener Lieferant komplette, vollautomatische Containerlagerhallen, um mehrere Hundert Seecontainer zu stauen und zu verwalten.

Alles aus einer Hand: Konstruktion, Fertigung, eigene Software und Inbetriebnahme vor Ort, abgerundet durch einen Rund-um-die-Uhr-Service.

Information

Gründungsjahr: 1997

Mitarbeiter: 35

Leistungsspektrum:
– Automatisierungstechnik
– Steuerungs- und
  Regelungstechnik
– Antriebstechnik
– eigene Fertigung
– Flurfördertechnik FTS, AGV
– vollautomatisierte
  Containerlagerhallen

Einsatzorte:

Die Produkte der HIT sind heute weltweit im Einsatz, u. a. in Deutschland, Spanien, Frankreich, England, Belgien, Russland, Polen, Türkei, USA, Indonesien, Japan, China und Singapur.

www.hit-germany.de

Year founded: 1997

Employees: 35

Range of services:
– automation technology
– control systems
– drive technology
– own manufacturing
– industrial trucks DTS/AGV
– fully automated container
  warehouses

Sites:

Today HIT's products are in use all over the world, including among others in Germany, Spain, France, England, Belgium, Russia, Poland, Turkey, USA, Indonesia, Japan, China and Singapore.

HIT wurde in Wilhelmshaven gegründet und ist seit 2002 in Wardenburg ansässig, um am neuen Standort noch effektiver und kundenorientierter arbeiten zu können.

HIT was founded in Wilhelmshaven and has been based in Wardenburg since 2002, where the company has scope to be even more effective with a more customer-oriented approach.

For 20 years, HIT Hafen- und Industrietechnik GmbH has been a renowned international provider of automation and drive technology together with control systems. It also has a comprehensive range of Move-e-Star driverless transport systems (DTS) for heavy loads from 3 to 200 tonnes.

HIT offers individually devised control technology to regulate physical variables such as pressure, temperature, speed, force or torque. Electrical and mechanical components are made and tested in the company's own production facility covering more than 2,500 square metres. The tested systems and vehicles are then implemented on site by our experienced team of installation experts and engineers. HIT works with its partners as an experienced supplier for complete, fully automated container warehouses for stowage and management of several hundred sea containers.

All from a single source: design, production, own software and commissioning on site, rounded off with 24/7 service.

PALFINGER
Tail Lifts GmbH

Information

Gründungsjahr: 1937
Werk Ganderkesee
Mitarbeiter: 295
Leistungsspektrum:
Hubladebühnen und Personeneinstiegssysteme für den öffentlichen Nah- und Fernverkehr
Standorte: PALFINGER Tail Lifts
ist neben Ganderkesee auch in
den USA, Großbritannien, Frankreich und der Slowakei vertreten.
www.palfinger.com

Year founded: 1937
Ganderkesee plant
Employees: 295
Range of services:
Tail lifts and passenger systems
for local and long-distance
public transport
Sites: Besides Ganderkesee,
PALFINGER Tail Lifts is also
represented in the USA, Great
Britain, France and Slovakia.

Seit über einem halben Jahrhundert entwickelt, produziert und vermarktet der PALFINGER-Standort in Ganderkesee nahe Bremen Hubladebühnen und Personeneinstiegssysteme für den weltweiten Einsatz.

Lange Zeit war das Unternehmen unter den Namen MBB bekannt bis es 2007 von der PALFINGER Gruppe – einem der weltweit führenden Anbieter von Hebelösungen für Nutzfahrzeuge und den maritimen Bereich – übernommen wurde. Besonderes Augenmerk legen wir bei PALFINGER auf die Zuverlässigkeit der Produkte im täglichen Einsatz und die Wirtschaftlichkeit für den Endkunden. Unsere Hubladebühnen werden in vielen Branchen wie der Logistik oder der Getränke- und Lebensmittelindustrie eingesetzt, um das Be- und Entladen von Nutzfahrzeugen zu erleichtern. Das Sortiment umfasst verschiedene Hubladebühnentypen mit einer Tragfähigkeit von 500 bis zu 4.000 kg.

Das Werk in Ganderkesee ist das Kompetenzzentrum für Aluminiumverarbeitung innerhalb der PALFINGER Gruppe und Vorreiter bei der Anwendung innovativer Produktionstechnologien. Höchste Qualität sowie eine zuverlässige und kundenorientierte Just-in-time-Fertigung sind im hochmodernen Bearbeitungszentrum selbstverständlicher Standard.

For more than half a century, tail lifts and passenger systems for worldwide use have been developed, produced and marketed at the PALFINGER site in Ganderkesee near Bremen.

For many years, the company was known under the name of MBB, until it was taken over in 2007 by the PALFINGER Group – one of the world's leading providers of lifting solutions for commercial vehicles and the maritime sector. Here at PALFINGER, we focus particularly on the reliability of our products in daily use and their economic efficiency for the final customer. Our tail lifts are used in many sectors such as logistics or the food and drinks industry to make it easier when loading and unloading trucks. The range encompasses various lift types with a load capacity from 500 to 4,000 kg.

The factory in Ganderkesee is the centre of excellence for aluminium processing in the PALFINGER Group and pioneers the use of innovative production technologies. It goes without saying that highest quality standards prevail in the state-of-the-art processing centre, together with reliable, customer-oriented just-in-time production.

Forming innovations

Der Oldenburger Verpackungsmaschinenhersteller Sealpac baut Maschinen für die automatisierte Verpackung von Lebensmitteln. Zum Fertigungsprogramm gehören sogenannte Traysealer, die das Produkt in einer vorhandenen Schale versiegeln, und Thermoformer, mit denen die jeweilige Verpackung hergestellt und das Lebensmittelprodukt anschließend verpackt wird.

Unsere Kunden können sich darauf verlassen, dass bei uns jedes ihrer Anliegen als Chefsache behandelt wird – ganz gleich, ob es die kleine Schlachterei um die Ecke ist, namhafte Lebensmittelhersteller aus Oldenburg oder große Fleischverarbeiter aus der ganzen Welt. Dafür sorgt ein ebenso erfahrenes und versiertes Team von Spezialisten, die jeden unserer Kunden umfassend beraten – von der Planung einer neuen Anlage bis zur Schulung des Personals. Dieser Mix aus technologischer Kompetenz, langjähriger Erfahrung, persönlicher Beratung und dem besonderen Gespür für persönliche Belange ist es, der Sealpac einzigartig macht.

Sealpac ist in über 50 Ländern aktiv. Für Forschung und Entwicklung wird auch mit Materialherstellern, Lebensmittelinstituten und Hochschulen kooperiert. Außerdem betreiben wir ein eigenes Technologiezentrum in Oldenburg. Am Anfang stand die Idee – und unser Anspruch, neue Maßstäbe im Bereich der industriellen Lebensmittelverpackung zu setzen. Dabei haben wir in vielen Jahren ein ebenso umfassendes wie spezifisches Know-how entwickelt.

„Developed in Germany, developed by Sealpac."

Immerhin handelt es sich bei kostbaren Lebensmitteln um leicht verderbliche Ware. Deshalb sind auch die Anforderungen an Hygiene und Reinheit in der Lebensmittelindustrie extrem hoch – vergleichbar mit denen in der Medizin. Das bedeutet für Sealpac, dass für Verpackungsmaschinen zum Beispiel nur korrosionsbeständige Materialien wie Edelstahl oder Aluminium verwendet

Information

Gründungsjahr: 2001
Mitarbeiter: ca. 250
Leistungsspektrum:

– Hightech-Maschinenbau, moderne Verpackungstechnologien, kreative und maßgeschneiderte Verpackungslösungen für die Lebensmittelindustrie
– umfassendes Servicepaket inkl. Wartung und Reparatur, Ersatzteile, Trainings, eigenes Entwicklungszentrum – Technikum

www.sealpac.de

Year founded: 2001
Employees: around 250
Range of services:

– high-tech machine construction, modern packaging technologies, creative customised packaging solutions for the food industry
– comprehensive range of services including maintenance and repair, spare parts, training courses, own Development Centre – technical centre

werden. Außerdem müssen die Maschinen leicht zu reinigen sein, um den anspruchsvollen Hygienevorschriften gerecht zu werden.

Wir bauen aber nicht nur Anlagen für die automatisierte Lebensmittelverpackung, sondern entwickeln auch selbst Verpackungen für alle Arten von Lebensmitteln. Dabei ist die Reduzierung der Lebensmittelverschwendung ein wichtiges Thema, weshalb sich Sealpac im Industrieverband VDMA engagiert und mit dem Fraunhofer-Institut kooperiert.

Ob InsideCut-Konturenschnitt, das Air Forming System oder das Kinetik-Central-Close-System – die Liste der von uns entwickelten Neuerungen ist lang. Möglich wird dies durch ein perfekt eingespieltes Team qualifizierter Mitarbeiter unterschiedlicher Fachrichtungen. Durch diesen Kompetenz-Mix setzen wir neue Maßstäbe: wirtschaftlich, fortschrittlich und effizient.

Forming innovations

The Oldenburg packaging machine manufacturer Sealpac makes machines for automated food packaging solutions. The production range includes so-called traysealers that seal the product in an existing tray, and thermoformers that produce the respective packaging and then pack the food product accordingly. Our customers can rely on us treating all their concerns as our top priority, regardless whether this is the small butcher's round the corner, renowned food manufacturers from Oldenburg or major meat processing firms from all over the world. Our experienced and skilled team of specialists provides each of our customers with comprehensive consulting services – from planning a new production facility to staff training. This blend of technological expertise, many years of experience, personal advice and a keen sense of personal needs is what makes Sealpac unique.

Sealpac is active in more than 50 countries, and pursues research and development in cooperation with material manufacturers, food institutes and universities. We also have our own Development Centre in Oldenburg. It began with an idea – and our ambition to set new standards in the field of industrial food packaging. Over the years, we have developed know-how that is both comprehensive and specific.

"Developed in Germany, developed by Sealpac."

After all, precious food products are easily perishable. That is why the food industry has extremely high requirements for hygiene and cleanliness, on a par with those in medicine. For Sealpac, this means that packaging machines may only be made of corrosion-resistant materials such as stainless steel or aluminium. Furthermore, the machines must be easy to clean in order to meet the demanding hygiene regulations.

But we do not just make machines for automated food packaging solutions: we also develop packaging for all kinds of food products. Reducing food waste is a key issue here, which is why Sealpac is involved in the industrial association VDMA and cooperates with the Fraunhofer Institute.

Whether inside cut contour cutting, the air forming system or the kinetic central close system, we have a long list of new technologies that we have developed. This is all thanks to a perfectly coordinated team of qualified employees from different disciplines. With this blend of expertise, we set new standards in terms of profitability, progress and efficiency.

Sealpac GmbH

Stahlwerk Augustfehn
Schmiede GmbH & Co. KG

Höchste Schmiedekunst im Dienste des Kunden

Die Ursprünge des Stahlwerks Augustfehn gehen zurück auf das Jahr 1872. Seitdem beliefern wir unsere Kunden mit geschmiedeten Qualitätsprodukten erster Güte – weil hier schon immer moderne Anlagen und Produktionsverfahren mit traditioneller, solider Handarbeit verbunden werden. So wachsen gute Beziehungen zu Kunden und Lieferanten und damit produktive Marktpartnerschaften.

Die nunmehr über 150-jährige Erfolgsgeschichte der Schmiede ist in den Anfängen die Geschichte des Gründers August Karl Friedrich Schultze und seit 1987 die des Geschäftsführers und Visionärs Peter Finkernagel (im Bild). Insbesondere seine vorausschauende Unternehmensführung hat das Unternehmen in den letzten Jahrzehnten zu einer der ersten Adressen in der Nischenfertigung gemacht. Mit dem Know-how aus Augustfehn entstehen kleine Stückzahlen und individuelle Qualitätserzeugnisse für den Maschinen- und Anlagenbau, die Recycling-Industrie und Hersteller von Baggern.

Die maßgefertigten Schmiedeteile aus Augustfehn behaupten sich erfolgreich im Technologiewettbewerb. Ihre überragenden Eigenschaften hinsichtlich Festigkeit, Zähigkeit und Zuverlässigkeit sind der Garant für stabile und erfolgreiche Geschäftsbeziehungen.

The art of forging on behalf of the customer

The origins of Stahlwerk Augustfehn go back to the year 1872. Since then, we have been supplying our customers with top quality forged products, because the company has always combined state-of-the-art machinery and production methods with traditional sound workmanship. This generates good relations to customers and suppliers, resulting in productive market partnerships. The company's success story covers a period of more than 150 years. Initially, this is the story of the founder August Karl Friedrich Schultze; since 1987, it has become the story of the managing director and visionary Peter Finkernagel (illustrated). His forward-looking style of management in particular has propelled the company in recent decades to become a top address for niche manufacturing. Stahlwerk Augustfehn uses its know-how to produce small quantities and individual quality products for machinery and plant construction, the recycling industry and excavator manufacturers. Tailor-made forged parts by Augustfehn perform successfully in the face of technological competition. Their outstanding strength, reliability and steadiness are the attributes that guarantee stable, successful business relations.

Information

Gründungsjahr: 1872	Year founded 1872
Mitarbeiter: rund 40	Employees: about 40

Leistungsspektrum:
- Verschleißteile für Zementindustrie und Recycling
- Verschleißteile für Nass- und Trockenbaggerei
- Kuppelstangen, Zugstangen, Kolbenstangen
- segmentierte Kugelbahnen und Zahnkränze
- Walzen, Rollen und Wellen
- Spezial-Schmiedeteile
- Lohnfertigung

Range of services:
- wear parts for recycling and mineral processing
- wear parts for dredging and excavation
- piston rods, tensile rods, coupling rods
- segmented ball-bearing races and gear rims
- rollers, reels and shafts
- special forged parts
- contract manufacturing

Unternehmensgruppe:
turboMech GmbH & Co. KG
Friesische Verschleißtechnik GmbH & Co. KG
Augustfehn Americas Inc.

Company group:
turboMech GmbH & Co. KG
Friesische Verschleißtechnik GmbH & Co. KG
Augustfehn Americas Inc.

www.stahlwerk-augustfehn.de

Zweckverband ecopark

Information

Gründungsjahr: 2002
Mitarbeiter im ecopark:
etwa 1.200
Leistungsspektrum:
Gewerbe- und Industriepark mit
besonderen Vorzügen an der
Hansalinie A 1
Zielgruppe:
Unternehmer aller Branchen
und aus allen Regionen, die auf
Expansionskurs sind und einen
attraktiven Standort suchen
www.ecopark.de

Year founded: 2002
Employees at ecopark:
approx. 1,200
Range of services:
commercial and industry park
offering special advantages on
the Hansalinie A 1 motorway
Target group:
companies in all industries and
from all regions looking for an
attractive site to expand

Dieser Name ist Programm: Der ecopark heißt nicht nur Park, er ist auch einer. Der Gewerbe- und Industriestandort an der Hansalinie A 1 im Landkreis Cloppenburg bietet dank Gestaltung und Pflege ein ideales Umfeld für gute Arbeit. Davon profitieren bereits mehr als 40 Firmen mit insgesamt etwa 1.200 Beschäftigten. Die Struktur der Unternehmen im 300 Hektar großen ecopark ist heterogen. Ob Produktion oder Dienstleistung, ob Logistik oder Handwerk, ob zwei Mitarbeiter oder 200 – der ecopark bietet allen wertvolle Vorteile. Auch die Verkehrsanbindung an der Schnittstelle Nord/Süd (A 1) und Ost/West (E 233) ist perfekt. Am Ausbau des benachbarten Kindergartens hat der ecopark sich finanziell beteiligt, auch damit Mitarbeiter, die nicht im Landkreis Cloppenburg leben, hier ihre Kinder betreuen lassen können.

The name says it all: the ecopark is not just called a park, it actually is a park. The commercial and industrial site on the Hansalinie A 1 motorway in the Cloppenburg district is well designed and cared for in order to offer an ideal setting for good work. More than 40 companies with altogether about 1,200 employees already profit from the facilities. The structure of businesses using the 300 hectare ecopark is highly heterogeneous. Manufacturing or services, logistics or the skilled crafts, just two employees or a workforce of 200 – all find valuable advantages in the ecopark. The location is also perfectly situated at the main North/South (A 1) and East/West (E 233) motorways. The ecopark is also financially involved in extending the neighbouring kindergarten to provide childcare for staff who do not live in the Cloppenburg district.

Information

Daten und Fakten:
– multimodaler
  Verkehrsknotenpunkt
– 285 ha zusammenhängende
  restriktionsarme Industrie-
  und Gewerbeflächen, teils
  zur sofortigen Bebauung
– 35.000 m² schwergutgeeignete
  Umschlags- und Lagerflächen
www.c-port-kuestenkanal.de

Facts and figures:
– multi-modal transport hub
– 285 ha of cohesive low restric-
  tion industrial and commercial
  land, some of which is available
  for immediate construction
– 35,000 m² of transhipment
  and storage facilities capable
  of handling heavy goods

c-Port cargo und Industrie am Küstenkanal

Der Aufschwung ist spürbar: Seit 2007 hat sich das Industrie- und Gewerbegebiet c-Port am Küstenkanal zu einem Standort entwickelt, der sich über die Region hinaus einen Namen gemacht hat. Mit 285 Hektar Fläche und einem leistungsfähigen Hafen ist er für Firmen aus fast allen Wirtschaftsbereichen zu einem attraktiven Zuhause geworden. c-Port – das steht heute für pragmatische Herangehensweisen, innovatives Denken, zukunftsorientiertes Handeln und Neugierde auf weitere Investoren. Die Zeichen stehen auf Wachstum. So entsteht eine grüne Raffinerie zur Produktion von ökologischen Kraftstoffen, auch der Hafen wird im Zuge des Ausbaus des Küstenkanals erweitert. c-Port-Geschäftsführer Arno Düren: „Unser Standort hat am Knotenpunkt der Bundesstraßen 401 und 72 eine exzellente Verkehrsanbindung und eine leistungsfähige Infrastruktur mit ultraschnellem Digitalnetz."

Noticeable upswing: since 2007, the c-Port industrial and commercial estate on the Coastal Canal has made a name for itself that extends way beyond the immediate region. With a surface area of 285 hectares and an efficient port, it has become an attractive home for companies from nearly all sectors of industry. c-Port – today that stands for a pragmatic approach, an innovative mindset, future-oriented action and a healthy curiosity about other investors. All the signs point to growth. For example, a green refinery is under construction for the production of ecological fuels, and the port is also being extended as part of the development of the Coastal Canal. Arno Düren, Managing Director of c-Port, puts it like this: "At the junction of the main federal roads B 401 and B 72, our site offers excellent transport links and an efficient infrastructure with a high-speed digital network."

Nietiedt-Gruppe

Nietiedt – Starke Leistung am Bau!

Nietiedt ist eines der großen inhabergeführten Unternehmen des Bau- und Ausbauhandwerks mit 13 Standorten und mehr als 600 eigenen Mitarbeitern. Es bietet seinen Kunden Gerüste aller Bauarten sowie Leistungen im Stahl- und Metallbau. Auf seinem Gebiet ist Nietiedt eines der führenden Maler- und Korrosionsschutzunternehmen. Das Portfolio umfasst Beton- und Korrosionsschutzarbeiten sowie Spezialbeschichtungen für Böden und Behälter, Schiffsanstriche und Oberflächenvorbereitungen. Abgerundet wird das Leistungsspektrum um Stahlreparaturen für den Schiffbau, Sanierungen von der Hausfassade bis zum komplexen Betonbauwerk, Fassadenwärmedämmungen, Renovierungen und dekorative Gestaltungen von Innenräumen sowie Bodenbelagsarbeiten.

Nietiedt – strong partner for the building trade!

Nietiedt is a large proprietor-run company on the skilled crafts sector with 13 sites and more than 600 own workers. It offers customers all kinds of scaffolding together with steel and metal construction services. Nietiedt is one of the leading painting and corrosion protection companies in its field. The portfolio includes concrete and corrosion protection work as well as special coatings for floors and tanks, marine coatings and surface preparation work. The range of services is rounded off with steel repairs for shipbuilding and house façade refurbishment, as well as complex concrete structures, façade heat insulation, renovation and decorative design of interiors as well as flooring work.

Information

Gründungsjahr: 1938
Mitarbeiter: mehr als 600
Leistungsspektrum:
– Gerüste aller Bauarten
– Stahl- und Metallbauarbeiten
– Maler- und Lackierarbeiten
– Bodenbelags- und
  Parkettarbeiten
– Korrosionsschutzarbeiten
– Betoninstandsetzungen
– Fassaden, Dämmungen
  und Putz
www.nietiedt.com

Year founded: 1938
Employees: more than 600
Range of services:
– scaffolding of all kinds
– steel and metal construction
– painting and varnishing work
– flooring and parquet work
– corrosion protection
– concrete refurbishment
– façades, insulation and
  plastering

Hermann Dallmann

Straßen- und Tiefbau GmbH & Co. KG

Mit umfassender Baukompetenz im Ingenieur- und Verkehrswegebau sowie im Tief- und Kanalbau bieten wir unseren Kunden ein ganzheitliches Leistungsspektrum. Unser Schwerpunkt liegt im Nordwesten. Mit unserem Hauptsitz in Bramsche bei Osnabrück und einer Niederlassung in Edewecht bei Oldenburg decken wir ein breites Einsatzgebiet zwischen Ruhrgebiet und Nordsee, zwischen Weser und holländischer Grenze ab. Wir setzen auf solide Werte: ein Fundament bestehend aus Engagement und langjähriger Erfahrung eines hoch qualifizierten Teams. Darauf können Sie bauen.

Our comprehensive building expertise in civil engineering and traffic route construction as well as underground engineering and sewer construction offers our customers a holistic range of services. Our focus is on the North West of Germany. With our headquarters in Bramsche near Osnabrück and a branch in Edewecht near Oldenburg, we cover a broad area between the Ruhr region and the North Sea, between the river Weser and the Dutch border. We advocate sound values, based on commitment and a highly qualified team that offers many years of experience. You can build on that.

Information

Leistungsspektrum:
– Verkehrswegebau
– Straßen-/Tiefbau
– Ingenieurtiefbau
– Kabel- und Leitungsbau
– Industriebau
– Wasserbau
– Erschließungsmaßnahmen
– Landwirtschaftliches Bauen
– Deponiebau
www.dallmann-bau.de

Range of services:
– traffic route construction
– road construction/under-
  ground engineering
– civil engineering
– cable and line construction
– industrial construction
– hydraulic engineering
– development measures
– agricultural construction
– landfill construction

ALBA Metall Nord GmbH
Betriebsstätte Wilhelmshaven

Information

Fläche: rund 60.000 m²

Leistungsspektrum:

Aufbereitungstechnik

– Shredder, Schere, Röntgen-
anlage, Granulieranlagen,
Rotorprallmühle, stationäre und
mobile Pressen, Kabelshredder

https://metall-nord.alba.info

Surface area: around 60,000 m²

Range of services:

Processing machinery

– shredders, shears, X-ray
machine, granulating unit,
rotor impact mill, stationary
and mobile presses, cable
shredders

Ihr Partner für Schrott, Metalle und Industriedienstleistungen in Niedersachsen

Die ALBA Metall Nord GmbH, ein Tochterunternehmen des internationalen Umweltdienstleisters und Rohstoffversorgers ALBA Group, ist seit nunmehr 50 Jahren am Standort Wilhelmshaven ein leistungsstarker und zuverlässiger Partner der Stahl und Metall produzierenden Industrie – regional, national wie auch international. Unsere Kernkompetenz ist die Erfassung, Rückgewinnung und Rückführung von hochwertigen Rohstoffen in den Materialkreislauf. Dabei zählt der private Lieferant genauso wie die industrielle Entfallstelle, der Autoverwerter und der Stahl- und Metallhandel zu unserem Lieferantenportfolio. Durch den Einsatz moderner Recyclingmethoden sowie einen hohen technischen Standard tragen wir maßgeblich dazu bei, ein Downcycling zu vermeiden und erzielen einen maximalen Beitrag für Klimaschutz und Nachhaltigkeit.

Die Betriebsstätte befindet sich in optimaler Lage direkt am Handelshafen mit einer Gleis- und Autobahnanbindung sowie in unmittelbarer Nähe zum Jade-WeserPort. Sie verfügt damit über einen unmittelbaren Zugang zur Nordsee und nach Übersee. Zusätzlich verfügt der Standort über eine 200 Meter lange Kai- und Umschlaganlage, die mit einem Brückenportalkran ausgestattet ist. Auf dem rund 60.000 m² großen Betriebsgelände sind etwa 100 Mitarbeiter beschäftigt.

Your partner for scrap, metal and industrial services in Lower Saxony

ALBA Metall Nord GmbH, a subsidiary of the international environmental services provider and raw materials trader ALBA Group, has been operating for more than 50 years in Wilhelmshaven as an efficient, reliable partner for the steel and metal manufacturing industry on a regional, national and international scale. Our area of expertise is collecting, recovering and recycling high quality raw materials for the materials cycle. Our supplier portfolio includes both private suppliers and industrial collection facilities, car recyclers and the steel and metals trade. With modern recycling methods and high technical standards, we help to avoid downcycling and make a major contribution towards climate protection and sustainability.

The company facility is in an ideal location right on the commercial port with rail and motorway links. It is also in the immediate vicinity of the JadeWesePort with direct access to the North Sea and to overseas. The site also has a 200 metres long quay and transhipment facility with a gantry crane. About 100 employees work on the company premises covering around 60,000 m².

Information

Gründungsjahr: 1896   **Mitarbeiter:** rund 120
Leistungsspektrum: Brücken, Kläranlagen, Tunnel und Tröge, sonstiger Ingenieurbau, Hochbau, Gewerbebau, Sanierung
Einsatzgebiet: Norddeutschland
Niederlassungen: Oldenburg und Schwerin
Auftraggeber: Bund, Länder und Kommunen, Industrie-/Gewerbe- unternehmen, Deutsche Bahn, Versorgungsunternehmen u. a.

Year founded: 1896   **Employees:** approx. 120
Range of services: bridges, wastewater treatment plants, tunnels and troughs, other civil engineering, structural engineering, commercial construction, refurbishment
Operation area: Northern Germany
Branches: Oldenburg and Schwerin
Clients: federal, state and local authorities, industrial/commercial companies, Deutsche Bahn, utility companies and many more

www.fritz-spieker.de

Fritz Spieker GmbH & Co. KG – Brücken- und Ingenieurbau

Wir bauen Werte. Seit 1896.   **Building value. Since 1896.**

Seit 125 Jahren steht unser Familienunternehmen für die Umsetzung innovativer Ingenieurleistungen. Das ist unsere Tradition und gleichzeitig unser Ansporn auf dem Weg in die Zukunft.

Wir errichten nicht nur solide Bauwerke, sondern legen großen Wert auf stabile und faire Partnerschaften: mit Kunden und Auftraggebern, Argepartnern, Nachunternehmen und Lieferanten. Sie alle verlassen sich seit vier Generationen auf die hohe Qualität unserer Leistungen und die termingerechte Fertigstellung aller Projekte.

Tradition und Innovation sind unser Fundament, unsere engagierten und erfahrenen Mitarbeiter bilden das Gerüst für unsere Marktführerschaft im Brückenbau und unseren nachhaltigen Erfolg. Seit 2006 leitet Dipl.-Ing. Jörn Spieker in nunmehr vierter Familiengeneration die Geschicke des Bauunternehmens mit Sitz in Oldenburg.

For 125 years, our family company has stood for implementing innovative engineering services. That is our tradition and at the same time our incentive for the future.

Besides building sound constructions, we also set great store by robust, fair partnerships with customers and clients, consortium partners, subcontractors and suppliers. For four generations, they have all relied on the top quality of our services and the punctual completion of all projects.

Tradition and innovation are our foundations, with a committed, experience workforce as the scaffold for our market leadership in bridge construction a nd our sustainable success. Dipl.-Ing. Jörn Spieker has been running the building firm based in Oldenburg since 2006 in the fourth generation of the family firm.

Alfred Döpker
GmbH & Co. KG Bauunternehmen

Zwei Dinge sind in unserer Baubranche von unschätzbarem Wert: langjährige Erfahrung und stetige Weiterentwicklung. Beides – Tradition und Bauinnovation – vereinen wir unter unserem Dach in Oldenburg und Bremen. In mehr als 55 Jahren haben wir als Generalunternehmer vielfältige Bauprojekte zum Erfolg geführt, ausgezeichnete Marktkenntnis erworben und einen Stamm hoch professioneller Partnerunternehmen aufgebaut. Von diesen gewachsenen Erfahrungen und Stärken profitieren in erster Linie unsere Kunden.

Dabei haben wir uns stets eine unkonventionelle, pragmatische und zielstrebige Arbeitsweise bewahrt. Sie macht uns begierig auf die neuesten technischen Entwicklungen und baulichen Trends. Gemeinsam mit unseren Kunden und Partnern wollen wir immer neue Wege gehen und die besten Ergebnisse erzielen. Unsere Baufirma pflegt eine Philosophie, die auf Vertrauen ruht, dem besten Fundament für eine langfristig erfolgreiche Zusammenarbeit. Doch Vertrauen kommt nicht von ungefähr; es muss verdient werden. Daher steht jedes Döpker-Bauprojekt unter einer Devise: Wir bauen Vertrauen.

Two things are of inestimable value in our building industry: years of experience and constant further development. In Oldenburg and Bremen, we combine both tradition and construction innovation under one and the same roof. We have worked as general contractor for more than 55 years, leading diverse construction projects to success, acquiring excellent knowledge of the market and setting up a network of highly professional partner companies. The experience and strengths that have evolved from this development benefit our customers first and foremost.

At the same time, we always maintain an unconventional, pragmatic and ambitious approach to our work, made evident in our eager desire to keep pace with the very latest technical developments and construction trends. Together with our customers and partners, we are always happy to explore new horizons and achieve the best results. Our corporate philosophy is based on trust and confidence as the best foundation for successful long-term cooperation. But confidence and trust are not a matter of chance: they have to be earned. This leads to the motto for every Döpker building project: We build trust and confidence.

Information

Gründungsjahr: 1965   **Mitarbeiter:** mehr als 50

Leistungsspektrum:
– Schlüsselfertiges Bauen (Büro- und Verwaltungsgebäude, Wohngebäude, Industriebauten, Einkaufsstätten, Pflegeeinrichtungen)
– Sanierung und Modernisierung (Altbau, energetisches Bauen, Fassaden, Fundamente, Gewölbe, Instandsetzungen, Dämmung)
– BIM (Building Information Modeling), Gebäudedaten-Modellierung

Year founded: 1965   **Employees:** more than 50

Range of services:
– Turnkey construction (office and administration buildings, residential buildings, industrial buildings, shopping centres, care facilities)
– Refurbishment and modernisation (old buildings, energy-efficient construction, facades, foundations, vaults, maintenance, insulation)
– BIM (Building Information Modeling)

www.team-doepker.de

DYNAPAC GmbH

Your Partner on the Road Ahead

DYNAPAC ist einer der weltweit führenden Hersteller von Maschinen und Geräten für den Bau von Straßen wie Straßenfertiger, Beschicker und Walzen. Das Unternehmen wurde 1934 in Schweden gegründet und ist derzeit mit Produktionsstätten in fünf Ländern weltweit präsent. Im Oktober 2017 wurde das Unternehmen von der französischen Fayat Gruppe übernommen.

Der Standort in Wardenburg hat für DYNAPAC eine besondere Bedeutung: mehr als 300 Mitarbeiter sind hier in der Produktion, im Kundencenter und in der Divisionsleitung beschäftigt. Sprich: Von Wardenburg aus – und nicht aus Schweden – wird die DYNAPAC-Gruppe geführt. Und der Standort soll in naher Zukunft weiter ausgebaut werden. Im Werk in Wardenburg werden jährlich rund 400 Straßenfertiger und Beschicker gebaut, Tendenz steigend.

Das Kundencenter in Wardenburg vereint die Bereiche Sales, Service und Schulung in einer zentralen Anlaufstelle für alle Fragen und Anliegen der Kunden. Die Experten im Straßenbau beraten kompetent in allen Themen der Maschinen- und Anwendungstechnik sowie zu Finanzierung und Service. Das DYNAPAC-Team im Kundendienst besteht aus ausgebildeten Technikern und Ingenieuren: Mit technischen Hilfestellungen, Tipps und Tricks geben sie ihr Know-how an die Monteure, Fertigerfahrer und Bediener der DYNAPAC-Baumaschinen weiter, die auf den Baustellen oder in den Werkstätten arbeiten. Außerdem organisiert der Kundendienst die rasche Ersatzteilversorgung.

Information

Gründungsjahr: 1934 in Karlskrona (Schweden); seit 2017 Teil der französischen Fayat-Gruppe

Mitarbeiter: rund 300 am Standort Wardenburg

Leistungsspektrum:
- Verdichtung (kleine und große Asphaltwalzen, Erdbauwalzen, statische und pneumatische Walzen; Stampfer und Vibrationsplatten) und leichte Verdichtung
- Straßenbau (Kompaktfertiger, City-Fertiger, Großradfertiger, Großkettenfertiger, Beschicker und Bohlen
- Serviceleistungen

Year founded: 1934 in Karlskrona (Sweden); part of the French Fayat Group since 2017

Employees: around 300 at the site in Wardenburg

Range of services:
- compaction (small and large asphalt rollers, soil compactors, static and pneumatic rollers; rammers and vibration plates) and compact equipment
- road construction (compact pavers, city pavers, large wheeled pavers, large tracked pavers, feeders and screeds)
- support services

www.dynapac.com

Your Partner on the Road Ahead

DYNAPAC is one of the world's leading manufacturers of machinery and equipment for road construction such as highway pavers, mobile feeders and rollers. The company was founded in Sweden in 1934 and currently has production sites in five countries worldwide. In October 2017, the company was taken over by the French Fayat Group.

The site in Wardenburg is particularly important for DYNAPAC, with more than 300 employees working here in production, the customer centre and division management. In other words, the DYNAPAC Group is run from Wardenburg, not from Sweden. And there are plans for further expansion of the site in the near future. Every year, around 400 highway pavers and mobile feeders are produced in the Wardenburg plant every year, and the numbers are increasing.

The customer centre in Wardenburg combines sales, service and training as a central point of contact for all questions and concerns of the customers. The road construction experts offer competent advice covering all aspects of machinery and applications engineering, as well as financing and service. The DYNAPAC customer service team consists of trained technicians and engineers who offer a wealth of technical assistance, tips and tricks for passing their know-how on to the fitters, paver drivers and operators of the DYNAPAC construction machinery working on the construction sites or in the workshops. The customer service also ensures fast spare parts provision.

DIE SPURENLEGERIN

The Tracemaker

AUTORIN:
ALKE ZUR MÜHLEN

BARBARA HASKAMP

In große elterliche Fußstapfen treten, die Richtung beibehalten und dennoch eigene Spuren hinterlassen: Barbara Haskamp gelingt dieses Kunststück. Die 44-jährige Edewechterin ist Prokuristin der Haskamp-Gruppe – unter anderem.

Sogar ihre Hausaufgaben habe sie oft in der Firma gemacht, erklärt Barbara Haskamp lachend, „wie man im Unternehmen aufwächst". Ihr Vater Heinz Haskamp hat sich 1978 selbstständig gemacht und sich auf die Fertigung von Aluminium-Glas-Fassaden, Fenster und Türen spezialisiert. Just in dieser Zeit wurde Barbara geboren. Ihre Mutter Christa gab mit der Firmengründung ihren Beruf als OP- und Krankenschwester auf und brachte sich im Betrieb ein – die Tochter immer dabei.

Dass daraus heute eine international agierende Unternehmensgruppe mit 215 Mitarbeitern hervorgegangen ist, ist eine Familienleistung. Die Liste der Großprojekte, die von Edewecht aus betreut wurden, ist lang: Das NATO-Hauptquartier in Brüssel zählt ebenso dazu wie der Luxemburger Flughafen. Und wenn im Kölner Tatort die Kranhäuser über den Rhein ragen, sind immer auch Fassaden von Haskamp im Bild.

Stepping in large footprints left by her parents, staying on course and still leaving her own traces: this is the feat achieved by Barbara Haskamp. Among others, the 44-year-old from Edewecht is general manager of the Haskamp Group.

Even her homework was often done on the company premises, says Barbara Haskamp with a laugh as she explains how you "grow up in a firm". Her father Heinz Haskamp set up his own business in 1978 as a specialist for making aluminium/glass façades, windows and doors. This was at the time when Barbara was born. Once the company was founded, her mother stopped working as a nurse and got involved in the business – with her daughter always at her side.

Meanwhile the firm has expanded into international group of companies with a workforce of 215 employees, which must be seen as a family achievement. There is a long list of major projects managed from Edewecht, including NATO headquarters in Brussels as well as Luxembourg airport. Façades made by Haskamp are also always in the picture when television films made in Cologne show the "crane houses" protruding across the Rhine.

Im Unternehmen ist man per Du. Viele Mitarbeiter kennen Barbara Haskamp von Kindesbeinen an. Der (selbstverständlich bezahlte) regelmäßige Ferienjob in der Werkstatt war für sie obligatorisch. „Die Firma ist meine erweiterte Familie. Ich war und bin jeden Tag hier." Gab es jemals die Option, nicht ins Familienunternehmen einzusteigen? „Klar!", kommt die Antwort wie aus der Pistole geschossen.

Perfekt (un-)geplant

Lehrerin für Mathematik und katholische Religion an der Grundschule sei lange Zeit ihr Traumjob gewesen. Die Unternehmensnachfolge hat sie zwar auch gereizt, sie war aber nie das Ziel. „Meine Eltern hätten mich bei allem unterstützt", ist sich die Unternehmerin sicher.

Vor dem Abitur sucht sie Abwechslung, jobbt in der Gastronomie. Das macht ihr nicht nur Spaß, sie profitiert bis heute davon. Serviceerfahrung hilft auch im Kundenkontakt, so ihre Überzeugung. Wann genau sie ihre Zukunftspläne geändert hat, weiß sie nicht mehr. Nur so viel: „Meine Ausbildung hat genau die richtige Basis gelegt." Überhaupt könne man mit einer Ausbildung nichts falsch machen. Sie absolviert ein Duales Studium zur Industriekauffrau und Wirtschaftsingenieurin beim Glashersteller Semco. Erst danach beschließen ihr (damals noch zukünftiger) Mann Mathias und sie, den Schritt ins Unternehmen zu wagen – und stellen mit der Familie die Weichen.

Erster Schritt: ein gemeinsames Duales Studium Bauingenieurwesen im baden-württembergischen Mosbach. Praktika führen sie an unterschiedliche Orte, das Auslandssemester gemeinsam nach Südamerika. In der Abschlussarbeit entwickeln die beiden, wie soll es anders sein, doppelschalige Fassaden weiter und schließen „sehr gut" ab. Barbara Haskamp ist Jahrgangsbeste.

Überhaupt sind sie ein starkes Team. Auch unter besonderen Bedingungen: Inzwischen verheiratet, werden sie noch im Studium Eltern. „Das war eine Herausforderung", blickt die 44-Jährige zurück. „Wir sind nachts aufgestanden, haben den Kleinen gefüttert und sind um 6 Uhr zur Uni gefahren." Es muss gehen – und funktioniert. Auch, weil Eltern und Schwiegereltern sich tagsüber um den Enkel kümmern. Rückblickend sagt Barbara Haskamp: „Es war anstrengend. Aber auch eine coole Zeit."

Fokus Mensch

Zurück in Edewecht. Barbara Haskamp steigt zunächst in Projekte ein. Mit wachsender Familie passt sie ihre Aufgabengebiete und Arbeitszeiten an. Ihr Fokus: Mitarbeiter und Ausbildung. Der Metall- und Elementebauer ist stolz auf lange Betriebszugehörigkeiten. Und darauf angewiesen. „Um unsere hohe Qualität im Fenster- und Fassadenbau zu halten, braucht es Spezialwissen. Wir bilden unsere Fachkräfte zu einem großen Teil selbst aus", erklärt die Unternehmerin. Seit Firmengründung haben 220 junge Menschen bei Haskamp ihre Ausbildung oder ein Duales Studium absolviert. 77 davon arbeiten heute noch oder wieder im Betrieb.

Zur Attraktivität als Arbeitgeber trägt neben klassischen Anreizen seit einiger Zeit die Möglichkeit der flexiblen Arbeitszeit für die Beschäftigten in der Verwaltung bei. „Das war nach alter Schule undenkbar, ist für unsere Generation aber selbstverständlich." Und es geht noch weiter:

Eine offene und freundliche Firmenkultur ist für das Edewechter Unternehmen Haskampf essenziell – das gilt nicht nur für die tägliche Arbeit, sondern auch für gemeinsame Freizeitaktivitäten oder soziale Engagements.

An open, friendly corporate culture is essential for the Haskamp Group in Edewecht. This applies not only to the daily work situation in the company but also to shared leisure activities and social commitment.

Baukonjunktur im Aufwind

Die Branche boomt – nicht nur in der Region. Dem konnte auch die Pandemie (bisher) nichts anhaben. Die Konjunkturprogramme nach der großen Krise vor zwölf Jahren haben gegriffen. Wichtigste Motoren sind die Investitionen vieler Unternehmen in Gewerbeimmobilien sowie der Wohnungsbau, der durch niedrige Zinsen und als Anlagemöglichkeit Fahrt aufnahm.

Vom Weltmarkt kamen hingegen zuletzt eher beunruhigende Nachrichten. So stiegen die Holzpreise in ungeahnte Höhen. Zudem konnte die Produktion von Baustahl nicht mit der in Ostasien explodierenden Nachfrage mithalten. Die Auswirkungen der Engpässe waren bis auf die kleinste Baustelle spürbar.

In der Region ist die Bauindustrie seit langem am stärksten in den Landkreisen Ammerland, Cloppenburg und Vechta sowie in der Stadt Oldenburg vertreten. Der Umsatz stieg im Jahr 2020 auf stolze 1,6 Milliarden Euro. Hoch- und Tiefbau trugen dazu den wesentlichen Anteil bei. Der öffentliche und Straßenbau spielte hingegen nur eine untergeordnete Rolle. Der Wohnungsbau hat sich dank einer Steigerung von 12,9 Prozent zur umsatzstärksten Hochbausparte entwickelt, lässt den Wirtschaftsbau mit gewerblichem und Industriebau hinter sich. Zulegen konnten insbesondere der öffentliche Baubereich mit einem Plus von 21,9 Prozent im Vergleich zum Vorjahr. Der Wirtschaftsbau war – der Pandemie geschuldet – leicht rückläufig.

Die Zahl der Beschäftigten in den 189 Bauunternehmen ab 20 Mitarbeitern im Gebiet der Oldenburgischen Industrie- und Handelskammer stieg im Jahresdurchschnitt leicht auf über 9.041. In der Gesamtheit betrachtet bewegt sich die regionale Bauwirtschaft im Niedersachsentrend. Das Bauhauptgewerbe war 2020 landesweit gesehen weder von Lockdowns noch von Kurzarbeit in nennenswertem Umfang betroffen.

Everyone in the company is on first-name terms. Many employees know Barbara Haskamp from childhood. The (naturally paid) regular holiday job in the workshop was "par for the course" for her. "The firm is my extended family. I was and am here every day." Was she ever given the option not to join the family business? "But of course!", she replies quick like a shot.

Perfectly (un-)planned

For a long time she dreamed of being a primary school teacher for maths and Catholic religious studies. Although she was also interested in the future of the company, it was but never her goal. "My parents would have supported me whatever I wanted to do", the entrepreneur is certain about that.

Before doing her university entrance exams, she gets a job in the hospitality trade for a bit of variety. She enjoys the work and still reaps the benefits today. She is convinced that experience in service also helps when dealing with customers. She can't really say exactly when she changed her plans for the future. Suffice to say that: "My training laid me the right foundations." Indeed, you can't go wrong with training. She does a dual education course in industrial management and business engineering with glass manufacturer Semco. It is only then that she and her (future) husband Mathias decide to take the plunge and join the business, thus paving the way for a future with the family firm.

The first step is to complete a dual education course together in civil engineering in Mosbach in Baden-Württemberg. Internships take them to many different places, including a semester abroad together in South America. Their final dissertations focussed on the further development of double-shell façades (what else?) with the grade "very good". Barbara Haskamp is the best of her vintage.

They are indeed a strong team. Even when things get a bit difficult: meanwhile married, they become parents while still in the middle of their course. "That was a real challenge", says the 44-year-old looking back. "We'd get up in the night, feed the baby and head for uni at 6 am." It has to work – and it does work. Also because the parents and in-laws take care of their grandchild during the day. In retrospect, Barbara Haskamp says: "It was hard work. But it was a good time as well."

Focus on people

Back in Edewecht. Initially, Barbara Haskamp begins with various projects. As the family grows, she adjusts her remit and her working hours. She focuses on the workforce and on training. The metal and element construction firm is proud of the long seniority record of its workforce. And depends on it too. "It takes specialist know-how to maintain our high standard of quality in window and façade construction. For the most part, we train our own skilled workers", explains the entrepreneur. Since the company was founded, 220 young people have completed an apprenticeship or dual education degree with Haskamp. 77 of them are still working with the company or have come back again.

Besides the usual perks, for some time now the firm's image as an employer has been enhanced by the possibility of flexible hours for

Booming building trade

The building trade is booming, and not just here in the region. Not even the pandemic has had an impact (up to now). The economy stimulus packages implemented after the major crisis twelve years ago had the desired effect. The main driving force is powered by investments made by many companies in commercial property as well as residential construction, where growth has been triggered by low interest rates and investment possibilities.

On the other hand, news from the global market is not so good. The price of wood has risen to meteoric heights. And the production of construction steel has failed to keep pace with the exploding demand from East Asia. Even the smallest construction sites have felt the effects of the resulting bottlenecks.

Here in the region, the building trade is strongest in the districts of Ammerland, Cloppenburg and Vechta and in the city of Oldenburg. Turnover increased to a proud 1.6 billion Euro in 2020, generated primarily by structural and civil engineering projects. By contrast public works and road construction only played a minor role. Residential construction increased by 12.9 percent to become the structural engineering sector with the highest turnover leaving commercial and industrial construction behind. Growth was particularly strong on the public sector with a year-on-year increase of 21.9 percent. Commercial construction declined slightly, due to the pandemic.

The 189 construction companies with more than 20 employees in the area covered by Oldenburg Chamber of Industry and Commerce saw a slight increase in the yearly average workforce numbers to reach 9,041. Altogether, the regional building trade is moving in the same direction as the state of Lower Saxony as a whole. Throughout the state, the primary construction industry was not affected by lockdowns or furlough schemes to any great extent during 2020.

Ein Entwicklungsprogramm mit externer Unterstützung stellt sicher, dass Firma und Personal ihre Potenziale ausschöpfen. Genauso wichtig ist die Bindung ans Unternehmen, auch über die Mitarbeitenden hinaus. So stellt Barbara Haskamp jährlich Aktionen für die Familien auf die Beine. Der Wikinger-Nachmittag ist auch für ihre eigenen Kinder ein Highlight. Einmal im Monat lädt die Belegschaft mittags auf eine Bratwurst ein. Die Chefin freut sich schon darauf, wenn die Umstände diesen lockeren Austausch wieder zulassen. Dann können auch Schulklassen erneut zum Schauen und Ausprobieren kommen.

Immer in Bewegung

Regelmäßige Bewegung ist für die passionierte Läuferin viel mehr als nur Abschalten. „Wenn ich keinen Sport machen kann, fehlt mir was", sagt sie. Das jährliche Sportabzeichen gehört für sie einfach dazu – nicht aus Ehrgeiz, vielmehr aus Freude am gemeinsamen Bewegen. So motiviert sie auch die Mitarbeiter. Durch ihre Kinder kommt sie zum Tennis. „Spielereltern werden bei Punktspielen als Schiedsrichter eingesetzt. Da habe ich mir gedacht: Das lerne ich am besten, wenn ich selbst spiele." Sie fängt Feuer und beteiligt sich seitdem am Spielbetrieb des örtlichen Vereins. „Hauptsächlich aus Spaß", wie sie lachend ergänzt.

Und sie trägt den Sport ins Unternehmen. „Mitarbeitersport ist eine tolle Möglichkeit, Kolleginnen und Kollegen besser kennenzulernen und Teams zu stärken." So gibt es heute eine Laufgruppe und Zuschüsse zu Startgeldern. Auch ein internes Tennisturnier hat sie schon organisiert. 28 „Profis" und „Amateure" nahmen teil, auch ihre Kinder. Die regelmäßige Teilnahme des Unternehmens am Sportabzeichen führte bereits zu einer Auszeichnung als „fitteste Firma". Die Haskamp-Stiftung setzt sich für örtliche Sportvereine ein.

Die Bedeutung des Ehrenamts hat Barbara Haskamp von ihrer Mutter vorgelebt bekommen. „Bei uns war immer was los, immer jemand mehr am Tisch", erinnert sie sich. In der Haskamp-Stiftung arbeiten beide heute zusammen. Seit 2011 unterstützt die Familie gemeinnützige und mildtätige Zwecke in der Region, von der Roboter AG des Gymnasiums bis zur Förderung von jungen Talenten. In der Kirchengemeinde, im Sportverein oder beim Flohmarkt-Team des Kindergartens zeigt die Unternehmerin persönlichen Einsatz. Seit über 20 Jahren ist sie mit ihrem Mann im Verein move e.V. aktiv. Und weil sie gut vernetzt ist, wird sie auch schon mal kurzfristig gefragt, ob sie nicht einer geflüchteten Familie beim Ankommen helfen kann. Natürlich sagt sie zu.

Ausbildung als Integration

Durch „einen Anruf aus dem Ort" kommt es dazu, dass Haskamp schon früh Geflüchteten eine Ausbildung ermöglicht und sie damit vor der Abschiebung bewahrt. Heute sind die jungen Männer unbefristet angestellt. „Wir haben durchweg gute Erfahrungen gemacht", freut sich die Chefin. Und hilft auch schon mal dabei, eine Wohnung zu finden oder den ersten großen Einkauf zu bewältigen.

the administrative staff. "That would have been inconceivable in the past, but it's something our generation takes for granted." And things don't stop here: a development programme with external support ensures that the company and its personnel make full use of their potential. Loyalty to the company is just as important, and goes beyond the employees themselves. Barbara Haskamp organises family events every year. The Viking Afternoon is a highlight also for her own children. Once a month, the workforce issue an invitation to enjoy a sausage at lunchtime. The company boss is looking forward to the point in time when circumstances will allow such informal encounters again. That will also be the time when school classes are encouraged to take a hands-on look at the firm.

Always on the move

For the avid runner, regular exercise is more than just a means of switching off. "I feel deprived if I haven't got any sport", she says. Doing the annual sports badge is simply part of it for her, not to satisfy any ambition but to enjoy exercising together. This also helps to motivate the staff. Her children get her involved in tennis. "The parents are roped in as umpires when they play a match. So I thought the best way to learn is to play tennis myself." She gets hooked and has played regularly with the local club since then. "It's mostly for fun", she says with a laugh.

She also brings sport into the firm. "Staff sport is a great way of getting to know the colleagues better and strengthening the teams." Today they have a running group and the company subsidises competition entry fees. She has also organised an internal tennis tournament. 28 "professionals" and "amateurs" took part, including her children. The company's regular participation in the sport badge programme has already seen it win the accolade of "fittest firm". The Haskamp foundation supports local sport clubs.

It was Barbara Haskamp's mother who showed her the importance of voluntary commitment. "There was always something going on at home, always someone extra at the meal table", she remembers. Today they work together in the Haskamp foundation. Since 2011, the family supports nonprofit and charitable projects in the region, from the grammar school robot club through to sponsoring young talents. The entrepreneur is personally involved in the local church, sports club or kindergarten flea market team. She and her husband have played an active role in move e. V. for more than 20 years. And thanks to her good connections, she also sometimes gets asked at short notice whether she can help a family of refugees on their arrival. Of course she says yes.

Training as integration

A call from the local authority ensures that Haskamp starts to offer training for refugees early on, thus preventing them from being deported. Meanwhile the young men have been taken on as permanent staff. "It has been a positive experience throughout", says the company boss. She also helps refugees find accommodation or takes them shopping for the first time.

Barbara Haskamp stellt jährlich Aktionen für die Familien auf die Beine. Der Wikinger-Nachmittag war auch für ihre eigenen Kinder immer ein Highlight.

Barbara Haskamp organises family events every year. The Viking Afternoon always was a highlight also for her own children.

Weil helfen zu ihrer Überzeugung gehört, rennt auch Lennart Lehmkuhl mit seiner Bewerbung offene Türen ein. Der junge Mann hat eine starke Sehschwäche. Barbara Haskamp erarbeitet mit der Personalabteilung eine individuelle Lösung: Unterstützende Technik, ein Rotationssystem, das stets Azubi-Teamarbeit ermöglicht, eine Fahrgemeinschaft und Hilfe in der Berufsschule schaffen die Voraussetzung, dass Lehmkuhl heute als ausgebildeter Industriekaufmann arbeitet.

Ihr Engagement hat Barbara Haskamp längst auch auf die IHK Oldenburg ausgedehnt. Seit 17 Jahren ist sie ehrenamtliche Prüferin, aktuell Vorsitzende eines Ausschusses. „Der Kontakt zu den vielen Auszubildenden und Unternehmen bereichert mich. Und es macht auch einfach Spaß."

Im abwechslungsreichen Alltag sind nicht nur die Generationen, sondern auch Firma und Privatleben eng miteinander verwoben. „Man nimmt die Arbeit mit nach Hause, das ist für mich okay", sagt die Unternehmerin. Lediglich Mahlzeiten sind Ruhepunkte. „Wir essen zusammen und sprechen am Tisch grundsätzlich nicht übers Geschäft. Diese Zeit gehört den Kindern." Auch für sie gilt übrigens: Nur wer will, macht später in der Firma mit. Bis es soweit ist, bleibt Barbara Haskamp bei ihren vielfältigen Aufgaben. „Ich bin glücklich und habe nicht vor, daran etwas zu ändern."

Because helping is her mindset, even the job application from Lennart Lehmkuhl finds open doors. The young man has severely impaired vision. Barbara Haskamp works with the human resources department to come up with an individual solution: assistive technology, a rotation system that a allows for trainees to work as a team, car sharing and support at the vocational college create the prerequisites for Lehmkuhl to be working now as a trained industrial clerk.

Barbara Haskamp has meanwhile extended her commitment to Oldenburg CCI. For 17 years now she has worked as a voluntary examiner and is currently also chair of a committee. "I find it enriching to have contact with the many trainees and companies. And I really enjoy it too."

Her highly varied daily routine is a close-knit construct not only of generations but also company and private life. "Sometimes we bring work home, but that's OK for me", says the entrepreneur. Mealtimes are the only exception: "We eat together and never talk about business at the table. This time belongs to the children." By the way, she sees their future like her parents did: they'll only be part of the firm if they really want to be. Until then, Barbara Haskamp keeps focused on her many tasks. "I'm happy with what I do and don't intend to change anything."

HASKAMP GmbH & Co. KG

Metallbau | Fassadentechnik

HASKAMP – der Maßstab in Metallbau und Fassadentechnik

1978 gründete Heinz Haskamp das Unternehmen – mit gerade einmal zwei Mitarbeitern. Mittlerweile arbeiten über 230 Mitarbeiter auf rund 18.000 Quadratmetern Produktions-, Lager- und Verwaltungsfläche. Die Erfolgsgeschichte einer Unternehmensgruppe, die stets der Drang nach Innovationen ausgezeichnet hat, verbunden mit höchstem Qualitätsbewusstsein und unbedingter Verlässlichkeit.

Seit über 40 Jahren fertigen wir hochwertige Fassaden, Fenster und Türen aus Aluminium, Glasdachkonstruktionen, Rauch- und Brandschutztüren sowie Sonderlösungen aus Aluminium. Wir verstehen uns als Partner unserer Kunden, mit dem gleichen Anspruch an Qualität sowie technischer und handwerklicher Präzision.

Dabei gehen Kreativität und Kostenbewusstsein Hand in Hand und selbst sehr spezifische Anforderungen lassen sich verwirklichen. „Wir von HASKAMP leben Handwerk – mit System!"

Information

Gründungsjahr: 1978	**Year founded:** 1978
Mitarbeiter: rund 230	**Employees:** around 230
Gruppe:	**Group:**
– Metall- und Elementbau HASKAMP GmbH & Co. KG	– Metall- und Elementbau HASKAMP GmbH & Co. KG
– HASKAMP Fassadentechnik GmbH & Co. KG	– HASKAMP Fassadentechnik GmbH & Co. KG
Leistungsspektrum:	**Range of services:**
– Fassaden	– façades
– Fenster	– windows
– Türen	– doors
– Wintergärten	– conservatories
Geschäftsfelder:	**Business units:**
– Großprojekte	– projects
– regionale Bürogebäude	– regional office buildings
– Privatkunden	– private

www.haskamp.de

HASKAMP – the benchmark in metal construction and façade technology

Heinz Haskamp founded the company in 1978 – with just two employees. In the meantime, more than 230 employees work on around 18,000 square meters of production, storage and administrative space. This is the success story of a group of companies that has always stood out with its drive for innovation, coupled with quality awareness and reliability.

For more than 40 years, we have been producing top quality aluminium façades, windows and doors, glass roof structures, smoke and fire doors together with special solutions made of aluminium. We see ourselves in the role of partnering our customers with the same aspirations in terms of quality as well as craftsmanship and technical precision. Creativity goes hand-in-hand with cost awareness, and even highly specific requirements can be implemented. "We at HASKAMP live craft – with a system!"

Von Delmenhorst in die Welt

Wir sind auf die Entwicklung, Montage und Distribution von elektrischen und LWL-Steckverbindern und -Systemen für raue Umgebungen spezialisiert. Unser hoch motiviertes und erfahrenes Team bietet maßgeschneiderte Lösungen und Produkte von höchster Qualität.

JOWO liefert Produkte für Schiffs- und Unterwasseranwendungen, Offshore- und Verteidigungstechnik, Broadcast-Lösungen, Luft- und Raumfahrttechnik sowie für Gefahrenbereiche (ATEX & IECEX). Unsere Produkte werden nach den individuellen Anforderungen unserer Kunden entworfen und von unseren Mitarbeitern in Handarbeit mit höchster Qualität gefertigt.

Die JOWO - Systemtechnik AG hat ihren Sitz in Delmenhorst, nahe Bremen, im schönen Norddeutschland. Wir sind stolz darauf, dass wir von hier aus unsere Produkte und Dienstleistungen in aller Welt anbieten können. Und das alles mit höchster Qualität – made in Germany gefertigt. JOWO wurde 1995 gegründet und hat sich in über 25 Jahren zu einem innovativen, flexiblen und sehr erfahrenen weltweiten Anbieter in der Steckverbinderbranche entwickelt.

JOWO - Systemtechnik AG

Information

Gründungsjahr: 1995

Mitarbeiter: rund 70

Produkte:

– VG & MIL Steckverbinder

– Unterwasser-Steckverbinder

– Luft- & Raumfahrt Steckverbinder

– ATEX & IECEX

– LWL-Steckverbinder

– Steckverbinder Zubehör

– Verschiedenes

– Kabel

– Konfektionierte Kabel

Marktsegmente:

– Verteidigung & Marine

– Luft- & Raumfahrt

– Öl & Gas

– Unterwasser & Offshore

– Broadcast

– Industrie

www.jowo.ag

Year founded: 1995

Employees: about 70

Products:

– VG & MIL connectors

– underwater connectors

– aerospace connectors

– ATEX & IECEX

– fibre optic connectors

– connector accessories

– miscellaneous

– cables

– cable assemblies

Market segments:

– defence & naval

– aerospace

– oil & gas

– underwater & offshore

– broadcast

– industrial

From Delmenhorst into the world

We are specialized in the development, assembly and distribution of electrical and fibre optic connectors and systems for harsh environments. Our highly motivated and experienced team provides customized solutions and high quality products.

JOWO supplies products for marine and underwater applications, offshore and defence technology, broadcast solutions, aerospace engineering and hazardous areas (ATEX & IECEX). Our products are designed according to the individual requirements of our customers and assembled by our employees with the highest quality.

JOWO - Systemtechnik AG is based in Delmenhorst, near by Bremen, in lovely North Germany. We are proud to offer products and services from here on a global scale, all in the very best quality, made in Germany. JOWO was founded in 1995 and has grown over the past 25 years into an innovative, flexible and highly experienced worldwide supplier in the connector business.

NKT GmbH

We connect a greener world

Unser Weg ist eine Geschichte der ständigen Innovation. Von den ersten Glühbirnen bis hin zu Hochspannungsmegawatt, die durch erneuerbare Energien erzeugt werden, war NKT ein zuverlässiger Partner, der die entscheidenden Verbindungen für die Energieversorgung der Welt geschaffen hat.

Die fortschreitende Technologie hat den Kabeln, höhere Spezifikationen und Leistungen abverlangt. Der wachsende Energiebedarf war beträchtlich, aber wurde gleichzeitig durch ein unaufhörliches Engagement für die Entwicklung gedeckt. Diese Motivation hat NKT viele Weltneuheiten beschert und das Unternehmen zu einem weltweit anerkannten Namen gemacht. Die flexiblen und zuverlässigen Lösungen der NKT bringen Strom in Verbundnetze, Wasser- und Kernkraftwerke sowie in Windparks an Land und auf See, auf Öl- und Gasplattformen und in die Solarenergie.

Heute ist NKT mit Standorten in mehr als 14 Ländern und Produktionsstätten in Deutschland, Schweden, Polen, der Tschechischen Republik, Norwegen und Dänemark ein weltweit führender Anbieter von Kabellösungen, der zum globalen Übergang zu erneuerbaren Energien beiträgt. Mit dem Fokus auf einer möglichst CO_2-neutralen Produktion und Abfallvermeidung ist der Schutz der Umwelt dabei ein wichtiges Anliegen. Deshalb investiert NKT in den hohen Standard der Produktionstechnologien. NKT verfügt weltweit über die modernsten, flexibelsten und kosteneffizientesten Fertigungsstätten.

NKT GmbH Kabelgarnituren in Nordenham

In Nordenham liegt der Schwerpunkt unserer Kompetenz auf Kabelgarnituren. Am Standort entwickeln und produzieren wir unser gesamtes hochwertiges Kabelgarniturensortiment. Damit ist Nordenham für NKT eine Drehscheibe, um unsere Pionierarbeit auf dem Gebiet des Silikonkautschuks fortzusetzen.

Information

Gründungsjahr: 1891
Mitarbeiter: 3400 (Konzern)
Produkte & Lösungen:
– Hochspannungskabel
– Hochspannungskabel-
  garnituren
– Mittelspannungskabel
– Mittelspannungskabel-
  garnituren
– Niederspannungskabel
– Kabelservice
– Technologieberatung
– Sichere Energieverteilung
Standorte:
Produktionsstätten in Nordenham, Köln und Schweden sowie in Dänemark (Hauptsitz), Norwegen, Tschechien und Polen
www.nkt.com

Year founded: 1891
Employees: 3,400 (Group)
Products & solutions:
– high voltage cables
– high voltage cable accessories
– medium voltage cables
– medium voltage cable
  accessories
– low voltage cables
– cable services
– technology consulting
– safe energy distribution
Sites:
Production facilities in Nordenham, Cologne and Sweden as well as Denmark (headquarters), Norway, Czech Republic and Poland

Unsere Kabelgarnituren bis 72 kV in modularer Bauweise zeichnen sich durch Sicherheit, Zuverlässigkeit und Vielseitigkeit aus. Durch unsere langjährige Erfahrung und kontinuierliche Produktentwicklung ist es uns möglich, Produkte in Mehrbereichstechnik anzubieten, die den aktuellen und zukünftigen Anforderungen an zuverlässige Systeme entsprechen. Unser aktuelles Sortiment umfasst Kabelmuffen, Kabelendverschlüsse und geschirmte Kabelsteckteile.

Wir sind ein dynamisches aufstrebendes Unternehmen und suchen stetig nach qualifizierten Mitarbeitern und bilden auch Azubis und duale Studenten aus. Unsere Ausbildungsberufe (m/w/d) sind Industriemechaniker, Elektroniker, Zerspanungsmechaniker, Verfahrensmechaniker, Fachkraft für Lagerlogistik, Technischer Produktdesigner und Industriekaufmann.

We connect a greener world

Our journey is a story of constant innovation. From the first light bulbs to the high-voltage megawatts generated by renewable energy, NKT has been a trusted partner in creating the vital links that power the world. Advancing technology has demanded higher specifications and cable performance. The growing demand for power was considerable, but has been met through an unceasing commitment to development. This drive has resulted in many world firsts for NKT so that the company has become a globally respected name. NKT's flexible, reliable solutions bring electricity in integrated grids, hydroelectric and nuclear power stations as well as onshore and offshore wind farms, oil and gas rigs and in solar energy.

Today with locations in more than 14 countries and manufacturing facilities in Germany, Sweden, Poland, Czech Republic, Norway and Denmark, NKT is a world-leader in cable technology contributing to the global transition to renewable energy. Focusing as far as possible on carbon-neutral production and waste prevention, protecting the environment is an important concern. This is why NKT invests in the high standard of its production technology. NKT offers the most advanced, flexible and cost efficient production facilities world-wide.

NKT cable accessories in Nordenham

The focus for our Nordenham site is on our cable accessory expertise. This is where we develop and produce our entire range of top quality cable accessories. Nordenham thus acts as a hub for NKT to continue our pioneering work in the field of silicone rubber.

Our modular cable accessories up to 72 kV offer outstanding safety, reliability and versatility. Our many years of experience and on-going product development put us in a position to offer multirange products complying with current and future requirements for reliable systems. Our current range includes cable joints, cable terminations and screened cable connectors.

We are a dynamic, growing company and are constantly looking for qualified employees; we also train apprentices as well as students on dual degree courses. We offer apprenticeships (m/f/d) for industrial mechanics, electronics technicians, cutting machine operators, process mechanics, qualified warehouse logistics personnel, technical product designers and industrial clerks.

Rund 300 NKT-Mitarbeiter am Standort Nordenham entwickeln, fertigen und vertreiben Kabelgarnituren

Around 300 NKT employees at the Nordenham location develop, manufacture and sell cable accessories.

HAWART Sondermaschinenbau GmbH

Die HAWART Sondermaschinenbau GmbH ist ein mittelständisches Unternehmen mit Sitz in Ganderkesee. Weltweit nutzen Hersteller in der Windenergiebranche die technisch führenden Lösungen und schätzen das Know-how, die Flexibilität und die Qualität der Marke HAWART.

HAWART ist Spezialist für die Produktion und Montage von Fertigungsmitteln für Rotorblätter und Transportsysteme für Großkomponenten. Die Produktpalette umfasst zudem Maschinen und Ausrüstungen für zahlreiche andere Industriebranchen. Dank unserer konsequenten Kundenorientierung finden wir stets die optimalen Konzepte und Lösungen für unsere Auftraggeber. Dieses Leistungsniveau erreichen wir gezielt durch eine eigene Entwicklungs- und Konstruktionsabteilung.

Höchste Qualität und Nachhaltigkeit sind das Leitmotiv für alle unsere Produkte und Dienstleistungen. An deren konsequenter Weiterentwicklung arbeiten wir jeden Tag, um die wachsenden Erwartungen unserer Kunden nach technischer Innovation und steigender Leistungsfähigkeit zu erfüllen.

HAWART Sondermaschinenbau GmbH is a medium-sized company based in Ganderkesee. All over the world, manufacturers working for the wind energy sector make use of the HAWART brand and its technically leading solutions, appreciating the know-how, flexibility and quality.

HAWART has specialised in the manufacture and assembly of production tools for rotor blades and transport systems for large components. The product range also includes machinery and equipment for numerous other sectors of industry. Our consistent customer orientation enables us to find the ideal concepts and solutions for our customers every time. We achieve this level of performance specifically through our own development and engineering department.

All our products and services are based on the guiding principle of supreme quality and sustainability. Continuous further development of our products and services is the focus of our activities every day in order to satisfy the growing expectations of our customers in terms of technical innovation and increasing efficiency.

Information

Leistungsspektrum:

– Transport und
  Logistikkomponenten
– Rotorblattproduktionsanlagen
– Montage Tools
– Überdachungen und
  Fahrgastunterstände

Range of services:

– transport and logistics
  components
– rotor blade manufacturing
  facilities
– assembly tools
– roofing and passenger shelters

www.hawart.de

Hartgen GmbH
Maschinen- und Mühlenbau

Information

Gründungsjahr: 1987   **Mitarbeiter:** rund 30
Schwerpunkte: Entwicklung und Fertigung von Förderanlagen für Schüttgüter, Anlagen zur Getreideverarbeitung, für die Ziegelindustrie, die Lebensmittelindustrie und die chemische Industrie

Year founded: 1987   **Employees:** about 30
Focal aspects: Development and production of materials handling systems for bulk goods, machinery for processing grain, for the brick industry, the food industry and the chemical industry

www.hartgen-maschinenbau.de

Höchste Präzision und Funktionalität in der Fördertechnik – dafür steht das Unternehmen Hartgen Maschinen- und Mühlenbau im norddeutschen Hude. Gegründet 1987 als Werkstatt für Trichter und Behälter, beschäftigt Hartgen heute rund 30 Mitarbeiter. Förderanlagen wie Transportschnecken, Behälterlifte oder Becherwerke für Schüttgüter sind die Kernkompetenz. Der kontinuierliche Ausbau des Maschinenparks, qualifizierte Fachleute und Innovationsgeist haben maßgeblich zur Entwicklung des Unternehmens beigetragen.

Ob komplette Anlagen, kleine Serien oder individuelle Einzelanfertigung, bei Hartgen entstehen technisch und ökonomisch sinnvolle Lösungen. Kraftfutterwerke, Ziegeleien, Lebensmittel- oder Chemieindustrie sind erfolgreiche Anwender von Maschinenbaulösungen aus Hude. „Just in time" ist keine Ausnahme, sondern eine Selbstverständlichkeit. Mit diesem Versprechen überzeugt das Unternehmen zahlreiche Kunden aus dem In- und Ausland. Und dieses Versprechen ist es auch, welches die Firmeninhaberin Helma Hartgen seit 1997 in alleiniger Verantwortung fortführt. Fachliche Qualifikation und kaufmännische Kompetenz verbindet sie mit Führungsqualitäten und persönlichem Engagement. Dafür wurde sie im Jahr 2010 von der deutschen Fachpublikation „handwerk magazin" als „Unternehmerfrau des Jahres" ausgezeichnet.

Absolute precision and functionality in materials handling systems: that is what Hartgen Maschinen- und Mühlenbau in Hude, North Germany, stands for. Founded in 1987 as a workshop for funnels and containers, today Hartgen has a workforce of around 30 employees, with core expertise in materials handling systems such as feeding screws, container lifts or bucket conveyors for bulk materials. Continuous expansion of the machinery, qualified experts and an innovative spirit have played a major role in the company's development. Whether complete plants, small series or individual custom-made units, Hartgen produces solutions that make technical and economic sense. Machine construction solutions from Hude are used successfully by concentrated feed manufacturing plants, brickworks, food producers or the chemical industry. "Just in time" is a matter of fact rather than an exception. It is a promise with which the company convinces numerous customers at home and abroad. And it is also the promise with which proprietor Helma Hartgen has been running the company under her sole responsibility since 1997. She combines professional qualification and commercial expertise with leadership skills and personal commitment. In recognition of her achievements, in 2010 she received the "Businesswoman of the Year" award from the German "handwerk magazine" trade journal.

Bilfinger
Engineering & Maintenance GmbH

Die Bilfinger Engineering & Maintenance GmbH ist Teil des internationalen Bilfinger Konzerns und Marktführer im Segment Industrieservice. Mit unseren mehr als 3.000 Mitarbeiter*innen planen und überwachen wir Anlagen in der Prozessindustrie. Wir bieten Dienstleistungen an, die den gesamten Lebenszyklus von Industrieanlagen begleiten, und konzentrieren uns dabei konsequent auf die individuellen Kundenanforderungen – von maßgeschneiderten Einzelleistungen bis hin zu integrierten Servicepaketen. Dabei steht das Bilfinger Maintenance Concept, kurz BMC, exemplarisch für die Innovationsführerschaft im Industrieservice. Zu unseren Kunden zählen Global Player aus den Branchen Erdgasindustrie, Chemie, Petrochemie und Pharma. Darüber hinaus sind wir auch in verschiedenen neuen Themenfeldern aktiv wie Flüssigerdgas- und Wasserstoff-Technologie.

Bilfinger Engineering & Maintenance GmbH is part of the international Bilfinger Group and leads the market in the industrial service segment. With our workforce of more than 3,000 employees, we plan and monitor plants in the process industry. We offer services that accompany the entire lifecycle of an industrial plant, with a consistent focus on specific customer requirements, from tailor-made individual services through to integrated packages. In this context, the Bilfinger Maintenance Concept (BMC) exemplifies our leading role in terms of innovation for industrial service. Our customers include global players in the gas, chemical, petrochemical and pharmaceutical industries. We also play an active role in various new topics, such as liquefied natural gas and hydrogen technology.

Information
Gründungsjahr: 1975
Mitarbeiter: ca. 3.000
Leistungsspektrum:
Engineering, Anlagenbau, Instandhaltung, Energy Transition, Digitale Lösungen
Branchen:
Erdgas, Chemie, Petrochemie, Pharma
https://bem.bilfinger.com

Year founded: 1975
Employees: approx. 3,000
Range of services:
engineering, plant construction, servicing, energy transition, digital solutions
Markets:
gas, chemical, petrochemical and pharmaceutical industries

J.H.K. Gruppe

Die J.H.K. Gruppe ist in der nunmehr vierten Generation eine Industrie- und Dienstleistungsgruppe mit sechs operativen Gesellschaften und einer breiten Expertise. Als mittelständisches Familienunternehmen überzeugen wir unsere Kunden mit zahlreichen Leistungen rund um den industriellen Rohrleitungs-, Sondermaschinen-, Stahl-, Behälter- und Apparatebau sowie Elektroanlagenbau, ergänzt um die entsprechenden Engineering-Kompetenzen. Weitere Geschäftsschwerpunkte sind der Gerüstbau, die Oberflächentechnik sowie die Mess- und Regelungstechnik im Bereich Mineralölumschlag.
An den Standorten Bremerhaven, Essen, Großenkneten-Ahlhorn und Hamburg setzen sich unsere rund 350 hoch motivierten und gut ausgebildeten Mitarbeiter für den Erfolg unserer Kunden ein.

The J.H.K. Group is an industrial and service group now in the fourth generation with six operative companies offering a wealth of expertise. As a medium-sized family business we convince our customers with various services related to industrial pipeline, steel, tank and apparatus construction as well as electrical systems engineering, together with the relevant engineering competence. Other key areas of business include scaffolding and surface technology as well as measurement and control systems for the mineral oil trade. About 350 highly motivated and well-trained employees work for the success of our customers at our sites in Bremerhaven, Essen, Großenkneten-Ahlhorn and Hamburg.

Information
Gründungsjahr/Year founded: 1901
Mitarbeiter/Employees: 350
Unternehmensgruppe/Company group:
– J.H.K. Anlagenbau und Industrieservice GmbH & Co. KG Bremerhaven
– J.H.K. Anlagenbau und Industrieservice GmbH & Co. KG Ahlhorn
– J.H.K. Industriebeschichtung GmbH & Co. KG
– M+F Technologies GmbH
– Regeniter Gruppe, Essen
www.jhk.de

Erich Stallkamp ESTA GmbH

Edelstahl: die wirtschaftliche Lösung!

Die Erich Stallkamp ESTA GmbH in Dinklage hat sich in den vergangenen vier Jahrzehnten aus einem Zwei-mannbetrieb zu einem innovativen, mittelständischen Spezialisten für die Konstruktion, Fertigung und Montage hochwertiger Edelstahlprodukte entwickelt. Zu den weltweit agierenden Kunden zählen insbesondere die Landwirtschaft, die Biogasbranche, Kommunen, die Lebensmittelindustrie, aber auch Papierfabriken oder die chemische Industrie. Egal ob einzelne Edelstahlbehälter von 30 m³ bis zu Komplettprojekten von Hochfermentern mit bis zu 100.000 m³, Pressschneckenseparatoren, Rührwerke, Langwellen-, Tauchmotor- oder Drehkolbenpumpen – Stallkamp steht für Qualität „Made in Germany". Das Erfolgsgeheimnis liegt in der hohen Qualität, Langlebigkeit und Robustheit von Produkten aus rostfreiem Edelstahl.

Stainless steel, the economic solution!

In the last four decades, Erich Stallkamp ESTA GmbH in Dinklage has developed from a two-man company into an innovative, medium-sized specialist for designing, manufacturing and installing top-quality stainless steel products. The global customer base includes in particular agriculture, the biogas industry, local authorities, the food industry and also paper mills and the chemical industry. Whether individual stainless steel tanks for 30 m³ or complete projects with tank reactors for up to 100,000 m³, press screw separators, agitators, long-shaft pumps, submersible pumps or rotary lobe pumps, Stallkamp stands for quality "made in Germany". The secret of the company's success consists in the high quality, durability and ruggedness of products made from stainless steel.

Information

Gründungsjahr: 1973	**Year founded:** 1973
Mitarbeiter: etwa 200	**Employees:** about 200
Leistungsspektrum:	**Range of services:**
– Edelstahlbehälter	– stainless steel tanks
– Separatoren	– separators
– Pumpen	– pumps
– Rührwerke	– agitators
Branchen: Agrar, Biogas, Industrie- und Prozessabwasser, kommunale Abwasseranlagen	**Markets:** agriculture, biogas, industry and process effluent, municipal wastewater systems

www.stallkamp.de

ALWID GmbH
Sondermaschinen

Die ALWID GmbH ist spezialisiert auf die kundenspezifische Entwicklung und Herstellung von Abfüll- und Verschließmaschinen für die Lebensmittel-, Chemie- und Pharmaindustrie. Die Abfüllmaschinen eignen sich dabei für fast alle Flüssigkeiten und Pasten, die nicht kohlensäurehaltig sind.
Die Verschließmaschinen verarbeiten neben diversen Schraubverschlüssen auch PP-Verschlüsse, Anrollverschlüsse, Kronkorken, Griffkorken, Naturkorken, Twist-off- und Trigger-Verschlüsse sowie diverse Ein- und Aufdrückverschlüsse. ALWID versteht sich als Problemlöser für kleine, mittlere und große Leistungsbereiche und entwickelt ganzheitliche Konzepte für komplette Abfüllstraßen. Die Qualität und Wirtschaftlichkeit der Anlagen hat sich weltweit herumgesprochen. ALWID exportiert seine Produkte in rund 60 Länder.

ALWID GmbH specialises in customer-specific development and the manufacture of filling and capping machines for the food, chemical and pharmaceutical industries. The filling machines are suitable for almost all non-carbonated fluids and pastes.
Besides various screw caps, the capping machines also process PP caps, roll-on caps, crown corks, grip corks, natural corks, twist-off and trigger caps, as well as different push-in and push-on caps.
ALWID considers itself to be a solution provider on a small, medium and large scale and develops integrated concepts for complete filling lines. The quality and efficiency of the systems are widely recognised all around the world. ALWID's products are exported to around 60 countries.

Information

Gründungsjahr: 1964	**Year founded:** 1964
Mitarbeiter: 70	**Employees:** 70
Leistungsspektrum:	**Range of services:**
Herstellung und Vertrieb von Abfüll- und Verschließmaschinen u. a. für die	manufacture and sales of filling and capping machines, for the following among others:
– Lebensmittelindustrie	– food industry
– Pharmaindustrie	– pharmaceutical industry
– chemische Industrie	– chemical industry
– Kosmetikindustrie	– cosmetic industry

www.alwid.de

DER MÖBELMINIMALIST

The Furniture Minimalist

AUTOR:
CLAUS SPITZER-
EWERSMANN

JOCHEN MÜLLER

Tradition bedeutet nicht, alles beim Alten zu belassen. Im Gegenteil. Tradition heißt, zu akzeptieren, dass sich die Erde weiterdreht und für das Bewährte Entsprechungen in der Zukunft gefunden werden müssen. Jochen Müller aus Bockhorn zeigt, wie das gelingen kann.

Geschäftstüchtig, ja, das sei er immer schon gewesen, sagt Jochen Müller mit einem breiten Schmunzeln und fröhlich funkelnden Augen. Schon als kleiner Junge sei er den Bauern gefolgt, wenn sie rund um Bockhorn ihre Äcker pflügten. Die dabei zutage geförderten Findlinge habe er eingesammelt und nach Hause transportiert. Und dann verkauft. Für eine Mark pro Stein. An seine Mutter. „Sie konnte sie gut für unseren Garten gebrauchen."

Dem Handel ist der 1973 Geborene bis heute treu geblieben. Allerdings geht es nun um Holz. Müller gerät ins Schwärmen: „Ein wunderbares Material. Und man benötigt nur wenig Werkzeug, um damit zu arbeiten." Begeisterung schwingt mit in seinen Worten – und doch bedauert er es kein bisschen, nicht selbst Tischler geworden zu sein. Obwohl er als Kind häufig in der elterlichen Werkstatt gespielt hatte, sah er sich nicht auf dem Holzweg. „Ich komme eher aus der Zahlenwelt", sagt der Betriebswirt, der einst im amerikanischen South Dakota als Austauschschüler lernte, auf eigenen Beinen zu stehen, und später im oberbayerischen Rosenheim studierte.

Tradition does not mean leaving everything as it was. On the contrary. Tradition means accepting that the world keeps on turning and that equivalents will have to be found in future for things that have proven their worth. Jochen Müller from Bockhorn shows how this can work.

He's always been rather enterprising, says Jochen Müller with a broad grid and a cheerful spark in his eyes. Even as a young boy he'd follow the farmers when they ploughed their fields around Bockhorn. He collected any boulders that were brought to the surface and took them home. Where he promptly sold them. For one mark per stone. To his mother. "She needed them for the garden."

Born in 1973, Jochen Müller has continued trading right through to the present day. But now he trades in wood. Müller is obviously passionate about it: "A wonderful material. And you only need one tool to work with wood." He's obviously passionate about it. But he's not sorry he didn't learn the carpenter's trade. Although he often played in his parent's workshop as a child, he didn't see this as his future. "Numbers are more my thing", says the business graduate, who learnt to stand on his own two feet while still a school boy on exchange in South Dakota, USA, before studying in Rosenheim, Bavaria.

Natürlich: Ein BWL-Studium bietet beste Voraussetzungen, um ein Familienunternehmen sicher durch die Gegenwart und behutsam in die Zukunft zu führen. So liegt es nahe, dass Jochen 2003 den 1869 von Gerhard Wilhelm Oetken gegründeten und zuletzt von seinem Vater Dierk in vierter Generation geleiteten Betrieb übernimmt – und nicht eine der beiden älteren Schwestern. Gemeinsam mit seiner Frau Katja nimmt er sich vor, „Müller Möbelwerkstätten" in die Jetztzeit zu überführen.

Erfolg mit einer Jahrhundertidee

Der Name verfügt in jenen Tagen bereits über einen guten Ruf in der Branche. Hatte man sich in der ersten Hälfte des vergangenen Jahrhunderts in der friesischen Manufaktur auf die Herstellung handwerklich anspruchsvoller Einzelstücke spezialisiert, konzentrierte man sich nun mehr und mehr auf die Produktion zeitgemäßer und praktischer Serienmöbel. Dabei arbeitete man erfolgreich mit renommierten Designern zusammen. Der Kontakt mit ihnen lief zum Teil auf einer sehr persönlichen und vertraulichen Ebene. Einige kamen gelegentlich sogar nach Bockhorn gereist und übernachteten hier auch, erinnert sich Jochen Müller.

Einer davon war Rolf Heide. „Der kam im Jahr ein- oder zweimal zu uns." Der berühmte Innenarchitekt und Industriedesigner entwarf 1966 den Prototypen einer Stapelliege, die drei Jahre später auf der Kölner Möbelmesse der Öffentlichkeit vorgestellt wurde und sich anschließend zu einem Klassiker des modernen Designs entwickelte. Müller baut und vertreibt sie noch heute exklusiv. Die Liege besteht lediglich aus vier aus Schichtholz gefertigten Teilen, spart Platz und lässt sich jederzeit leicht und schnell aufbauen. Also das perfekte Möbel für unerwartete Übernachtungsgäste oder die kleine Wohnung.

Müller selbst hielt bis zu Heides Tod im Sommer 2020 den Kontakt aufrecht. Die Jahrhundertidee des Designers spiegelt punktgenau seine Philosophie wider: „Wir stellen grundsätzlich die Funktion in den Mittelpunkt unserer Überlegungen und hoffen danach, dass es auch noch gut aussieht." Klare Sache: Müllermöbel müssen vor allem praktisch sein und einen Nutzwert besitzen. Weiter fallen Begriffe wie „Schlichtheit", „Minimalismus" und auch „Geradlinigkeit".

Ständiger Kontakt zu den Designern

Kein Schnickschnack und funktionsorientiert – das alles klingt sehr nach den Konzepten des Bauhauses. Gibt es da tiefere Verbindungen? „Ja, doch", bestätigt der Firmenchef, „schon mein Opa und mein Vater haben solche Impulse gern aufgegriffen." Und die Designer, mit denen er selbst heute bevorzugt arbeitet, folgen dieser Linie, wie Müller nicht nur anhand ihrer Entwürfe feststellen kann. Regelmäßig führt er Gespräche mit ihnen, besucht sie sogar zu Hause. „Einerseits müssen wir in unserer Denke übereinstimmen. Andererseits hält der direkte Kontakt insbesondere zu den Designstudenten mich jung und zeigt mir, wie viele gute neue Ideen es gibt."

Über einer grübelt er seit einer Weile selbst. Schon mehrfach habe er gehört, die Rolf Heides Stapelliege sei eventuell ein bisschen zu schwer. Eine Antwort auf die Frage, ob es nicht ein paar Kilogramm weniger sein könnten, hat Jochen Müller bis heute noch nicht gefunden. Aber er nimmt die Sache ernst und sucht danach. „Ich denke immer in Chancen und Lösungen", bekräftigt er. Und da wird sich in jedem Fall eine finden lassen.

Einblicke in die Endmontage. Alle Möbel werden in Eigenregie seit über 150 Jahren in Bockhorn hergestellt.

Glimpses into final assembly. All the furniture has been made here on the premises in Bockhorn for more than 150 years.

Differenziert betrachten

Das Handwerk ist auch im 21. Jahrhundert einer der bedeutendsten Wirtschaftszweige unseres Landes. 2019 wurden in Deutschland mehr als eine Million Betriebe gezählt; im Bereich der Handwerkskammer Oldenburg waren es 7881.

Zu den großen Stärken des Handwerks gehört die enorme Vielfalt der Berufe. Junge Menschen können sich in mehr als 130 ausbilden lassen. Auf der Liste der Männer stehen nach Angaben des Bundesinstituts für Berufsbildung seit Jahren Kfz-Mechatroniker, Elektroniker und Anlagenmechaniker für Sanitär-, Heizungs- und Klimatechnik ganz oben. Frauen favorisieren demnach eher eine Ausbildung zur Friseurin, zur Fachverkäuferin im Lebensmittelhandwerk oder zur Augenoptikerin.

Zugleich macht diese Heterogenität es aber auch fast unmöglich, einen Gesamtüberblick der wirtschaftlichen Situation zu geben. Gerade in der Corona-Zeit muss deshalb differenziert werden. Ein Großteil der Betriebe hat zum Teil erhebliche Umsatzeinbußen hinnehmen müssen, etwa die Gesundheits- oder die Lebensmittelhandwerke. Andere hingegen sind relativ gut durch die Krise gekommen. So konnte beispielsweise die Bauwirtschaft vielfach beinahe ungestört weiterarbeiten. Weniger hart traf es vor allem Firmen, die sich flexibel der Lage anpassen und Produktionsumstellungen vornehmen konnten.

Ein großes Thema im Handwerk bleibt der Fachkräftemangel. Aktuellen Einschätzungen zufolge fehlen in den Betrieben zurzeit rund 250 000 qualifizierte Mitarbeiter. Das hat Folgen: Da es am Personal fehlt, müssen Kunden nicht selten mit Wartezeiten von mehreren Wochen oder gar Monaten rechnen. Viele Firmen arbeiten deshalb an neuen Konzepten, um gute Fachkräfte für sich zu gewinnen und jungen Menschen eine Ausbildung im Handwerk schmackhaft zu machen.

A differentiated approach

Even in the 21st century, the skilled crafts are still one of the most important branches of the economy in our country. Germany had more than one million skilled craft businesses in 2019, with 7,881 in the region covered by Oldenburg Chamber of Skilled Crafts.

One of the big strengths of the skilled crafts is the wide range of trades that can be learnt. Young people find more than 130 possibilities for training and apprenticeships. According to the Federal Institute for Vocational Training, for years now men's favourites include learning to be a car mechanic, an electronics technician and a plant mechanic for sanitary, heating and air conditioning systems. Women tend to prefer to train as hairdressers, opticians or sales staff in the specialist food sector.

At the same time, the skilled crafts are so heterogeneous that it is almost impossible to give a general overview of the economic situation. A differentiated approach is necessary, particularly during the Covid pandemic. Most companies are facing considerable sales losses, especially in the specialist healthcare or food sector. By contrast, others have managed to keep going fairly well. Many in the building trade for example have carried on working almost without interruption. Companies that have been able to respond flexibly to the situation with corresponding production adjustments have been less severely affected.

The skills shortage remains a major issue in the skilled crafts. Current estimates indicate that companies currently have a shortfall of around 250,000 qualified staff. As a result, customers often have to wait for several weeks or months due to the lack of workers. Many companies are therefore looking at new concepts for attracting good skilled staff and tempting young people to train in the skilled crafts.

A degree in business administration naturally gives you the best prerequisites for leading a family company safely through the present and carefully into the future. So it made sense in 2003 that it was Jochen Müller rather than one of his two older sisters who took over the company founded by Gerhard Wilhelm Oetken in 1857 from the capable hands of his father Dierk. He now represents the fourth generation to be running the business. Together with his wife Katja, he intends to take "Müller Möbelwerkstätten" into the here and now.

Successful idea of the century

The company already has a good name in the industry. During the first half of the 20th century, the Frisian manufactory had specialised in making one-off pieces with intricate craftsmanship. But now the focus shifted increasingly to contemporary, practical mass-produced furniture, working in successful collaboration with renowned designers. Often this entailed highly personal, confidential contact. Jochen Müller remembers that some designers actually came out to Bockhorn and stayed overnight.

Take Rolf Heide, for example. "He came to visit once or twice a year." In 1966, the famous interior and industrial designer created the prototype for a stacking recliner. Three years later it was presented to the general public at the Furniture Fair in Cologne before becoming a classic example of modern design. Müller still makes and sells them exclusively today. The recliner consists of just four plywood parts in a space-saving design that is quick and easy to set up at any time. It is therefore the ideal piece of furniture for unexpected overnight guests or small apartments.

Müller remained in contact with Rolf Heide until he died in summer 2020. He finds his own philosophy precisely reflected in the designer's idea of the century: "Functionality is always the focus of our discussions. Then we hope it will look good too." One thing is clear. Above all, Müllermöbel must be practical and have a utility value. Expressions such as "simple", "minimal" and "straightforward" also come to mind.

Constant contact with the designers

No frills and fully functional: it sounds like Bauhaus. Does that go any deeper? "Yes it does", says the company boss. "My grandfather and father liked these ideas." And his preferred designers also follow the same concept, which Müller sees not just in their designs. He has regular meetings with them and even visits them at home. "On the one hand we must make sure we're thinking along the same lines. On the other hand, direct contact particularly with design students helps to keep me young and shows me how many good new ideas there are out there."

One such idea has been on his mind for a while now. He has often heard people say that Rolf Heide's stacking recliner may possibly be a bit too heavy. Jochen Müller still hasn't found out how to take a few kilos off the weight, but he's taking it seriously and is searching for the right answer. "I always think in chances and solutions", he says. And he's sure to find one here too.

Regardless of the weight issue, Rolf Heide's masterpiece remains one of the best sellers from Bockhorn. Orders come in from Korea and Singapore, from the USA and the whole of Europe, in fact from every single continent. "I think the only place we haven't sent one to is the Antarctic", says Müller, admitting that he has every intention of closing

Unabhängig von der Frage des Gewichts bleibt Rolf Heides Meisterwerk der Bestseller aus Bockhorn. Bestellungen treffen aus Korea und Singapur, aus den USA und ganz Europa ein, eigentlich von allen Kontinenten. „Ich glaube, nur in die Antarktis haben wir noch nicht geliefert", meint Müller – und gibt zu, dass er durchaus den Ehrgeiz habe, diese Lücke eines Tages zu schließen. Momentan bereitet ihm aber der Transport in Richtung Südpol noch Kopfschmerzen.

Nur eine kleine Verrücktheit? Nein. Wer sich mit Jochen Müller unterhält, merkt schnell: Dieser Mann hat die Zukunft im Blick. Und so manches, was vielleicht zunächst leicht spleenig wirkt, entpuppt sich als weitsichtig. „Wir sind ja trotz allem ein eher kleiner Produzent", erklärt er. „Deshalb brauchen wir Produkte, die besonders sind und auffallen." Man müsse cleverer und flexibler sein als die Wettbewerber, dabei aber ehrlich und verlässlich bleiben.

Im richtigen Moment die Weichen stellen

Die kontinuierliche Entwicklung des Unternehmens liegt dem zweifachen Familienvater deshalb besonders am Herzen. „Das Tagesgeschäft kann ich im Wesentlichen meinen Leuten überlassen", weiß er, „ich kümmere mich in erster Linie um morgen und übermorgen". Sein Denken gilt ebenso der Reputation in der Branche wie dem Ruf als Arbeitgeber. Scheidet ein Mitarbeiter aus dem Betrieb aus, bekommt er stets einen würdigen und respektvollen Abschied. Das sei als Dankeschön zu verstehen und halte zusätzlich die Tür für eine Rückkehr offen.

Jochen Müller erweist sich als Mann der Prinzipien. Kein Widerspruch ist es, dass dazu auch der Wille zählt, im richtigen Moment die Weichen anders zu stellen. So hielt er vor einigen Jahren einen umfangreichen Relaunch der Marke Müller für unerlässlich. „Es gab damals ein Schlüsselerlebnis", erinnert er sich. Ein Interessent habe sich auf der Messe nach dem Preis eines Schreibtisches gefragt. „600 Euro", lautete die Antwort. „Das ist aber teuer!", kam es mit leichter Empörung in der Stimme zurück. Müller wollte es nicht glauben. Noch heute sagt er: „Hätte der Name eines weltbekannten Herstellers auf unserem Schreibtisch geklebt, hätte der Kunde ohne mit der Wimper zu zucken das Doppelte akzeptiert."

Müller ärgerte sich nur kurz, überlegte und entschied dann, Konsequenzen zu ziehen. „Ich hatte das Gefühl, dass irgendwas nicht stimmen kann. Man hat uns offenbar nicht als Marke wahrgenommen, sondern als einen x-beliebigen Hersteller." Bis dahin hatte er sich selbst um das Marketing gekümmert und eigentlich geglaubt, dabei einen guten Job zu machen. Nun aber war es an der Zeit für den kritischen, unabhängigen Blick von außen und einen ganz neuen Ansatz, gestand er sich ein. Er beauftragte eine Oldenburger Agentur mit der Analyse und Vorschlägen für Veränderungen.

this gap one day. But at the moment, the issue of transport to the South Pole is still a problem.

Is this all just a little bit of madness? Definitely not. When you talk to Jochen Müller, you soon realise that he has the future in his sights. And some things that may seem a bit crazy at first turn out to be far-sighted. "After all, we're just a little manufacturer", he says. "That's why our products have to be something special that attract attention." It's a case of being cleverer and more flexible than the competition, while remain honest and reliable.

Adjusting course at the right moment

The father of two children therefore focuses particularly on the company's on-going development. "For the most part, I can leave everyday business to my team", he knows, "so that I can concentrate primarily on tomorrow and the day after." His thoughts circle around the company's name in the industry and also its reputation as an employer. When employees leave the company, they are given a dignified, respectful send-off as a sign of gratitude and also to keep the door open for a possible return.

Jochen Müller is a man of principles. The fact that he also has the will to change course at the right moment in time is by no means a contradiction. A few years ago, he felt that a comprehensive relaunch of the Müller brand was simply indispensable. "It was triggered by a defining moment", he remembers. A potential customer visiting the company's stand at the Furniture Fair asked what a desk would cost. The answer was "600 Euro". "But that's far too much" was the slightly indignant reaction. Müller couldn't believe it. Today he still believes that "the customer would have accepted twice as much without flinching if the name of a world-famous manufacturer were on the desk."

Müller was annoyed for only a brief moment before thinking about the situation and deciding what to do next. "I had the feeling that something wasn't quite right. Apparently, we were seen as any old run-of-the-mill manufacturer and not as a brand." Up to that point in time, he was personally in charge of marketing and actually thought he'd been doing a good job. But now he admitted that the time had come for a critical, independent look from the outside with a completely new approach. He instructed an agency in Oldenburg to proceed with a corresponding analysis and make suggestions for changes.

The motto for the future: Small Living

As a result, the craft firm from Bockhorn with its long, rich tradition now comes across with a visibly refreshed brand. The company website is convincing with clever content and an appropriately contemporary look. The company logo is an eye-catcher with the Ü-dots on top of each other rather than side by side. The glossy catalogue with its 212 pages leaves nothing to be desired.

Das Credo der Zukunft: Small Living

Im Ergebnis zeigt sich das traditionsreiche Bockhorner Handwerksunternehmen heute als sichtbar aufgefrischte Marke. Die Präsentation im Internet überzeugt mit klugen Inhalten und einer angemessen zeitgemäßen Optik das Firmenlogo mit zwei übereinander gestapelten Ü-Pünktchen. Der 212 Seiten starke Katalog ist hochwertig und wird allen Ansprüchen gerecht.

Und Jochen Müller beweist darüber hinaus Mut zu einem neuen Firmennamen, der deutlich werden lässt, welchem Credo er folgt: „Müller Small Living". Ausgangspunkt, so erläutert der Firmenchef, sei die Erkenntnis gewesen, „dass viele Menschen nach kleineren Wohnungen suchen und eine intelligente Grundrissgestaltung sowie eine maximal komprimierte Innenausstattung immer wichtiger wird." Genau dort sieht er die Zukunft seines Unternehmens. Geschäftstüchtig war Müller ja schon immer.

And Jochen Müller has even taken the courageous step of changing the company name to clearly state his motto: "Müller Small Living". It's all based on the fact that "many people are downsizing their homes, so it's more important than ever to make intelligent use of the space with suitably condensed interior fittings". And this is exactly where he sees the future of his company. Müller always was an enterprising guy.

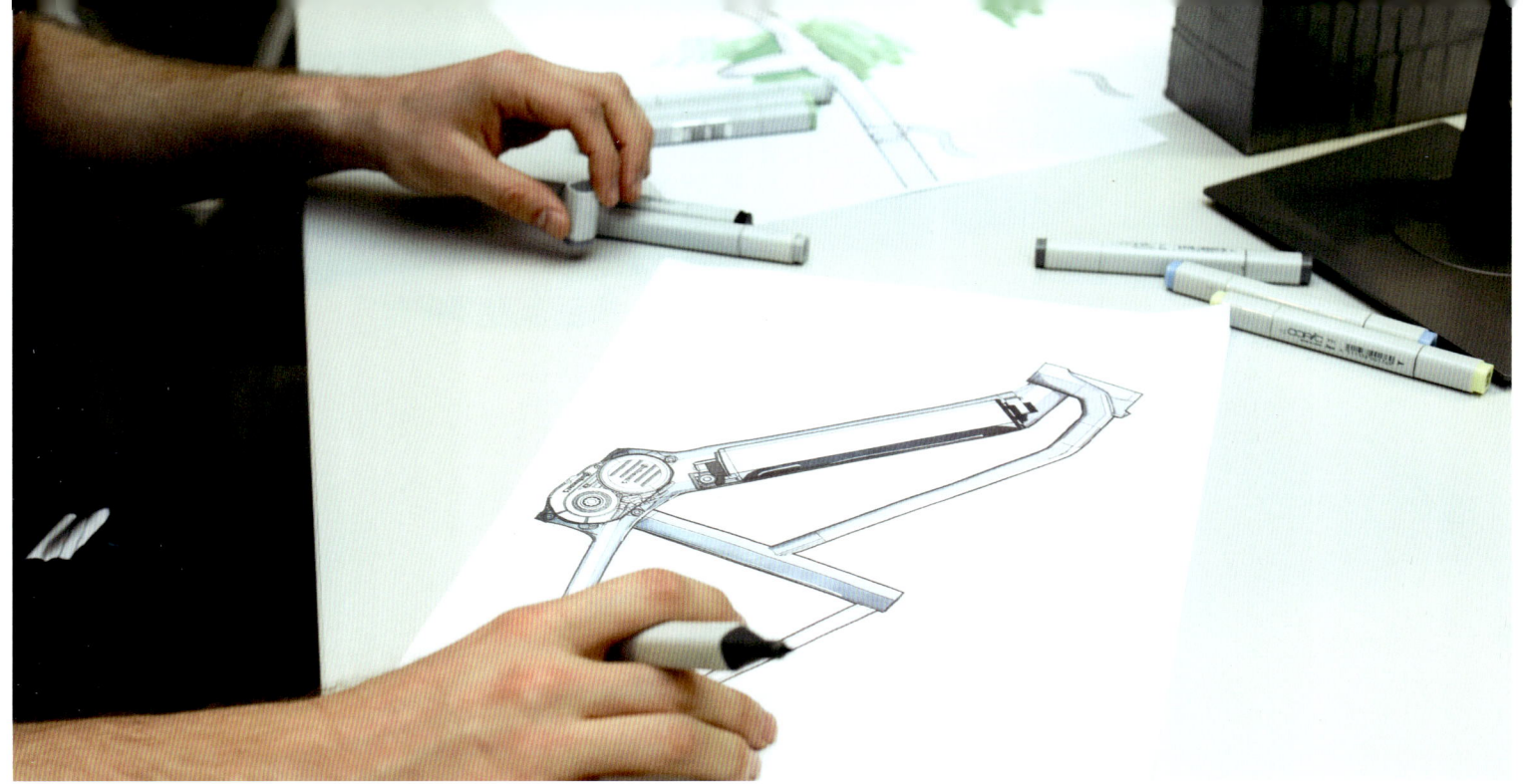

Kalkhoff Bikes

Hochlaufzeit bei Kalkhoff Bikes

Das große Thema für den Fahrradhersteller Kalkhoff im Jahr 2022 ist das Ramp up in der Europa-Allee. Dann ist in den neuen Kalkhoff-Hallen die Produktion hochgefahren. Mehr als 600 Mitarbeiterinnen und Mitarbeiter werden ab dann Fahrradteile lackieren und montieren, schrauben und auf Funktionalität und Sicherheit prüfen – alles in solider Handarbeit. Ein Fahrrad besteht aus über 1.000 Einzelteilen, die mit viel Liebe für das Produkt und Leidenschaft für das Radfahren zu einem der unverwechselbaren eBikes von Kalkhoff entwickelt und zusammengebaut werden.

Diese liefert Kalkhoff heute in 25 Länder weltweit. Das eBike ist eines der Verkehrsmittel der Zukunft. Die Nachfrage nach den motorisierten Rädern ist gerade in den letzten Jahren enorm gewachsen, sodass Kalkhoff seine Produktionszahlen stetig erhöht.

Kalkhoff-Räder sind „made in Cloppenburg". Im Ecopark bei Cloppenburg entsteht bis 2022 die modernste Fahrradfabrik Europas. Und alle Beschäftigten von Kalkhoff erfüllen beim Umzug in die neue Fabrikhalle eine wichtige Funktion. So auch Fabian, der den Projektmanager des Neubaus der Kalkhoff-Hallen und den Umzug der Produktion von der Siemensstraße in Cloppenburg in den Ecopark unterstützt. 2014 begann Fabian seine berufliche Karriere bei Kalkhoff als Auszubildender zum Industriekaufmann. Nach einem Aufenthalt bei der Schwestermarke FOCUS in Stuttgart studiert er jetzt parallel zu seiner Tätigkeit Wirtschaftsingenieurwesen (Dualer Studiengang). Aktuell fiebert Fabian wie das gesamte Team dem „Ramp up" entgegen. Dies ist ein entscheidender Schritt für das zukunftsorientierte Unternehmen Kalkhoff.

Auch Amelie ist an der Entstehung der neuen Hallen ganz nah dran. Die Entscheidung für den neuen Standort fiel in der Projektgruppe, in der Amelie als Business Development Managerin federführend mitgewirkt hat. Heute ist Amelie Director of Engineering and Product Management und entwickelt mit ihrem eigenen Team das moderne und innovative eBike von Kalkhoff, welches den Kunden grenzenlose Freiheit bietet.

Ramp-up time at Kalkhoff Bikes

The big topic for bike manufacturer Kalkhoff in 2022 will be the ramp up on Europa-Allee, with the start of production in the new Kalkhoff buildings. More than 600 employees will then be painting, assembling and screwing bike parts, checking functionality and safety, all in good craftsmanship. A bike consists of more than 1,000 individual parts, developed and assembled with a great love for the product and passion for cycling before becoming one of the unmistakable eBikes by Kalkhoff.

Today they are supplied by Kalkhoff in 25 countries around the world. The eBike is one of the means of transport of the future. The last few years have seen such huge demand for the motorised bikes that Kalkhoff is constantly increasing its production output.

Kalkhoff bikes are "made in Cloppenburg". Europe's most advanced bicycle factory is under construction on the Ecopark commercial estate near Cloppenburg, with completion scheduled for 2022. All the Kalkhoff employees will have an important role to play when the company moves to the new premises.

This also includes Fabian, who assists the project manager responsible for construction of the new Kalkhoff buildings and for moving production from Siemensstraße in Cloppenburg to the Ecopark. Fabian began his career at Kalkhoff in 2014 as a trainee industrial clerk. After working for a while at the sister brand FOCUS in Stuttgart, he is now studying industrial engineering on a sandwich course parallel to his job in the company. Like the whole team, Fabian is now eagerly awaiting the ramp up. This will be a crucial step for the future-oriented company Kalkhoff.

Amelie has also been closely involved in the new buildings. The decision in favour of the new site was taken in the project group where she played a leading role as Business Development Manager. Today Amelie is Director of Engineering and Product Management with her own team that is responsible for developing Kalkhoff's modern, innovative eBikes that offer customers unlimited freedom.

Information

Gründungsjahr: 1919; seit 2012 gehört Kalkhoff Bikes zur niederländischen Marke Pon

Year founded: 1919; since 2012, Kalkhoff Bikes has been part of the Dutch Pon brand

Mitarbeiter: rund 1.000 in Cloppenburg

Employees about 1,000 in Cloppenburg

Leistungsspektrum: Premium eBike Marke Produktion von hochwertigen eBikes und Fahrrädern

Range of services: Premium eBike brand production of high-quality eBikes and bicycles

www.kalkhoff-bikes.com/karriere

Franz Holthaus Elektro GmbH

www.elektro-holthaus.de

Holthaus ist ein Innungsfachbetrieb in Lohne mit einer mehr als 100-jährigen Familientradition. Mit rund 55 Mitarbeitern betreuen wir unsere Kunden schwerpunktmäßig in den Bereichen Elektroinstallation, Maschinenbau, Automatisierungstechnik und Energieanlagenbau. Unsere Spezialisten entwickeln, bauen, programmieren und montieren nach den Vorgaben und Anforderungen unserer Kunden – darunter sind private Hausbesitzer ebenso vertreten wie mittelständische Gewerbebetriebe oder große Industrieunternehmen. Wir bei Holthaus haben für alle Wünsche clevere Lösungen. Die Montage und Inbetriebnahme kann von uns standortunabhängig weltweit ausgeführt werden.

Holthaus is an affiliated guild company in Lohne with a family tradition extending back for more than 100 years. With our workforce of around 55 employees, the services we offer our customers mainly include electrical installation, mechanical engineering, automation systems and energy systems construction. Our specialists proceed with developing, building, programming and installation according to the specifications and requirements of our customers, from private households to medium-sized businesses and large industrial companies. Here at Holthaus, we have smart solutions to meet all requests. We proceed with installation and initial commissioning worldwide, regardless of the location.

The company based in Cappeln has invested considerable sums of money in the last two years to forge ahead with digitisation as well as implementing new technologies and processes to put it on a competitive footing for the future. The new warehouse covering around 3750 square metres was completed in 2019 and the company moved into its new administration building twelve months later. 2020 was also the year in which Wilhelm Sieverding junior joined the family company in the third generation with every intention of continuing the successful story of this medium-sized company that is firmly rooted in the skilled crafts.

Sieverding Heizungs- und Sanitärtechnik GmbH

Das Cappelner Unternehmen hat in den vergangenen beiden Jahren erhebliche Investitionen getätigt, um die Digitalisierung sowie die Implementierung neuer Technologien und Prozesse voranzutreiben und für die Zukunft wettbewerbsfähig aufgestellt zu sein. 2019 wurde die neue, rund 3750 Quadratmeter große Lagerhalle fertiggestellt, ein Jahr später konnte das neue Verwaltungsgebäude bezogen werden. Und schließlich stieg auch im Jahr 2020 mit Wilhelm Sieverding junior die dritte Generation in das familiengeführte Unternehmen ein und schickt sich an, die erfolgreiche Geschichte des mittelständischen Betriebes mit seinen Wurzeln im Handwerk fortzuschreiben.

Information	Year founded: 1954
Gründungsjahr: 1954	**Employees:** around 380
Mitarbeiter: rund 380	**Range of services:**
Leistungsspektrum:	– plumbing, gas and water installation
– Klempnerei, Gas- und Wasserinstallation	– sanitary and heating engineering
– Sanitär- und Heizungstechnik	– electrical engineering and control systems
– Elektro- und Regeltechnik	– cable laying and pipeline construction
– Kabel- und Rohrleitungsbau	– gas instrumentation and control systems
– Gasmess- und Regeltechnik	

www.sieverding.de

BRÖTJE: Seit über 100 Jahren am Markt mit Weitblick auf zukünftige Technologien

Das Unternehmen BRÖTJE kann auf über 100 Jahre Erfahrung bei der Entwicklung und Vermarktung von Heiztechnik sowie Service- und Dienstleistungen im Heizungsbereich zurückblicken. Innovationen und Zukunftsorientierung stehen stets auf der Unternehmensagenda. Neben den bewährten Brennwertgeräten für den Einsatz fossiler Energieträger, ist der Heizungsspezialist mit Innovationen im Wärmepumpenproduktsegment, in der Solarthermie sowie in der Wasserstoffnutzung für die Energietransformation in der Zukunft bestens aufgestellt.

Der einst kleine Familienbetrieb aus Rastede ist Teil der international agierenden BDR Thermea Gruppe. Durch die enge interne Zusammenarbeit und den Erfahrungsaustausch können zukunftsweisende Lösungen schneller vorangetrieben werden. Allen voran, die Möglichkeiten der Wasserstoffnutzung. BRÖTJE wird sich auch weiterhin auf den Ausbau und die Optimierung seiner Systeme konzentrieren – gepaart mit intelligentem Zubehör für das smarte Zuhause. Weitere Informationen aus dem Hause BRÖTJE unter www.broetje.de.

August Brötje GmbH

Information

Gründungsjahr: 1919   Mitarbeiter: ca. 500

Leistungsspektrum: Gasheizungen, Ölheizungen, Wärmepumpen, Solarsysteme, Trinkwassererwärmer, Wasseraufbereitung, Heizkörper

Year founded: 1919   Employees: about 500

Range of services: gas heating systems, oil heating systems, heat pumps, solar energy systems, domestic water heaters, water treatment systems, radiators

www.broetje.de

BRÖTJE: Established for more than 100 years with sights set on future technologies

BRÖTJE looks back on more than 100 years of experience in the development and marketing of heating technology, together with related support and services. The focus is always on innovation and a seminal approach. Besides proven condensing systems for fossil fuels, the heating specialists are also developing innovations with heat pumps, solar technology and the use of hydrogen for future energy transformation to keep the business fit for the future.

What used to be a small family company from Rastede is meanwhile part of the international BDR Thermea Group. Close internal collaboration and the sharing of knowledge and experience drives progress with trendsetting solutions. This refers particularly to the possibilities of using hydrogen. BRÖTJE will continue to focus on expanding and optimising its systems, in combination with intelligent accessories for the smart home. For more information about BRÖTJE, go to www.broetje.de.

Bestmöglicher Komfort und Service für seine Kunden: Seit über 100 Jahren entwickelt und produziert das Unternehmen BRÖTJE innovative Heiztechnik.

Best possible comfort and service for its customers: BRÖTJE has been developing and producing innovative heating technology for over 100 years.

Jähnig ist Spezialist für Signal- und Schrankenanlagen sowie Parkraumabsicherung.

Jähnig specialises in signalling and barrier systems together with car park security.

Kurt Jähnig

GmbH & Co. KG

www.jaehnig.de

Seit rund 110 Jahren stellen wir Signalanlagen für Schiene und Straße her. Höchste Produktqualität sichern wir dabei durch die Zusammenarbeit mit den jeweiligen Markt- und Weltmarktführern. Dem entspricht unsere Servicestärke bei Montage, Wartung und Instandhaltung. Deshalb schließen 90 Prozent unserer Kunden für unsere technischen Anlagen Serviceverträge ab: für besonders langlebige Funktionssicherheit. Parkraumabsicherung und Bewirtschaftung ist seit über 40 Jahren eine weitere Kernkompetenz von uns. Mit gleichbleibend hoher Produkt- und Servicequalität haben wir hier viele Kunden überzeugt und sind Marktführer im Nordwesten.

For around 110 years, we have been making signalling systems for road and rail, working with market and global leaders to safeguard top product quality. We also offer equally efficient installation, maintenance and repair services. 90 percent of our customers therefore conclude service agreements for our technical systems, in the interests of particularly long-lasting functional reliability. Car park security and management is another area of expertise that we have offered for more than 40 years: we convince many customers with a consistently high standard of product and service quality, leading the market in the North West.

ETB Gehrmann GmbH

Manchmal kommt es anders als man denkt

Das Familienunternehmen E.T.B. wurde 1977 von Horst Gehrmann e.K. gegründet und produzierte zeitweise mit mehr als 200 Mitarbeiter:innen elektrotechnische Bauteile für namhafte TV-Hersteller. Als die Bildröhre bei der Herstellung von Fernsehgeräten ausgedient hatte, wollte der Firmengründer sich eigentlich zur Ruhe setzen. Doch es kam anders: Ein attraktives Angebot veränderte die Zukunftsaussichten entscheidend und die gesamte Familie Gehrmann engagierte sich, um das Unternehmen E.T.B. weiterzuführen. Seitdem befasst sich die Oldenburger Firma mit der Produktion und dem Vertrieb von Schaltanlagentechnik. 2020 übergab der 85-jährige Horst Gehrmann das Zepter an die nächste Familiengeneration. Diese führt unter dem Namen ETB Gehrmann GmbH das Unternehmen innovativ und kreativ weiter.

Sometimes things turn out differently

Information

Produktionsbereich: elektrotechnische Konfektion/ Schaltanlagentechnik	**Production range:** electronic assembly/ switchgear technology
Produktionsstätten: regional, sozial, integrativ	**Production sites:** regional, social, integrative
Qualitätssicherung: durch eigenes Fachpersonal	**Quality assurance:** by the company's own skilled staff
Absatz: Lohnfertigung	**Sales:** job order production
Vertrieb: durch eigenen Fuhrpark	**Distribution:** by the company's own fleet

The family company E.T.B. was founded by Horst Gehrmann e.K. in 1977, producing electronic components for renowned TV manufacturers with a workforce that numbered more than 200 employees at times. Once picture tubes were no longer needed to make television sets, the company founder actually wanted to retire. But things turned out differently: an attractive offer drastically changed the future prospects, and the whole Gehrmann family got involved in keeping E.T.B. alive. Since then, the Oldenburg company has focused on producing and selling switchgear. In 2020, Horst Gehrmann, at the age of 85, handed over the reins to the next generation. With an innovative, creative approach, the family is keeping business going at ETB Gehrmann GmbH.

Clemens Osterhus
GmbH & Co. KG

Information

Gründungsjahr: 1952	**Year founded:** 1952
Mitarbeiter: 150	**Employees:** 150
Leistungsspektrum:	**Range of services:**

Leistungsspektrum:
- Kabel- und Rohrleitungsbau
- Horizontalbohrtechnik
- Haustechnik (Elektro, Sanitär, Gas, Wasser)
- Kleinkläranlagen
- CAD und GIS
- Vermessung
- DTP und WEB-Design
- Drucken, Plotten und Scannen

www.osterhus.de

Range of services:
- cable laying and pipeline construction
- horizontal drilling
- building services (electricity, plumbing, gas and water)
- small sewage treatment plants
- CAD and GIS
- surveying
- DTP and WEB design
- printing, plotting and scanning

Alles unter einem Dach

Die Elektroinstallationsfirma Clemens Osterhus aus Molbergen ist ein bodenständiges, dabei aber hoch innovatives und flexibles Handwerksunternehmen mit einer fast 70-jährigen Tradition. 1952 gegründet, ist Clemens Osterhus in den Bereichen Elektrotechnik, Gas- und Wasserinstallation, Freileitungsbau sowie Zeichenbüro und Vermessung tätig.

Die Hauptaufgabe des Leitungsbetriebes sind die Verlegung und Instandhaltung der Rohrnetze im Auftrag verschiedener Kunden, darunter vor allem Energieversorger. Komplexes Wissen, Zuverlässigkeit und Kompetenz sind tragende Säulen unseres expandierenden Unternehmens. Die Firma Clemens Osterhus kann mittlerweile viele Unternehmen, Behörden sowie private Verbraucher zu seinem festen Kundenstamm zählen.

All from a single source

The electrical installation company Clemens Osterhus from Molbergen is a down-to-earth and yet highly innovative and flexible skilled crafts company with traditions going back nearly 70 years. Founded in 1952, Clemens Osterhus works in the fields of electrical engineering, gas and water installation, overhead line construction, drawing office and surveying.

The main task for the pipeline division consists of the installation and maintenance of pipeline networks on behalf of various customers, including energy supply companies primarily. Complex know-how, reliability and expertise are the mainstays of our expanding company. Clemens Osterhus counts many companies, authorities and private consumers as its regular customers.

DIE STARTHELFERIN

The Start-up Helper

AUTOR:
MAREIKE LANGE

Durchstarterin, Anpassungstalent, Steuerfrau – für Alexandra Wurm ließen sich noch viele weitere Bezeichnungen finden. Zu manch anderem Wort hat die gebürtige Sauerländerin wiederum wenig bis keinen Bezug, etwa „Urlaub" oder „Stehenbleiben". Sie ist immer in Bewegung, immer in Weiterentwicklung begriffen.

Klarer Blick mit vergnügten Fältchen um die Augen. Feste Stimme mit wohltuendem Timbre. Gerade Haltung mit weichen Konturen. Dass Alexandra Wurm von sich sagt, Durchsetzungsfähigkeit und Optimismus seien ihre prägendsten persönlichen Eigenschaften, nimmt man ihr sofort ab. Wenn sie als Projektleiterin des Oldenburger „GO! Start-up Zentrum" im Technologie- und Gründerzentrum Oldenburg (TGO) Strukturen aufbaut und Inhalte festlegt, muss sie ihre Entscheidungen mit Bestimmtheit vertreten. Immerhin legt sie damit das Fundament für die Zukunft der Gründerinnen und Gründer, die über das Accelerator-Programm ihre Geschäftsidee zur Marktreife bringen wollen. Keine geringe Verantwortung.

Mit ihrer positiven Einstellung wiederum versucht sie, Menschen mitzureißen. Genauer: Sie versucht es nicht nur, sie schafft es auch. „Bei ihren vielen Herausforderungen könnten die GO!-Teilnehmerinnen und -Teilnehmer oft den Kopf in den Sand stecken", erzählt Alexandra Wurm, Gründungscoach und studierte Psychologin. Sie zu motivieren und in schwierigen Phasen emotional aufzufangen, sei wesentlich. Ihre offene, kommunikative Art hilft ihr außerdem dabei, Kontakte zu knüpfen und zu pflegen. Und natürlich, dass sie Menschen mag und den Austausch mit ihnen.

Kick-starter, talented fixer-upper, helmswoman: there are many words to describe what Alexandra Wurm does. On the other hand, there's lots of things the lady from the Sauerland doesn't do at all – such as going on holiday, or standing still. She's always on the move, always driving developments forward.

She has a clear view of things, with laughter lines around her eyes revealing her sense of humour. She speaks firmly with a pleasant timbre to her voice. She comes across as someone with a softly contoured upright stance. When Alexandra Wurm says assertiveness and optimism are her key personal characteristics, you believe her straight away. It takes resolute determination to stand by her decisions when setting up structures and stipulating contents as project manager at Oldenburg's "GO! Start-Up Centre" (TGO). After all, this is when she lays the foundations for the future of the young entrepreneurs who are taking part in the Accelerator Programme to get their busines s ideas ready for the market. Not a minor responsibility.

On the other hand, her positive outlook is what enthuses and motivates people. And this is something she's really good at. "The GO! participants might be tempted to bury their heads in the sand, faced with all the challenges", says Alexandra Wurm, start-up coach and graduate psychologist. Getting them motivated and keeping them going emotionally when things turn difficult is key to the whole programme. Her open, communicative manner also helps her to make and cultivate contacts, together with the fact that she likes people and enjoys sharing with them.

Fachlich und zwischenmenschlich kompetent

Das war von Beginn ihres Berufslebens an so. Während ihrer Ausbildung zur Investmentfondskauffrau in Frankfurt am Main wurde den Vorgesetzten schnell klar, dass Alexandra Wurm nicht nur fachlich einen guten Job macht, sondern auch zwischenmenschliche Kompetenz zeigt. Sie war immer an den Ideen der Kollegen interessiert, suchte den Kontakt und wollte wissen, „was die anderen zu den Projekten denken". Das ließ sie herausragen und zum hochgefragten Mitglied jedes Teams werden.

Die Zeit in Frankfurt hat sie geprägt. „Diese Ausbildung absolviert man nicht nebenbei", betont sie. Selbst Auszubildenden wurde deutlich vermittelt: Wer nicht 16 Stunden am Stück arbeiten könne, der brauche gar nicht erst wiederzukommen. Heute profitiert Wurm von der Härte der Finanzbranche: „Diese Disziplin aufbringen zu können, hilft mir jetzt sehr." Und auch in anderen Hinsichten wurden viele Bausteine gelegt, die ihr auf dem weiteren Berufsweg zum Vorteil gereichten. Darunter vor allem: strategisches Denken. Deswegen bereut sie die Entscheidung für die Ausbildung keinesfalls: „Ich würde es immer wieder so machen!"

Nicht nur Hirn, sondern auch Haltung

Dem Bankwesen hat sie dennoch den Rücken gekehrt. Zu ihrer eigenen Überraschung. „Ich hätte damals geschworen, dass ich für die Großstadt gemacht bin. Ich wollte im Hosenanzug arbeiten und die Welt erobern." Aber ihr „moralischer Kompass" hätte dagegengesprochen. Alexandra Wurm hat eben nicht nur Hirn, sondern auch Haltung.

Die Welt hat sie trotzdem ein Stück weit erobert. Wie nicht anders zu erwarten bei einer, die – wenn nicht bereits mit dem Lebenslauf, dann endgültig – mit ihrer starken Persönlichkeit überzeugt. In Berlin hat sie ein Start-up bei der Gründung begleitet und bei der Unternehmensberatung CARLO Consulting die Personal- und Strategieberatung für sich entdeckt. Im nächsten Schritt unterstützte sie die Entwicklung eines internen Schulungssystems für die Academy der Broetje-Automation GmbH in Rastede, die Sondermaschinen und Montageanlagen für die Luft- und Raumfahrt herstellt. Die (zunächst) letzte Herausforderung: der Aufbau des „GO! Start-up-Zentrum".

Im Februar 2018 übernahm sie – gerade 30 geworden – die Projektleitung und damit Führungsverantwortung. Die Zügel in der Hand zu haben passt zu ihr. Oder besser gesagt die Taue: Alexandra Wurm hat einen Sportbootführerschein. Bis zur Pressekonferenz Ende März hatten sie und ihr Team Zeit, um das Coaching-Programm mitsamt Inhalten und Trainer-Pool, den Bewerbungsaufruf und die Kommunikationsstrategie mit Marke und Kanälen zu entwickeln. 27 Tage blieben dafür, das weiß sie noch genau. „Wir haben wenig geschlafen in dieser Phase", erzählt die Start-up-Kennerin augenzwinkernd. Sie schuf Strukturen, konzipierte das Coaching, sorgte – auch in Persona – für die Außendarstellung und sprach sich mit den Beiratsmitgliedern rück, darunter Hochkaräter der regionalen Wirtschaft.

Auf Augenhöhe mit Hochkarätern

In Momenten wie diesen entspannt sein zu können, rührt aus ihren Erfahrungen in Frankfurt. Ihr Mentor habe ihr damals mit auf den Weg gegeben, Bildungsstatus und Gehaltsstufe würden nichts über die Gesamtkompetenz, das Verhalten anderen gegenüber oder den Humor

eines Menschen aussagen. „Das hat mir die Angst genommen." Ihr heutiger Chef Jürgen Bath, Geschäftsführer des TGO, sagt über sie, sie sei die perfekte Person, um gleichermaßen mit Gründern und Wirtschaftsgrößen zu reden.

Und sicherlich nicht nur für Netzwerkpflege und -erweiterung – das ist erwiesen. Seit Frühjahr 2018 haben über 30 Start-ups das Accelerator-Programm durchlaufen, wurden über 1 Mio. Euro an Investments eingeworben sowie über 20 Gründungsstipendien vergeben. „Eine enorme Entlastung für die Gründerinnen und Gründer", weiß ihr womöglich wichtigster Coach. Mittlerweile gehen sogar aus Afrika Bewerbungen ein. Für Alexandra Wurm persönlich war jedoch insbesondere die Rückmeldung aus dem Beirat wichtig, es habe eine sichtbare Weiterentwicklung gegeben. „Das war das beste Kompliment überhaupt!", freut sie sich.

Ostfriesland als wohltuendes Kontrastprogramm

Bei aller Begeisterung für ihren Job weiß Alexandra Wurm auch gelegentliche Ruhemomente zu schätzen: „Ich arbeite gerne intensiv und bin beruflich auf Abendveranstaltungen. Aber wenn ich danach zurück nach Ostfriesland fahre, ist das ein schönes Kontrastprogramm." Das platte Land, wo sie in einem kleinen Dorf bei Leer wohnt, hat für sie seinen eigenen Reiz. Obwohl sie bis zum zwölften Lebensjahr im Sauerland aufgewachsen ist und selbst zwei Jahrzehnte später noch die

Keine Angst vorm Gründen

Der Nordwesten Deutschlands hat sich zu einer Hochburg der Existenzgründer entwickelt. Bezogen auf 10.000 Einwohner gab es im ersten Halbjahr 2020 im Oldenburger Land 34 Firmengründungen – deutlich mehr als in anderen Regionen Niedersachsens. An der Spitze liegen mit Vechta (38) und Cloppenburg (37,4) zwei Landkreise, die für gewöhnlich eher als bodenständig denn als innovativ angesehen werden. Aber gerade in diesen beiden Kreisen, die zusammen das Oldenburger Münsterland bilden, hat sich in den letzten Jahren viel getan, was auch junge Gründer inspiriert.

Um der Entwicklung in ihrer Region noch weitere Schubkraft zu geben, wollen die beiden Kreise gemeinsam mit der Stadt Vechta sowie der dortigen Universität Einrichtungen etablieren, in denen Gründer sich beraten lassen können. Vorbild dafür ist das Technologie- und Gründerzentrum Oldenburg (TGO), in dem Gründer nicht nur auf ihre Bedürfnisse zugeschnittene Räumlichkeiten, sondern auch Gleichgesinnte finden, mit denen sie sich austauschen können. Unterstützung erhalten Start-ups heute von vielen Seiten, etwa auch von der Industrie- und Handelskammer oder den örtlichen Wirtschaftsförderungen.

Bemerkenswert: Das Gründen ist auch im ländlichen Raum schon lange kein No-Go mehr. Einer Studie der Hochschule Landshut zufolge sind Gründer auf dem Land in der Regel jünger als die in den Städten, häufig haben sie auch keinen akademischen Hintergrund. Stattdessen bringen sie Berufserfahrung mit, nicht selten als Führungskräfte in der Industrie, wo sie mit ihren Ideen in den Unternehmen nicht mehr weiterkommen – und sich dann entscheiden, etwas Eigenes zu machen. Ferner fühlen sie sich stärker ihrem Standort verbunden. Wer in einer Großstadt ist, kann auch in eine andere gehen. Aber wer auf dem Land gründet, tut es bewusst genau dort. Viele Gründer in kleineren Kommunen setzen vor allem eigenes oder aus dem Familien- bzw. Freundeskreis stammendes Kapital ein und sehen die Finanzierungssituation als wenig dramatisch an. Sie konnten bereits Reserven aufbauen.

Not afraid of starting up

North West Germany has become a start-up hot-spot. There were 34 companies per 10,000 inhabitants launched in the Olden-burger Land during the first six months of 2020 – far more than in other parts of Lower Saxony. Vechta takes the lead (38), followed by Cloppenburg (37.4) - two areas that in the past tended to be down-to-earth rather than innovative. But these two districts in particular, that come together to form the Oldenburger Münster-land, have seen a lot happening in recent years to inspire young entrepreneurs.

To give their region a further boost, the two districts together with the town of Vechta and its university want to establish facilities that provide advice and support for start-ups. The role model is Oldenburg Technology and Start-Up Centre (TGO), which offers young entrepreneurs not only tailor-made premises but also an opportunity for sharing with kindred spirits. Start-ups receive support today from many sides, including the Chamber of Commerce and Industry or the local economic development agencies.

It's also worth noting that start-ups have also been welcome in rural areas for some time now. A study by Landshut University of Applied Sciences has revealed that as a rule, start-up entre-preneurs in rural areas tend to be younger than in the cities and often have no academic background. Instead, they come with professional experience, often enough from leading positions in industry, working for companies that offered no future for their own ideas so they decide to start their own business. Furthermore, they often feel stronger links to their particular location. Someone based in a city can easily move to another. But someone starting up business in the rural setting does so as a quite deliberate choice. Many start-ups in smaller municipalities invest their own money or that of their families or friends, making their financial situation is less dramatic: they have already established reserves.

Professional expert with the necessary soft skills

This is the way it has always been ever since the start of her career. During her training as an investment fund trader in Frankfurt am Main, her superiors soon saw that Alexandra Wurm was not only good at her job but also had a wealth of soft skills. She was always interested in what other colleagues thought and their ideas, was highly communi-cative and keen to know "what the others thought of the projects". This made her stand out from the rest and she was soon in great demand for every team.

The time in Frankfurt left its mark on her: "It's not the kind of training you do half-heartedly", she says. Even trainees were told in no uncertain terms that if they couldn't work 16 hours on the trot, they didn't need to come back. Today Wurm benefits from the tough life in the finance sector. "It's a great advantage to be so disciplined". During this time, many other cornerstones were also put in place that have helped her with her career. Strategic thinking must be one of the main ones. And so she doesn't regret doing that particular training at all: "I'd do it again every time!"

Berge vermisst. Mit ihrem Golden Retriever Harvey macht sie lange Spaziergänge im Wald. Das ist ihre Pause, ihre Möglichkeit, zwischendurch einmal Abstand von allem zu nehmen.

Um dann wieder voller Power durchzustarten. Wer so hoch qualifiziert, mental flexibel, teamfähig und mittlerweile branchen- und bereichsübergreifend erfahren ist, den könnte man auch in den Metropolen dieser Welt verorten. Wieso also Oldenburg? „In meinem Job beim ‚GO!' fühle ich mich total angekommen", sagt die Projektleiterin mit Überzeugung. Hier entstehe etwas Großes, und dabei auch immer wieder Neues. „Ich habe sozusagen eine ‚grüne Wiese', auf der ich mich austoben darf." Und das mit voller Rückendeckung von Chef Jürgen Bath.

Langeweile? Geht nicht und gibt's nicht!

Alexandra Wurm bleibt also erst einmal beim „GO!". Wobei „bleiben" bei ihr weit entfernt ist von „stehen bleiben". Im Kopf ist sie nämlich immer schon einen Schritt weiter und überlegt, wie sie ihre Kompetenzen ergänzen und ihr Profil schärfen kann. Entsprechend lang ist die Liste mit universitären Abschlüssen und Zusatzqualifikationen. Beispiele: Bachelor in Wirtschaftswissenschaften und Bachelor in Psychologie – Letzteres wohlgemerkt berufsbegleitend –, Master in Management Consulting, Schulungen in Rhetorik und Präsentationskompetenzen. Bei dem Pensum liegt die Frage nahe: warum? Die Antwort kommt prompt: „Ich hasse Langeweile!", weiß die 33-Jährige von sich. Und auch: „Wenn ich mich für etwas entscheide, dann ziehe ich es auch durch."

Zum Erfolg äußert sich Alexandra Wurm immer bescheiden. „Den Aufbau des Start-up-Zentrums hätte ich nie alleine geschafft", betont sie. Ein gutes Team zu haben, sei die Basis. „Außerdem mag ich Menschen nicht, die die Arbeit anderer für die eigene ausgeben." Da ist sie wieder: die klare Haltung, die Alexandra Wurm zu einer weithin geschätzten Person macht – egal ob als Teammitglied oder Gesprächspartnerin beim Netzwerkabend, als Mitarbeiterin oder einfach als Mitmensch. Geradlinig, reflektiert, verlässlich.

Fragt man Alexandra Wurm nach ihren Zukunftsplänen, nennt sie genau zwei. Einer ist privater Natur: Sie wolle endlich ihren Hund erziehen, lacht sie. Und einer – klar – im Beruflichen verankert: Eher mittel- als langfristig will sie „das ‚GO!' noch mehr zum Strahlen bringen, ihm mehr Schlagkraft verleihen". Eine ihrer vielen Ideen besteht darin, sich selbst zur Mediatorin ausbilden zu lassen. Sie ist eben unaufhaltsam.

Stance as well as brain

Even so, she turned her back on the banks. To her own surprise. "Back then, I could have sworn that I was made for the city life. I wanted to work in smart trouser suits and conquer the world." But her moral compass didn't agree. Alexandra Wurm has stance as well as a brain.

Nevertheless, she has still conquered a bit of the world. Which is only to be expected from someone whose strong personality will soon convince if her resumé isn't already enough. In Berlin she accompanied a start-up through the initial phases and discovered the world of personal and strategy consultancy with CARLO Consulting. She then supported the development of an internal training system for the Academy of Broetje-Automation GmbH in Rastede, a company making special machines and assembly systems for the aerospace industry. Her last challenge (for now) was to set up the "GO! Start-Up Centre".

Just turned 30, it was in February 2018 that she started managing the project, which put her in a leading role. It suits her to hold the reins. Or better the ropes: Alexandra Wurm has a sport boat licence. She and her team were given time until the press conference at the end of March to develop the coaching programme with contents and trainer pool, the call for applications and the communication strategy with brand and channels. Just 27 days. She still knows exactly how long they had. "We didn't get much sleep for a while", says the start-up expert with a wink. She created structures, devised the coaching, took personal charge of the whole public image aspect and kept talking with the members of the advisory council, including big names in the regional economy.

On equal terms with big names

It's all thanks to her time in Frankfurt that she remains relaxed at such moments. Her mentors back then told her that education or salary had nothing to do with someone's overall skills, conduct towards others or sense of humour. "That stopped any kind of anxiety". Today her boss, Jürgen Bath, CEO of TGO, also says she's the perfect person to talk with both start-ups and big names.

Her skills definitely go beyond just cultivating and growing networks – that's a proven fact. Since spring 2018, more than 30 start-ups completed the Accelerator Programme, investments were acquired worth more than one million Euro and more than 20 start-up grants were awarded. "That's a huge relief for start-up entrepreneurs", says the one who is quite possibly their most important coach. Meanwhile applications come in from places as far away as Africa. But what mattered most for Alexandra Wurm personally was when the advisory council said there had been visible further development. "That was the best compliment of all!", she says.

East Frisia: just the contrast she needs

Although she loves her job, Alexandra Wurm also loves the occasional break: "I like working hard and often attend business events in the evening. But the drive back home to East Frisia afterwards is all the contrast I need." The wide, flat land where she lives in a little village near Leer has its own special charm, although she grew up in the Sauerland until the age of 12 and still misses the hills two decades later. Harvey, her Golden Retriever, is her faithful companion on long walks in the woods. This is where she takes a break and steps back from everything for a moment.

This enables her to kick-start with full power again afterwards. Someone with her qualifications, mental flexibility, team spirit and cross-sectoral experience could have settled in any of the great cities anywhere in the world. Why Oldenburg? "My job at ‚GO!' is just what I want", says the project manager, full of conviction. Here she's involved in creating something great, something constantly new. "You could say I've got a ‚green field' where I can simply let rip." With full backing from the boss Jürgen Bath.

Bored? Not here, and not her!

So Alexandra Wurm will be staying at "GO!" for the time being. Although staying doesn't mean standing still. In her mind she's always one step ahead, pondering how to supplement her skills and refine her profile. She comes with an impressive, long list of university degrees and additional qualifications. Examples: Bachelor's degree in economics and another one in psychology – the latter on a part-time basis

Das „GO!"-Team Daniel de Oliveira Prudêncio, Jürgen Bath, Alexandra Wurm und Oliver Benkel (v. l.)

The „GO!"-Team Daniel de Oliveira Prudêncio, Jürgen Bath, Alexandra Wurm und Oliver Benkel (from left to right)

next to a full-time job – Master's degree in management consulting, courses in rhetoric and presentation skills. It makes you want to ask: why? And you don't have to wait for the answer: "I hate being bored!" says the 33-year old. What's more, "when I decide to do something then I keep going until I've finished!"

Alexandra Wurm is always modest about her success. "I'd never have managed to get ‚GO!' up and running on my own", she emphasises. Having a good time is key. „And I don't like people who claim other people's work as their own". There it is again. It's this clear stance that means Alexandra Wurm is still highly esteemed: as a team member, on the panel at the network event, as an employee or simply as a person. Straightforward, thoughtful, reliable.

If you ask Alexandra Wurm about her plans for the future, she has just two. One is private: it's about time she trained her dog properly, she laughs. And the other, obviously is to do with work: in the medium rather than long term, she wants "GO!" to become even more effective and have more punch. One of her ideas is to get some training as a mediator. She never stops.

Lager 3000 GmbH

LAGER 3000 mit Hauptsitz im ammerländischen Wiefelstede ist eines der führenden Unternehmen für das vollumfängliche Archivmanagement. Zahlreiche Banken, Behörden, Gerichte, Versicherungen sowie Handels- und Industriekunden sehen in LAGER 3000 den effizienten Outsourcing-Partner für das gesamte Leistungsspektrum rund um die digitale und papierhafte Akte.

Das Portfolio umfasst unter anderem den abgesicherten Service für die Aktenbestandsübernahme nebst Logistik via eigener Speditionen, die DV-gestützte Aktenarchivierung sowie anschließende barcodegestützte Einlagerung in Spezialcontainer und die Aktenvernichtung in der eigenen Schredderanlage bis hin zur vollständigen Digitalisierungslösung des gesamten Aktenarchivs nebst Posteingang-Digitalisierung. Ein wirtschaftlich interessanter Scan-On-Demand verbindet die digitale und die papierhafte Aktenwelt.

Die Qualität sämtlicher Dienstleistungen der LAGER 3000 GmbH zählt zu den besten auf dem Markt. Alle Bereiche werden von geschulten und qualifizierten Mitarbeiter*innen durchgeführt. Alle Prozesse entsprechen höchstmöglichen Sicherheitsstandards und sind vollumfänglich ISO-zertifiziert.

Getreu dem Motto „alles aus einer Hand" wird für den Kunden das Rundum-sorglos-Paket gebildet.

Information

Gründungsjahr: 1999
Mitarbeiter: 90
Leistungsspektrum:
Archivmanagement
– Archivconsulting
– Aktenarchivierung
– Aktenlagerung
– Aktenvernichtung
– Aktendigitalisierung
– Posteingang-Digitalisierung
– Scan-On-Demand
– Logistik
– Containerlagerung
– Umzugslogistik
– Umzugsgutlagerung
– Containervertrieb

www.lager3000.de

Year founded: 1999
Employees: 90
Range of services:
Records management
– archive consulting
– file archiving
– offsite storage
– shredding services
– document scanning
– mail scanning services
– scan-on-demand
– logistics
– container storage
– removal logistics
– removal goods storage
– container sales

LAGER 3000 based in Wiefelstede in the Ammerland is a leading company for full-scale records management. Numerous banks, authorities, courts, insurance companies and retail and trade customers see LAGER 3000 as an efficient outsourcing partner for the entire range of services covering all aspects of digital and paper files.

Among others, the portfolio includes a secure service for taking over stocks of files including logistics with the company's own haulier, computerized file archiving and subsequent bar-coded storage in special containers and file destruction in the company's own shredder, through to total digitization of the whole file archive including mail scanning services. The digital and paper file worlds are connected by economically interesting scan-on-demand.

The quality of all services provided by LAGER 3000 GmbH is among the best on the market. All types of work are performed by trained, qualified employees. All processes comply with the highest security standards and are fully ISO-certified.

Customers are offered an all-in package from a single source.

NORD/LB
Norddeutsche Landesbank
Girozentrale

Information

Die NORD/LB ist eine regional ausgerichtete Universalbank mit Sitz in Norddeutschland und zählt zu den national systemrelevanten Banken.

NORD/LB is a universal bank on the regional level based in North Germany. It is one of the systemically relevant banks in Germany.

www.nordlb.de / www.nordlb.com

Die NORD/LB Norddeutsche Landesbank gehört mit einer Bilanzsumme von 120 Milliarden Euro zu den führenden deutschen Geschäftsbanken. Die Bank mit Sitz in Hannover unterhält mit Oldenburg einen wichtigen Marktstandort. Neben den Bereichen Privat- und Geschäftskunden sowie Firmenkunden ist hier auch der Bereich Structured Finance angesiedelt.

Die NORD/LB engagiert sich schon seit Mitte der 1990er-Jahre als Finanzierer für Projekte im Bereich Erneuerbare Energien und hat bei Windkraftfinanzierungen Pionierarbeit geleistet. Mit zahlreichen Projektfinanzierungen und Beratungsmandaten für Windparks – zu Land und zu Wasser – sowie Solarparks ist sie einer der Top-Arranger auf den nationalen und internationalen Märkten.

NORD/LB Norddeutsche Landesbank is one of Germany's leading business banks, with a balance sheet total of 120 billion Euro. Along side the bank's headquarters in Hanover, its branch in Oldenburg is also a significant market site and home to the structured finance division, in addition to the private, business and corporate customer divisions.

Already since the mid 1990s, NORD/LB has been committed to financing projects for renewable energies and has been a pioneer in wind energy financing. By providing project funding and consultancy for both onshore and offshore wind farms and solar parks, the bank is one of the top financial arrangers on the national and international markets.

DER SOFTWARE-VISIONÄR

The Software Visionary

AUTORIN:
LISA KNOLL

„Und dann sind wir spontan ins Silicon Valley geflogen. Wir wollten einfach mal schauen, ob man dort wirklich so schnell Anknüpfungspunkte findet." So beginnt die wohl verrückteste Anekdote aus dem Leben von Jascha Stein – und zugleich ein Meilenstein in der Geschichte von OmniBot. Heute zählt das kleine Oldenburger Start-up auf dem europäischen Markt zu den erfolgreichsten Unternehmen im Bereich der Sprachassistenten mit künstlicher Intelligenz.

Einer der Köpfe dahinter ist Jascha Stein. Schon in der Schulzeit interessierte sich der gebürtige Hannoveraner für das „Neuland" Internet, entwickelte erste Websites. „Meine Eltern wollten, dass ich etwas Solides lerne. Und als solide galt das Internet damals nun wirklich noch nicht", erinnert sich der 38-Jährige schmunzelnd.

Ein Start-up aufbauen? Diesen Begriff kannten damals nur sehr wenige in Deutschland. „In klassischen Unternehmenshierarchien fühlte ich mich nicht wohl, auch wenn ich später als Strategieberater und Projektleiter zumindest teilweise innerhalb dieser arbeitete. Deshalb habe ich mich für die Freiheit des eigenen Gestaltens entschieden." Nach einer IT-Ausbildung folgten Stationen in München und Bielefeld, wo Stein 2005 eine der ersten Google-zertifizierten Digitalagenturen Deutschlands aufbaute. Ein paar Jahre später verschlug es den selbsternannten Nerd schließlich nach Oldenburg. Als Mitgründer und Director E-Commerce begleitete er den Launch des erfolgreichen Online-Optikers Brille24.

"And then, quite spontaneously, we flew to Silicon Valley. We just wanted to see whether it really is so easy to find points of contact over there." That's the start of what must be the craziest anecdote from Jascha Stein's life – and at the same time a milestone in the history of OmniBot. Today, the small start-up from Oldenburg counts among Europe's most successful companies when it comes to voice assistants with artificial intelligence.

One of the brains behind it is Jascha Stein. While he was still at school, Hanover-born Jascha was interested in the "uncharted territory" of the internet and already started developing websites. "My parents wanted me to learn something 'proper'. And the internet wasn't really seen as bring proper in those days", recalls the 38-year old with a grin.

Launching a start-up? In those days, not many people in Germany knew what that meant. "I wasn't happy in a traditional corporate hierarchy, even though I would be working within such hierarchies later on at least some of the time as a strategy consultant and project leader. That's why I opted for the freedom of setting up my own business." After training in IT, he worked in Munich and Bielefeld, where he set up one of Germany's first Google-certified digital agencies in 2005. A few years later, the self-named nerd finally arrived in Oldenburg. He accompanied the launch of the successful online optician Brille24 as co-founder and Director E-Commerce.

Die Schnittstelle Mensch-Maschine

Ganz und gar nicht „typisch Nerd" war hingegen sein berufsbegleitendes Langzeitprojekt: eine psychologische Ausbildung. Gründe dafür gab es viele, einer lag für ihn auf der Hand, denn im Businessmanagement sei eine gewisse Sozialkompetenz schließlich von Vorteil. 3.400 Stunden später darf sich Jascha Stein Psychologischer Coach und Gestalttherapeut nennen – und hat nicht zuletzt deshalb die Idee für die Gründung von OmniBot: „Mich hat die Schnittstelle Mensch-Maschine immer gereizt. Technik trifft Psychologie – wie spannend ist das denn?" Zusammen mit Geschäftspartner Alexander Rauser tüftelt er fortan im Technologie- und Gründerzentrum (TGO) an einer Projektidee, aus der später die OmniBot-Plattform geboren werden sollte: ein Sprach-Interface für praktisch jeden Anwendungsfall.

Als Text-Sprach-Schnittstelle kann das System komplexe Software für Menschen einfach bedienbar machen oder etwa die Funktionalitäten eines Callcenters abbilden. Als die OmniBot-Technologie bereits ausgereift war, begann Stein das gleichnamige Unternehmen international zu vernetzen. 2017 flog er kurzerhand nach Mumbai, traf sich dort auf gut Glück mit ein paar Softwareentwicklern. „Das war wirklich eine ganz schön hemdsärmelige Aktion", erinnert sich Stein. „Ich war vorher noch nie in Indien und habe alles auf mich zukommen lassen." Und das mit Erfolg: Eine der Firmen, bei denen er sich damals vorstellte, arbeitet noch heute eng mit OmniBot zusammen.

Sympathien für das Unvoreingenommene

Beschwingt vom erfolgreichen Deal an der indischen Westküste, ging es für Stein und sein Team weiter an die US-amerikanische, nach San Francisco. Im Silicon Valley, dem Innovationsmekka der IT- und Hightech-Industrie, spielte den Oldenburger Entwicklern der Zufall in die Karten. Auf einer Investorenkonferenz trafen sie auf ein Start-up, das ebenfalls an einer Sprachassistenten-Plattform tüftelte. „Wir hatten zu diesem Zeitpunkt schon viel Arbeit in die erste Version der OmniBot-Plattform gesteckt und eine recht vorzeigbare Version parat", berichtet Stein. „Also haben wir sie präsentiert."

Von der „Oldenburger Lösung" zeigte man sich im Silicon Valley tief beeindruckt. Auch Jeff Adams, ehemaliger Kopf hinter Amazons Alexa und heute CEO eines der führenden Unternehmen in der Sprachtechnologieforschung, war überzeugt. „Ihm war unsere unbedarfte Herangehensweise von Anfang an sympathisch, außerdem sah er großes Potenzial in unserer Idee. Ab diesem Zeitpunkt war die Sache klar." Adams stieg kurzerhand als Partner bei OmniBot ein. „Cultural Fit" sei sofort vorhanden gewesen, denn als Sohn eines US-Soldaten hatte er einen Teil seiner Jugend in Bremerhaven verbracht und spricht noch immer recht gut Deutsch.

Bisher lief also alles gut für OmniBot. An seiner Vision zweifelt Jascha Stein dennoch jeden Tag. Denn wer aufhöre zu zweifeln oder zu hinterfragen, sei nicht mehr wachsam genug, um erfolgreich zu sein. Man mache Fehler, höre Freunden und Geschäftspartnern mitunter nicht mehr ausreichend zu. Das räche sich sehr schnell. Ein amerikanischer Investor bezeichnete ihn wohl völlig zu Recht als „coachable": bereit zu lernen, vom Feedback anderer zu profitieren und sich dabei auch von harter Kritik nicht demotivieren zu lassen. Diese Haltung hat der OmniBot-Gründer längst verinnerlicht: „Es ist eine der ältes-

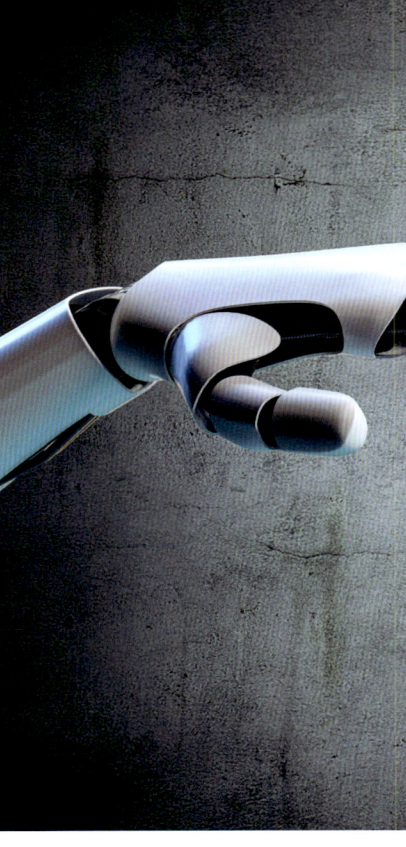

Die Schnittstelle Mensch-Maschine steht im Fokus aller OmniBot-Geschäftsaktivitäten.

The human-machine interface is the focus of all OmniBot business activities.

KI auf dem Vormarsch

Die Oldenburger Digital-Agentur Quantumfrog gewinnt mit einer Eigenentwicklung den Deutschen Computerspielpreis in der Kategorie „Familienspiel". Omnibot sichert sich mit seiner auf Künstlicher Intelligenz (KI) basierten Konversationsplattform und der Zusammenarbeit mit dem früheren Amazon-Entwickler Jeff Adams internationale Aufmerksamkeit. Die Kreishandwerkerschaft Cloppenburg hat einen Chatbot entwickeln lassen, der Handwerker bei der Bewältigung der alltäglichen Routine unterstützen kann. Keine Frage: Die Informationstechnologie hat auch im Nordwesten die nächste Stufe erreicht.

Die Kreishandwerkerschaft ist – wie beispielsweise auch die Handwerkskammer Hannover – darüber hinaus Teil des vom Bundesministerium für Arbeit und Soziales geförderten KomKI-Verbundprojekts (Kompetenzen über Künstliche Intelligenz). Darin geht es in erster Linie um eine effizientere Arbeits- und Einsatzplanung in kleinen und mittleren Unternehmen sowie eine Verringerung der körperlichen Belastung von Beschäftigten. Die einzelnen Module werden im Rahmen praxisnaher KI-Werkstätten gemeinsam mit Handwerksbetrieben entwickelt, erprobt und umgesetzt.

Kompetenz aus dem Nordwesten ist auch beim Projekt „5G Nachhaltige Agrarwirtschaft" gefragt. Es sieht vor, dass sich das Oldenburger Münsterland in den kommenden Jahren zu einem Reallabor für die Integration Künstlicher Intelligenz entwickelt. Mithilfe der Mobilfunktechnologie 5G und Künstlicher Intelligenz soll beispielsweise mehr Tierwohl und ein nachhaltigerer Umgang mit dem Anfall von Gülle und Trockenmist ermöglicht werden. Antragsteller für die Förderung des Vorhabens durch das Bundesministerium für Verkehr und digitale Infrastruktur waren die Transformationsstelle Agrar (trafo:agrar) an der Universität Vechta sowie die Wirtschaftsförderung des Landkreises Vechta. Unterstützung erfährt das Vorhaben durch mehrere renommierte Unternehmen aus der Region.

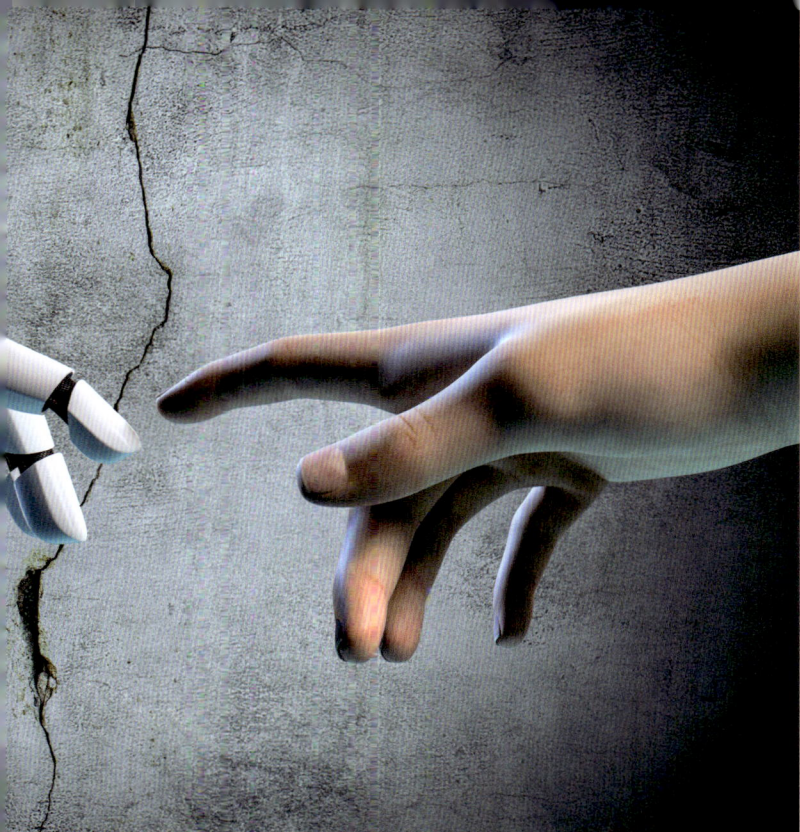

AI on the advance

The digital agency Quantumfrog in Oldenburg wins the German computer game prize in the "family game" category with a proprietary development. OmniBot attracts international attention with its conversation platform based on artificial intelligence (AI) and its cooperation with former Amazon developer Jeff Adams. Cloppenburg District Skilled Crafts Association has had a chatbot developed to help skilled craftsmen in dealing with their daily routines. There's no doubt that information technology has reached the next level, also in the North West.

The District Skilled Crafts Association – like Hanover Chamber of Skilled Crafts, for example – is also part of the "KomKI" project (Expertise through Artificial Intelligence) funded by the Federal Ministry of Labour and Social Affairs. First and foremost, the aim is to make work and deployment planning more efficient in small and medium-sized companies and to reduce the physical pressure on employees. The individual modules are developed, tested and implemented with skilled crafts companies in the framework of practical AI workshops.

Expertise from the North West is also in demand for the project "5G Sustainable Agriculture". Here the intention is over the next few years to turn the Oldenburger Münsterland into a real-life laboratory for the integration of artificial intelligence. For example, 5G cellular technology and artificial intelligence should bring about more animal welfare and a more sustainable approach to dealing with wet and dry manure. Funding for the project from the Federal Ministry of Transport and Digital Infrastructure was applied for by the Agriculture Transformation Department (trafoagrar) at the University of Vechta and the economic development agency of Vechta rural district. Several renowned companies in the region are supporting the project.

The human-machine interface

On the other hand, parallel to his career he had a long-term project running that was anything but "nerdy": he trained in psychology. There were many reasons to do this, one of which was paramount to him, given the benefits of having certain social skills in business management. 3,400 hours later, Jascha Stein is now entitled to call himself a psychological coach and Gestalt therapist. Last but not least, this gave him the idea for founding OmniBot: "The human-machine interface has always fascinated me. Technology meets psychology: you can't get more exciting than that!" Together with his business partner Alexander Rauser, he worked away at a project idea that would eventually give birth to the OmniBot platform: a voice interface for practically every application, using the premises of the Technologie- und Gründerzentrum (TGO – Technology and Start-up Centre).

As text-voice interface, the system makes it easy for people to handle complex software, or depicts call centre functionalities, for instance. Once the OmniBot technology was sufficiently mature, Stein started networking the eponymous company on an international scale. 2017 he flew without further ado to Mumbai, where, on the off chance, he met up with a few software developers. "It was all rather informal", Stein remembers. "I'd never been to India before and I just decided to see what would happen." And indeed, it all went well: one of the companies he met up with on that visit still works closely with OmniBot today.

Appreciation for impartiality

Elated by the successful deal on the Indian West Coast, Stein and his team then headed for the American West Coast and San Francisco. In Silicon Valley, the innovation mecca of the IT and high-tech industry, fate played into the hand of the developers from Oldenburg. At an investor conference, they came across a start-up that was also working on a voice assistant platform. "At this point in time, we had already put a lot of work into the first version of the OmniBot platform and had a really presentable version at the ready", reports Stein. "So we showed them what we had."

Silicon Valley was very impressed with the "Oldenburg solution". Jeff Adams, former head of Amazon's Alexa and meanwhile CEO of one of the leading companies involved in voice technology research, was also convinced. "He appreciated our ingenuous approach right from the start and saw great potential in our idea. From then on, everything was clear." Adams became an OmniBot partner there and then. There was a "cultural fit" right from the start: as the son of a US soldier, Adams had spent some of his youth in Bremerhaven and still speaks fairly good German.

So up to that point in time, things were going well for OmniBot. However, Jascha Stein still has doubts about his vision on a daily basis. Because if you stop having doubts or queries, you won't be alert enough to be successful. You'll make mistakes and no longer listen properly to what friends and business partners are saying. A mistake you'll have to pay for pretty soon. An American investor was quite right in describing him as being "coachable" willing to learn, to benefit from the feedback of others and also not to be discouraged by harsh criticism. An attitude that the OmniBot founder has long assimilated: "It's one of the oldest

ten Start-up-Weisheiten: Arbeite nicht allein, sondern mit starken Partnern." Nur so könne ein Unternehmen seine Agilität bewahren und trotzdem schnell wachsen. Am Erfolg von OmniBot sind rund 40 Menschen beteiligt, darunter viele Softwareentwickler aus dem Ausland.

Schon früh Lust auf eigene Wege

Schon jetzt gehört das Oldenburger Unternehmen zu den wichtigsten Sprachassistenten-Plattformen Europas. Bei einer der größten Supermarktketten in der DACH-Region werden heute bis zu 80.000 Anrufe pro Monat auf den Sprachassistenten umgeleitet. „Das entlastet das Personal im Callcenter, denn OmniBot filtert gezielt die komplexen Anliegen heraus und gibt sie an einen geschulten Mitarbeiter weiter", erklärt der Experte. Immer wiederkehrende und simple Anliegen erledigt das Programm hingegen selbst.

Und auch aus dem Ausland wächst das Interesse an der Sprachtechnologie made in Oldenburg. Vor einigen Monaten konnte eine Partnerschaft mit dem Callcenter-Betreiber Majorel, mit 64.000 Mitarbeitern globaler Marktführer im Bereich Customer Experience Management und seit kurzem börsennotiert, besiegelt werden. Accenture, eine der weltweit größten Unternehmens- und Strategieberatungen, wählte die OmniBot-Technologie gar für die japanische Regierung in Tokio aus.

Dass der Sprung vom IT-Azubi zum CEO eines international erfolgreichen Start-ups gelungen ist, schreibt Stein nicht zuletzt seiner Risikobereitschaft zu. „Ich war eben verrückt genug, zu denken, dass ich auch eigene Wege gehen kann." Seine Arbeit sei ein dauerhafter Lernprozess mit dem Ziel, mindestens 70 Prozent der Arbeitszeit das zu tun, was ihm Spaß mache. Auch deshalb besteht zu vielen Geschäftskontakten eine freundschaftliche Verbindung.

Viel Ausgleich zu seinen beruflichen Herausforderungen braucht Jascha Stein nicht. Seine Freizeit verbringt er gern an der Nordsee, auf dem Golfplatz oder mit Reisen. An seiner Wahlheimat Oldenburg schätzt er nicht nur die breit aufgestellte Kulturlandschaft, sondern auch die entspannte Lebensart der Menschen. „Ich habe in vielen Städten Deutschlands gelebt, aber Oldenburg ist die Stadt, in der ich mich das erste Mal wirklich zu Hause gefühlt habe. Hier ist es so norddeutsch wie nötig, aber so menschlich wie möglich."

Mitarbeit im Weltwirtschaftsforum

Mit seinem Start-up auch langfristig in Oldenburg zu bleiben, steht für Stein trotz des internationalen Erfolgs außer Frage. Im KI-Bundesverband, Deutschlands größtem Netzwerk für Künstliche Intelligenz, ist er Leiter der Regionalgruppe Nordwest für Niedersachsen und Bremen. „In puncto Künstliche Intelligenz hat der Nordwesten Deutschlands Nachholbedarf. Wir wollen uns deshalb in und mit der Region entwickeln. Vor der eigenen Haustür, aber trotzdem mit globalem Potenzial."

bits of wisdom for start-ups: work with strong partners, and not on your own." This is the only way for a company to remain agile and still grow at the same time. Around 40 people are involved in OmniBot's success, including many software developers from abroad.

Wanting to do his own thing from an early age

The Oldenburg company is meanwhile already one of Europe's most important voice assistant platforms. The voice assistant already deals with up to 80,000 phone calls each month for one of the largest supermarket chains in the DACH region. "This relieves the pressure on the call centre staff, with OmniBot filtering out the complex issues and forwarding them to a trained member of staff", explains the expert. Recurring, simple issues on the other hand are handled directly by the program itself.

Other countries are also showing a growing interest in voice technology made in Oldenburg. A few months ago, a partnership was confirmed with the call centre operator Majorel, a global market leader for customer experience management with a workforce of 64,000 employees and recently listed on the stock exchange. Accenture, one of the world's largest corporate and strategy consultancies, even chose OmniBot technology for the Japanese government in Tokyo.

Among others, Stein attributes his successful leap from IT trainee to CEO of an internationally successful start-up to his willingness to take risks. "I was crazy enough to think I could go ahead and do my own thing." His work has been a continuous learning process, with the aim of spending at least 70 percent of his working hours having fun. This is just one reason why he enjoys friendly relationships with many business contacts.

Jascha Stein doesn't need much of a counterweight to his professional challenges. He likes to spend his free time at the North Sea, on the golf course or travelling. What he appreciates about his adopted home of Oldenburg is not only the broad cultural landscape but also the laidback lifestyle of the people who live here. "I've lived in many places in Germany, but Oldenburg is the town where I've really felt at home for the first time. It's as North German as necessary, but as human as possible."

Involved in the World Economic Forum

Despite all the international success, Stein is in no doubt that he and his start-up will be staying in Oldenburg in the long term. At the German AI Association, the country's largest network for artificial intelligence, he is head of the regional group North West for Lower Saxony and Bremen. "When it comes to artificial intelligence, North West Germany has some catching up to do. That's why we want to develop in and with the region. On our own doorstep, but with global potential nevertheless."

Schon jetzt gehört das Oldenburger Unternehmen zu den wichtigsten Sprachassistenten-Plattformen Europas.

The Oldenburg company's meanwhile already one of Europe's most important voice assistant platforms.

Die Möglichkeiten im Bereich Künstliche Intelligenz sind noch längst nicht ausgeschöpft. Stein ist sicher: „Das kommende Jahrzehnt dürfte spannend werden – für die Branche, aber nicht zuletzt auch für jeden Einzelnen, denn KI wird unseren Alltag immer mehr verändern.“

Als „Global Innovator" des Weltwirtschaftsforums nahm er in diesem Jahr als einer von weltweit 2.200 Teilnehmern an der Davos Agenda teil und war Teil verschiedener Arbeitsgruppen. Unter anderem entwickelte Stein eine Health Care Policy „ChatBot RESET" mit, die sich mit den Möglichkeiten der Einbindung von Chatbots im Gesundheitswesen beschäftigt. So soll Künstliche Intelligenz und damit OmniBot bald bei der Unterstützung von Patienten eingesetzt werden, zum Beispiel durch regelmäßige Erinnerungsanrufe für Demenzkranke oder Fernanleitungen bei medizinischen Notfällen.

Der Spontanbesuch im Silicon Valley hat sich also gelohnt. Und Alexa-Erfinder Jeff Adams kennt inzwischen nicht nur Bremerhaven, sondern auch Oldenburg

The possibilities offered by artificial intelligence are far from being exhausted. Stein is sure: "The next decade should be exciting – for the branch but also for every individual, because AI will be changing our everyday lives more and more."

As "Global Innovator" of the World Economic Forum he was one of 2,200 participants worldwide to attend the Davos Agenda and was part of various working groups. Among others, Stein was involved in developing a Health Care Policy "ChatBot RESET" that looks at the possibilities of integrating chatbots in the healthcare sector. The aim is for artificial intelligence and thus also OmniBot to be used soon to assist patients, for example by making regular reminder calls to those suffering from dementia or giving remote instructions in medical emergencies.

And so the spontaneous visit to Silicon Valley was worthwhile. And Alexa inventor Jeff Adams meanwhile knows Oldenburg as well as Bremerhaven.

MULTI DATA
Wedemann Vertriebs GmbH

MULTI DATA importiert seit mehr als 40 Jahren Kassensysteme und POS-Geräte vorwiegend aus Fernost. Ein Meilenstein in der Firmenhistorie war die Einführung der weltweit ersten elektronischen Registrierkasse von Fujitsu in Europa. Sorgfältige und kompetente Marktbeobachtung und Bewertung bilden das Fundament für den erfolgreichen Vertrieb unserer Produkte auch ins europäische Ausland. MULTI DATA tritt als Generalimporteur für Sam4s (ehemals Samsung-Kassensysteme) auf und bietet mit seiner Eigenmarke SAMPOS Kassensysteme mit ausgezeichnetem Preis-/Leistungsverhältnis an.

Unsere Kunden rekrutieren sich aus dem Registrierkassen-Fachhandel, dem Büromaschinen-Fachhandel mit Schwerpunkt Registrierkassen, POS-Distributoren, EDV-Systemhäuser sowie Kassensystemhäuser.

Das 1978 in Oldenburg gegründete Unternehmen beschäftigt heute 22 Mitarbeiter in den Teams Vertrieb, Verwaltung, Lager, Technik, Support, Research & Development und Geschäftsleitung.

For more than 40 years, MULTI DATA has been importing cash registers and POS systems primarily from the Far East. One milestone in the company's history was the introduction to Europe of the world's first electronic cash register by Fujitsu. The successful sales of our products also to other European countries is based on meticulous, competent market observation and analysis. MULTI DATA operates as exclusive importer for Sam4s (formerly Samsung cash registers) and offers excellent value for money with its own brand of SAMPOS cash registers.

Our customers include cash register dealers, office machine dealers specialising in cash registers, POS distributors, IT system houses and cash register system houses.

The company founded in Oldenburg in 1978 today has 22 employees working in teams responsible for sales, administration, warehouse, technical support, customer support, research & development and management.

Information

Leistungsspektrum:
– Generalimporteur für Sam4s (ehemals Samsung-Kassensysteme)
– technische Dokumentation, Support und Softwareentwicklung

Range of services:
– exclusive importer for Sam4s (formerly Samsung cash registers)
– technical documentation, support and software development

www.multidata-kassen.de

Information

Gründungsjahr: 1971	**Year founded:** 1971
Mitarbeiter: rund 400	**Employees:** around 400
Leistungsspektrum:	**Range of services:**

Leistungsspektrum:

- Entwicklung, Integration und Pflege passgenauer Softwarelösungen für die kommunale IT
- Optimierung von IT-Infrastrukturen
- Begleitung strategischer Reformprozesse
- ISO-zertifiziertes Hochleistungsrechenzentrum
- Cloudlösungen
- Druck- und Kuvertierzentrum
- Datenschutz und Informationssicherheit
- KDO-AKADEMIE: Schulungen, Workshops und kommunale Weiterbildung

Range of services:

- developing, integrating and updating tailor-made software solutions for municipal IT
- optimising IT infrastructures
- accompanying strategic reform processes
- ISO-certified high-performance data centre
- cloud solutions
- printing and enveloping centre
- data protection and information security
- KDO ACADEMY: training, workshops and municipal further training

www.kdo.de

Zweckverband Kommunale Datenverarbeitung Oldenburg (KDO)

Wir gestalten kommunale Zukunft

Der Zweckverband Kommunale Datenverarbeitung Oldenburg (KDO) ist Innovations- und Technologiedienstleister für Verwaltungsprozesse und Ansprechpartner für Kommunen in ganz Deutschland. Die KDO deckt mit ihrem Portfolio das gesamte Anforderungsprofil öffentlicher IT ab: von der Entwicklung und Integration passgenauer Software und Lösungen für Verwaltungsdigitalisierung über Datenschutz und Informationssicherheit bis hin zur Übernahme der kompletten IT in das moderne Hochleistungsrechenzentrum.

Seit ihrer Gründung 1971 ist die KDO kontinuierlich gewachsen und heute der größte kommunale IT-Dienstleister in Niedersachsen. Fast 400 Mitarbeiter*innen betreuen vom Stammsitz in Oldenburg und in Servicecentern innerhalb Niedersachsens aus nahezu 700 Vertragskund*innen bundesweit. Zum Kundenkreis gehören kleine Gemeinden ebenso wie große und kreisfreie Städte, Landkreise sowie Krankenhäuser, Verbände und kommunale Eigenbetriebe.

We shape the municipal future

The Zweckverband Kommunale Datenverarbeitung Oldenburg (KDO – municipal data processing association) is an innovation and technology service provider for administrative processes and the contact partner for municipal authorities throughout Germany. The range of services offered by KDO covers all requirements of public IT, from the development and integration of tailor-made software and solutions for administration digitisation via data protection and information security through to taking on complete IT in the state-of-the-art data centre.

KDO has grown constantly since it was founded in 1971 and is today the largest municipal IT service provider in Lower Saxony. Nearly 400 employees at the headquarters in Oldenburg and in service centres throughout Lower Saxony take care of almost 700 contract customers nationwide. The customer base is made up of small municipal authorities and large cities, independent towns and rural districts as well as hospitals, associations and municipal undertakings.

Wir leben Partnerschaft

Wir sind stark organisiert in einer (freiberuflichen) Partnerschaftsgesellschaft mit beschränkter Berufshaftung. Die Vielzahl an Gesellschaftern sowie Mitarbeiterinnen und Mitarbeiter mit Spezialwissen auf allen Beratungsgebieten des Steuer- und Handelsrechts garantiert Ihnen eine schnelle und qualifizierte Bearbeitung jeder Fragestellung aus Ihrer Betriebsführung.

Wir betreuen unsere Mandanten – Unternehmer, Freiberufler und Arbeitnehmer – professionell, gleich welche Anforderungen sie an uns richten. Wir verstehen die Wünsche und Notwendigkeiten der Unternehmer ebenso wie die der Freiberufler und betreuen diese praxisorientiert, persönlich und perspektivisch. Einer unserer Kernbereiche ist der unternehmergeführte Mittelstand. Durch unsere Spezialisierung sind wir in der Lage, viele verschiedene Branchen zu betreuen und maßgeschneiderte Dienstleistungen anzubieten.

Wir stehen für Qualität, Termintreue und Zukunftsorientierung. Unsere Angebotspalette ist so umfassend angelegt, dass sie maßgebliche unternehmerische, freiberufliche oder arbeitnehmerische Problemstellungen abdeckt. Damit entfallen für Sie langwierige Abstimmungs- und Koordinationsprozesse oder die mühsame Suche nach der richtigen Lösung.

Unser Qualitätsanspruch ist hoch. Unsere Partner sind Steuerberaterinnen und Steuerberater, vielfach mit Mehrfachqualifikation als Rechtsanwalt, vereidigter Buchprüfer, Wirtschaftsprüfer oder Landwirtschaftliche Buchstelle. Wir bieten die Fachberatung für Sanierung und Insolvenzberatung (DStV e. V.).

Living partnership

We are organised as a strong (freelance) partnership with limited professional liability. The large number of partners and employees with special know-how in all areas of fiscal and commercial law give you the guarantee of swift, qualified handling of every issue arising from the management of your company. We provide our clients – entrepreneurs, freelancers and employees – with professional support, no matter what their requirements are. We understand the wishes and needs of both entrepreneurs and freelancers, offering practical, personal advice with a perspective. Proprietor-run SME companies are one of our core areas. With our specialisation, we are in a position to support many different sectors and offer tailored services.

Voss Schnitger Steenken Bünger & Partner PartG mbB

Information
Gründungsjahr: 1967
Mitarbeiter: 250
Branchenschwerpunkte: Bäcker und Konditoren, Ärzte und Heilberufe, Bauhandwerk, Kraftfahrzeuggewerbe, Handelsgewerbe, Industrie, Kommunale Unternehmen, Soziale Einrichtungen
Kooperationspartner:
buda Steuerberatungsgesellschaft mbH (Beratung für die östlichen Bundesländer), OBIC Revision GmbH Wirtschaftsprüfungsgesellschaft

Year founded: 1967
Employees: 250
Main sectors: bakers and confectioners, doctors and healthcare professionals, building trade, automotive trade, commerce and trade, industry, municipal companies, social organisations
Cooperation partners:
buda Steuerberatungsgesellschaft mbH (tax consultants for east German states), OBIC Revision GmbH Wirtschaftsprüfungsgesellschaft (auditing company)

www.obic-steuerrecht.de

We stand for quality and adhere to deadlines while keeping a focus on the future. The range of services we offer is so comprehensive that it covers all major problems that entrepreneurs, freelancers or employees have to deal with. This saves you from tedious coordination processes or laborious searches for the right solution.

We have high quality aspirations. Our partners are tax consultants, often with additional qualifications as lawyers, certified auditors, chartered accountants or farm accountants. We offer specialised restructuring consulting and insolvency advice (DStV e. V.).

Selos Informationssysteme GmbH

Information
Gründungsjahr 1993
Mitarbeiter: 12
Leistungsspektrum:
– IT-Infrastruktur
– Server/Client-Systeme
– Datensicherung/
 Datenschutz
– Virtualisierung
– Telekommunikation
– Web Design/CMS

Year founded: 1993
Employees: 12
Range of services:
– T infrastructure
– server/client systems
– data protection/data privacy
– virtualisation
– telecommunication
– web design/CMS

www.selos.de

Selos
it systemhaus

IT-Dienstleistungen aus Wilhelmshaven
für den Jade-Weser-Raum seit 1992

* Computer und Netzwerke

* IT- und Telekommunikation

* Service und Support

* Mu timed asysteme

* IT-Outsourcing

Die Selos Informationssysteme GmbH in Wilhelmshaven wurde 1993 als technisches Systemhaus gegründet und wird durch die beiden Geschäftsführer Jan Lucklum und Jörg Johann Müller vertreten.

Die langjährige Erfahrung des stetig wachsenden Teams – bestehend aus kompetenten Technikern und Kaufleuten – gewährleistet eine umfassende Unterstützung in den Bereichen der IT und den daraus resultierenden Anforderungen. Mit ihrem umfangreichen Dienstleistungsangebot bietet die Selos ganzheitliche Lösungen, welche sich an den spezifischen Bedürfnissen, Wünschen und Nutzen des Kunden orientieren. Sie begleitet von der Planung über die Beschaffung und Installation bis hin zum Betrieb und der anschließenden Betreuung den Prozess ganzheitlich. Hieraus entsteht die Grundlage für erfolgreiche, langjährige Geschäftsbeziehungen.

Zu den Kunden im Raum Weser-Ems zählen Kommunal- und Bundesbehörden, die Hafenwirtschaft, Industrie und Gewerbe, Handels- und Dienstleistungsunternehmen sowie Ärzte, Rechtsanwälte und Steuerberater.

Selos Informationssysteme GmbH in Wilhelmshaven was founded in 1993 as a technical systems house and is represented by the two managing directors Jan Lucklum and Jörg Johann Müller.

The long-standing experience of the constantly growing team, consisting of skilled technicians and business experts, warrants comprehensive support in all areas of IT and the resulting requirements. With its extensive range of services, Selos offers holistic solutions geared to the customer's specific needs, requests and benefit. The company provides holistic process support from initial planning via procurement and installation through to operation and aftercare.

This generates the basis for successful, long-term customer relations. Customers in the Weser-Ems region include municipal and federal authorities, the port services sector, commerce and industry, retail and service companies together with doctors, lawyers and tax consultants.

DER GENUSSTRONOM

The Connoisseur-Restaurateur

AUTOR:
CLAUS SPITZER-
EWERSMANN

In der Gastronomie ist ein steter Wechsel von guten und schlechten Zeiten normal. Heiner Ahrmann hat im Gut Altona in Dötlingen vor allem gute erlebt – und einen richtigen Schreckensmoment. Nach über 40 Jahren übergibt er das Haus nun an die nächste Inhabergeneration. Und fühlt sich richtig wohl dabei.

Der Schock ist mitten in der Nacht plötzlich da. „Wir hörten die Feuerwehrsirenen, aber man denkt ja zunächst nichts Böses und überlegt, wo die wohl hinfahren", erinnert sich Heiner Ahrmann. Dann aber kommt auch das Flackern der Blaulichter immer näher. Und als die Fahrzeuge tatsächlich auf sein Anwesen einbiegen, macht sich Hektik breit. „Da haben wir gesehen, dass unser Haupthaus in Flammen stand."

Als klappe das ganze Leben weg

Nicht einmal eine halbe Stunde später sind mehr als 300 Feuerwehrleute aus der ganzen Region vor Ort, Löschwasser wird aus dem nahen Mühlbach und dem Annasee herangepumpt. Ein Großeinsatz, wie er im Buche steht. Der aber nur mit einem Teilerfolg endet. Die Brandbekämpfer können zwar ein Übergreifen des Feuers auf die Nebengebäude verhindern, aber das über 100 Jahre alte Haupthaus von Gut Altona ist nicht zu retten. Auch ein neuerer Anbau fällt den Flammen zum Opfer. Grund: ein Kurzschluss in der Elektrik. Kleine Ursache, verheerende Wirkung. Zum Glück kommen keine Menschen zu Schaden.

In the hospitality industry, it's quite normal for good times to alternate with bad times. For Heiner Ahrmann and his "Gut Altona" hotel and restaurant in Dötlingen, times have mainly been good – apart from one really dreadful moment. Now after more than 40 years in the business, he is ready to hand over to the next generation of proprietors. He feels it is the right thing to do.

The shock came all of a sudden in the middle of the night. "We heard the sirens of the fire engines, but you don't think the worst thing to start with and we just wondered where they were going", recalls Heiner Ahrmann. But then the flashing blue lights came closer. And when the vehicles actually turned onto his property, things suddenly got hectic. "We saw that our main building was in flames."

As if life was suddenly falling away

Less than half an hour later, more than 300 fire-fighters had arrived from all over the region, pumping water from the nearby Mühlbach stream and lake Annasee. A major incident like you find in the textbooks. But it was only partly successful. Although the fire-fighters managed to prevent the fire from spreading to the auxiliary buildings, it was not possible to save the 100-year-old main building of Gut Altona. A more recent annex was also lost to the flames. The reason for the fire: a short-circuit in the electrical system. Small cause, with a devastating effect. Fortunately, no-one was hurt.

Ganz scheint sich Heiner Ahrmann auch nach fünfeinhalb Jahren noch nicht von jener Schreckensnacht im September 2016 erholt zu haben. „So etwas wünscht man wirklich niemandem, und das braucht man auch kein zweites Mal", sagt er leise. „Man fühlt sich, als klappe gerade das ganze eigene Leben unter einem weg." Alles, was man selbst aufgebaut hat und wofür schon die Generationen zuvor geackert haben, liegt von einem Moment auf den anderen in Schutt und Asche. Es droht der Fall ins Bodenlose. Keine Frage, es gibt nicht wenige Menschen, die an einem solchen Erlebnis zerbrechen.

Nicht so die Ahrmanns. Schnell regt sich bei der Dötlinger Familie der Überlebenswille. Freunde bieten ihre Unterstützung an. Zu tun gibt es genug. Zwar gleicht das Grundstück einem Trümmerfeld, doch die verbliebenen Gäste müssen untergebracht, fest gebuchte Familienfeiern und Tagungen umgelegt, erste Gespräche mit der Versicherung geführt werden. Das lenkt ab. Aufgeben kommt trotz des Millionenschadens nicht infrage. Schon drei Tage nach dem Brand geht der Hotelbetrieb weiter – natürlich unter erschwerten Bedingungen und mit viel Improvisationsgeschick. Aber: „Meiner Frau und mir war einfach klar, dass das nicht das Ende von Gut Altona sein kann."

Erster Berufswunsch: Landwirt

Der Anfang datiert auf das Jahr 1888. Genau 63.000 Goldmark zahlte Heiner Ahrmanns Urgroßvater Johann-Heinrich dem Vorbesitzer für das Anwesen mit der prägnanten, Mitte des 16. Jahrhunderts erbauten Mühle. Sie hatte zuvor lange als Zollstelle zwischen der Stadt Wildeshausen und der früheren Vogtei Hatten gedient. Mit einer Schankwirtschaft wollten sich Ahrmann und seine Frau Elise an dieser strategisch günstigen Stelle ein zweites Standbein aufbauen. Ursprünglich stammte die Familie aus Ueffeln.

Die bei Bramsche gelegene, sogenannte „Streusiedlung" ist auch der Heimatort von Heiner Ahrmann. Hier kam er 1953 zur Welt. Es war die Zeit des Wirtschaftswunders, der mehr und mehr aufblühenden Bundesrepublik. Jungs wollten Lokomotivführer oder Pilot, Schauspieler oder Polizist werden. Nicht so der kleine Heiner. „Das interessierte mich alles nicht", winkt er ab. Sein Traumberuf: Landwirt. Den ganzen Tag draußen auf dem Feld, in der freien Natur, wunderbar. Am liebsten natürlich im heimischen Betrieb.

Mit 13 war die Sache erst einmal vorbei. Der Ahrmannsche Hof in Ueffeln wurde verpachtet. Heiners Mutter – der Vater war früh verstorben – zog mit dem Junior nach Dötlingen. Hier hatte sich das Gut Altona bereits gut entwickelt. Ausflügler legten gern einen Stopp ein, der Saal wurde häufig für Bälle und andere Festivitäten gebucht. Heiner Ahrmann fand Gefallen an dem emsigen Treiben. „Als ich 21 war, habe ich mich festgelegt: Ich will etwas in der Gastronomie machen."

Es folgte der in jenen Tagen klassische Weg: erstmal eine Ausbildung zum Hotel- und Gaststättengehilfen. Dafür ging es jeden Tag nach Bremen ins Hotel Columbus am Hauptbahnhof, seinerzeit eine der ersten Adressen am Platz. „Das war für einen Landmenschen wie mich schon eine andere Welt." Danach die Bundeswehr und die renommierte Hotelfachschule in Rottach-Egern am Tegernsee. Und schließlich nach einer Zwischenstation im Harz, die Ausbildung zum Koch im Jagdhaus Eiden in Bad Zwischenahn.

Das traditionsreiche Gut Altona der Familie Ahrmann in Dötlingen

Ahrmann: The traditional Gut Altona of the Ahrmann family in Dötlingen

Existenzen gefährdet

Gastronomie und Hotellerie gehören zu den Branchen, die von der Corona-Krise am härtesten getroffen wurden. Wie auch immer die Beschlüsse der Politik aussehen: Allein im Oldenburger Land sind davon rund 4.000 Betriebe betroffen. Schätzungen des Statistischen Bundesamtes zufolge gingen 2020 die Umsätze um durchschnittlich 36 Prozent zurück. Besonders hart war es im April 2020: Nach Angaben der Statistiker sanken die Umsätze hier um 68 Prozent.

Nicht alle Restaurants, Hotels oder Gaststätten konnten in guten Zeiten ausreichend Rücklagen bilden. So ist kaum jemand in der Lage, die wochen- bzw. monatelangen Ausfälle zu kompensieren. Die vielfach ins Leben gerufenen Abhol- und Bringangebote waren deshalb nicht mehr als ein Tropfen auf den heißen Stein. Nicht selten halfen sie aber dabei, zumindest das Team bei Laune zu halten.

Der Deutsche Hotel- und Gaststättenverband geht davon aus, dass bundesweit etwa 70.000 Betriebe die Krise nicht überleben werden. Kaum einer, der nicht um seine Existenz bangt – und das betrifft alle Bereiche der Branche, bis hin zu den vermeintlich großen Playern der Systemgastronomie. Vielen machte zudem zu schaffen, dass die eigentlich als Rettungsanker gedachten staatlichen Unterstützungsmaßnahmen wie die Novemberhilfe nur sehr schleppend ausgezahlt wurden. Oder sie kamen nur einmal, obwohl ein Gastronom mehrere Betriebe schließen musste.

Perspektivisch glauben viele Kenner der Branche, dass die sogenannte Offsite-Gastronomie nach Ende der Pandemie einen hohen Stellenwert behalten wird. Das heißt, die Menschen werden sich weiterhin Speisen bestellen und sich liefern lassen. Ob sich dabei professionelle Lieferdienste weiter etablieren werden, oder ob einzelne Gastronomen mit eigenen Angeboten erfolgreich sind, wird sich zeigen – und letztlich von Qualität und Werbung abhängig sein.

Livelihoods at risk

The hospitality trade is one of the industries that has been hardest hit by the corona crisis. No matter what decisions the politicians take, in the Oldenburger Land alone, around 4,000 business are affected. Estimates by the Federal Statistical Office indicate that turnover has declined by 36 percent on average during 2020. April 2020 was particularly difficult, with turnover falling by 68 percent in this month, according to the statistics.

Not all restaurants, hotels, pubs or cafés had managed to generate enough reserves during better times, and scarcely anyone is in a position to compensate for weeks or months of losses. Although many places have been offering collection and take-away services, this is usually no more than a drop in the ocean. On the other hand, at least it has been a way of keeping the team happy.

The German Hotel and Catering Federation expects that about 70,000 businesses won't survive the crisis. Almost everyone in the industry is worried about their existence – and this refers to the industry as a whole, right through to the supposed big players with their catering chains. Many are also struggling with the extensive delays being encountered in receiving the state aid payments such as the November Aid that was supposed to give them a lifeline. Or the payments were only made once, even though a restaurateur was forced to close several businesses.

In the long term, many industry experts expect so-called off-site catering to remain popular even after the end of the pandemic. In other words, people will continue to order meals for delivery. Whether this will see the further emergence of professional delivery services or whether individual restaurants will establish their own services remains to be seen. In the end, it will depend on quality and advertising.

Even now, five and a half years later, Heiner Ahrmann still does not seem to have recovered completely from that dreadful night back in September 2016. "You really wouldn't wish that kind of thing on your worst enemy, and it's not something you'd want to go through a second time", he says quietly. "It feels like your whole life is falling away." At a moment's notice, everything he had worked for and everything that had been built up by generations before him lay in ruins. It would be so easy to fall into the abyss. Without doubt, more than just a few people would go to pieces in a moment like this.

But not the Ahrmanns. Quickly the family from Dötlingen found the will to survive. Friends offered to help. There was certainly plenty to do. Despite the devastation all around, accommodation had to be found for the remaining guests, bookings for family celebrations and conferences had to be postponed and initial talks held with the insurance company. That helped to distract them. Although the damage went into millions, there was no question of giving up. Just three days after the fire, the hotel was back in business – under adverse conditions of course, and with a great deal of improvisation. But: "My wife and I were absolutely convinced that this cannot be the end of Gut Altona."

Initial career choice: farmer

The beginnings go back to 1888. Exactly 63,000 gold marks was the sum paid by Heiner Ahrmann's great-grandfather Johann-Heinrich to the former owner of the estate with the striking mill built in the middle of the 16th century. It formerly served as customs post between the town of Wildeshausen and the former bailiwick of Hatten. Ahrmann and his wife Elise wanted to establish a tavern as a second mainstay at this strategically favourable point. Originally the family came from Ueffeln.

The scattered settlement near Bramsche is also Heiner Ahrmann's home. He was born here in 1953. It was the time of Germany's economic miracle that saw the country flourishing more and more. Boys wanted to be train drivers or pilots, actors or policeman. But not little Heiner. "I wasn't interested in all that", he says, waving the idea aside. His dream job was to be a farmer. To spend all day outside in the fields, out in the countryside: that's what he wanted! Preferably on the family farm, of course.

But that dream came to an end when he was 13. Someone else took on the tenancy of the Ahrmann's farm in Ueffeln. Following the early death of Heiner's father, mother and son moved to Dötlingen, where Gut Altona was already well established. It was popular place for day trippers to call in for refreshments and the hall was frequently booked for balls and other celebrations. Heiner Ahrmann liked the busy hustle and bustle. "When I was 21, I decided I wanted to do something in the hospitality trade."

In those days, that meant the traditional approach, training to be a hotel and restaurant assistant. Every day he went to Bremen as an apprentice in Hotel Columbus at the central station, in those days one of the top addresses in town. "For a country boy like me, it was like a completely different world." This was followed by his military service and further

Als Krisenmanager gefordert

Bestens für den gastronomischen Alltag gerüstet steigt Heiner Ahrmann 1977 in den Familienbetrieb ein und übernimmt sogleich die Aufgaben des Geschäftsführers – mit nur 24 Jahren. Radikalen Veränderungen kann er zwar nichts abgewinnen, dennoch brechen neue Zeiten an. Es gilt, einerseits die Tradition zu wahren, andererseits zusätzliche Gäste anzusprechen. Das Hotel wird behutsam erweitert, das Tagungsgeschäft ausgebaut. Der Restaurantbetrieb erhält ein stärkeres Gewicht. Ihn selbst, räumt der heute 67-Jährige ein, zieht es allerdings trotz seiner Ausbildung nur sehr selten in die Küche.

Die Dinge fügen sich gut zusammen. Die Geschäfte laufen, der Ruf von Gut Altona reicht weit über das Oldenburger Land hinaus. Zudem werden Ahrmann und seine Frau Inka gleich dreimal Eltern. Vincent, Malte und Nele heißen die Kinder – und sie lassen schon bald erkennen, dass sie die gastronomische Familientradition eines Tages fortführten wollen.

Also alles bestens? Nein. Denn im September 2016 fällt Heiner Ahrmann ohne Vorwarnung eine neue Aufgabe zu, die des Krisenmanagers. „Diese Rolle kannte ich bis dahin noch gar nicht." Heute kann er darüber schmunzeln, damals war es harte Arbeit. Selbstverständlich habe man nach dem Brand erst einmal den Familienrat zusammengetrommelt. Ein Wiederaufbau braucht schließlich eine Perspektive. „Hätten unsere Kinder andere Pläne gehabt, wären wir sicherlich ins Grübeln geraten", betont der Seniorchef. Aber so kommt es nicht – und deshalb rücken schon im Herbst des Jahres die Bagger an, um alle Spuren der Ruine endgültig zu beseitigen.

Zwei Jahre dauert der Wiederaufbau. Im Herbst 2018 läuft der Betrieb wieder an. Deutlich wird: Die Plan- und Bauteams haben ganze Arbeit geleistet. Das Gebäude wurde im Gutshausstil neu errichtet, der Eingang von der Straßenseite weg verlegt und im Innern allerlei an Akzenten gesetzt. Die Gäste können sich etwa an dekorativen Pendelleuchten, chinesischem Blausteinboden und einer Vielzahl schmückender Holzelemente erfreuen. Deutlich wird ferner, dass Altes auch immer zu Neuem taugt: Etliche Steine aus dem abgebrannten Gebäude konnten beim Bau des Kamins wiederverwendet werden.

Krakau, Rom und dann nach Kalifornien

Heiner Ahrmann ist sichtlich stolz auf das Erreichte. Und er freut sich, ein freundlich, hochwertig und zeitgemäß eingerichtetes Haus an die nächste Generation übergeben zu dürfen. „Der Gedanke daran hat meiner Frau und mir in den schweren Momenten die nötige Kraft gegeben", sagt er.

Aber kann jemand, der über 40 Jahre lang die Geschicke des Traditionsbetriebs bestimmte, tatsächlich loslassen? Die Antwort kommt wie aus der Pistole geschossen: „Kein Problem, lieber heute als

training at the renowned college of hotel management in Rottach-Egern on lake Tegernsee. Then finally, after a spell in the Harz, he completed his training as a chef in Jagdhaus Eiden in Bad Zwischenahn.

Learning to deal with a crisis

Well-prepared for everyday life in the hospitality trade, Heiner Ahrmann joined the family business in 1977, immediately taking on the tasks of managing director at the age of just 24 years. Although he was not one for making radical changes, nevertheless it was the start of a new era. While preserving traditions, at the same time the hotel needed to reach out and attract additional guests. Heiner Ahrmann proceeded with cautious extensions and started to expand the conference business. The restaurant was given a greater role. Despite his training, now at the age of 67 years he admits that he is rarely to be found in the kitchen.

Things have all worked out well. Business is good. Gut Altona's reputation extends way beyond the Oldenburger Land. Ahrmann and his wife Inka also have three children: Vincent, Malte and Nele, who soon show their intentions to continue the family's hospitality tradition one day in the future.

So everything is fine? No. In September 2016, Heiner Ahrmann suddenly found himself in the new role of crisis manager. "It's something I hadn't had to do at all up to then." Today he can smile about it. Back then, it was hard work. Needless to say that after the fire, the first thing was to hold a family council. After all, reconstruction needs a perspective. "If our children had had other plans, we would certainly have had to think things over", emphasises the boss. But that isn't what happened. And so that autumn, the bulldozers arrived to finally remove all remaining traces of the ruins.

The reconstruction took two years. In autumn 2018, they opened for business again. It was soon quite clear that the planning and construction teams had done a grand job. The building was rebuilt in the manor house style and the entrance was relocated away from the roadside. All kinds of accents have been set in the interior. Decorative pendant lamps, Chinese bluestone floors and a large number of decorative wooden elements delight the hearts of hotel guests. It is also quite clear that old and new are equally appreciated: many bricks from the burnt-out building have been put to good use in constructing the chimney.

Kraków, Rome and then California

Heiner Ahrmann is visibly proud of what has been achieved. And he is pleased to pass on a friendly, top quality, contemporarily furnished establishment to the next generation. "It was this thought that gave my wife and myself the necessary power to keep going when things got tough", he says.

Der große Festsaal ist für Feiern bis zu 250 Personen ausgelegt.

Up to 250 people can attend events in the large ballroom.

morgen." Man dürfe doch nicht das Leben neben der Gastronomie vergessen. Urlaub zum Beispiel. Einen Besuch im polnischen Krakau hat der Mallorca-Liebhaber weit oben auf seiner Liste stehen, ebenso Rom und Florenz. Und außerhalb Europas? Ahrmann wiegt den Kopf hin und her. „Ich mag eigentlich keine Langstreckenflüge." Eigentlich? „Naja, die amerikanische Westküste würde mich schon reizen, einmal Kalifornien sehen." Das sollte sich doch machen lassen.

Zudem beabsichtigt er, sich in Zukunft mehr um die umliegenden, der Familie gehörenden Wälder zu kümmern und wieder mehr Golf zu spielen. „Das habe ich ein wenig vernachlässigt", gibt er zu. Auch seinem Oldtimer-Hobby will der Besitzer eines Fiat 124 Sport mehr Zeit widmen, Ausflüge machen, sich auf feines Essen und einen guten Tropfen Wein freuen. Er sei ein Genussmensch, sagt er. Kein Zweifel.

But can he really let go after more than 40 years of running the traditional business? The answer comes quick like a shot: "That's absolutely no problem, sooner rather than later!" After all, life also exists outside the hotel doors. Holiday, for example. The Majorca fan has a to-do list with Kraków in Poland near the top, as well as Rome and Florence. And what about outside Europe? Ahrmann wags his head. "Actually, I don't really like long-distance flights." But? "But well yes, I'd rather like to see the American West Coast and have a look at California." Well, that ought to be possible.

In future, he also intends to take more care of the woods that belong to the family and hopes to play more golf. "I've had to neglect that a bit", he admits. The owner of a Fiat 124 Sport also wants to devote more time to his vintage car hobby, and looks forward to fine dining with a good drop of wine. He's someone who appreciates the good things in life, he says. No doubt about that.

DIE REHA-SPEZIALISTIN

The Rehabilitation Specialist

AUTOR:
TORBEN ROSENBOHM

Hektik soll hier nicht aufkommen. Ein gutes Stück abseits des geschäftigen Treibens rund um das Oldenburger Klinikum und damit in vergleichsweise ruhiger Lage ist eine Institution des städtischen Gesundheitswesens beheimatet: das Reha-Zentrum. Am Ende der Brandenburger Straße in Kreyenbrück befindet sich die Einrichtung, die 2022 ihren 25. Geburtstag begeht. Die gebürtige Oldenburgerin Karin Vogel ist hier seit mehr als 20 Jahren die Geschäftsführerin.

Ein Grund zum Feiern? „Auf jeden Fall!", sagt Karin Vogel mit einem überzeugenden Lachen, das auch die obligatorische Maske in Corona-Zeiten nicht verbergen kann. „Das Feiern sind wir vor allem unseren Mitarbeiterinnen und Mitarbeitern schuldig, ohne die das alles hier nicht funktionieren würde." Die Oldenburgerin muss es wissen: Seit 1998 und damit seit kurz nach Eröffnung des Zentrums ist sie im Hause tätig. Wer über die Geschichte dieses besonderen Projekts spricht, kann auch ihren persönlichen Weg nicht ausblenden.

1959 erblickt sie als Kind der Region, der sie bis heute verbunden ist, das Licht der Welt. Auf die Grundschule in Wardenburg und das Abitur am Graf-Anton-Günther-Gymnasium in Oldenburg folgt zunächst eine kaufmännische Ausbildung, bevor der Gang an die Universität den späteren Weg ebnet: In Osnabrück studiert Karin Vogel Betriebswirtschaftslehre im Gesundheitswesen. „Damit stand fest, in welche Richtung es gehen soll."

Everything is calm and peaceful here. Well away from the hustle and bustle of daily life at Oldenburg hospital, in a comparatively calm location, this is where we find a facility belonging to the city's healthcare sector: the Rehabilitation Centre. It is housed at the end of Brandenburger Straße in Kreyenbrück and will be celebrating its 25th birthday in 2022. Karin Vogel, a native of Oldenburg, has been managing director here for more than 20 years.

A reason to celebrate? "Quite definitely!", says Karin Vogel with a convincing smile that not even the obligatory corona mask can conceal. "We owe it to our employees to celebrate: nothing here would work without them." She knows what she's talking about, having worked here since 1998 just after the centre opened. Any discussion about the history of this special project has to include her personal journey.

She was born here in 1959, in the region where she is still well-rooted today. After primary school in Wardenburg and A-levels at Graf Anton Günther grammar school in Oldenburg, she did commercial training first before going on to university. In Osnabrück, Karin Vogel set the course for her future career, studying business management in the healthcare sector. "That dictated the path I would follow."

Alles für den einzelnen Patienten

Nach dem Abschluss erfolgt der Eintritt ins Berufsleben bei einer Oldenburger Wirtschaftsprüfungsgesellschaft. „Danach habe ich die Seiten gewechselt", blickt sie zurück. Für diesen Seitenwechsel muss sie das von ihr sehr geschätzte Oldenburger Land nicht verlassen, denn in Bad Zwischenahn übernimmt sie die kaufmännische Leitung der Nachsorgeklinik Niemoeller. Der Umstand, dass diese ihre Türen schließen muss, führt sie 1998 dorthin, wo sie bis heute – „mit anhaltend großer Begeisterung" – tätig ist: ins Reha-Zentrum Oldenburg. Zunächst als Prokuristin, ab 2000 schließlich als Geschäftsführerin (Rehabilitationszentrum Oldenburg GmbH und Ambulantes Rehabilitationszentrum Oldenburg gGmbH).

Vier Fachbereiche werden an der Brandenburger Straße heute klinisch abgedeckt: Kardiologie, Neurologie, Geriatrie und Orthopädie/Unfallchirurgie. Im Mittelpunkt stehe immer „der einzelne Patient", betont Karin Vogel. Die Kernkompetenzen aller Beteiligten in der Rehabilitation zielten darauf ab, Menschen zurück ins Berufsleben zu bringen bzw. Pflegebedürftigkeit zu verhindern. Daran arbeitet ein großes Team in den unterschiedlichsten Bereichen. Dass die Zusammenarbeit aller Kräfte der Schlüssel zum Erfolg sei, habe sie früh festgestellt. „Ich habe schon im Studium die verschiedenen Seiten wahrgenommen", erinnert sie sich an ihre Zeit an der Universität. „Es geht alles nur miteinander. Nur so lässt sich im vorgegebenen Rahmen die bestmögliche Qualität erzielen."

Schritt für Schritt entwickelt sich Karin Vogel ab dem Ende der 1990er-Jahre weiter, Stein für Stein und Mitarbeiter für Mitarbeiter wächst auch das Reha-Zentrum selbst in einem fort. Bei seiner Eröffnung 1997 bilden die Klinik für Neurologie und die Klinik für Kardiologie die ersten Einheiten, mit denen der Betrieb aufgenommen wird. Endgültig zum „Oldenburger Modell" wird das Zentrum 2004, als die orthopädische Klinik hinzukommt und fortan mit dem Pius-Hospital alle drei Oldenburger Krankenhäuser an der Trägerschaft beteiligt sind. „Die Besonderheit besteht darin, dass ein kommunales Haus und zwei konfessionelle Häuser unterschiedlicher Konfession in der Trägerschaft sind." Damit nicht genug, denn: „Die wiederum gehören zum medizinischen Campus der European Medical School der Universität Oldenburg."

Das Gesundheitswesen als Impulsgeber

Das Reha-Zentrum hat seine Rolle in der Kliniklandschaft der Region definiert und sieht sich auch für neue Anforderungen gerüstet: „Die strategische Weiterentwicklung ist immer nach dem Bedarf in der Patientenversorgung ausgerichtet, selbstverständlich in Abhängigkeit der politischen Rahmenbedingungen. Wir in Oldenburg sind insbesondere mit der Verbindung zu den Akuthäusern und darüber zur Unimedizin gut aufgestellt, um uns den zukünftigen Herausforderungen auch unter Berücksichtigung der demografischen Entwicklung zu stellen und uns danach auszurichten", erklärt die Geschäftsführerin.

Menschen zurück ins Berufsleben bringen bzw. Pflegebedürftigkeit verhindern: daran arbeitet ein großes Team in den unterschiedlichsten Bereichen im Rehabilitationszentrum Oldenburg.

Enabling people to return to their working lives or to prevent them from becoming dependent on care. This involves a large team working in the many different areas at Oldenburg Rehabilitation Centre.

Auch in Zukunft ein Jobmotor

Im Fokus der Öffentlichkeit steht das deutsche Gesundheitswesen immer wieder. Spätestens im Verlauf der Corona-Pandemie wurde dabei die herausragende Relevanz für die Gesellschaft deutlich. Denn insbesondere die Situation in den Kliniken wurde bei vielen Verordnungen als entscheidender Maßstab betrachtet. Offensichtlich wurde aber auch, dass im Bereich der personellen Ausstattung vielerorts Handlungsbedarf besteht.

Derweil ist das Gesundheitswesen in Deutschland ein wahrer Jobmotor. Fast sechs Millionen Beschäftigte sind hier nach Angaben des Bundesgesundheitsministeriums tätig – das ist immerhin jeder achte Erwerbstätige. Die demografische Entwicklung lässt erwarten, dass der Bedarf an Arbeitskräften in Zukunft eher noch steigen wird. Unterschieden wird per Definition zwischen dem ersten und dem zweiten Gesundheitsmarkt: Der erste umfasst die „klassischen" Bereiche, die überwiegend durch gesetzliche und private Kranken- und Pflegeversicherungen finanziert werden. Im zweiten Gesundheitsmarkt sind die Angrenzungen nicht immer klar gesetzt, im Wesentlichen werden hier aber beispielsweise individuelle Gesundheitsleistungen, Fitness und Wellness mit aufgeführt.

Wie viele andere Branchen auch, hat das Gesundheitswesen mit einem Fachkräftemangel zu kämpfen. Die Verantwortlichen versuchen, diesem mit innovativen Ideen zu begegnen. Zuletzt wurden beispielsweise in der Pflege neue Wege beschritten: Eine Ausbildung findet nicht mehr jeweils in den bewährten Bereichen statt, sondern fasst die Felder Kranken-, Alten- und Kinderkrankenpflege in einer generalistischen Ausbildung zusammen.

Everything for the individual patient

After graduating, her career began with an auditing firm in Olden-burg. "Then I changed sides", she says looking back. This did not entail leaving her beloved Oldenburger Land: instead, she took up a position as commercial manager for Niemoeller after-care clinic in Bad Zwischenahn. When this clinic was forced to close down in 1998, she moved to where she still works today "as passionately as ever", in Oldenburg Rehabilitation Centre. Initially as general manager then since 2000 as managing director (Rehabilitationszentrum Olden-burg GmbH and Ambulantes Rehabilitationszentrum Oldenburg gGmbH).

Today the Rehabilitation Centre on Brandenburger Straße covers four specialist areas: cardiology, neurology, geriatrics and orthopaedics/trauma surgery. The focus is always on "the individual patient", emphasises Karin Vogel. All those involved in the rehabilitation process devote their core expertise to enable people to return to their working lives or to prevent them from becoming dependent on care. This in-volves a large team working in the many different areas. Right from an early point in time she realised that the key to success consists in pooling all the forces. "I had already become aware of the various different sides during my degree course", she says, recalling her time at university. "It only works if everyone pulls together. That's the only way to achieve the best possible quality in the given setting."

Karin Vogel pursued her personal development step-by-step from the end of the 1990s; stone-by-stone and employee-by-employee is the way that the Rehabilitation Centre itself also went about its own develop-ment. It opened in 1997 with the neurology clinic and the cardiology clinic as the first units. The "Oldenburg Model" then emerged in 2004 with the addition of the orthopaedic clinic. From then on, the organising body behind the centre consisted of all three hospitals in Oldenburg including the Pius hospital. "The special thing about the organising body is that it consists of one municipal hospital and two religious hospitals of different denominations." What's more. "In turn, they belong to the medical campus of the European Medical School at Oldenburg University."

Healthcare sector as catalyst

The rehabilitation centre plays a defined role in the region's clinic land-scape and sees itself as being fit for the future also when it comes to new requirements: "On-going strategic development is always geared to providing what patients need, also of course in accordance with general political conditions. Here in Oldenburg we are well situated, particularly with our links to the acute care hospitals and to the Univer-sity Hospital as well, in order to address and adjust to future challenges also in terms of demographic developments", explains the managing director.

Job motor also in future

The German healthcare sector keeps on hitting the headlines. Its outstanding relevance for society has become quite clear at the latest during the corona pandemic, with the situation in the hospi-tals acting as a crucial benchmark for many of the regulations that have been imposed. But it has also become apparent that there is a need for action in terms of staffing in many places.

Meanwhile the healthcare sector in Germany is a real job motor. According to the Federal Ministry of Health, nearly six million peo-ple work in healthcare, or one in eight of the working population. Demographic developments mean that the demand for workers is more likely to grow further in future. The healthcare sector is divided by definition into two markets: the first healthcare market encompasses the „classic" areas funded primarily by statutory and private health and care insurance. In the second healthcare market, the distinctions are not always so clear, but it mainly includes individual healthcare services, fitness and wellness.

Like many other parts of the economy, the healthcare sector is also struggling with a skills shortage. Those in positions of res-ponsibility are trying to solve the problem with innovative ideas. For example, new approaches have recently been introduced to care and nursing, where training is no longer specialised accor-ding to established areas but encompasses nursing, geriatric care and paediatric nursing in one generalised course of training.

Kaum überraschend ist derweil, dass Karin Vogel das Reha-Zentrum als attraktiven Arbeitgeber einstuft. Der aber gleichzeitig auch mit den branchenbekannten Problemen zu kämpfen hat, wie ein Blick auf den angesprochenen Fachkräftemangel beweist. „Wir sind ein sicherer Standort", betont sie und wirbt bei jungen Menschen dafür, sich in den Überlegungen für die Zukunftsplanung intensiv mit dem Sektor auseinanderzusetzen. „Das Gesundheitswesen ist schon heute ein attraktiver Impulsgeber auf dem Arbeitsmarkt. Es ist einer der zukunftsträchtigsten und innovativsten Sektoren mit viel Potenzial für Arbeitskräfte." Außerdem biete Oldenburg „alle Möglichkeiten der Aus- und Weiterbildung in den Gesundheitsberufen".

Dass Oldenburg ohnehin viel zu bieten habe, stellt auch für Karin Vogel kein Geheimnis dar. Kein Wunder, dass sie als hier Geborene nach dem Intermezzo in Studientagen wieder zurückgekehrt ist. „Liebevoll, urban und grün" – so bringt sie die Vorzüge der Stadt auf den Punkt. Und während in Zeiten der Corona-Pandemie viele Menschen bei der Frage nach den größten Entbehrungen das Reisen weit vorne platzieren, sieht sie die Umgebung in dieser Hinsicht als großes Plus: „Natürlich reise ich auch sehr gerne, aber hier im Umland gibt es so viel zu erleben, dass sich das alles gut aushalten lässt."

Das Leitbild mit Leben füllen

Um abschalten zu können, reiche ihr grundsätzlich schon ihr schönes Zuhause vor den Toren der Stadt. Hinzu kommen ihre Begeisterung für das Lesen und sportliche Betätigungen. Als begeisterte Kulturinteressierte schmerzen die coronabedingten Einschränkungen aber doch, schließlich mussten das von ihr hochgeschätzte Staatstheater oder das Theater Laboratorium ihre Türen schließen.

Das enorme Arbeitspensum in Einklang mit dem Familienleben zu bringen, sei durchaus stets eine große Herausforderung gewesen. „Mein Ehemann hat mitgezogen", sagt sie lachend. Zwei erwachsene Kinder mit klaren Vorstellungen seien das Ergebnis dieser Anstrengungen. Und natürlich auch die anhaltend hohe Motivation, sich für das Oldenburger Reha-Zentrum im Speziellen und die Rehabilitationsmedizin im Allgemeinen mit voller Kraft einzusetzen.

Ihre Erfahrungen aus den vielen Jahren im Berufsleben und aus der Teamarbeit mit Vertretern der unterschiedlichen Disziplinen lassen sich übrigens auch gut daraus ablesen, wie das Reha-Zentrum mit dem eigenen Leitbild umgeht. Das existiere eben nicht nur auf dem Papier, sondern werden von allen mit Leben gefüllt. „Unser Leitbild wurde unter Beteiligung aller Mitarbeiterinnen und Mitarbeiter des Reha-Zentrums erarbeitet", unterstreicht Karin Vogel. Mitarbeiterbefragungen würden regelmäßig durchgeführt, „um die Aktualität der Werte und Ziele" zu prüfen. So finde eine kritische Auseinandersetzung statt, an der alle beteiligt blieben. Das Projekt „Transparenz und Beteiligung", das von einem externen Team begleitet werde, ermögliche es den Mitarbeiterinnen und Mitarbeitern, sich selbst einzubringen. Das trage zur Mitarbeiterzufriedenheit bei – „was die Kennzahlen aus den Befragungen auch widerspiegeln", so Karin Vogel.

It is meanwhile no great surprise that Karin Vogel sees the Rehabilitation Centre as an attractive employer. At the same time, the facility is also struggling with the same problems as the rest of the healthcare sector, such as the skills shortage that has already been mentioned. "This is a safe and secure place to be", she emphasises, and encourages young people to take an intensive look at the healthcare sector when considering their plans for the future. "Today the healthcare sector already acts as an attractive catalyst on the job market. It is one of the most seminal and innovative sectors, with plenty of potential for workers." Oldenburg also offers "the full range of possibilities in terms of initial and advanced training for healthcare professionals".

It is no great secret for Karin Vogel that fact that Oldenburg has a lot to offer in general. It is therefore not surprising that the native of Oldenburg came back again after studying elsewhere. "Friendly, urban and green" is how she sums up the city's best points. And while many people put travel at the top of their to-do lists after the many sacrifices made during the corona pandemic, she sees a great advantage in her immediate surroundings under these circumstances: "Of course I love travelling, but there's so much to do in the surrounding area that it makes it easier to cope."

Filling the vision with life

To switch off, all she really needs is her lovely home just outside the city. She also enjoys reading and sport. But she's really feeling the corona restrictions when it comes to her cultural preferences, with her beloved State Theatre and the Theatre Laboratory both having to close their doors.

Achieving some kind of balance between her huge work load and the demands of family life has always been a real challenge. "My husband did his bit", she says with a laugh. Two grown-up children with their own clear ideas are the result of their efforts. And of course the continued high motivation to devote herself to rehabilitation medicine in general and Oldenburg's Rehabilitation Centre in particular.

The experience she has gained from the many years of her career and from working in a multidisciplinary team is also reflected in the Rehabilitation Centre's approach to its own vision. The vision does not just exist on paper but is filled with life by everyone involved. "All employees at the Rehabilitation Centre played a role in producing the vision", emphasises Karin Vogel. Regular employee surveys help check "that the values and goals remain up to date". This is a critical process that everyone remains involved in. The "transparency and involvement" project that is being facilitated by an external team gives the employees a chance to make their own contribution. This helps to keep the employees satisfied, "as reflected in the results of the surveys", says Karin Vogel.

No boredom in future either

And how does she see her own future after meanwhile two decades at the Rehabilitation Centre? Well, she certainly does not like to think

Rehabilitationszentrum Oldenburg

Oldenburg Rehabilitation Centre

Auch in Zukunft keine Langeweile

Und wie urteilt sie über ihren weiteren Weg nach inzwischen über zwei Jahrzehnten im Hause? Ans Aufhören jedenfalls mag sie noch nicht allzu oft denken. Außerdem muss ja auch noch gefeiert werden – 2022 nämlich, wenn das Zentrum seinen 25. Geburtstag begeht und dabei gewiss nicht nur auf die Entwicklung des Hauses zurückgeblickt wird, sondern auch auf die Rolle von Karin Vogel. Sie hat die Entwicklung schließlich fast von Beginn an mitgeprägt. „Immer gemeinsam mit den Chefärzten und den vielen Mitarbeitern", wie sie explizit betont.

Übrigens: Um ihr Netzwerk stetig zu erweitern und auch, „um politisch Einfluss zu nehmen", engagiert sich die Oldenburgerin zusätzlich in der Verbandsarbeit, unter anderem im Vorstand des Verbandes der Privatkliniken Niedersachsen und Bremen und als Mitglied im IHK-Be rat der Stadt Oldenburg. „Langweilig wird es nicht", sagt sie mit ihrem Lachen, das glücklicherweise keine Maske verhindern kann.

too much about stopping just yet. And there's a big celebration on the horizon in 2022 for the centre's 25th birthday, which is sure to offer an opportunity to look back not just at the development of the facility itself but also at the role that Karin Vogel has played. After all, she has helped shape its development almost right from the start. "Always together with the senior consultants and the many employees", as she stresses explicitly.

By the way, to continue expanding her network and also "have some political influence", Karin Vogel is involved in association work as well, including among others the management board of the association of private hospitals Lower Saxony and Bremen and as a member of the CIC advisory board for the city of Oldenburg. "I'm not going to get bored", she says with her laugh that, fortunately, no mask can prevent.

Information

Mit insgesamt neun Kliniken, zwei Belegabteilungen und 17 medizinischen Kompetenzzentren ist die Ammerland-Klinik GmbH in Westerstede eine Klinik der Schwerpunktversorgung mit regionalem und überregionalem Einzugsgebiet. Mit ca. 1.500 Mitarbeitenden und 145 Auszubildenden in 12 Ausbildungsberufen ist die Ammerland-Klinik zudem einer der größten Arbeitgeber im Landkreis Ammerland.

With altogether nine clinics, two private wards for affiliated physicians and 17 medical centres of excellence, Ammerland-Klinik GmbH in Westerstede is a tertiary care hospital serving a regional and supraregional catchment area. Furthermore, Ammerland-Klinik is also one of the largest employers in Ammerland district with approx. 1,500 employees and 145 trainees in 12 skilled occupations.

www.ammerland-klinik.de

Ammerland-Klinik GmbH

Im Jahr 1950 übernahm der Landkreis Ammerland das Kreiskrankenhaus, damals mit 100 Betten. Inzwischen blickt die Ammerland-Klinik – Akademisches Lehrkrankenhaus der Medizinischen Hochschule Hannover – auf eine mehr als 70-jährige Geschichte zurück. Als moderne Akutklinik mit 375 Betten werden heute jährlich rund 80.000 Patienten versorgt. Die hochwertige Behandlung basiert auf der fachlichen Kompetenz gut ausgebildeter und qualifizierter Mitarbeitender, dem Einsatz moderner technischer Geräte und einer umfassenden Begleitung und Betreuung.

In zertifizierten Krebszentren (Onkologisches Zentrum, Brust-, Darm- und Prostatazentrum) und zahlreichen zertifizierten Kompetenzzentren (zum Beispiel Endometriosezentrum und Stroke-Unit) wird mit gebündeltem Expertenwissen das optimale Behandlungskonzept für jeden Patienten erarbeitet. Außerdem betreibt die Klinik eine zertifizierte Chest-Pain-Unit und bietet zudem eine Neurologische Frühreha der Phase B. Deutschlandweit einzigartig ist die Kooperation mit dem Bundeswehrkrankenhaus Westerstede als Klinikzentrum Westerstede.

Getreu dem Gedanken „Gemeinsam für Gesundheit" arbeitet das regional verbundene Team mit Leidenschaft auf allen Ebenen zusammen, um die bestmögliche Versorgung der Patienten sicherzustellen.

In 1950, Ammerland district took over the district hospital with 100 beds in those days. Meanwhile, Ammerland-Klinik – academic teaching hospital of Hanover Medical School – looks back on more than 70 years of history. Today it is a modern acute care hospital with 375 beds and treats around 80,000 patients every year. The top quality treatment is based on the professional expertise of well trained and qualified staff, the use of modern technical equipment and comprehensive support and care.

The certified cancer centres (Oncology Centre, Breast Centre, Bowel Centre and Prostate Centre) and numerous certified centres of excellence (such as the Endometriosis Centre and the Stroke Unit) pool their expert knowledge to ensure every patient is offered the best possible treatment concept. The clinic also has a certified Chest Pain Unit and offers early phase B neurological rehabilitation. It also cooperates with the Armed Forces Hospital Westerstede in the Clinic Centre Westerstede as the only venture of its kind in Germany.

True to the spirit of "Together for Health", the regionally rooted team cooperates passionately on all levels to safeguard the best possible patient care.

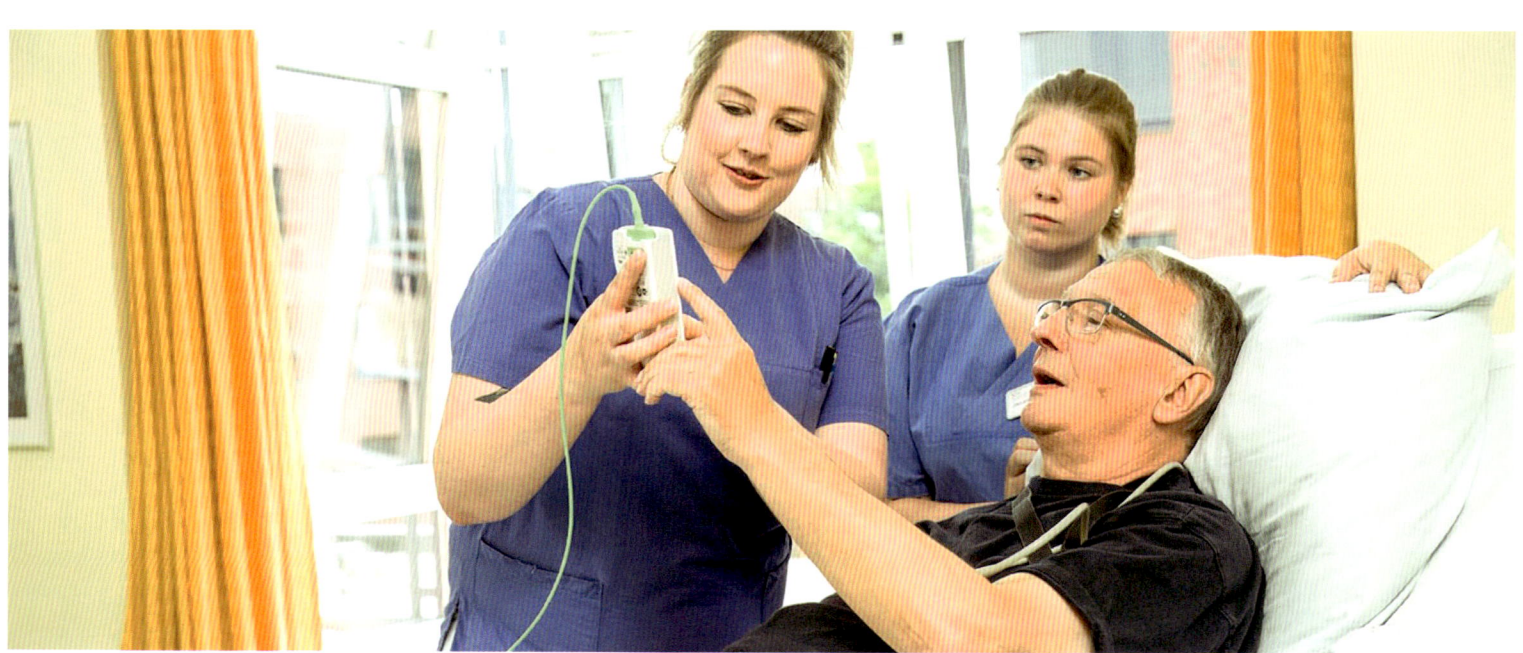

Zukunft aktiv gestalten

NWP geht zurück auf die Gründung der Bürogemeinschaft „Nord-West-Plan" Anfang 1979. Seit 1987 firmiert das Unternehmen als NWP Planungsgesellschaft mbH – Gesellschaft für räumliche Planung und Forschung.

Die NWP Planungsgesellschaft mbH ist heute ein interdisziplinär besetztes Ingenieur- und Planungsbüro mit einem Stamm von rund 35 bewährten Mitarbeiterinnen und Mitarbeitern und einem Tätigkeitsschwerpunkt in Norddeutschland. Im NWP-Team sind querschnittsorientiert alle Fachrichtungen vertreten, die in der räumlichen Planung gefordert sind und eine umfassende Planung und Beratung aus einer Hand ermöglichen.

Kerngeschäft ist seit 40 Jahren die Bauleitplanung. Hier erarbeitet und betreut NWP alle nach Baugesetzbuch vorgesehenen förmlichen öffentlich-rechtlichen räumlichen Planungen für Kommunen und private Investoren.

Actively shaping the future

NWP goes back to the start of 1979 when the office partnership "Nord-West-Plan" was founded. Since 1987, the company has been operating under the name NWP Planungsgesellschaft mbH (company for spatial planning and research).

NWP Planungsgesellschaft mbH today is an interdisciplinary engineering and planning firm with a workforce of around 35 proven employees, focusing its activities in North Germany. NWP's cross-sectional team covers all disciplines required for spatial planning, allowing for comprehensive planning and consulting from a single source.

For 40 years, the core business has been urban land-use planning. Here NWP elaborates and accompanies all formal public-law spatial planning for local authorities and private investors as stipulated in the building code.

NWP
Planungsgesellschaft mbH

Information

Gründungsjahr: 1979

Beschäftigte: etwa 35

Leistungsspektrum:
– Bauleitplanung
– Landschafts- und
  Umweltplanung
– räumliche
  Entwicklungsplanung
– Stadtplanung/Städtebau
– Freiraumplanung
– Dorfentwicklungsplanung
– Regionalplanung
– Organisation von
  Vergabeverfahren

www.nwp-ol.de

Year founded: 1979

Employees: about 35

Range of services:
– urban land-use planning
– landscape and environment
  planning
– spatial development planning
– urban planning/
  urban development
– open space planning
– village development planning
– regional planning
– organising contract awarding
  procedures

DIE LEUCHTTURM-WÄRTERIN

The Lighthouse Keeper

AUTORIN:
ALKE ZUR MÜHLEN

Kirchturmdenken und zukunftsorientierter Tourismus? Nein, das geht nicht zusammen – starke Regionen bündeln heute ihre Kräfte und Vorzüge. Dem gemeinsamen Auftreten geht oft ein intensiver Prozess voraus. Sonja Janßen hat sich mit der Destination Nordsee auf diesen Weg gemacht. Und ist überzeugt: Leuchttürme gibt es hier wahrlich genug, es müssen nur alle an einem Strang ziehen.

Ja, durch und durch Friesin sei sie, bestätigt Sonja Janßen. Sie liebe die Weite, das Meer, sogar das spontan umschlagende Wetter. „Wie das eigene Leben, man weiß nie was kommt." In Jever geboren, hat sie in Wilhelmshaven Tourismus studiert und wohnt heute in Hooksiel. Wer jetzt an das Klischee der in Stein gemeißelten Teezeit und wortkarge Menschen von sturem Gemüt denkt, den belehrt die 51-Jährige eines Besseren. Und ist selbst das Paradebeispiel. „Wir sind offen, hilfsbereit und direkt. Anonymität wie in den Großstädten kennen wir nicht." Wenn es früher dicke Luft gab, habe man sich getroffen und die Sache ausdiskutiert. Selbst wenn es dabei manchmal heiß herging, konnten sich danach alle wieder in die Augen sehen. „Heute werden gleich Bürgerinitiativen gegründet, statt sich an einen Tisch zu setzen", fügt sie nachdenklich hinzu.

Parish-pump mentality and future-oriented tourism? No, they don't go together. Today, strong regions pool their strengths and advantages. An intensive process is often involved before they reach this point. Sonja Janßen has set off on this path with the Destination North Sea. She is convinced that there are literally enough lighthouses here. It's just a case of getting everyone to pull together.

Yes, she is quintessentially a Frisian, confirms Sonja Janßen. She loves the wide horizons, the sea, the spontaneous changes in the weather. "It's like life itself: you never know what's coming." Born in Jever, she studied tourism in Wilhelmshaven and now lives in Hooksiel. The 51-year old soon dispels all carved-in-stone notions of teatime and taciturn, stubborn people. In fact, she's the very best example: "We are open-minded, direct, and always willing to help. Life's not anonymous here, not like in the big cities." When there was trouble brewing in the past, people would get together and talk about it. Even if it sometimes got a bit heated, at least you could look people in the eye afterwards. "But nowadays they get an action group going instead of sitting round a table", she adds thoughtfully.

Vielleicht hilft Nordseeluft den Einheimischen, einen kühlen Kopf zu bewahren. Sonja Janßen hat ihn jedenfalls. Diskutiert wird stets die Sache, das ist ihr wichtig. Nicht Befindlichkeiten, sondern das gemeinsame Ziel im Blick. Als Geschäftsführerin der Nordsee GmbH reicht der immerhin von Otterndorf bis Greetsiel. Sieben Küstenorte, zwei maritime Städte und ein Fährunternehmen betreiben unter dieser Marke überregionales Destinationsmarketing und versprechen Gästen ganzjährig Urlaubserlebnisse der besonderen Art. Bei Sonja Janßen laufen die Fäden zusammen – und nicht nur die der Dachmarketingorganisation.

Gestalten und nach vorne bringen

Im Mai 2020, mitten in den ersten Corona-Monaten, hat sie das Ruder übernommen. Sozusagen im Auge des Sturms. „Hier hat permanent das Telefon geklingelt", erinnert sie sich. Presse, Mitglieder, Verbände und Institutionen fragen nach Stellungnahmen, Rücksprache, Abstimmungen. Von Null auf Lockdown ohne Übergabe, denn ihre Position war länger unbesetzt. Aber kein Problem für die langjährige Geschäftsführerin des übergeordneten Tourismusverbands Nordsee, der im Gegensatz zur Nordsee GmbH keine Marketingaufgaben übernimmt. Sie kennt sich aus. Und kann sich beim operativen Marketing auf ihre Mitarbeiter verlassen. So fällt die Bilanz nach dem ersten halben Jahr positiv aus: „Es macht Spaß! Das Team ist sehr engagiert, die Zusammenarbeit mit den Küstenorten und Städten toll." Sie schätzt den Austausch, und dass sie „gestalten und nach vorne bringen" kann.

Der Sport hat Sonja Janßens Leben geprägt – auf viele Arten. „Mein Vater war Fußballer und Trainer, ich war sonntags immer mit auf dem Platz", erinnert sie sich. Bis Mitte 30 hat sie Handball gespielt und gelernt auf mehreren Positionen aktiv zu sein. „Aber nie als Führungsspielerin. Ich bin eher der Typ Zuspielerin." Immer ehrgeizig, immer im Hintergrund. Die Vorlagen liefern und das Team zusammenhalten. Eigenschaften, die Sonja Janßen ins Berufsleben mitgenommen hat. „Wenn ich in Sitzungen bin, an Besprechungen teilnehme oder sie leite, versuche ich jede Person mit ihren Bedürfnissen zu verstehen. Und dann überlege ich, wie wir es schaffen können, alle an einem Strang zu ziehen." Weggefährten schätzen sie dafür.

Kehrtwende und Neustart mit 28

Vater Handwerker, Mutter im Pflegebereich tätig, später Badefrau in einer Kureinrichtung – das Leben der Familie Janßen war stets auf Sicherheit und Planbarkeit ausgerichtet. So ließ Sonja sich zur Bürogehilfin ausbilden, auch wenn es sie eigentlich in die „große weite Welt" zog. Zunächst kein Platz für Selbstverwirklichung. Sie heiratete früh, wurde Mutter, konnte auch dem Leben als Hausfrau etwas abgewinnen. Doch die Ehe scheiterte, Sonja Janßen stand mit 28 Jahren vor dem Neustart. Alleinerziehend und alleinverantwortlich. Für das Arbeitsamt war sie im ursprünglich gelernten Beruf angesichts des technologischen Fortschritts nicht mehr vermittelbar. „Ich musste mein Leben komplett ändern."

Ihre Entscheidung: Flucht nach vorn, mit Abitur und Studium Tourismusmanagement. Zu einer Zeit, in der an Ganztagsbetreuung nicht zu denken war. Einige Mitmenschen belächelten ihre Pläne – sie zeigte es ihnen. Organisierte die Kinderbetreuung erst mit Freunden, gründete später einen Elternverein mit privatem Hort. Hausaufgaben und

Strandkörbe sind typisch für die Küstenorte der Region und beliebt bei Alt und Jung.

"Strandkörbe" (wicker seats with sides and tops to offer protection from the elements) are typical for the region's seaside resorts and popular with old and young.

Butjadingen statt Balneario

In Deutschland sind 2,92 Millionen Erwerbstätige direkt in der Tourismusbranche beschäftigt – über 290.000 Arbeitsplätze sichert die Branche allein in Niedersachsen. Von der bundesweiten Bruttowertschöpfung in Höhe von 105,3 Mrd. Euro werden etwa 20,7 Mrd. Euro zwischen Hannover und Nordseeküste erwirtschaftet. In der neuen nationalen Tourismusstrategie wird die Bedeutung der Branche nicht nur für die inländische Wertschöpfung, sondern auch für die Lebensqualität der in Deutschland lebenden Menschen und die internationale Stabilität betont.

Die Nordseeküste zählt mit fast 14 Millionen Übernachtungen zu den beliebtesten Urlaubsregionen im Lande. Im Bundesvergleich liegt sie damit an vierter Stelle. Im September 2014 wurde die Niedersächsische Nordsee die erste zertifizierte Thalasso-Region Europas. Das typische Reizklima ist seitdem zur etablierten Marke geworden. Und damit doppelt wertvoll. Auch die Auszeichnung des Wattenmeeres als UNESCO-Welterbe spielt den Verantwortlichen in die Karten.

Schon in „normalen" Jahren regelmäßig ausgebucht, wird die Küste im Pandemie-Jahr 2020 zum Sehnsuchtsort neuer Inlandsurlauber. Butjadingen statt Balneario – wo, wenn nicht hier, lässt sich entspannt durchatmen. „Aufenthalt in der Natur" und „Spazierengehen" stehen bei den Lieblingsaktivitäten deutscher Urlauber ohnehin mit an oberster Stelle. Die Deutschen sind im eigenen Land weiterhin die wichtigste Reisegruppe – Tendenz durch Corona steigend.

2020 war – nach zehn Rekordjahren in Folge – für den Tourismus dennoch ein Jahr herber Verluste. Bundesweit rechnete der Deutsche Tourismusverband allein für die Monate März, April und Mai Umsatzausfälle in Höhe von 35 Mrd. Euro hoch. Etwa 20 Mrd. davon fehlten durch ausbleibende Tagesgäste, die im Schnitt 28,80 Euro an deutschen Zielorten für Verpflegung, Einkäufe oder Unterhaltung ausgeben.

Butjadingen instead of Balneario

Germany has 2.92 million employees working directly in the tourism sector, which accounts for more than 290,000 jobs in Lower Saxony alone. Of Germany's total gross value creation amounting to 105.3 billion Euro, about 20.7 billion Euro are generated between Hanover and the North Sea coast. The new national tourism strategy emphasises the sector's significance not just for domestic value creation but also for the quality of life for people living in Germany, as well as international stability.

The North Sea coast with nearly 14 million overnight stays is one of the most popular holiday regions in the country, ranking fourth in a national comparison. In September 2014, Lower Saxony's North Sea cost became the first certified thalasso region in Europe. Since then, the typical bracing climate has become an established brand. Which makes it twice as valuable. And having the Wadden Sea declared a UNESCO's World Heritage Site plays into the hands of those in charge.

Regularly booked to capacity in "normal" years, during the 2020 pandemic the coast became a new place of longing for German holidaymakers, now that going abroad was no longer an option. Butjadinger instead of Balneario – where else are conditions so ideal for taking a relaxed breather? When all is said and done, "spending time in nature" and "going for a walk" are among the favourite things German holidaymakers like to do. After all, the Germans themselves are the most important tourist group in their own country, and the trend continues to increase thanks to corona.

Even so, 2020 was a bitter year of negative figures for the tourism sector, following ten record-breaking years in succession. On a national scale, the German Tourism Association calculated short-falls in sales of 35 billion Euro just for the months of March, April and May. Of this total, about 20 billion Euro was accounted for by the absence of daytrippers, who on average spend 28.80 Euro at German destinations on food, shopping or entertainment.

Perhaps the North Sea air helps locals to keep a clear head. Sonja Janßen has a clear head at least. What matters to her is that people discuss the actual issue. Not focussing on feelings or sensitivities but with an eye on the shared objective. As CEO of Nordsee GmbH, she has to keep her eye on an area extending from Otterndorf to Greetsiel. This is the destination marketing brand for seven coastal towns, two maritime cities and a ferry company, attracting visitors by promising a special holiday experience all year round. Sonja Janßen holds the reins in her hands, and not just for the marketing organisation.

Shaping things and moving them forward

It was in May 2020 that she took the helm, in the middle of the first corona months. You could say in the eye of the storm. "The telephone was ringing all the time", she remembers. The press, members, associations and institutions all wanted statements, feedback, consultations. From zero to lockdown with no proper handover because the job had been vacant for quite some time. In fact, it wasn't a problem for the long-standing CEO of the higher level North Sea Tourism Association which does no marketing, in contrast to Nordsee GmbH. She knows what she's doing. And she knows she can rely on her staff when it comes to operative marketing. And so on the bottom line at the end of six months, it's all quite positive: "It's fun! The team is highly committed, and working with the coastal towns is going really well." She enjoys the contact and sharing, and the fact that she's "shaping things and moving them forward".

Sonja Janßen's life has been shaped by sport – in many different ways. "My father loved football and was a coach, so I spent Sundays at the football ground", she recalls. She herself was an active handball player until her mid-30s, and learnt to play in various different positions. "But I never took the lead. I'd rather keep passing the ball around." Always ambitious, always in the background. Making good moves and keeping the team together. Qualities that serve Sonja Janßen well in her professional life. "When I attend or chair meetings, I try to understand every one sitting round the table with their individual needs. And then I think about what we can do to get us all to pull together." That's something people like about her.

U-turn and new start aged 28

Her father was a skilled craftsman, her mother worked in healthcare and was later a bathing attendant in a spa. The life of the Janßens was always secure and well planned. So Sonja trained as an office clerk, although she felt the pull to see the "big wide world". Initially, she simply didn't have time to do her own thing. She married early and had a child, started to see that life as a housewife could be good. But the marriage failed and Sonja Janßen had to start over again at the age of 28 years. On her own, as a single mum and responsible for everything. The employment agency said she was no longer employable in her original job due to technical progress. "I had to change my life round completely."

She decided to take the plunge and did her A-levels, followed by a degree in tourism management. This was all at a time when full-time childcare was out of the question. Some people ridiculed her plans, but she soon showed them. Friends helped to look after her child at first, before she founded a parent's association with private childcare. In the evening,

Prüfungsvorbereitungen erledigte sie abends, neben Jobs in der Gastronomie und als Pflegehelferin im Klinikum Sanderbusch. Das Geld war immer knapp. „Bei allem wollte ich meinem Sohn trotzdem eine unbeschwerte Kindheit ermöglichen", sagt sie heute. Und erinnert sich, dass sie auch mal kurz ans Aufgeben gedacht habe. „Aber das ist nicht meine Mentalität."

Sie biss sich durch, das Studieren machte Spaß. Zu ihren Professoren pflegt sie noch heute ein gutes Verhältnis. Aus „Neugierde zu Menschen und Themen" begann sie sich politisch zu engagieren, zog für die SPD in den Wangerländer Rat. Fraktionszwang? Im Vordergrund der politischen Arbeit steht sie zu ihren Überzeugungen und hat dabei immer den Blick auf die ganze Region. Stark war mitunter der Gegenwind – und er kostete auch Freundschaften. Auf vordere Listenplätze verzichtete sie, wollte lieber als Person gewählt werden.

Nächste Aufgabe: Kräfte bündeln

Lange hat Sonja Janßen andere in den Fokus gestellt – irgendwann wurde es zu viel. Ob die stetig steigenden Wochenstunden, die fehlende Vertretung, das politische Engagement oder die Verantwortung für ihr Kind ausschlaggebend waren, kann sie rückblickend nicht mehr sagen. Nur so viel: 2014 kam die Erkenntnis, „dass ich mehr für mich tun muss". Sie wurde nachsichtiger mit sich, schuf Freiräume. Für Freundschaften, für Spaziergänge, für Sport. Sie begann, über Lebensziele nachzudenken, verwirklichte sich noch einen Jugendtraum: das Kitesurfen zu lernen.

Heute wirkt Sonja Janßen sehr reflektiert. Sie weiß, was sie vom Leben erwartet, will die Heimat und die Vorzüge der Region genießen. Urlaub gehört dazu, vielleicht mal eine kleine Weltreise. Die kulturelle Intensität New Yorks reizt sie genauso, wie der Besuch eines Formel-1-Rennens in Abu Dhabi. Sie liebt ihre Jobs weiterhin, aber die Jobs sind nicht mehr ihr ganzes Leben.

Der Posten der Geschäftsführung bei der Nordsee GmbH ist keine Vollzeitstelle. Um Operatives kümmert sich ihr Team. Für Sonja Janßen kam der Job daher im Mai 2020 „on top". Mehr Stunden arbeitet sie beim Tourismusverband Nordsee e. V., den sie seit 2006 führt. Dessen Kernaufgabe: die Lobbyarbeit für den Standort- und Wirtschaftsfaktor Tourismus. Doch damit nicht genug: Auch die Geschäftsführung des Tourismusverbands Niedersachsen e. V. liegt seit 2009 in ihren Händen.

Vielleicht ist es der langjährige Einblick in die Veränderung touristischer Destinationen, der sie in ihrem aktuell wichtigsten Projekt aus Überzeugung „am eigenen Ast sägen" lässt. So nennt sie es selbst. „Einzelne Gemeinden können sich überregionale Sichtbarkeit nämlich nicht leisten", betont sie. Und von außen falle es schwer, die vielen Marken zu verstehen. „Wir wollen deshalb die Kräfte auf einer zentralen Ebene

she did her homework and revised for the exams, as well as working in the hospitality trade and as a care assistant in Sanderbush hospital. There was never enough money. "Despite it all, I still wanted to give my son a carefree childhood", she says today. And remembers there were times when she briefly thought of giving up. "But that's not my mindset."

She gritted her teeth together, and enjoyed life as a student. She still has a good relationship with her professors to this day. Her "curiosity about people and issues" saw her start to get involved in politics and was elected to Wangerland local council for the SPD. Was she forced to toe the party line? Well, her political activities are based more on her own convictions, always with an eye to the region as a whole. The headwind was strong at times and even cost friendships. She refrained from being shortlisted for the party, preferring to be elected as a person instead.

Next task: pooling forces

For a long time, Sonja Janßen always focused on others, before it all eventually got too much. Whether it was the constantly longer working hours, no-one to stand in for her, her political commitment or the responsibility for her child – exactly what it was she cannot say in retrospect. Suffice to say that in 2014 she realised "I need to do more for myself". She started being less hard on herself and gave herself more space. Space for friendships, for going for walks, for sport. She started to reconsider her aims in life and actually fulfilled a dream from her youth and learned how to do kitesurfing.

Today Sonja Janßen comes across as a discerning person. She knows what she expects from life, she wants to enjoy her home and all the region has to offer. Holidays, yes, or possibly even a little trip around the world. She would love to experience the cultural intensity of New York, or go to a Formula 1 car race in Abu Dhabi. She is still passionate about her work, but it no longer dictates her whole life.

Being CEO of Nordsee GmbH is not a full-time job. Her team deal with the operative side of things. For Sonja Janßen, the job came "on top" in May 2020. She spends more time working for the North Sea Tourism Association, where she has been in charge since 2006. The main task here entails lobbying for tourism and the role it plays for the location and economy. But that's not all: since 2009, she's also been CEO of Lower Saxony Tourism Association.

Perhaps it's her longstanding insights into the changes in tourism destinations that give her the conviction to "undermine her own position" in what is currently her most important project. At least that's the way she puts it. "Some places simply cannot afford to be visible on a broader scale"; she says. And the many brands can be confusing for outsiders. "The aim is therefore to pool forces on a central level for a stronger overall image." The tourism association and its members are

Sonnenuntergang bei Hooksiel

Sunset near Hooksiel

bündeln und gemeinsam stärker auftreten." Daher arbeitet der Tourismusverband gemeinsam mit seinen Mitgliedern intensiv an einem Prozess zum Aufbau eines neuen Destinationsmanagements.

Gemeinsam mit dem Verbandsvorsitzenden Landrat Sven Ambrosy, Friesland, koordiniert Sonja Janßen dieses Projekt als Geschäftsführerin des Tourismusverbands Nordsee – eine Mammutaufgabe und gleichzeitig ihr Meisterstück in Sachen „alle an einen Tisch bringen". Dennoch: An zukünftige Führungsaufgaben denkt sie nicht. In einen Bundesverband zieht es sie ebenso wenig. Und Macht oder Gehalt allein reizen sie nicht. Was dann? „Auch ein Fußball-Bundestrainer kann irgendwann keine Impulse mehr geben", ist die gebürtige Frieslanderin überzeugt. „Vielleicht wechsle ich 2021 einfach den Verein."

therefore currently working hard at establishing a new kind of destination management.

Together with Sven Ambrosy, the association chairman and district administrator for Frisia, Sonja Janßen is coordinating this project as CEO of the North Sea Tourism Association. It's a huge task, and at the same time her masterpiece in terms of "getting everyone round the table". Even so, she's not thinking about taking on further management roles. Nor is she interested in anything on a national level. And power or money alone aren't the attraction. So what is it then? "Even the best coaches reach a point where they've no longer got anything to give", says the born Frisian with conviction. "Perhaps I'll simply change the club in 2021."

Das Wasserwerk Großenkneten ist eines von insgesamt 15 Wasserwerken des OOWV, die rund um die Uhr frisches Trinkwasser liefern.

The waterwork in Großenkneten is one of altogether 15 waterworks operated by the OOWV, supplying fresh drinking water 24/7.

Information

Gründungsjahr: 1948; Abwasserentsorgung seit 1999
Mitarbeiter: rund 875, davon 50 Auszubildende
Versorgungsgebiet Trinkwasser: 7.524 Quadratkilometer
Versorgte Einwohner: 1,105 Mio.
Trinkwasserabgabe: rund 85 Mio. Kubikmeter/Jahr
Gereinigtes Abwasser: rund 30 Mio. Kubikmeter/Jahr

Year founded: 1948; wastewater disposal since 1999
Employees: approx. 875, including 50 trainees
Supply area for drinking water: 7,524 square kilometres
Supplied population: 1.105 million people
Supplied drinking water: around 85 million cubic metres p.a.
Treated wastewater: around 30 million cubic metres p.a.
www.oowv.de

Starker Partner rund ums Wasser

Qualitativ hochwertiges Trinkwasser und umweltgerecht gereinigtes Abwasser – dafür steht der OOWV. Der Wasser- und Bodenverband ist ein zuverlässiger Partner in der kommunalen Trinkwasserversorgung. Mit 15 Wasserwerken versorgen wir Haushalte, Industrie, Gewerbe, Landwirtschaft und kommunale Einrichtungen. In 46 Kläranlagen reinigen wir das Abwasser mit moderner und energiesparender Technik. Mit rund 875 Mitarbeiterinnen und Mitarbeitern gehört der Oldenburgisch-Ostfriesische Wasserverband zu den wichtigen Arbeitgebern im Nordwesten.

Der OOWV setzt auf effiziente Technik, umfassende Fachkenntnis und investiert fortlaufend in die Instandhaltung, Modernisierung und den zukunftsfähigen Ausbau der Anlagen und des Leitungsnetzes. So schafft der OOWV die Voraussetzung für Wachstum und eine weiterhin zuverlässige Trinkwasser- und Abwasserentsorgung.

OOWV
Oldenburgisch-Ostfriesischer Wasserverband

Strong partner for water

Top quality drinking water and environmentally friendly wastewater treatment: that is what OOWV stands for. The Water and Soil Association is a reliable partner for ensuring supplies of municipal drinking water, with 15 waterworks working to meet the demand from households, industry, trade, agriculture and municipal facilities. 46 sewage plants treat wastewater with modern, energy-saving technology. The OOWV (Oldenburgisch-Ostfriesischer Wasserverband) has a workforce of approx. 875 employees, making it one of the key employers in the North West.

It advocates efficient technology as well as comprehensive technical know-how and is constantly investing in the maintenance, modernisation and future-oriented extension of the plants and pipe network. The OOWV thus creates the prerequisites for growth and for constantly reliable drinking water supplies and wastewater disposal.

II. Oldenburgischer Deichband

Deichbau und Küstenschutz

Das Verbandsgebiet des II. Oldenburgischen Deichbandes umfasst rund 84.300 Hektar und liegt bis zu zwei Meter unter dem Meeresspiegel. Die gesamte Deichstrecke in Verantwortung des II. Oldenburgischen Deichbandes beträgt 142 Kilometer. Der Hauptdeich beginnt in Oldenburg und verläuft an der Hunte (linkes Ufer) bis zum Huntesperrwerk, entlang der Weser sowie entlang der Nordsee und weiter entlang des Jadebusens bis Dangast.

Der aktive Küstenschutz wird in Zeichen der Prognose steigender Meeresspiegel in Zukunft immer wichtiger. Die Deiche für ihre zukünftigen Schutzaufgaben in der Standfestigkeit zu ertüchtigen und bei Bedarf zu erhöhen, ist eine der Hauptaufgaben des Verbandes und nicht selten eine besondere ingenieurtechnische Herausforderung.

So auch bei der Deicherhöhung im südlichen Jadebusen am Jade-Wapeler Siel (im Bild). Im Vorfeld mussten das Sielbauwerk mit den zwei Sielzügen Ost und zwei Sielzügen West je 70 Meter Länge sowie die Auslaufleitungen des Mündungsschöpfwerk Schöpfwerk bautechnisch an die zukünftigen Gegebenheiten angepasst werden. Beide Bauwerke müssen auf ihrer Küstenseite Hochwasser und Sturmfluten abwehren und gleichzeitig die Oberflächenentwässerung des Hinterlandes sicherstellen.

Information

Gründungsjahr: 1855
Mitarbeiter: 12
Aufgaben: Deichbau, Deich-unterhaltung, Küstenschutz, Deichschäfereien

Daten:
- ca. 142 km Deichstrecke
- ca. 84.300 ha Schutzgebiet
- ca. 61.500 Einzelgrundstücke
- Schutz von ca. 135.000 Arbeitsplätzen
- Schutz von ca. 220.000 Menschen

Year founded: 1855
Employees: 12
Tasks: dike construction and maintenance, coastal protection, sheep-farming on the dikes

Data:
- approx. 142 km of dikes
- approx. 84.300 protected area
- approx. 61.500 individual plots of land
- protection for approx. 135.000 jobs
- protection for approx. 220.000 people

www.zweiter-oldenburgischer-deichband.de

Dyke construction and coastal protection

The territory covered by the II. Oldenburgischer Deichband (2nd Oldenburg Dyke Association) encompasses around 84,300 hectares and is up to two metres below sea level in places. The II. Oldenburgischer Deichband is responsible for altogether 142 kilometres of dykes. The main dyke begins in Oldenburg and runs along the river Hunte (left bank) to the Hunte flood barrier, along the river Weser and then along the North Sea coast to Dangast on the Jade Bay. Active coastal protection will become increasingly significant in future in the context of rising sea levels. One of the main tasks for the association consists in strengthening the stability of dykes to make them fit for their future protection tasks and making them higher if necessary, something that more often than not presents particular engineering challenges.

This was demonstrated for example in raising the level of the dyke at the Jade-Wapel lock gates (illustrated) in the south part of Jade Bay. Firstly, it was necessary to adjust the construction of the tidal lock with the two gates to the east and the two gates to the west each measuring 70 in length, together with the discharge outlets of the estuary pumping station, to bring them in line with the future conditions. Both structures have to offer protection from flooding and storm surges from the North Sea, while at the same time ensuring surface drainage from the land behind the dyke.

HK GmbH

Vermessung und Dokumentation

Unser Portfolio umfasst Vermessungsarbeiten, Bodenortungen sowie CAD-, BIM- und GIS-Arbeiten aller Art. Insbesondere für Energieversorger und Telekommunikationsanbieter sind wir ein namhafter und verlässlicher Dienstleister.

Von unseren fünf deutschen Standorten in Niedersachsen, Brandenburg und Bremen aus betreut unser fachkundiges Personal unsere Kunden mit neuester Technik und Software.

Im Bereich Geoinformation treiben wir die Digitalisierung, den Breitbandausbau und die Energiewende in Deutschland voran.

Our range encompasses surveying work and ground inspections together with CAD, BIM and GIS work of all kinds. We are a renowned, reliable service provider particularly for utility and telecommunication companies.

From our five German sites in Lower Saxony, Brandenburg and Bremen, our expert staff support our customers with the very latest technology and software.

When it comes to geoinformation, we are a driving force behind Germany's digitalisation, broadband expansion and energy transition.

Information

Gründungsjahr: 1983	**Year founded:** 1983
Mitarbeiter: über 90	**Employees:** more than 90
Leistungsspektrum:	**Range of services:**
– Vermessungsarbeiten	– surveying work
– Bodenortung	– ground inspection
– Dokumentation und Digitalisierung von Geodaten für verschiedenste Branchen	– documenting and digitalising geodata for many different branches

www.hk-gmbh.info

Atlas Airfield GmbH

Der Flugplatz Ganderkesee bietet nicht nur einen hohen Freizeitwert, sondern ist auch ein wichtiger Wirtschaftsfaktor für die Gemeinde Ganderkesee und die gesamte Region. Rund 20 Unternehmen und Vereine haben sich im Laufe der Jahre am Atlas Airfield angesiedelt mit insgesamt mehr als 100 Beschäftigten, die am Flugplatz Ganderkesee ihre berufliche Heimat gefunden haben. Die Atlas Airfield GmbH (AAG) betreibt seit über 50 Jahren die Flugleitung inkl. Tankstelle und ist verantwortlich für alle fliegerischen Belange am Flugplatz Ganderkesee. 2015 wurde der Flugschul- und Charterbetrieb aufgenommen. Dafür stehen den Piloten und Flugschülern 6 Flugzeuge unterschiedlicher Muster zur Verfügung. Außerdem sind Motor-, Segel-, Ultraleicht-, Drachen-, Gleitschirm- und Modellflieger sowie Ballonfahrer und Fallschirmspringer in Ganderkesee zu Hause.

Ganderkesee airfield not only offers high recreational value but is also an important economic factor for the eponymous municipality and for the whole region. In the course of time, around 20 companies and associations have settled at Atlas Airfield, providing a working home for altogether more than 100 employees. For more than 50 years, Atlas Airfield GmbH (AAG) has been responsible for air traffic control and operates the filling station, as well as managing all aeronautical aspects of Ganderkesee airfield. Flying schools and charter business began here in 2015, offering pilots and student pilots 6 aircraft of different types. Ganderkesee is also home to gliders, powered airplanes and ultralight aircraft, hang-gliders, paragliders and model airplanes as well as balloon pilots and skydiving enthusiasts.

Information

Inbetriebnahme: 1969	**Commissioned:** 1969
Mitarbeiter: In den verschiedenen Unternehmen und Vereinen auf dem Gelände sind rund 100 Personen beschäftigt.	**Employees:** around 100 people work in the various companies and associations on the airfield.
Infrastruktur: Flugschulen, Vereine, Charter, Vermietung, Tankstelle, Hotel & Restaurant, Veranstaltungen, Eventhangar u. v. m.	**Infrastructure:** flying schools, associations, charter, airplane hire, filling station, hotel & restaurant, events, event hangar and much more besides

www.flugplatz-ganderkesee.de

Delmenhorst-Harpstedter Eisenbahn GmbH (DHE)

Persönlich. Flexibel. Leistungsstark.
Seit 1912 sorgt die DHE für serviceorientierte Mobilität auf Schienen und Straßen unserer Region und auch darüber hinaus. Kundennähe und Servicequalität werden bei uns großgeschrieben – und das stellen wir im ÖPNV mit unseren Linienbussen jeden Tag aufs Neue unter Beweis: vom Bürgerbus und dem Nachtschwärmer bis hin zu Sonderfahrten. Im Reisebusverkehr organisiert die DHE Betriebsausflüge, Leserreisen, Klubtouren oder Klassenfahrten – innerhalb Deutschlands und ins europäische Ausland. Als Eisenbahn-Verkehrsunternehmen bieten wir unseren Güterverkehrskunden auf rund 25 Kilometern eigener Gleise einen attraktiven Schienengüterverkehr zwischen Delmenhorst und Harpstedt.

Personal. Flexible. Efficient.
Since 1912, DHE has stood for service-oriented mobility by rail and road in our region and beyond. We focus particularly on customer proximity and service quality, as demonstrated everyday anew with our local public transport buses. We also operate "citizens buses" and night services as well as special trips. DHE also offers coaches for company excursions, book tours, club tours or school outings, in Germany and also to other European countries. As a railway undertaking, we offer our freight customers attractive rail freight transport between Delmenhorst and Harpstedt on our own tracks covering a distance of around 25 kilometres.

Information

Gründungsjahr: 1912	**Year founded:** 1912
Mitarbeiter: etwa 45	**Employees:** about 45
Leistungsspektrum:	**Range of services:**
– Linienbusverkehr	– public service buses
– Reisebusverkehr	– coach services
– Schienengüterverkehr	– rail freight transport
– Werkstatt für Straßen- und Schienenfahrzeuge	– workshop for road and rail vehicles

www.dhe-reisen.de

Fähren Bremen-Stedingen GmbH

Information

Gründungsjahr: 1993	**Year founded:** 1993
Mitarbeiter: etwa 80	**Employees:** around 80
Fährverbindungen:	**Ferry connections:**
Farge–Berne	Farge–Berne
Blumenthal–Motzen	Blumenthal–Motzen
Vegesack–Lemwerder	Vegesack–Lemwerder
Anteilseigner:	**Shareholders:**
Land Bremen	State of Bremen
Landkreis Wesermarsch	Wesermarsch district

www.faehren-bremen.de

Die Fähren Bremen-Stedingen GmbH betreibt die Fährverbindungen zwischen dem Stadtgebiet Bremen-Nord und den gegenüberliegenden niedersächsischen Gemeinden im Landkreis Wesermarsch. Über 13.000 Menschen nutzen täglich unsere drei Weserfähren Farge–Berne, Blumenthal–Motzen und Vegesack–Lemwerder. Der Fährverkehr wird an 365 Tagen im Jahr durchgeführt.

Unsere Fährkunden kommen insbesondere aus der Metropolregion Bremen-Oldenburg im Nordwesten mit seinen zehn Landkreisen und fünf kreisfreien Städten bzw. Stadtgemeinden sowie dem Landkreis Rotenburg/Wümme rechts der Weser und den Landkreisen Wittmund, Aurich, Leer, Emsland und der Stadt Emden links der Weser.

The ferry company Fähren Bremen-Stedingen GmbH operates the ferries between the North of Bremen and the municipalities of the Wesermarsch district in Lower Saxony on the other side of the river Weser. Every day, more than 13,000 people use our three Weser ferries Farge–Berne, Blumenthal–Motzen and Vegesack–Lemwerder. The ferries operate 365 days a year.

Our passengers come particularly from the Metropolitan Region Bremen-Oldenburg in the North West with its ten districts and five independent towns or boroughs as well as the Rotenburg/Wümme district on the right side of the river and the districts of Wittmund, Aurich, Leer, Emsland and the city of Emden on the left side of the river.

DER WELTVERBESSERER

The Global Philanthropist

AUTOR:
THORSTEN LANGE

Die Wissenschaft ist werturteilsfrei. Es geht um Objektivität, Validität und Reliabilität. Ist in diesem neutralen Umfeld auch Platz für Meinung und Mission? „Nein!", sagen die Traditionalisten. „Ja!", sagt dagegen Professor Dr. Nick Lin-Hi, Inhaber der Professur für Wirtschaft und Ethik an der Universität Vechta. Er forscht nicht der reinen Erkenntnis wegen – er forscht, um die Welt zu verändern. Damit ist er sehr erfolgreich. Doch: Damit eckt er auch an.

Alles begann mit der Dotcom-Blase. Eigentlich wollte Nick Lin-Hi, geboren 1980 in Offenbach und aufgewachsen in Hildesheim, Mediziner werden. Doch dann spekulierte er Ende der 1990er-Jahre am Neuen Markt. Er beschäftigte sich mit Märkten, Branchen, Unternehmen – und entschied sich für ein BWL-Studium. Dort drängte sich die Wirtschaftsethik zunächst nicht auf. „Anfangs habe ich gedacht: Was für ein Quatschthema", erinnert er sich. Doch schließlich fand er einen Zugang.

Lin-His Kommilitonen wurden Investmentbanker und Unternehmensberater, er setzte voll auf Nachhaltigkeit und schwamm damit gegen Strom und Schwarm. Das zahlte sich aus: Noch während der Arbeit an seiner Dissertation wurde erstmals im großen Maßstab über die Klimaverantwortung von Unternehmen diskutiert. Die großen Konzerne suchten plötzlich händeringend nach Experten. Davon gab es in Deutschland nur wenige, unter ihnen aber: Nick Lin-Hi.

Science isn't about judgements It's about objectivity, validity and reliability. Is this neutral approach also to opinion and mission? "No!" say the traditionalists. "Yes!" counters Prof. Dr. Nick Lin-Hi, Professor for Business and Ethics at the University of Vechta. He doesn't pursue research to generate pure knowledge. He pursues research to change the world. And he does it very well. But he also causes offence.

It all began with the dot-com bubble. Born in Offenbach in 1980 and grew up in Hildesheim. Actually, he wanted to become a doctor. But then at the end of the 1990s he started speculating on the New Market. He looked at the markets, industries and companies – and decided to do a business degree. Business ethics wasn't really on his horizon at first. "Initially I thought 'What a lot of rubbish!'", he remembers. But eventually he found a way of dealing with it.

Lin-Hi's fellow graduates became investment bankers and management consultants, he opted for sustainability, thus going against the flow and the crowd. It paid off: even before he finished his dissertation, discussions about corporate responsibility for the climate had already begun on a large scale. Major companies suddenly started searching desperately for experts. There weren't many in Germany, but one of them was Nick Lin-Hi.

Durch seine Arbeit erlangte er große Bekanntheit; und die sollte sich bald noch steigern. Am 17. September 2008 meldete die US-Investmentbank Lehmann Brothers Insolvenz an und stürzte die globalen Finanzmärkte ins Chaos. Unweigerlich wurde auch hier die Frage nach der gesellschaftlichen Verantwortung der Konzerne gestellt. Zu genau diesem Zeitpunkt vollendete Lin-Hi in Leipzig seine Doktorarbeit. Titel: „Eine Theorie der Unternehmensverantwortung: Die Verknüpfung von Gewinnerzielung und gesellschaftlichen Interessen". Damit war er einmal mehr der Mann der Stunde.

Der Erweckungsmoment der Wirtschaftsethik

Warum war Lin-Hi der Zeit immer voraus? Er zuckt mit den Schultern. „Es ist eigentlich ganz einfach: Ich beschäftige mich Themen, die ich gesellschaftlich für wichtig halte," erklärt er. „Mein Treiber war immer Nachhaltigkeit. Ich will positiv wirken, etwas verändern. Bei bald zehn Milliarden Menschen, wachsendem Wohlstand und begrenzten Ressourcen ist eines klar: So wie es ist, kann es nicht weitergehen."

Weiter ging es aber für ihn. Nur wenige Monate nach der Promotion folgte der Ruf an die Universität Mannheim. Dort baute Lin-Hi die Juniorprofessur für Corporate Social Responsibility (CSR) auf. Die Finanzkrise war der Erweckungsmoment der Wirtschaftsethik – nun wurde sie in die Tat umgesetzt. „Ich war live dabei, als das Thema durch die Decke ging", freut er sich noch heute. Und er war nicht nur dabei – er prägte es entscheidend. „Ich habe immer um die Ecke gedacht, etwas anders als die anderen", erklärt er. „Dafür braucht man Selbstbewusstsein und Risikofreude, dafür braucht man aber auch Frustrationstoleranz. Weil längst nicht alles funktioniert." So galt lange Zeit der Konsument als Auslöser für Veränderungen – doch der leidet an einer Doppelmoral: Er hat gute Vorsätze, hält sich aber nicht daran. „Der Konsument ist ein Bremser", konstatiert Lin-Hi bewusst provokant.

Vieles andere funktionierte allerdings. So konnte Lin-Hi in der Textilindustrie zeigen, dass sich eine Verbesserung der Arbeitsbedingungen in den Fabriken positiv auf die Wettbewerbsfähigkeit auswirkt. Zudem skalierte er die Verantwortung neu: Ihm ging es nicht um Sozialprojekte oder Scheckübergaben. „Die Konzernlenker mussten erstmal verstehen, dass es ums Kerngeschäft geht", erzählt er. Das heißt: keine Korruption, keine Menschenrechtsverletzungen in der Lieferkette, keine Umweltverschmutzung. Damals empfanden das viele als anstrengend – heute ist es längst etabliert.

Vechta bietet Raum für Kopfarbeit

Zwischenbilanz: Diplom mit 24, Promotion mit 28, Habilitation mit 35, Stammgast bei DAX-Konzernen, in Ministerien und Staatskanzleien, und sogar in Zeitschriften wie „Capital" und „GQ". Sie zählten Nick Lin-Hi zu „Deutschlands junger Elite" bzw. den „40 wichtigsten Männern in Deutschland unter 40 Jahren". Wie erreicht man so schnell so viel? Ein Antrieb liegt vielleicht in der Familie: Sein Großvater flüchtete im chinesischen Bürgerkrieg nach Madagaskar, sein Vater kam über ein Carl-Duisberg-Stipendium nach Deutschland. Doch Lin-Hi nennt andere Gründe: „Realistisch gesehen: Glück und Naivität." Das klingt angenehm bescheiden, aber man muss es entschlüsseln: Glück steht dafür, zur richtigen Zeit das Richtige zu tun. Und Naivität meint den Mut, sich festzulegen und klar zu positionieren. Beides erfordert viele weitere Talente und Kompetenzen.

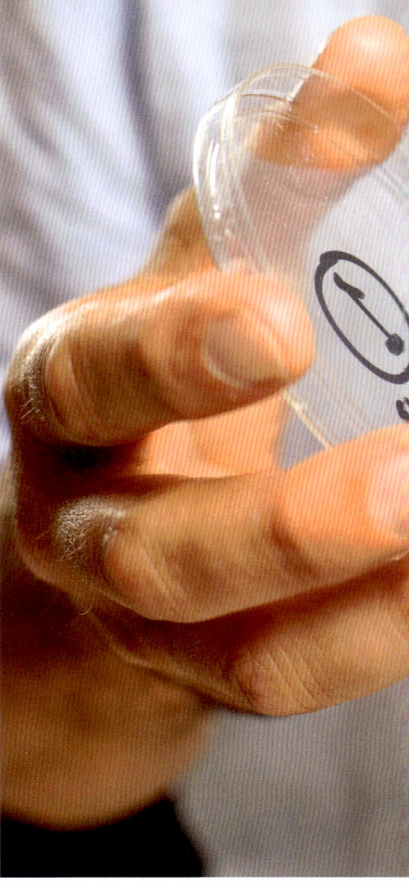

Nach Professor Lin-His Überzeugung liegt die Zukunft der Ernährungswirtschaft in kultiviertem Fleisch.

Professor Lin-Hi believes that the future of the food industry lies in cultured meat.

Neue Strahlkraft aus Nordwest

Die Leuchttürme des Oldenburger Landes standen lange Zeit ausschließlich an der Küste, nicht auf einem Campus. Das hat sich geändert. Die Bedeutung der Wissenschaft hat in der jüngeren Vergangenheit erheblich zugenommen. Das stärkste Signal dafür mag Oldenburgs Auszeichnung als deutsche „Stadt der Wissenschaft" im Jahr 2009 gewesen sein. Doch es gibt weitere.

Über 18.000 Studierende sind in Oldenburg an der Carl von Ossietzky Universität und der Jade Hochschule eingeschrieben, etwa 5.500 an der Universität Vechta und der Privaten Hochschule für Wirtschaft und Technik. Das sind 11 bzw. 16 Prozent der jeweiligen Bevölkerung. Zu den stärksten Studiengängen zählen jene mit gesellschaftlichen Effekten: Bildungs- und Sozialwissenschaften, Umweltwissenschaften und Nachhaltigkeit, Zukunftsfragen und Transformationsprozesse. Ein weiterer roter Faden ist der Praxisbezug: Es geht nicht nur um Forschung, sondern auch um Transfer und Anwendung. Über Projekte wie die „Innovative Hochschule" wird eine enge Verzahnung mit Wirtschaft, Gesellschaft, Behörden und Kultur angestrebt. Kein Zweifel: Die Wissenschaft versteht sich als integraler Bestandteil der Region – und der Campus ist ein moderner Marktplatz des Wissens.

Die gewachsene Bedeutung hat auch konkrete Effekte. So wird das starke Wachstum Oldenburgs – bei Bevölkerung und Gewerbesteuer – immer wieder auf die Innovationskraft der Hochschulen zurückgeführt. In ihrem Dunstkreis entstanden viele Start-ups, die heute Motor der wirtschaftlichen Entwicklung sind. Ein ähnliches Bild in Vechta: Junge Talente zieht es weniger in die Metropolen, sie bleiben vielfach vor Ort. Es dürfte kein Zufall sein, dass die Gründerkultur in Vechta besonders ausgeprägt ist.

Die meisten Leuchttürme des Oldenburger Landes stehen nach wie vor an der Küste. Doch im Landesinneren sind einige hinzugekommen – und sie strahlen besonders hell. Um sie herum ist ein Wissenschaftssektor entstanden, der einerseits wichtige Entwicklungen vor Ort anstößt, andererseits weit über die Grenzen der Region hinauswirkt. Das ist die neue Strahlkraft aus Nordwest.

His work brought him widespread recognition, which was soon set to increase even further. On 17 September 2008, the US investment bank Lehmann Brothers filed for bankruptcy, plunging the global financial markets into chaos. Inevitably, here too the question about corporate social responsibility arose. It was exactly at this point in time that Lin-Hi completed his doctoral thesis in Leipzig. Title: "A theory of corporate responsibility: linking the generation of profits with the interests of society". Once again, he was the man of the hour.

The wake-up call for business ethics

Why was Lin-Hi always ahead of his time? He shrugs his shoulders. "It's actually quite easy: I'm totally focused on topics that I think have social significance," he explains. "I've always been driven by sustainability. I want to have a positive effect, to change something. If you take the fact that the world's population is approaching 10 billion people, together with growing prosperity and limited resources, one thing is quite clear: things can't continue as they are."

But things did continue for him. Just a few months after receiving his doctorate, he was called to the University of Mannheim. Here Lin-Hi established the junior professorship for Corporate Social Responsibility (CSR). The financial crisis acted as the wake-up call for business ethics. Now was the time to put it into practice. "I was there on the spot when the whole thing took off", he recalls with pleasure even today. And he wasn't just on the spot: he played a crucial role. "I've always thought outside the box, differently to the others", he explains. "It takes plenty of confidence, you must be willing to take risks but you also have to be able to tolerate frustration. Because not everything is going to work well." For a long time, consumers were seen as the trigger of change. But consumers struggle with double standards: they have good intentions, but don't always live up to them. "Consumers act as a brake", says Lin-Hi, deliberately provocative.

But lots of other things do work well. In the textile industry for example, Lin-Hi was able to show that improving the working conditions in the factories would have a positive impact on competitiveness. He also put responsibility on a new scale: he wasn't concerned with social projects or handing over cheques. "First of all, company leaders had to understand that it's about their core business", he says. In other words, no corruption, no violations of human rights in the supply chain, no pollution. Back then, this was a real challenge for many. Today, it is well established.

Vechta offers space for brainwork

Meanwhile: degree with 24, doctorate with 28, professor's qualification with 35, regular guest at DAX-listed companies, ministries and state chancelleries, and even in magazines such as "Capital" and "GQ". Nick Lin-Hi has been ranked among "Germany's Young Elite" or the "40 most important men in Germany younger than 40 years". How can someone achieve so much so quickly? It may be in the family: his grandfather fled from the Chinese civil war to Madagascar, while a Carl Duisberg scholarship brought his father to Germany. But Lin-Hi knows of other reasons: "To be quite realistic: I was lucky. and I was

New radiant power from the North West

For a long time, lighthouses in the Oldenburger Land were only found on the coast, not on a campus. But that has changed. Science has recently started to play a far more significant role. The strongest signal may be Oldenburg's award as the German "City of Science" in 2009. But there are other signs too.

In Oldenburg, more than 18,000 students are enrolled at the Carl von Ossietzky University and at Jade University of Applied Sciences, together with about 5,500 at the University of Vechta and the private PHWT University. They account for 11 or 16 percent of the respective population. The most popular degrees include those with a social slant: education and social sciences, environmental sciences and sustainability, future studies and transformation processes. The practical approach runs through them all like a red thread. It's not just about research: it's also about transfer and application. Projects such as the "Innovative University" are aimed at close integration with business, society, authorities and culture. Without any doubt, the academic sector with its knowledge and science sees itself as an integral part of the region. And the campus is a modern market place for knowledge.

The growing significance also has quite specific effects. Oldenburg's strong growth, in terms of population and trade tax, is repeatedly attributed to the innovative powers of the universities. Many start-ups have emerged from their orbit and act today as the driving force behind economic development. The situation in Vechta is similar: young talents are less likely to be drawn to the big cities, they simply stay where they are. It cannot be a coincidence that Vechta has a pronounced start-up culture.

Most lighthouses in the Oldenburger Land are still to be found on the coast. But they have been joined by a few further inland that shine with a particularly bright radiance. Around and about them, a science sector has developed that triggers important local developments while also having an impact that extends way beyond the borders of the region. That is the new radiant power from the North West.

Nach der Habilitation folgte im Jahr 2015 der Wechsel ins beschauliche Vechta. Warum? „Das Angebot kam genau zum richtigen Zeitpunkt – und die Stelle passte inhaltlich perfekt", erklärt Lin-Hi. Und wie sieht ein typischer Tag des Professors aus? „Nach dem Aufstehen geht es gleich an den Schreibtisch. Hier arbeite ich dann zügig die To-Dos des Tages ab." Der Rest der Zeit bewegt sich zwischen unsichtbarer Denk- und Konzeptionsarbeit – auch mal beim Kleepflücken auf der Wiese – und beinahe manischen Schreibphasen. „Dann bin ich vollkommen im Tunnel, total konzentriert."

Die Nähe zur Agrar- und Ernährungsbranche empfindet Lin-Hi als Glücksfall: „Hier steht die nächste riesige Transformation zur Nachhaltigkeit an. Ich darf so einen umwälzenden Prozess jetzt zum zweiten Mal mitmachen!" Allerdings gibt es derzeit noch viel Widerspruch. Wenn man Schweinebauern prophezeit, die Zukunft der Ernährung liege im künstlich erzeugten Fleisch, dann fliegen einem die Herzen nicht unbedingt zu. Aber das ficht Lin-Hi nicht an. Er ist überzeugt, dass disruptive Veränderungen nötig sind. „Mein Tipp ist immer: Seht mich als Hofnarr. Der durfte Wahrheiten aussprechen, ohne bestraft zu werden." Und seine Wahrheit ist: Entweder gestaltet man den Wandel aktiv mit – oder man wird irgendwann mitgerissen. „Transformation geht nicht behutsam. Das hat zuletzt die Autoindustrie gedacht – und dann kam Tesla." Seine Überzeugung: Die aktuellen Probleme kann man nicht mit dem vorhandenen Instrumentarium lösen; sonst wären sie gar nicht da. Der Schlüssel sind Innovationen wie das kultivierte Fleisch, die große ökologische und ethische Vorteile bieten. Generell geht es Lin-Hi um eine größere Akzeptanz von Veränderungen: „Wir diskutieren immer nur die Risiken von Technologien. Ich will aber auch über das Risiko sprechen, wenn wir Technologien nicht nutzen!"

Der Traum vom Olympiastadion

Diese Haltung will er verbreiten, die Menschen sollen sie verstehen. Dafür gibt er zahllose Interviews und hält Vorträge mit Titeln wie „Darwinismus im Kuhstall – was die Milchwirtschaft von Tesla lernen sollte". Damit seine Botschaft ankommt, muss er vereinfachen und zuspitzen. Das ist dünnes Eis. Würde die Boulevardpresse berichten, stünde auf der Titelseite: „Chinesischer Professor nimmt uns das Schnitzel weg!" Dennoch fühlt sich Lin-Hi wohl auf der Bühne. Er spricht verständlich, eindringlich und unterhaltsam. „Wenn ich ins Olympiastadion mit 80.000 Leuten müsste, das würde mir gefallen", schmunzelt er. Und die Wertfreiheit der Wissenschaft – sieht er keinen Verstoß? „Nein. Die Forschung hat ein Instrumentarium für die Kommunikation, das nutze ich." Es brauche natürlich eine wissenschaftliche Basis. Sei die vorhanden, könne man durchaus versuchen, etwas zu verändern. „Ich habe zwei Töchter. Denen habe ich gesagt: Papa kümmert sich darum, dass ihr eine Zukunft habt. Ich stehe da also in der Pflicht."

naive." That sounds pleasantly modest, but needs some explanation. Being lucky means doing the right thing at the right time. And being naive means having the courage to make a commitment and take a clear stand. Both demand many other talents and skills.

After qualifying as a professor, he moved to the tranquil setting of Vechta in 2015. Why Vechta? "The offer came at exactly the right time, and the job is exactly what I wanted", ecplains Lin-Hi. And what does a typical day look like for the professor? "After getting up, I'll go straight to the desk and work quickly through the tasks of the day." The rest of the time is taken up with invisible thinking and conceptual work. This can also include picking clover in the meadow, and phases of writing that can be almost manic. "When I start writing, I'm so concentrated it's like I'm in a tunnel."

Lin-Hi sees the proximity to the agrifood sector as a stroke of good luck: "This is where the next huge transformation towards sustainability will happen. This is the second time I've been part of such a revolutionary process!" But in the meantime, there is also a lot of opposition. Pig farmers don't like being told that the future of the food industry lies in artificial meat. But Lin-Hi doesn't contest this. He is convinced that disruptive changes are needed. "I always tell people to see me as the jester. A jester is allowed to tell the truth without being punished." And his truth is: either you play an active role in shaping change, or you it will simply drag you along in its wake. "You can't do transformation by being cautious. That's what the car industry thought: then Tesla arrived." He is convinced that the current problems can't be solved with the existing instruments, otherwise the problems wouldn't be there. The key to innovation is cultivated meat that offers great ecological and ethical advantages. In general terms, Lin-Hi would like to see a greater acceptance of change: "All we do is discuss the risks of technology. But I also want to talk about the risks if we don't use technology!"

Dreaming of the Olympic stadium

He wants to spread this viewpoint and help people to understand it. Besides countless interviews, he also gives lectures with titles such as "Darwinism in the cowshed – what dairy farming can learn from Tesla". He has to simplify and hone what he says to make sure the message gets through. He's moving on thin ice. If the tabloids were to report about this, the front pages would claim: "Chinese professor takes away our schnitzels!" Even so, Lin-Hi feels at ease on a stage. What he says is understandable, penetrating and entertaining. "A venue like the Olympic stadium with an audience of 80,000 would be great", he grins. And what about the fact that science doesn't make judgements: is that not an infringement? "No. Research has a set of instruments for communication, that's what I use." A scientific basis is of course prerequisite. Once that's there, that's when you can start trying to change things. "I have two daughters. I said to them: I'm going to make sure that you have a future. So I've put myself under an obligation."

In der Textilindustrie konnte Professor Lin-Hi zeigen, dass sich eine Verbesserung der Arbeitsbedingungen in den Fabriken positiv auf die Wettbewerbsfähigkeit auswirkt.

In the textile industry for example, Professor Lin-Hi was able to show that improving the working conditions in the factories would have a positive impact on competitiveness.

Die technologische Zukunft sieht Nick Lin-Hi oft genau voraus – aber wie ist es mit der eigenen? Was würde ihn reizen? „Definitiv der Mars! Da wäre auch kultiviertes Fleisch gefragt." Und sonst? „Die Fusion von Ernährung und Medizin – über implantierte Chips und Echtzeit-Analyse von Vitaldaten durch einen Algorithmus in der Cloud. Oder Rassismus gegenüber humanoiden Robotern." Das klingt nach Science-Fiction. Aber eines hat man bei Lin-Hi schnell gelernt: Alles kommt früher, als man denkt.

Was also ist Professor Dr. Nick Lin-Hi – Pionier? Missionar? Futurist? Agent provocateur? Vielleicht all das, aber ganz sicher eines: ein Weltverbesserer – im wortwörtlichen Sinne. Dank seiner Vorstöße kann die Gesellschaft Wandel gestalten, bevor er sie mitreißt. Und Probleme lösen, bevor sie entstehen. Mit seinem Tempo und Temperament eckt Lin-Hi zwar manchmal an. Doch das gehört bei Weltverbesserern eben dazu.

Nick Lin-Hi often predicts exactly where the technological future is going. But what about his own future? What would he really like to do? "Oh, definitely go to Mars! That would need cultivated meat too." And what else? "I'd like to see a fusion of food and medicine, with implanted chips and real-time analysis of vital data using an algorithm in the cloud. Or racism against humanoid robots." Now it's starting to sound like Science Fiction. But there's one thing we've quickly learnt from Lin-Hi everything happens sooner than you expect.

So what is Professor Dr. Nick Lin-Hi? A pioneer? A missionary? A futurist? An agent provocateur? Perhaps all those things, but he is also quite definitely one thing a philanthropist, someone who wants to improve the world. Thanks to his initiatives, society is able to shape change before it simply gets dragged along. And change problems before they occur. Lin-Hi with his pace and temperature sometimes causes offence. But that's simply "par for the course" for philanthropists.

DER ENTWICKLER

The Developer

AUTOR:
CLAUS SPITZER-
EWERSMANN

Es klingt ein wenig wie bei Asterix und Obelix: „Wir sind das kleine gallische Dorf und zeigen es dem Rest der Welt." So beschreibt Wolfgang Nebel seine Motivation, Oldenburg dauerhaft einen Platz auf der Landkarte der wichtigsten Informatikstandorte zu sichern. Mit der Idee des IT-Campus dürfte ihm das gelingen.

Oldenburg? Nein, die Stadt sei ihm damals völlig unbekannt gewesen, sagt Wolfgang Nebel mit leichtem Schmunzeln. Er habe erst einmal nachschauen müssen, wo sie überhaupt liegt – damals, 1993, als er einen Ruf auf eine Professur am Fachbereich Informatik an der hiesigen Universität erhielt. Allerdings: „Kaum vor Ort, habe ich mich sofort in die Stadt verliebt."

Und diese Liebe hat Bestand bis heute: „Oldenburg ist für mich der beste Lebensmittelpunkt." Zudem zählt der in Wanne-Eickel Geborene und in Bad Pyrmont Aufgewachsene längst zu den Persönlichkeiten, die mit ihren Ideen und ihrem Wirken die Stadt an der Hunte maßgeblich prägen.

It sounds a bit like Asterix and Obelix: "We are like that small village of indomitable Gauls still holding out against the rest of the world." That's how Wolfgang Nebel describes his motivation for making sure Oldenburg has a permanent place on the map of key IT places. The IT Campus is what should make it happen.

Oldenburg? Well, actually, to start with he knew nothing about it, says Wolfgang Nebel with a slight grin. He had to look the place up to see where it was, back then in 1993 when he was called to be professor for IT at Oldenburg University. But then, "as soon as I arrived, I found myself falling in love with the place".

A love that lasts to the present day: "Oldenburg is the best place I can think of to live." After starting life in Wanne-Eickel and growing up in Bad Pyrmont, today he has become one of those inspiring personalities whose ideas and activities play a major contribution in shaping the city on the river Hunte.

Ein Trostpflaster aus der Landeshauptstadt

Als Oberbürgermeister Jürgen Krogmann dem 64-Jährigen im Dezember 2020 den Wirtschaftspreis „Oldenburger Bulle" überreicht, lobt er dessen Engagement als „standortfördernd, nachhaltig und weitsichtig". Es sei „von unschätzbarem Wert für den Ruf der Stadt Oldenburg", heißt es in der Laudatio. Die Auszeichnung habe ihn sehr berührt, bekennt Nebel wenige Wochen später. Vor allem, weil er sie nicht nur als Anerkennung seiner persönlichen Leistung sieht, sondern ebenso als Würdigung der gesamten Oldenburger Informatik.

Tatsächlich wäre ein Einzelner wohl kaum in der Lage gewesen, der Informatik zu dem Stellenwert zu verhelfen, den sie heute innehat. „Das war damals nur ein kleiner, eher mäßig ausgestatteter Fachbereich", weiß Wolfgang Nebel zu berichten. Oldenburg hatte den Zuschlag für den Studiengang 1984 erhalten – mehr oder minder als Trostpflaster dafür, dass der Niedersächsische Landtag die erhoffte Einrichtung eines Fachbereichs Jura abgelehnt hatte. Denkbar knapp mit 85 zu 83 Stimmen. So nahmen zum Wintersemester 1985/1986 die ersten 55 Abiturienten ihr Studium der Informatik in Oldenburg auf.

Der nächste wichtige Schritt bestand in der Gründung des Oldenburger Forschungs- und Entwicklungsinstituts für Informatikwerkzeuge und -systeme, kurz: OFFIS. Es wurde 1991 gegründet, in einer Zeit ohne Smartphones und weltweite Vernetzung. Ziel war es, zwischen der universitären Grundlagenforschung und der Wirtschaft mit ihrem Bedarf an innovativen Produkten und Dienstleistungen eine Brücke zu schlagen. Die Sache ließ sich gut an. So gut, dass man im Sommer 1995 von angemieteten Räumen im Haarenesch ins frisch errichtete eigene Gebäude auf dem alten Fleiwa-Gelände im Ziegelhofviertel umzog und hier den Grundstein für Oldenburgs neues IT-Quartier legte.

Über Rheinland-Pfalz und Hamburg zum beruflichen Gipfel

Wolfgang Nebel verweist auf die treibenden Kräfte jener Tage: „Ohne Professor Volker Claus und Professor Hans-Jürgen Appelrath gäbe es das alles hier nicht." Die beiden Professoren hatten die Nische erkannt, in der Oldenburg sich positionieren konnte, und dann die richtigen strategischen Überlegungen angestellt. Insbesondere der 2016 verstorbene Appelrath – übrigens 2005 ebenfalls mit dem „Oldenburger Bullen" geehrt – habe tiefe Spuren hinterlassen. Und er war es auch, der Nebel einst fragte, ob er ihm nicht als Vorstandsvorsitzender von OFFIS folgen wolle.

Der Familienvater war damit auf dem Höhepunkt seiner beruflichen Laufbahn angelangt. Auf das erfolgreich absolvierte Studium der Elektrotechnik in Hannover hatte er 1986 die Promotion am Fachbereich Informatik der Universität Kaiserslautern folgen lassen zu einem Thema aus dem Bereich der Mikroelektronik. Es schlossen sich eine sechsjährige Industrietätigkeit bei Philips Semiconductors in Hamburg und Lehraufträge an der TU Hamburg Harburg an. Einen Ruf an die Universität im österreichischen Linz lehnte Nebel ab. „Denn ich hatte festgestellt, dass ich mich in Norddeutschland ein bisschen wohler fühle", räumt er rückblickend ein. So kam der Ruf nach Oldenburg genau zur rechten Zeit.

Nach dem Ja für das Bleiben im Norden nimmt die Karriere weiter Fahrt auf. Von 1996 bis 1998 ist Wolfgang Nebel Dekan des Fachbereichs Informatik, in den Jahren 2001 und 2002 Vizepräsident der Universität Oldenburg. Bereits seit 1998 zählt er zum damals drei-

Das Labor für intelligente Energiesimulation und -automatisierung (Smart Energy Simulation and Automation, kurz: SESA) am Oldenburger OFFIS – Institut für Informatik

The Smart Energy Simulation and Automation laboratory (or SESA for short) at the OFFIS Institute for Information Technology in Oldenburg.

IT-Branche erwartet 2021 Wachstumsschub

Der Bundesverband Informationswirtschaft, Telekommunikation und neue Medien e. V. (Bitkom) geht für das Jahr 2021 von einem Wachstum um 2,7 Prozent auf 174,4 Mrd. Euro aus. Bis zum Ende des Jahres werden die Unternehmen in Deutschland voraussichtlich 20.000 zusätzliche Jobs schaffen. Aktuell sind 1,2 Millionen Menschen in der Branche beschäftigt. Aber es könnten noch weit mehr sein, denn rund 124.000 Stellen blieben nach Bitkom-Angaben Ende des Vorjahres unbesetzt.

Die IT-Branche klagt seit Jahren über einen massiven Fachkräftemangel. Er wirkt sich längst auch auf das Tempo der Digitalisierung aus, zudem bleiben in vielen Unternehmen Aufträge unerledigt. Einer der Gründe liegt im nach wie vor geringen Anteil an Frauen. Nicht einmal drei von zehn Beschäftigten in Niedersachsen sind weiblich. Die Informationstechnologie gilt weiterhin als Männerdomäne.

Der Branchenverband erwartet im Bereich der Informationstechnik rasante Zuwächse. Die Corona-Krise habe in vielen Unternehmen gezeigt, wo Nachholbedarf besteht. So geht man davon aus, dass bei der IT-Hardware – also insbesondere bei Computern, Servern und Peripheriegeräten – nachgerüstet wird, ebenso wie bei der Software. Auch Schulungs- und Beratungsdienstleistungen werden 2021 zulegen. Weitere Wachstumstreiber liegen in der verstärkten Hinwendung zu Cloudlösungen sowie im Konzept „Miete statt Kauf". Das Geschäft mit gemieteten Servern, Netzwerk- und Speicherkapazitäten verzeichnete zuletzt bereits jährliche Zuwachsraten von bis zu 40 Prozent und ist mittlerweile ein Milliardenmarkt.

Im globalen Vergleich spielt der deutsche Markt weiterhin eine eher untergeordnete Rolle. Die Experten von Bitkom rechnen 2021 mit einem Anteil von lediglich 3,9 Prozent. Die Tendenz sei eher rückläufig, heißt es, weil die Investitionen und Ausgaben in anderen Ländern schneller wachsen, besonders im asiatischen Raum. Wachstumsspitzenreiter sind Indien (+13,5 Prozent) und China (+7,1 Prozent).

2021: IT sector experts to see a surge in growth

Bitkom, Germany's digital association, expects to see growth of 2.7 percent to reach 174.4 billion Euro in 2021. By the end of the year, IT companies in Germany are expected to create 20,000 additional jobs, in an industry currently employing 1.2 million people. But there could be so many more, with around 124,000 jobs still vacant at the end of last year according to Bitkom.

A massive skills shortage has been plaguing the IT sector for years and is meanwhile impacting on the pace of digitisation, while jobs are simply not getting done in many companies. One of the reasons for this is the low share of women. Less than three of ten employees in Lower Saxony are women. The IT sector continues to be a man's world.

Bitkom is forecasting rapid growth in the field of information technology. The corona crisis has shown many companies where their deficits are. It is expected that there will be a great demand for IT hardware, particularly for computers, servers and peripheral devices, as well as software. Training and consulting services are also expected to grow in 2021. The increased usage of cloud solutions and "renting instead of buying" options are other factors driving growth. Business with rented servers, networks and memory capacities has already reported annual growth rates of up to 40 percent and is meanwhile worth billions.

The German market continues to play a minor role in a global comparison. The Bitkom experts expect to see a share of only 3.9 percent in 2021. The trend is even on the decrease due to the faster growth in investment and expenditure in other countries, particularly in Asia. Growth leaders are India (+13.5 percent) and China +7.1 percent).

Consolation prize from the state capital

When Mayor Jürgen Krogmann presented the 64-year old with the "Oldenburg Bull" business award in December 2020, he paid tribute to him as a visionary committed to sustainability promoting the city. The Mayor's speech praised him as being of "inestimable value for the name of Oldenburg". He felt truly honoured by the award, Nebel admits a few weeks later, mainly because he sees it as commendation for the whole IT scene in Oldenburg and not just recognition of his personal achievements.

Indeed, one person on their own could scarcely have raised IT to its current position of significance. "In those days, it was just a small, poorly equipped department", recalls Wolfgang Nebel. Oldenburg was granted permission to launch the IT course in 1984, more or less as consolation prize for the state parliament rejecting the initial request to establish a law department. A close decision with 85 to 83 votes. And so the first 55 students were welcomed on Oldenburg's IT course in the winter semester 1985/1986.

The next important step was to found OFFIS as a research and development institute for IT tools and systems. OFFIS was founded in 1991, long before smart phones and long before the world wide web. The aim was to act as a bridge between pure academic research and the business sector with its demand for innovative products and services. It went well right from the start. So well that in summer 1995 OFFIS moved from rented premises on "Haarenesch" to its own newly built facilities on the former Fleiwa grounds in the "Ziegelhofviertel", laying the cornerstone for Oldenburg's new IT district.

Via Rhineland-Palatinate and Hamburg to the pinnacle of his career

Wolfgang Nebel gives a special mention to the main personalities involved in driving the developments back then: "None of this would exist without Professor Volker Claus and Professor Hans-Jürgen Appelrath". The two professors saw the niche emerging for Oldenburg and then implemented the right strategy. Appelrath in particular, who died in 2016 and was also awarded the title "Oldenburg Bull" in 2005, had a profound influence on developments. He was also the one who approached Nebel about succeeding him as Chairman of the Board at OFFIS.

This brought the family father to the pinnacle of his career. After studying electrical engineering in Hannover, he gained his PhD in IT at the University of Kaiserslautern with a dissertation on microelectronics. This was followed by six years of working in industry for Philips Semiconductors in Hamburg as well as teaching at TU Hamburg Harburg. Nebel turned down the opportunity of moving to Linz University in Austria. "Meanwhile I realised that North Germany suited me better", he admits looking back. And so the appointment in Oldenburg came at just the right time.

After deciding to stay in the north, his career continued to pick up speed. From 1996 to 1998 Wolfgang Nebel was dean of the IT depart-

köpfigen Vorstand des OFFIS-Instituts. Und er übernimmt im Juni 2005 die Aufgaben des Vorstandsvorsitzenden, so wie von seinem Vorgänger Hans-Jürgen Appelrath erhofft.

Weg vom Bauchladen, hin zum Profil

In den Folgejahren kümmert sich Nebel vorrangig um eine Konzentration auf die Kernaufgaben. Oldenburg hat sich dank OFFIS fürs Erste als IT-Standort etablieren können, wie 2009 selbst August-Wilhelm Scheer, der damalige Präsident des Branchenverbands Bitkom, bei der Eröffnung der CeBIT-Messe in Hannover betont. Nun geht es darum, die richtigen Akzente zu setzen. Man will weg vom digitalen Bauchladen und sich ein klareres, zukunftsorientiertes Profil schaffen. So fokussiert sich OFFIS mehr und mehr auf vier Forschungs- und Entwicklungsschwerpunkte: Energie, Gesundheit, Produktion und Verkehr. In allen Bereichen gehört die Informatik zu den entscheidenden Innovationsmotoren.

Doch damit nicht genug. Wolfgang Nebel ist schon ein Stück weiter. Er denkt stets etwas größer als andere, entwickelt Visionen und glaubt an ihre Realisierbarkeit. Oldenburg habe gute Voraussetzungen, um dauerhaft einen Platz auf der Landkarte der wichtigsten Informatikstandorte zu finden, bekräftigt er. Sein Plan: ein IT-Campus. Er soll zum Innovationsquartier für Digitalisierung und Gesellschaft werden. Ende November 2020 kommt die Nachricht aus Berlin, dass der Bund das ambitionierte Projekt mit 35 Mio. Euro fördern wird.

Vordenker Nebel, der sich selbst als „durchaus ungeduldig" einschätzt, sieht sich bestätigt. „Der Campus soll mein Abschlussprojekt sein", sagt er. Noch bevor der Bescheid aus der Hauptstadt eingetroffen ist, hat er nämlich die Weichen neu gestellt, sich vom OFFIS-Vorsitz zurückgezogen und den Staffelstab an Professor Sebastian Lehnhoff weitergereicht. Im Vorstand will er noch bis 2022 bleiben und das Projekt IT-Campus weiter vorantreiben. Und danach? „Um den IT-Campus werden sich dann Sebastian Lehnhoff mit Holger Peinemann und der OFFIS-Vorstand kümmern." Aber zur Eröffnungsfeier, vermutlich im Jahr 2024, möchte er gern kommen.

Vom Segeln und Fotografieren

Die Zeit bis dahin und darüber hinaus wird er sinnvoll nutzen und neben mehreren weiteren Mandaten in Wissenschaft und Wirtschaft vor allem dem Privaten mehr Raum geben. Weit oben auf der Liste der Hobbys steht das Segeln. Gern auch in etwas raueren Gewässern. Unternehmer Peter Waskönig, den er als „väterlichen Freund" bezeichnet, habe ihn mehrmals mit auf Nord- und Ostseetörns genommen. Auch den Atlantik hat er bereits überquert. „Eine tolle Erfahrung, das würde ich sofort wieder machen." Aber während Nebel im Job auf Teamwork setzt, ist er im Boot am liebsten mit seiner Frau allein. „Wir können uns hundertprozentig aufeinander verlassen." Kein Wunder: Beide kennen sich seit gut 50 Jahren.

ment at Oldenburg University, where he was Vice President in 2001 and 2002. He has been one of the then three-man Executive Board at OFFIS since 1998, assuming the role of Chairman in June 2005, as hoped for by his predecessor Hans-Jürgen Appelrath.

Less of a pick-and-mix, more of a defined profile

Since then, Nebel has turned his attention to the core tasks. Thanks to OFFIS, Oldenburg has become established as a top place for IT, as emphasised by August-Wilhelm Scheer, former President of Bitkom, Germany's digital association, at the opening of the 2006 CeBIT trade fair in Hanover. Now it's a case of setting the right accents. The aim is to move away from being a digital pick-and-mix and to establish a clear, future-oriented profile. Increasingly OFFIS focuses on four main aspects of research and development: energy, health, manufacturing and transportation, with IT being one of the crucial innovation motors in all areas.

But there's more too. Wolfgang Nebel has already taken the next step. He always thinks bigger than others, developing visions and believing in their feasibility. Oldenburg has good prerequisites to get established on the map of key IT places, he affirms. His plan is for an IT Campus as an innovation district for digitisation and society. At the end of November 2020, news is received from Berlin that the German government is going to support the project with funds amounting to 35 million Euro.

Pleasing confirmation for visionary Nebel, who admits that he can often get "a bit impatient". "The Campus will be my final project", he says. Even before notification of funding arrived from Berlin, he has already made the necessary readjustments, retiring from his position as chairman of the OFFIS Executive Board and passing the baton on to Professor Sebastian Lehnhoff. He wants to stay on the Board until 2022 while devoting his attention to the IT Campus. And then? "Then it will be up to Sebastian Lehnhoff with Holger Peinemann and the OFFIS Board to take care of the IT Campus." But he very much hopes to attend the opening ceremony, probably in 2024.

Sailing and photography

Until then and beyond, he will be devoting his time not only to numerous other academic and business roles and activities but also hopefully finding more scope for his private life. Sailing ranks high on his list of hobbies, even when the water gets rough. Entrepreneur and "fatherly friend" Peter Waskönig used to take him sailing on both the Baltic and the North Sea. He has even crossed the Atlantic. "Now that was an amazing experience, I'd love to do it again." But while Nebel likes to have a team around him at work, when sailing he'd rather be alone with his wife. "We trust each other absolutely." Not surprising, seeing that they've known each other for a good 50 years.

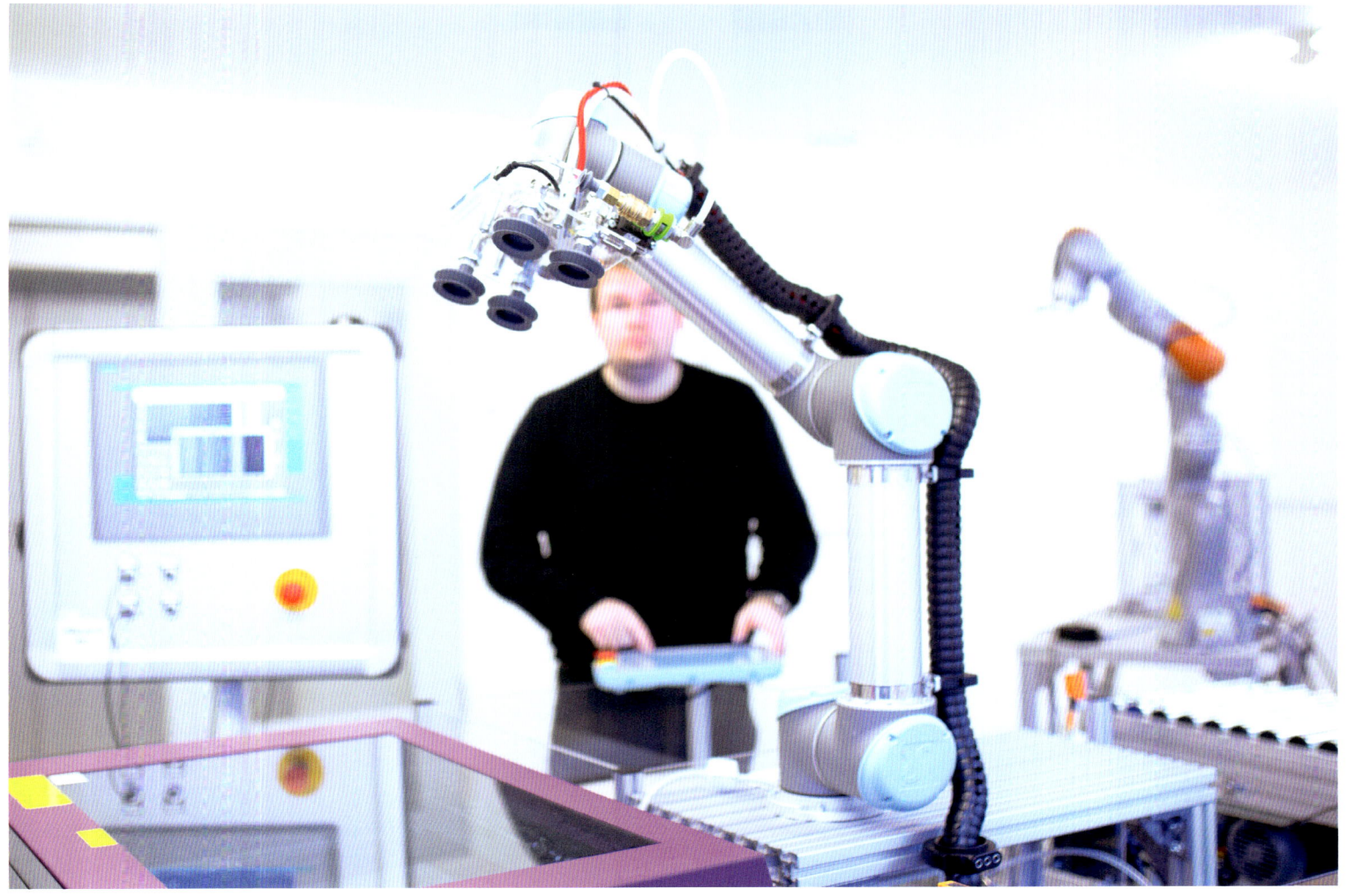

Die Gruppe Smart Human Robot Collaboration arbeitet daran, eine enge Zusammenarbeit von Mensch und Roboter zu ermöglichen.

The Smart Human Robot Collaboration group is working on collaboration between human beings and robots.

Eine zweite Leidenschaft gehört dem Fotografieren. Wobei: Sie lag fast 40 Jahre brach. „Wir hatten in Hannover an der Uni eine AG, in der wir uns sehr intensiv mit der Fotografie beschäftigten", erinnert sich Nebel. Später fehlte die Zeit, ganz aber erlosch die Flamme nicht. Der Siegeszug des Smartphones sorgte dafür, dass sie wieder aufflackerte: „Mit geringem zeitlichem Aufwand konnte ich Projekte verfolgen und erste regionale Ausstellungen bespielen."

Bei Handyfotos blieb es indes nicht. Im Gegenteil. Zuletzt entwickelte Wolfgang Nebel das Konzept für eine Serie unter dem Titel „Transformation". In großformatigen Aufnahmen zeigt er Orte in Deutschland, die in den vergangenen Jahren eine ganz andere Bestimmung als die ursprüngliche erhalten haben. Etwa eine ehemalige Luftschiffhalle, die heute als tropischer Vergnügungspark dient. Das frühere Atomkraftwerk, in dessen Kühltürmen sich inzwischen die Kettenkarussells drehen. Oder das lange Zeit größte Kalibergwerk der Welt, in dem nun Konzerte stattfinden.

Eine beeindruckende Serie. Ein Ort allerdings fehlt: die einst größte Fleischwarenfabrik Europas, auf deren Gelände in Oldenburg heute das Herz der norddeutschen Informatikszene schlägt. Und an deren Erfolg Wolfgang Nebel maßgeblichen Anteil hat.

His second passion is photography. Mind you, it was neglected for nearly 40 years. "At uni in Hanover we had a photography club, that gave me an intensive introduction", Nebel recalls. Although time was lacking later on, the spark never quite went out and was revived by the arrival of the smart phone: "All of a sudden it was so much easier to pursue projects with far less time involved, even including regional exhibitions."

He soon moved beyond photos on his phone. On the contrary, Wolfgang Nebel recently developed the concept for a series called "Transformation". Large pictures show places in Germany that are currently being used for a completely different purpose than originally intended. An airship hanger that is now being used as a tropical theme park. A nuclear power station with swing carousels spinning round inside. Or what used to be the world's largest potash mine that is now a concert venue.

An impressive series. But there's one place missing: the meat factory that was once the largest in Europe but whose premises in Oldenburg are being converted to the heart of North German IT. And whose success is down to Wolfgang Nebel to a great extent.

Wir denken Zukunft

OFFIS ist ein anwendungsorientiertes Forschungs- und Entwicklungsinstitut für Informatik mit Sitz in Oldenburg. In durchschnittlich 70 laufenden Projekten pro Jahr unterstützt OFFIS Unternehmen bei der Konzipierung und Umsetzung innovativer Lösungen auf höchstem internationalem Niveau. Der Fokus liegt dabei insbesondere auf den Fachbereichen Energie, Gesundheit, Produktion und Verkehr. Dafür kooperiert OFFIS weltweit mit über 700 Partnern aus Wirtschaft und Wissenschaft. Regionalpolitisch verstehen wir uns als Innovationsmotor, durch den Wissen vor Ort bleibt und neue zukunftsfähige Arbeitsplätze für den Nordwesten geschaffen werden.

Forschungsprojekte mit oder ohne öffentliche Förderung können auch für Ihr Unternehmen der Schlüssel zur Umsetzung innovativer Ideen und zum Einstieg in neue Technologien für eine erfolgreiche Zukunft sein. OFFIS verfügt über einen breiten Pool an Spezialist*innen und unterstützt Sie von der ersten Projektidee hin zur Antragsstellung, Koordination und Projektdurchführung.

OFFIS e. V.
Institut für Informatik

Information
Gründungsjahr: 1991
Beschäftigte: über 300 aus rund 25 Nationen
Leistungsspektrum: Forschung und Entwicklung in der Informationtechnik
www.offis.de

Year founded: 1991
Employees: more than 300 from 25 countries all over the world
Range of services: research and development in information technology

We think ahead

OFFIS is an application-oriented research and development institute for information technology based in Oldenburg. In an average of 70 ongoing projects per year, OFFIS supports companies in the conception and implementation of innovative solutions at the highest international level. The focus is particularly on the specialist areas of energy, health, manufacturing and transportation. OFFIS cooperates worldwide with over 700 partners from industry and science. From a regional policy perspective, we see ourselves as an innovation engine that keeps knowledge in the region and creates new sustainable jobs for the Northwest.

Research projects with or without public funding can also be the key for your company to implement innovative ideas and to enter new technologies for a successful future. OFFIS has a broad pool of specialists at its disposal and supports you from the initial project idea through to application, coordination and project implementation.

IBS IT & Business School Oldenburg

Information

Kleingruppen von max. 30 Studierenden pro Studiengang und Jahr, persönlicher Kontakt zu Lehrenden, 24/7-Zugang zu den Räumen, regelmäßige Spitzenposition im CHE-Hochschulranking und Best-bewertungen in Akkreditierungen

Small groups of max. 30 students per degree course and year, personal contact to teaching staff, 24/7 access to the facilities, regular leading positions in CHE University Ranking and top marks in accreditation processes

www.ibs-ol.de

Fachkräfte für die Region: Die gemeinnützige IBS IT & Business School Oldenburg bietet duale Studienprogramme für Betriebswirtschaft und Wirtschaftsinformatik an. Das Lernen in kleinen Gruppen von maximal 30 Studierenden, mit neuesten Materialien und Informationstechnologien, ist an der IBS Oldenburg selbstverständlich. Die Absolventinnen und Absolventen sind durch die Verknüpfung von Studien- und Praxisphasen während des Studiums für die weitere berufliche Zukunft überdurchschnittlich gut aufgestellt. Dies wird u. a. in Akkreditierungen oder dem CHE-Hochschulranking regelmäßig bestätigt.

Neben den Gründungsunternehmen, darunter zum Beispiel EWE, BTC, CEWE, OLB sowie das OFFIS, sind mittlerweile ca. 50 Unternehmen der Region Weser-Ems und Bremen in Kooperation getreten, um ihren Fachkräftenachwuchs sicherzustellen. So entsenden zum Beispiel Stadt Oldenburg, Ulla Popken, KDO, Rügenwalder Mühle, Lufthansa Ind., Media Markt, Stadtwerke Achim und Nanu-Nana dual Studierende an die IBS Oldenburg.

Skilled workers for the region: the non-profit IBS IT & Business School Oldenburg offers dual degree programs for business management and business informatics. Learning in small groups of maximum 30 students with state-of-the-art resources and IT facilities can be taken for granted at the IBS Oldenburg. Each course of study offers closely integrated theory and practice so that the graduates are well prepared for their future careers. This is confirmed in regular accreditation processes or the CHE University Ranking.

Besides the founding companies, including e.g. EWE, BTC, CEWE, OLB and OFFIS, around 50 companies in the Weser-Ems region and Bremen have entered into cooperation with IBS to safeguard their future needs when it comes to the next generation of skilled specialists. Students on dual degree programs at IBS Oldenburg come among others from the City of Oldenburg, Ulla Popken, KDO, Rügenwalder Mühle, Lufthansa Ind., Media Markt, Stadtwerke Achim and Nanu-Nana.

GWS Großmann GmbH
Wach- und Sicherheitsdienst

Information

Gründungsjahr: 2001
Mitarbeiter: rund 600
Leistungsspektrum:
– Sicherheitsdienst
– Revierdienst
– Werk- und Objektschutz
– Mietservice
– Kurierdienste
– Detektivaufgaben
– Qualitätsmanagement
– Eventsicherheit/Technik
Standorte:
Molbergen und Zeven
Zertifizierungen:
DIN EN ISO 9001
DIN 77200-5 Stufe 2
DIN 77200-1:2017-11
www.ws-grossmann.de

Year founded: 2001
Employees: around 600
Range of services:
– security service
– patrolling service
– site and property protection
– hire service
– courier services
– investigation tasks
– quality management
– event security/equipment
Sites:
Molbergen and Zeven
Certifications:
DIN EN ISO 9001
DIN 77200-5 step 2
DIN 77200-1:2017-11

Eine sichere Wahl.

Ganz gleich, ob es um klassische Detektivarbeit, Eventsecurity, Überwachungstechnik oder Spezialeinsätze geht: Gruppenschulungen und Ausbildungen in sämtlichen Sicherheitsbereichen gehören ebenso zu unseren Stärken wie der Fullservice für Veranstaltungssicherheit und der Objektschutz. Dank eines breit gefächerten Tätigkeitsfeldes kann unser Team für nahezu jede Anforderung eine maßgeschneiderte Lösung anbieten.

Frei nach dem Motto „Stillstand ist Rückschritt" sind wir bestrebt, unsere Qualität immer weiter zu steigern. Durch ständige Kontrollen und Qualitätssicherungsmaßnahmen wird nicht nur theoretisches Verständnis bei unseren Mitarbeitern hervorgerufen, sondern sichergestellt, dass die Vorgaben auch wirklich in die Praxis umgesetzt werden – für effiziente Prozesse in der Zusammenarbeit mit den Kunden.

Als erfolgreiches mittelständisches Unternehmen sind wir stets an ambitionierten Nachwuchskräften interessiert und bilden seit dem Jahr 2018 jährlich Fachkräfte für Schutz und Sicherheit aus. Die erste Generation hat 2021 ihre Ausbildung erfolgreich abgeschlossen.

A secure choice.

Whether classic investigation work, event security, surveillance technology or special assignments, our strengths include group training and instruction courses in all areas of security as well as offering full service for event security and property protection. The team covers a broad range of tasks and offers a tailor-made solution for practically every requirement.

Along the lines of "stagnation is regression", we endeavour to keep on improving our quality. Constant checks and quality assurance not only generate a theoretical understanding among our employees but also ensure that stipulations really are put into practice, for efficient processes in cooperation with the customers.

As a successful medium-sized company, we are always interested in ambitious young talents and have been providing training for specialist protection and security personnel every year since 2018, with the first generation completing their training successfully in 2021.

An der Jade Hochschule zeichnen sich Lehre und Forschung durch innovative Ansätze, kooperative Zusammenarbeit und eine zugewandte Haltung aus. In allen Bereichen fördert die Hochschule entsprechend ihres Leitbildes Kompetenz und Vielfalt. In Rankings überzeugt sie seit Jahren mit ihrem Praxisbezug, dem engen Kontakt zur Wirtschaft sowie Abschlüssen, die in einer angemessenen Studienzeit erreicht werden.

Unter den rund 50 Studiengängen – über Architektur, Bauwesen, Geoinformation, Gesundheit, Informatik, Maritimes und Logistik, Medien und Journalismus, Elektrotechnik, Maschinenbau, Mechatronik, Tourismus, Wirtschaft, Management und neu Logopädie, Angewandte Pflegewissenschaft, Hebammenwissenschaft, Bauinformationstechnologie bis zu Urban Design – ist für viele Interessen etwas dabei, das unterschiedlichen Neigungen und Wünschen entspricht.

An der Jade Hochschule studiert keiner alleine. In einer fast familiären Atmosphäre finden Studierende schnell Anschluss. Ihnen stehen viele Unterstützungsangebote zur Verfügung, die sie durchs ganze Studium begleiten. Auch die Professorinnen und Professoren sind jederzeit ansprechbar. Die Dozentinnen und Dozenten kommen ohne Einschränkung aus der Praxis und halten den Kontakt zur Wirtschaft. Davon profitieren die Studierenden immer wieder. Die Jade Hochschule ist eine familienfreundliche Hochschule, die dafür sorgt, dass alle Hochschulangehörigen Lehren, Lernen und Arbeiten mit den Anforderungen des Familienlebens bestmöglich verbinden können. Dazu gehören flexible Arbeitszeiten und Kinderbetreuungsangebote.

Die Jade Hochschule wurde 2009 mit der Zusammenführung zweier ehemaliger Fachhochschulen gegründet. Ihre Ausbildungstradition reicht jedoch bis auf das Jahr 1832 zurück.

Jade Hochschule
Wilhelmshaven/Oldenburg/Elsfleth

Information
Gründungsjahr: 2009
Studierende: 4200 (in Wilhelmshaven),
2200 (in Oldenburg), 600 (in Elsfleth)
Fachbereiche: Architektur, Bauwesen/Geoinformation/Gesundheitstechnologie, Ingenieurwissenschaften, Management/Information/Technologie (MIT), Seefahrt und Logistik sowie Wirtschaft mit insgesamt 37 Bachelor- und 15 Masterstudiengängen

Year founded: 2009
Students: 4,200 (in Wilhelmshaven),
2,200 (in Oldenburg), 600 (in Elsfleth)
Departments: Architecture, Civil Engineering/Geoinformation/Health Technology, Engineering, Management/IT/Technology (MIT), Maritime Studies and Logistics as well as Economics offering altogether 37 Bachelor's degrees and 15 Master's degrees

www.jade-hs.de

At Jade University of Applied Sciences, what makes teaching and research stand out is a combination of an innovation culture, cooperative collaboration and a supportive environment. In all areas, the University promotes expertise and diversity in accordance with the principles of its core values. For years now it has performed well in ranking tables with its practical approach, close contacts with business and graduation within a reasonable timescale.

Around 50 degree courses, including Architecture, Civil Engineering, Geoinformation, Healthcare, Computer Science, Maritime Studies and Logistics, Media and Journalism, Electrical Engineering, Mechanical Engineering, Mechatronics, Tourism, Economics and Management as well as new courses such as Speech Therapy, Applied Nursing Science, Midwifery, Computer Science in Construction or Urban Design, offer something for a wide variety of interests and ambitions.

At Jade University of Applied Sciences, nobody studies on their own. In an almost family-like atmosphere, students find friends easily and can draw on lots of support programs that help them throughout their studies. The professors are always available for a chat with students. Our teaching staff all come from a practical background and maintain contacts with business. Students constantly benefit from this. Jade University of Applied Sciences is a family-friendly university that makes sure all its staff and students can teach, learn and work while maintaining a good work-life balance. That includes flexible working hours as well as childcare facilities.

Jade University of Applied Sciences was founded in 2009 following the merger of two technical colleges, but it draws on an educational tradition that extends right back to 1832.

DER PUPPENSPIELER

The Puppeteer

AUTOR:
THORSTEN BRUNS

Die Kleine Straße macht ihrem Namen alle Ehre. Nur eine Handvoll Häuser steht hier. Und doch gehört sie zu den bekanntesten Adressen Oldenburgs. Genauer gesagt: die Hausnummer 8. Hier – in der 1869 erbauten ehemaligen Turnhalle des OTB – residiert eines der bedeutendsten Figurentheater Deutschlands: das Theater Laboratorium von Pavel Möller-Lück.

Es ist ein ungemütlicher Vormittag in Oldenburg, nass und kalt. Betritt man jedoch das Gebäude, lässt man mehr als nur das Wetter hinter sich. Wir finden uns wieder in einem opulenten Café, das sehr viel erhabener wirkt, als man es vom Vorraum eines Theatersaals erwarten dürfte. Die detailverliebte Einrichtung gleicht einem „Best-of" europäischer Kaffeehauskultur. Man spürt sofort: Das Theatererlebnis beginnt hier nicht mit dem Heben des Vorhangs – es beginnt mit Überschreiten der Türschwelle.

Studium und Praxis perfekt verzahnt

An einem der Tische sitzt der Spiritus Rector dieses Kleinods im Oldenburger Ziegelhofviertel: Pavel Möller-Lück. Geboren 1959 in Eutin, romantischer Abenteurer, verträumter Anarchist und begnadeter Erzähler. Anders ausgedrückt: Theatermacher mit Leib und Seele. Mit dem Laboratorium hat er – gemeinsam mit seiner Frau Barbara Schmitz-Lenders – einen „Seelenort" geschaffen, dessen Ruf weit über die Grenzen der Region reicht.

The Kleine Straße is a small road that suits its name, with just a handful of houses. Even so, it is one of Oldenburg's most famous addresses. Or at least Number 8 is. Here in the former OTB sports hall built in 1869 we find one of Germany's most important puppet theatres: Pavel Möller-Lück's Theatre Laboratory.

It's an unpleasant morning in Oldenburg, cold and wet. But we leave more than the weather behind as we enter the building. We find ourselves in a sumptuous café that seems much grander than you would expect from a theatre lobby. The furnishings show a love of detail that is almost a "best of" European coffeehouse culture. Right from the start, it's obvious that theatre here starts long before the curtain goes up and starts as soon as people cross the threshold.

Perfect mixture of studying and practice

At one of the tables we find the guiding spirit of this little jewel in Oldenburg's "Ziegelhofviertel": Pavel Möller-Lück. Born in Eutin in 1959, romantic adventurer, spell-bound anarchist and gifted storyteller. In other words, a theatremaker with heart and soul. Together with his wife Barbara Schmitz-Lenders, he has created the Theatre Laboratory as a choice venue with a reputation going way beyond the region itself.

Rund 60.000 Gäste verzeichnet das Haus pro Jahr, beinahe alle Vorstellungen sind ausverkauft. Wer eine davon besucht hat, weiß sofort warum – kann es aber meist nicht in Worte fassen. Die Stücke sind fantasievoll, poetisch, emotional, atmosphärisch, nachdenklich, krachend komisch. Doch kein Attribut scheint ausreichend zu beschreiben, was das Besondere ist. Alle treffen zu; aber selbst ihre Summe wird dem Erlebnis kaum gerecht.

Wie lernt man, so etwas zu kreieren? Seit 1983 gibt es in Stuttgart einen Studiengang für Figurentheater. Doch Möller-Lück hat ihn nicht etwa besucht. „Ich habe ihn mit aufgebaut", erklärt er schmunzelnd. Wie bitte? Zu dieser Zeit müsste er 24 Jahre alt gewesen sein. „Ja, genau. Und erst wollte ich auch nicht. Mir war das nämlich nicht genug, um dafür nach Stuttgart gehen. Ich wollte auch die Leitung des Figurentheaters." Reichlich selbstbewusst für jemanden, der als junger Puppenspieler zwar eine gewisse Bekanntheit erlangt hatte, auf dem Papier aber nur ein Schauspielschüler war. Doch Möller-Lück bekam, was er wollte und konnte Studium und Praxis perfekt miteinander verzahnen. Gleichzeitig stellte er sich gegen die Traditionalisten und definierte das Figurentheater neu: als ernstzunehmende Sparte für jedes Alter. „Nötige Dehnübungen" nennt er das heute.

Diese Episode verrät viel über den Menschen und Macher Pavel Möller-Lück. Über sein Selbstbewusstsein, über seine Anspruchshaltung und über seine Vorstellungskraft. Eingerahmt von kreisrunden Brillengläsern funkeln seine Augen, wenn er davon erzählt. Das tun sie eigentlich durchgehend, als wäre er ständig aufs Neue inspiriert. Immer wieder rutscht er auf dem Stuhl nach vorn, stützt die Arme auf den Tisch und erzählt eindringlich. Kein Zweifel: Hier hat jemand Freude an dem, was er tut.

Zwischen Frankreich und Schweden

Nach Oldenburg wollte Möller-Lück eigentlich nicht. Zumindest nicht ursprünglich. „Aber dann war ich mal hier. Und ich wurde gefragt, ob ich nicht bleiben wollte." Das entscheidende Lockmittel war die erste Spielstätte, eine ehemalige Isolierbaracke hinter dem Kulturzentrum PFL. „Für die Stadt war das ein Abrissobjekt, für uns ein Traum", erinnert er sich. Und so wurde der Vagabund nach unzähligen Theatertouren durch Europa schließlich sesshaft. So sehr, dass nach 13 Jahren der Umzug in die Kleine Straße erfolgte – und später sogar die Erweiterung um die benachbarte Limonadenfabrik.

Bereut hat er die Entscheidung nie. Und das, obwohl er mit seinem Theater – nach Ansicht von Experten – in jeder Metropole der Welt bestehen könnte? „Mag sein. Aber die Menschen hier haben einen großen Vorsprung gegenüber allen anderen. Sie haben uns vom ersten Tag an die Bude eingerannt. Das vergesse ich nie." Und nach einem kurzen Moment ergänzt er: „Ich liebe Frankreich, ich liebe Schweden – und Oldenburg liegt doch in vieler Hinsicht genau dazwischen."

Mittlerweile ist er länger hier als an irgendeinem anderen Ort: über ein Vierteljahrhundert. Das liegt auch daran, dass sich Oldenburg in dieser Zeit verändert hat. „Man erkennt immer mehr, wie wichtig die sogenannten weichen Faktoren sind. Städte müssen leben. Und dafür braucht es Kultur." Möller-Lück ist nicht so vermessen, einen Anteil daran auf sich zurückzuführen. Abstreiten würde er es aber auch nicht.

Der Wettbewerb um Fachkräfte und Zukunftsfähigkeit entscheidet sich eben nicht nur in Büros, sondern auch auf Bühnen. Da schadet es nicht, wenn man ein Laboratorium zu bieten hat.

Eine Form des fantastischen Realismus

Für Möller-Lück geht es aber um mehr. Die Menschen, die das Laboratorium besuchen, sollen nicht nur in eine andere Welt eintauchen. Sie sollen von dort auch etwas mitnehmen. „Wir wollen verstehen lernen – und ein Stück heiler werden in dieser Welt", beschreibt er den Effekt. Aber wie erreicht man das? Wie entstehen die Geschichten? „Immer im Team", erzählt er. „Wir sind etwa zehn Leute, setzen uns gemeinsam an einen großen Tisch und dann geht's los!"

Man spürt selbst bei dieser schlichten Beschreibung, wie viel Spaß ihm das macht – und dass er diese Runde am liebsten augenblicklich wieder einberufen würde. Die Mitglieder des Teams haben ihre Expertise beim Film, in der Fotografie oder im Schauspiel. Jeder hat eine andere Perspektive auf den Stoff. Durch das gemeinsame „Laborieren" bekommt das Stück seine Konturen. „Im Figuren- und Objekttheater haben wir den großen Vorteil, dass wir unserer Fantasie freien Lauf lassen können", erklärt Möller-Lück. „Wir schaffen eine Form des fantastischen Realismus."

Als Wirtschaftsfaktor anerkannt

Wenn ein Theatermacher in einer Wirtschaftsmonographie auftaucht, kann das zwei Gründe haben. Erstens: Sein Theater ist so erfolgreich, dass es einen ökonomisch relevanten Faktor darstellt. Das ist hier zwar der Fall, doch es geht um zweitens: Kunst und Kultur sind mittlerweile als Wirtschafts- und Standortfaktoren anerkannt.

Das ist in dieser Klarheit noch nicht allgemeiner Konsens. Jedoch lässt sich – immerhin – ein Trend ablesen. Früher betrachtete man die Kunst im Einzelfall und verstand sie als persönliche Leidenschaft, bei der finanzielle Sicherheit die Kreativität bedrohte. Heute sieht man zunehmend das große Ganze – und damit einerseits unverzichtbaren kreativen Stimulus für die Bevölkerung und andererseits die enormen volkswirtschaftlichen Dimensionen.

Paradoxerweise führte uns ausgerechnet die Corona-Krise den Wert der Kultur vor Augen. Ihre Abwesenheit hinterließ eine Lücke, die durch nichts anderes zu füllen war. Wie groß diese Lücke war, wurde vielen erst bewusst, als die Eckdaten der Branche in einer breiteren Öffentlichkeit diskutiert wurden: 1,2 Millionen Beschäftigte sind dem Kultursektor zuzurechnen, seine jährliche Bruttowertschöpfung liegt bei über 100 Mrd. Euro. Das ist mehr als die gesamte chemische Industrie oder die deutsche Energieversorgung. Dieser volkswirtschaftliche Gigant lag monatelang vollständig brach. Und das führte zu einer Bewusstwerdung – bei den Kulturschaffenden ebenso wie bei ihrer Kundschaft.

Trotz ihrer Größe musste die Kultur immer um ihre wirtschaftliche Anerkennung kämpfen. Bezeichnenderweise wurde ihre Bedeutung häufig über die Umwegrentabilität definiert – also über Geld, das letztlich in Handel, Gastronomie und Hotelgewerbe ausgegeben wurde. Vor dem Hintergrund neuer Erkenntnisse zum „Selbstwert" der Kultur und deren Rolle in der kommunalen Profilierung wandelt sich jedoch die Wahrnehmung. Der weiche Standortfaktor Kultur härtet langsam aus. Und die Theater bilden in diesem Prozess Identifikations- und Kristallisationspunkte.

Acknowledged economic factor

There can be two reasons for including a theatremaker in a
business monograph. Firstly: his theatre is so successful that it is
an economically relevant factor. Although that is the case here,
there is also a second reason: art and culture are meanwhile
acknowledged economic and location factors.

Not everyone has realised this yet. But even so, a trend can be
perceived. Art used to be seen in isolation as a personal passion
where creativity was felt to be threatened by financial security.
Today, people increasingly see the whole picture, on the one
hand as an indispensable creative stimulus for the population in
general, and on the other hand as having huge economic dimensions.

It is a paradox that it just happens to be the corona crisis that is
making us realise the true value of culture. The lack of culture has
left a void that nothing else can fill. The sheer dimensions of this
void only emerged gradually when people started to discuss the
sector's statistics: the culture industry is said to have 1.2 million
employees with annual gross value production of more than 100
billion Euro. That is more than the entire chemical industry or the
German power supply. This economic giant came to a complete
standstill for months on end. Which led to a greater awareness,
both in the creative artists and in their audience.

Despite its size, the culture industry has always had to fight for
economic recognition. It is quite significant that its meaning
frequently used to be defined in terms of profitability, i.e. the
money spent in retail, catering and hospitality. New findings about
the intrinsic value of culture and its role in municipal profiling
are gradually triggering a change in awareness and perception.
Culture as a soft location factor is going through a hardening process, in which theatres are both identification and crystallisation
points.

Around 60,000 guests come here every year, almost all the perform-
ances are sold out. People who've attended one will know exactly why,
but probably struggle to find the right words. The plays are imaginative, poetic, emotional, atmospheric, reflective and so funny you'll split
your sides laughing. But no single attribute manages to conjure up
exactly what you're trying to say. They are all accurate but even taken
altogether they're still not really enough.

How can you learn to create something like this? There has been a course
of study for puppeteers in Stuttgart since 1983. But Möller-Lück didn't
do the course. "I helped to get it going"; he explains with a grin. Pardon?
He can't have been more than 24 years old back then. "Yes, that's right.
And I didn't really want to get involved at first. The course on its own
simply wasn't a good enough reason for me to move to Stuttgart.
I wanted to run the puppet theatre as well." Pretty assertive for someone
who may have acquired a certain name as a young puppeteer but who
on paper was just a drama student, after all. But Möller-Lück got what
he wanted and managed to achieve a perfect mixture of studying and
practice. At the same time he took a stand against the traditionalists and
redefined the puppet theatre, turning it into a serious genre for every
age group. "Necessary stretching exercises", he calls it looking back.

Es scheint diese Offenheit zu sein, die es ermöglicht, auch sensible Themen wie Krankheit und Sterblichkeit gefühlvoll zu thematisieren – wie zum Beispiel in „Die Bremer Stadtmusikanten", mit insgesamt 180.000 Gästen das erfolgreichste Stück. Wie kommt es zum Entschluss, diese Stoffe aufzugreifen? „Das liegt oft an persönlicher Betroffenheit. Manchmal denke ich: Die Themen suchen uns, nicht wir sie." Das ist auch einer der Gründe, warum die schwierige Gratwanderung zwischen Emotionalität und Leichtigkeit so gut gelingt. „Man darf Angst zulassen, aber sich ihr nicht ergeben. Wir spielen mit ihr." Für Möller-Lück sind Melancholie und Humor Geschwister, immer nah beisammen. „Nach der Vorstellung sind die Gäste oft in guter Stimmung, sie haben viel gelacht. Aber wir geben ihnen die Nachdenklichkeit trotzdem mit; wie eine große Tüte, in die noch was reingepackt wird. Zum Mitnehmen. ‚Melancholie to go'."

Der Kaspar als Kabarettist

Möller-Lück versteht das Theater aber nicht nur als emotionalen, sondern auch als politischen Ort. „Figurentheater hatte immer eine politische DNA", erklärt er. „Der Kasper zum Beispiel war ein Kabarettist. Er konnte sagen, was andere nicht sagen durften. Er war das geduldete Enfant Terrible." Möller-Lück sieht sich in dieser Tradition. „Ich spiele niemals das gleiche Stück. Wenn tagespolitisch was passiert ist, wenn die Leute sich über was aufregen – dann gehört das mit rein. Dann will ich das mit ihnen besprechen." Dabei hält er seine eigene Meinung nicht zurück. „Theater muss sich einmischen", ist er überzeugt.

Wenn man Pavel Möller-Lück so hört, wünscht man sich beinahe, etwas von seiner Strahlungswärme würde abfärben und man dürfte sie nach Hause mitnehmen. Aber letztlich ist es genau das, was im Theater Laboratorium passiert. Möller-Lück und sein Team haben eine Sprache gefunden, die ihre vielen Gäste berührt; von der sie sich gern berühren lassen; und die widerhallt in ihren Köpfen, wenn sie das Theater längst verlassen haben.

Ein Blick durch die großen Fenster verrät: Immer noch prasseln Regentropfen nieder. Bevor es wieder hinausgeht in die Kälte, drängt sich noch eine Frage auf: Wie geht's weiter? Mit Anfang 60 zählen manche schon die Tage bis zur Rente. „Ich sicher nicht! Ich habe noch genug Energie", wehrt Möller-Lück ab. Dennoch schwebt ihm eine Art Altersteilzeit vor: „Jedes Jahr drei Monate Frankreich, drei Monate Schweden – und dazwischen Oldenburg. Das fände ich gut!" Der Puppenspieler bleibt der Region also erhalten – und mit ihm eines der bedeutendsten Figurentheater Deutschlands.

This episode tells us a lot about the person and puppeteer Pavel Möller-Lück. About his self-confidence, his expectations and his imagination. Behind the round spectacles, his eyes twinkle while he talks. In fact, they twinkle all the time as if he is constantly being inspired. He keeps sliding forwards on his chair, leans on his arms and the table and tells his story vividly. No doubt about it: here is someone who loves his job.

Between France and Sweden

Möller-Lück didn't really want to come to Oldenburg. Or at least, not to start with. "But then all of a sudden I was here. And they asked me to stay." The first venue played a crucial role in his decision. This was a former isolation hut behind the PFL culture centre. "The city wanted to demolish it, but it was ideal for us", he remembers. And so after many theatre tours through Europe, the vagabond eventually settled down. So much so that after 13 years they moved to Kleine Straße, subsequently even adding the neighbouring soft drinks factory to their premises.

He has never regretted his decision. Even though experts reckon his theatre could have been a success in any city of the world? "May be. But the people here offer something nobody else can. They've filled the seats and stalls and rows right from Day One. That's something I'll never forget." A moment later he adds: "I love France and I love Sweden. And Oldenburg is kind of between the two. In many respects."

Meanwhile he has been here longer than anywhere else: more than twenty five years. That's also because Oldenburg itself has changed in this time. "Time and again you realise how important the so-called soft factors are. A city has to live. And it needs culture to do that." Möller-Lück isn't so presumptuous to claim any of this for himself. But he wouldn't dispute it either. When it comes to skilled workers and future viability, decisions are often taken on the stage and not just in the office. So it's not a bad thing if you have a laboratory on offer.

A kind of imaginative realism

But for Möller-Lück it's about much more than that. When people come to his Theatre Laboratory, he wants them to do more than just escape to another world for a while. They should take something away with them. "We want to learn how to understand – and experience a bit of healing in this world", is how he describes the effect. But how can he do that? How do the stories come about? "It's always teamwork", he says. "There are about ten of us, we get together around a big table and off we go!"

Even this simple description reveals how much fun he has in the process – and that he'd preferably get the team together again straight away. The individual members have their own expertise in the world of cinema, photography or acting. Everyone sees the subject matter from a different point of view. And by "labouring" away at it together, they start shaping the play. "The advantage of the puppet and object theatre is that we can give free rein to our imagination", explains Möller-Lück. "We create a kind of imaginative realism".

Apparently, it is this open approach that lets them deal sensitively even with difficult topics such as illness and dying, as they did for example with "The Town Musicians of Bremen", their most successful production with altogether 180,000 spectators. What makes them decide to go in a certain direction? "It's often a very personal decision. Sometimes I think the topics find us, not the other way round." That's also one of the reasons why they are so good at staying on the narrow path between all the emotions and keeping it light. "You're allowed to feel anxious, but you mustn't give in to it. We play with it." For Möller-Lück, melancholy and humour are always closely related. "After the show, people often leave the building in a good mood, having laughed a lot. But we also give them plenty to think about, in a big bag to take home with them: ,Melancholy to go'."

Punch the cabaret artist

But for Möller-Lück, the theatre is not just an emotional but also a political place. "Puppet theatre has always had a political DNA", he says. "Punch for example was a cabaret artist. He could say things others couldn't. They tolerated him as an enfant terrible." Möller-Lück sees himself as following on in the same tradition. "I never do the same play twice. Whatever's happening in the politics of the day, whatever people are getting worked up about – we put it all in the show. That's what we want to talk about." And he's happy to say exactly what he thinks. ,Theatre must get involved", is his conviction.

Die Inszenierungen von Pavel Möller-Lück und seinem Team sind kreativ, fordernd und auf eine berührende Weise unterhaltsam.

The productions by Pavel Möller-Lück and his team are creative, challenging and touchingly entertaining.

When you hear Pavel Möller-Lück talk like this, you wish some of his enthusiasm could rub off on you so you could take it home. And that is just what happens in the Theatre Laboratory. Möller-Lück and his team have found a language that touches many of their spectators: a language that goes to their hearts and resounds in their heads long after they've left the building.

A glimpse through the big windows tells us it's still pouring with rain out there. Before we go back out into the cold, we have one last question: Where does he go from here? Some people start thinking about retiring when they turn 60. "You must be joking! I've still got plenty of energy", parries Möller-Lück. Even so, he could envisage a kind of semi-retirement "I could split the year between France and Sweden: three months in each, and Oldenburg in between. That would be good!" So the puppeteer will be remaining in the region, and with him one of Germany's most important puppet theatres.

191

DIE VORREITERIN

The Outrider

AUTOR:
CLAUS SPITZER-
EWERSMANN

Der Pferdesport spielt im Oldenburger Land seit Jahrzehnten eine große Rolle. Der aktuell wohl bekannteste Name gehört Kristina Bröring-Sprehe, dreifache Medaillengewinnerin bei den Olympischen Spielen. Nach Babypause und Corona-Stopp geht die Dressurreiterin ihre neuen Ziele an.

Olympia – für Sportler in aller Welt nach wie vor ein Zauberwort mit ganz besonderem Klang. Kristina Bröring-Sprehe hat es zwei Mal zu den Spielen geschafft und sich damit einen Jugendtraum erfüllt. 2012 war sie in London dabei, vier Jahre später auch in Rio de Janeiro. „Unvergessliche Tage", erinnert sich die Dressurreiterin aus Dinklage. Unvergesslich nicht nur wegen der insgesamt drei Medaillen, die sie mit nach Hause brachte.

Die Ergebnisse stimmten schließlich ebenso wie die Erlebnisse. „Ich habe im Olympischen Dorf gewohnt, das ganze Flair und die Atmosphäre genossen und mir nach meinen Wettkämpfen viele andere Sportarten angesehen: Turmspringen, Hockey, Bahnradfahren." Und Leichtathletik. Da hat sie auch den Superstar der Szene getroffen: Usain Bolt, den Sprinter aus Jamaika. Usain Bolt! Mehr geht nicht. „Stimmt", sagt sie und freut sich.

Equestrian sport has played a major role in the Oldenburger Land for decades. The best-known name at the moment must be Kristina Bröring-Sprehe, who won three Olympic medals. After maternity leave and the Corona-related hiatus, the dressage rider has now set her sights on new goals.

The Olympic Games: these words still spell magic of a very special kind for athletes all over the world. Kristina Bröring-Sprehe made it to the Games twice, thus fulfilling one of her childhood dreams. She was at the Games in 2012 in London, and four years later also in Rio de Janeiro. "Memorable times", recalls the dressage rider from Dinklage. Memorable not just because of the total haul of three medals that she brought home.

It was the experience that counted as much as the results. "I lived in the Olympic Village and loved the whole flair and atmosphere, as well as the opportunity to watch many other disciplines once I'd finished my own events, such as diving, hockey and track cycling." And athletics, where she even met the scene's superstar: Usain Bolt, the Jamaican sprinter. Usain Bolt! Can't beat that! "True", she says with evident pleasure.

Ein Pony zum Karrierestart

Angefangen hat alles im Alter von vier Jahren mit einem Geschenk ihres Vaters. Auf dem Pony Nathan lernen die Zwillingsschwestern Kristina und Tanja reiten. Schon ihr Großvater war Reitlehrer und Züchter, Papa Paul führt das familieneigene Gestüt in Löningen. „Die Liebe zu den Pferden wurde mir einfach in die Wiege gelegt", kommentiert Kristina. Während ihre Schwester vor allem Gefallen am Springreiten findet, entscheidet sie sich für die Dressur – und nimmt mit Nathan 2002 erstmals an der Deutschen Meisterschaft teil. Der Start einer großen Karriere.

Aber nochmal kurz zurück: Warum diese Leidenschaft für die Dressur? „Weil es mich fasziniert, wie zwischen Reiterin und Pferd eine Verbindung entsteht, die ausschließlich auf Vertrauen aufbaut." Während der Ausbildung und während des Trainings lasse sich mehr und mehr beobachten, wie sich das Zusammenwachsen weiterentwickelt. Zudem, so fügt sie an, bereite es ihr große Freude, den Zuschauern das Gefühl zu vermitteln, es gehe alles ganz leicht. „Ich gebe ja immer nur ein paar unsichtbare Hilfen."

Das Talent des Mädchens aus dem Oldenburger Münsterland bleibt nicht unbemerkt. Als sogenannte „Junge Reiterin" reiht Kristina Erfolg an Erfolg. 2010 nimmt sie den Hannoveraner Hengst Desperados unter ihre Fittiche. Er wird ihr schon bald zum endgültigen Durchbruch verhelfen. Es dauert am Ende nur einige Monate, bis sie im A-Kader der deutschen Dressurreiter und auf der Kandidatenliste für Olympia in London steht.

Fast 40 Grand-Prix-Siege mit Desperados

„Ich hatte einfach zum richtigen Zeitpunkt immer die passenden Pferde", sagt Bröring-Sprehe mit dem Abstand von einigen Jahren. Welche Eigenschaften muss denn ein vierbeiniger Partner mitbringen, mit dem sie klarkommt? Auf jeden Fall Sensibilität und Ehrgeiz, lautet die Antwort. „Und er muss so richtig arbeiten wollen." Dann merke sie schnell, „wer Talent hat und das Potenzial für die Lektionen mitbringt".

Sie selbst bietet dafür ebenfalls Ehrgeiz, viel Ehrgeiz. Nicht das Optimum herausholen zu können, das würde sie ärgern. Dafür arbeitet sie die vollen sieben Tage in der Woche zielstrebig mit ihren Pferden. Auch heute noch. Daneben hält sie Verlässlichkeit für entscheidend. Sie fühlt sich verantwortlich für jedes ihrer Tiere. „Ein Pferd ist ja kein Tennisschläger, den ich einfach in die Ecke pfeffern kann, wenn ich nicht mehr mag", wagt sie einen drastischen Vergleich.

Bei Desperados passt es perfekt. Ein echter Glücksfall. Anfangs allerdings habe man sich gar nicht so gut verstanden. „Er war ein dominanter, ein sehr charakterstarker Hengst, eher ein Männerpferd und gern auch mal ein Macho. Wir haben viel miteinander trainiert und sind uns dabei immer nähergekommen." So nahe, dass sie nicht nur von Dressur-Experten als ideal aufeinander eingespielte Einheit wahrgenommen werden. Gemeinsam erringen sie fast 40 internationale Siege auf Grand-Prix-Niveau.

Kristina Bröring-Sprehe aus Dinklage gehört zu den erfolgreichsten deutschen Dressurreiterinnen.

Kristina Bröring-Sprehe from Dinklage is one of Germany's most successful dressage riders.

Wirtschaftsfaktor auf vier Beinen

Der exzellente Ruf der Pferdezucht im Oldenburger Land geht zurück bis in die Zeit von Graf Anton Günther, der im 17. Jahrhundert als großer Kenner und Förderer galt. Wurde das Oldenburger Pferd danach lange Jahre eher als Kutsch- und Zugpferd in der Landwirtschaft eingesetzt, ist es heute in erster Linie als Sportpferd gefragt. Die eleganten und charakterstarken Oldenburger werden von der internationalen Reitelite hoch geschätzt – bei der Dressur ebenso wie beim Springreiten.

Als größte Interessenvertretung hat sich der 1923 gegründete Oldenburger Pferdezuchtverband mit Sitz in Vechta einen Namen gemacht. Darin sind alle renommierten Züchter aus der Region vertreten. Die rund 4.500 hier jährlich geborenen Fohlen haben ihren ersten öffentlichen Auftritt bei den Brennterminen zwischen Mitte April und Ende Juli. Dort erhält der Nachwuchs mit Abstammungsnachweis das Brandzeichen und einen Mikrochip.

Vier Mal im Jahr kommen bei Auktionen in Vechta Fachleute, Züchter und Käufer zusammen: Anfang April und Anfang Oktober lassen sich bei den Elite-Auktionen besonders talentierte Oldenburger Spring- und Dressurpferde ersteigern. Die Summer und Winter Mixed Sales bieten Anfang Juni und Anfang Dezember neben Top-Vierbeinern auch weniger hochpreisige Sportpferde an. Bei der Eliteauktion im Frühjahr 2021 wurde bei 31 Reitpferden ein Umsatz von rund 1,5 Millionen Euro erzielt. Die Hälfte der Tiere ging ins Ausland.

Die Organisation der Auktionen ist hochprofessionell. Um das Risiko zu minimieren, steht zunächst ein Gesundheitscheck auf dem Programm. Die Röntgenbilder und tierärztlichen Bescheinigungen sind für potenzielle Käufer einsehbar. Zudem kann jeder Interessent während des Trainings seine Wunschkandidaten begutachten und reiten. Und danach geht es dann direkt in den Bieterwettstreit – vor Ort oder am Telefon.

It all begins when she is four years old with a present from her father. It is on pony Nathan that the twin sisters Kristina and Tanja learn to ride. Their grandfather had already been a riding instructor and breeder, and their father Paul runs the family's own stud in Löningen. "I was simply destined to love horses from birth", says Kristina. While her sister likes show jumping best of all, she prefers dressage, taking part in the German championships with Nathan for the first time in 2002: this is the start of a great career.

But let's just go back a bit: why this passion for dressage? "I am fascinated by the connection that is generated between horse and rider. It's based entirely on trust." The way this relationship grows and develops can be observed during initial schooling and ongoing training. Furthermore, she adds, she loves giving the spectators the feeling that it's all so easy. "All I do is just give a bit of invisible assistance here and there."

The girl from the Oldenburger Münsterland and her talent do not go unnoticed. As a so-called "Young Rider", Kristina goes from one success to the next. In 2010 she starts working with Desperados, a Hanoverian stallion. He soon helps her to achieve her final breakthrough, and within just a few months, she makes it into the A-squad of German dressage riders and onto the list of candidates for the Olympic Games in London.

Nearly 40 Grand Prix wins with Desperados

"I just always had the right horses at the right time", says Bröring-Sprehe looking back several years later. So what characteristics does she like to see in her four-legged partners? Definitely sensitivity and ambition, comes the reply. "And the horse must really want to work", before adding quickly "and have the talent and the potential for the lessons".

She herself is certainly also ambitious, very ambitious. Not getting the very best out of things would annoy her. That's why she works resolutely with her horses seven days a week. And still does so today. For her, reliability is crucial. She feels responsible for each and every one of her animals. "A horse isn't a tennis racket that I can fling away in the corner when I've had enough", she says in a drastic comparison.

Desperados is perfect for her. A real stroke of luck. But they didn't get on so well in the beginning. "He was a dominant stallion with a very strong character, more a man's horse and also a bit macho. We trained together a lot and this brought us closer together." So close that not only dressage experts see them as an ideally coordinated team. Together they win nearly 40 international titles on the Grand Prix level.

Participating in the 2012 and 2016 Olympic Games was of course an absolute highlight. "I was only 25 when they nominated me for the London Games. It all happened so quickly that I couldn't really take it all in." That doesn't matter: with her teammates Dorothee Schneider and Helen Langehanenberg she wins a surprising second place in the team competition. That's the silver medal! Four years la-

Economic factor on four legs

The excellent reputation enjoyed by horse breeding in the Oldenburger Land goes back to the days of Count Anton Günther, who was a great expert and promoter back in the 17th century. While for a long time the Oldenburger horse was used to draw coaches and agricultural machinery, today it is primarily in demand for equestrian sport. The elegant Oldenburger horse with its strong character is highly esteemed by the international riding elite, for both dressage and show jumping.

The Oldenburger Horse Breeding Association founded in 1923 and based in Vechta has made a name for itself as the main lobby, representing all renowned breeders in the region. Roughly 4,500 foals are born here every year. Their first public appearance is at the branding events between mid-April and the end of July, when the next generation with pedigree certificate receives its brand mark and microchip.

Auctions are held four times a year in Vechta, bringing together experts, breeders and buyers. Highly talented Oldenburger show jumping and dressage horses are featured at the Elite Auctions in early April and early October. The summer and winter Mixed Sales include both top sport horses and also less highly priced ones. At the Elite Auction in spring 2021, 31 riding horses generated turnover of around 1.5 million Euro. Half of the animals went abroad.

The auctions are highly professional. They always begin with a health check to minimise the risk. The X-rays and vet's certificates can be seen by potential buyers. Furthermore, they can view and ride their favourites during a training session, followed immediately by the bidding contest, either on the spot or by phone.

Höhepunkte sind natürlich die beiden Olympiateilnahmen 2012 und 2016. „Als ich für die Spiele in London nominiert wurde, war ich erst 25. Das ging alles so schnell, dass ich es gar nicht richtig realisieren konnte." Macht nichts, denn mit ihren Kolleginnen Dorothee Schneider und Helen Langehanenberg belegt sie in der Teamwertung überraschend Rang 2. Silber! Vier Jahre später geht es – erneut mit Desperados – nach Brasilien. In Rio gewinnt Kristina Bröring-Sprehe mit der Mannschaft sogar Gold. Als Zugabe kommt in der Einzelwertung noch Bronze für den dritten Platz hinzu. Der olympische Medaillensatz ist komplett.

Höhen und Tiefen im Wechsel

Und jetzt? Eigentlich würde nun ein neuer Vierjahreszyklus mit dem Ziel Olympia in Tokio beginnen. Manchmal jedoch macht das Leben den Plänen einen Strich durch die Rechnung. Und so verschieben sich in Dinklage die Prioritäten.

Bereits im Sommer 2015 hatte Kristina ihre Jugendliebe Christian Bröring geheiratet – eingebettet zwischen Turnierterminen und den Schulferien des Lehrers. Die Boulevardpresse war entzückt, zeigte ausgiebige Fotostrecken von der „Traumhochzeit". Im Sommer 2019 wird Töchterchen Mila geboren. Und die, so betont die Mutter, „soll nicht zu kurz kommen". Sie legt – so gut es ihre Leidenschaft zulässt – eine Babypause ein. Dass Mila ein echtes Pferdemädchen wird, versteht sich von selbst. Inzwischen hat sie bereits das eine oder andere Mal auf dem Pony gesessen und dabei Spaß gehabt, berichtet ihre Mutter schmunzelnd.

Bei ihren Ambitionen, so bald wie möglich wieder ins Dressurviereck zurückzukehren, findet sie große Unterstützung in der Familie. „So kann ich mich morgens um meine Pferde kümmern, ab Mittag zählt dann nur noch Mila." Das Konzept geht auf. Anfang 2020 steht Kristina Bröring-Sprehes Name erstmals wieder in den Teilnehmerlisten von Turnieren.

Ihr Comeback in Münster bestreitet sie mit dem Desperados-Sohn Destiny. Von Westfalen geht es weiter nach Schleswig-Holstein. In Neumünster gewinnt sie ihren ersten Grand Prix nach dem Neustart. Doch in die Freude platzt die Nachricht vom Tod ihres Herzenspferdes. Die Reiterin ist geschockt. „Gerade erst hatten wir uns entschieden, ihn wegen seines Alters und seiner tollen Erfolge in Rente zu schicken, aber er hatte ja noch nicht mal seinen Abschied von der sportlichen Bühne gefeiert", sagt sie später. „Dass Desperados während des Sieges seines Sohnes starb, fühlt sich für mich rückblickend so an, als hätte er darauf gewartet, seinem Sohn nun das Zepter zu überlassen."

Fernziel: Olympia 2024 in Paris

Und die Hiobsbotschaften nehmen kein Ende. 2020 hält noch eine weitere Prüfung bereit: Corona. Die Pandemie bringt die Turnierserien zum Erliegen. Für Kristina Bröring-Sprehe und ihr Team stellen sich plötzlich ganz neue Fragen: Wie halten wir unsere Pferde fit? Wie dosieren wir das Training? Wie lassen sich Leistungen einschätzen, wenn es keine Wettkämpfe gibt? Das Problem: „Dressurpferde brauchen

ter, she goes to the 2016 Olympic Games in Brazil, again with Desperados. In Rio, Kristina Bröring-Sprehe wins the gold medal in the team competition, together with a bronze medal for third place in the individual competition. Her set of Olympic medals is thus complete.

Alternating ups and downs

And now? Normally this kind of achievement would be followed by a new four-year cycle aiming for the Olympic Games in Tokyo. But sometimes life puts a spoke in the wheel of the best-laid plans. And so there's a change of priorities in Dinklage.

Back in summer 2015, Christina had married her childhood sweetheart Christian Bröring, squeezed in between equestrian events and the teacher's school holidays. The tabloids loved it and showed lots of pictures of the "dream wedding". Daughter Mila was born in summer 2019. Wanting to have plenty of time with her baby, the young mother took a break from equestrian sport, as far as her passion would allow. It goes without saying that Mila will also grow up with horses. Meanwhile she's already sat on her pony a few times and "just loves it", reports her mother with a grin.

The family is right behind her ambition to get back to the dressage arena as soon as possible. "I spend the morning looking after my horses, then from lunch onwards I devote my time to Mila." The concept is working. Early 2020 sees Kristina Bröring-Sprehe's name back on the lists of contestants at equestrian events.

For her comeback in Münster she rides Desperado's son Destiny. From Westphalia then on to Schleswig-Holstein. In Neumünster she wins her first Grand Prix since returning to the sport. But her joy is overshadowed by the news that her favourite horse has died. The rider is shocked. "We'd only just decided to retire him due to his age and all his great achievements, but he hadn't even celebrated his departure from the sporting stage", she says later. "Looking back, the fact that Desperados died while his son was winning shows me that he was waiting to hand the baton over to his son."

Long-term goal 2024 Olympic Games in Paris

And the bad news just keeps on coming. 2020 has another trial just round the corner: Corona. The pandemic brings the equestrian season to a halt. Kristina Bröring-Sprehe and her team are suddenly confronted by a whole number of new questions: How can we keep our horses fit? How should we quantify the training? How can we assess performance levels when there are no contests? The problem: "Dressage horses need routine, particularly the young ones." Furthermore, in the early stages it is not at all clear how the sponsors will react when there are no public appearances. Bröring-Sprehe is a professional: equestrian sport is her livelihood. As a former business administration student, she knows exactly what happens when there's no income.

Mit ihrem Pferd „Desperados"
nahm Kristina Bröring-Sprehe u.
a. an den Olympischen Spielen in
Rio de Janeiro teil und wurde dort
Olympiasiegerin mit der Mannschaft.
Im Einzelwettbewerb gewann sie
zudem die Bronzemedaille.

With her horse „Desperados",
Kristina Bröring-Sprehe competed
among others at the Olympic Games
in Rio de Janeiro winning the gold
medal in the team competition.
She also won the bronze medal in
the individual event.

Routine, gerade die jungen." Zudem ist zunächst auch unklar, wie die Sponsoren reagieren, wenn es keine Auftritte gibt. Bröring-Sprehe ist Profi, sie lebt vom Pferdesport. Als ehemalige BWL-Studentin weiß sie genau, was passiert, wenn die Einnahmen ausbleiben.

Einige Monate später hat sich die Situation beruhigt. Die Förderer haben zu ihr gehalten, der Hausbau in Dinklage wurde erfolgreich beendet. „Ich bin jetzt wieder richtig motiviert", stellt die inzwischen 34-Jährige klar. Ihr großer Hoffnungsträger ist Destiny, der immer besser wird. „Wir sind noch lange nicht am Limit", weiß sie. Mit ihm will sie wieder die Spitze angreifen, es zurück in den A-Kader und zu den internationalen Championaten schaffen. Fernziel sind die Olympischen Spiele 2024 in Paris. Sprintkönig Usain Bolt hat längst abgedankt, Kristina Bröring-Sprehe will dann wieder dabei sein. Zum dritter Mal.

A few months later the situation has calmed down a bit. The sponsors have stood by her, and the construction work on her house in Dinklage has been finished. "I'm now really motivated again", says the meanwhile 34-year-old rider. She places all her hopes in Destiny, who is getting better all the time. "We've still not reached our limit", she says. With Destiny, she wants to aim for the top again, back in the A-squad and back to the international championships. Her long-term goal is to take part in the 2024 Olympic Games in Paris. Sprint king Usain Bolt has long since retired, but, Kristina Bröring-Sprehe wants to be back there again. For the third time.

ZWEI DOPPELTE CHEFS

Two Double Bosses

HERMANN SCHÜLLER

STEFAN NIEMEYER

INTERVIEW:
TORBEN ROSENBOHM

Der eine hat seinen Unternehmenssitz in Westerstede, der andere in Essen/Oldb. Über ihre Rolle als Firmenchefs hinaus verbindet sie ihr Engagement im Sport – Hermann Schüller leitet die Geschicke bei den EWE Baskets Oldenburg, Stefan Niemeyer bei RASTA Vechta. Beide äußern sich im Doppelinterview zum Zusammenwirken von Wirtschaft und Sport.

One runs a company in Westerstede, the other in Essen/Oldb. Going beyond their standing in business, they also share a commitment to sport: Hermann Schüller is in charge at EWE Baskets Oldenburg, Stefan Niemeyer at RASTA Vechta. During the following double interview they both speak about how business and sport interact.

Herr Schüller und Herr Niemeyer, Sie sind beide sehr erfolgreiche und vielbeschäftigte Unternehmer. Doch damit nicht genug: Sie sind auch noch Geschäftsführer jeweils eines Basketball-Bundesligisten. Warum tun Sie sich das an?

Hermann Schüller: (lacht) Ich antworte einfach mal zuerst, ich bin ja mit dem Basketball-Engagement etwas eher als Stefan gestartet, 1995 war das. Ab 1977 habe ich zunächst einmal das Unternehmen aufgebaut. Später kam dann die Überlegung, was ich mir suche, um mich zusätzlich in der Gesellschaft zu verantworten. Man macht dann in der Regel das, was einem sehr liegt – und ich war schon immer leidenschaftlicher Basketballer. Mit dem Zusammenschluss der Basketballabteilungen der TSG Westerstede und des Oldenburger TB haben wir den Grundstein gelegt. Wir haben gesehen, dass man damit gute Chancen hat. Ich wollte etwas bewegen, den Standort attraktiver machen und den Menschen etwas anbieten.

Stefan Niemeyer: Als Unternehmer habe ich 1989 begonnen, darüber hinaus bin ich nun aber auch schon im 30. Jahr Vorsitzender des Vereins SC RASTA Vechta e. V. Ich habe selbst Basketball gespielt, wenngleich nicht auf Bundesliga-Niveau wie Hermann. Es ist doch so: Wenn man Unternehmer ist, dann unternimmt man was – man schaut, was zu erreichen möglich ist. So war es für mich bei RASTA immer und so ist es bis heute. Ich hatte das große Glück, ein erfolgreicher Unternehmer zu sein, daher waren die Mittel, um Basketball nachhaltig zu fördern, auch entsprechend vorhanden. Ich behaupte keinesfalls, von Anfang an das Ziel gehabt zu haben, einmal in der Bundesliga zu landen. Das ist auch ganz vielen Zufällen geschuldet, so ehrlich müssen wir sein. Stadt und Region haben voll mitgezogen, auch die Politik war von Beginn an im Boot. Ein echtes Zusammenspiel aller Kräfte. Daher ist es keine Frage: Ich tue mir das nach wie vor sehr gerne an.

Vergleichbare Werte bei Sport und Wirtschaft

Was nehmen Sie nach diesen vielen Jahren in der Wirtschaft und im Sport aus dem jeweils einen Bereich in den anderen mit?

Schüller: Dass grundlegende Abläufe ähnlich sind, wurde lange vermutet. Ich nenne ein Beispiel: Als wir uns 2015 von unserem Trainer Sebastian Machowski trennen mussten, fiel unsere Wahl auf Mladen Drijencic. Er war damals im Profigeschäft ein unbeschriebenes Blatt, war im Nachwuchs tätig und hat dort die Jungs begeistert. Erst herrschte Skepsis, aber dann hat er alle überzeugt. Mit seiner intuitiven Art hat er eine besondere, werteorientierte Teamkultur eingeführt. Daraus haben wir ein Programm entwickelt, das wir in die Unternehmen tragen. Denn das Fundament in der Wirtschaft ist das gleiche wie im Sport: Wie geht man miteinander um? Genau dort steckt das Potenzial, um sich weiterzuentwickeln.

Niemeyer: Da kann ich nur beipflichten. Das Unternehmen RASTA Vechta, und genau so muss man die Profiabteilung nennen, funktioniert ähnlich wie ein reguläres Unternehmen. Es geht um vergleichbare Werte, aber auch Störfaktoren. Das ist nicht immer einfach, das auch entsprechend zu vermitteln. Und es kommt ja noch eine Besonderheit hinzu: Im Profibereich muss man auch schon mal die Richtung ganz klar vorgeben, das geht in einer klassischen Vereinsstruktur natürlich nicht. Am Ende geht es aber um Teamarbeit. Und da ist es auch wichtig, dass beispielsweise der Trainer nicht der Alleinentscheider ist.

Spiele zwischen den EWE Baskets und RASTA Vechta haben stets eine besondere Atmosphäre.

Matches between EWE Baskets and RASTA Vechta always have a special atmosphere.

Aus der Region für die Region: Hermann Schüller und Stefan Niemeyer

Sie sind Geschäftsführer erfolgreicher Wirtschaftsunternehmen in der Region und darüber hinaus im Spitzenbasketball engagiert: Hermann Schüller und Stefan Niemeyer. Tief im Norden verwurzelt, ist es beiden eine Herzensangelegenheit, nicht nur ihre Unternehmen voranzubringen, sondern auch Bundesligabasketball im Nordwesten kontinuierlich zu stärken.

Der Westersteder Unternehmer Hermann Schüller, der einst selbst in der Bundesliga auf Körbejagd ging, ist geschäftsführender Gesellschafter der Semcoglas-Gruppe, die 1997 durch den Zusammenschluss der beiden Unternehmen Schüller Qualitätsglas aus Westerstede und der Isoglas-Gruppe aus Nordhorn entstand. Im Mittelpunkt stehen Flachglaserzeugung und -veredelung. Der Stammsitz ist in Westerstede, inzwischen gibt es insgesamt 19 Standorte.

Hermann Schüller ist darüber hinaus geschäftsführender Gesellschafter des Basketball-Bundesligisten EWE Baskets Oldenburg. Der Club stieg im Jahr 2000, damals noch als Oldenburger Turnerbund, in die erste Liga auf, wurde 2009 Deutscher Meister und 2015 Deutscher Pokalsieger. Seit 2001 gehen die Oldenburger Basketballer in der deutschen Eliteklasse als EWE Baskets an den Start.

Südlich von Oldenburg zu Hause ist das Unternehmen Miavit. Stefan Niemeyer ist Geschäftsführer des Spezialisten für Futtermittel, Zusatzstoffe, Mineralstoffe und Vitamine. Das Unternehmen wurde 1964 gegründet und liefert seine Produkte inzwischen weltweit in über 80 Länder.

Ebenso wie Hermann Schüller engagiert sich auch Stefan Niemeyer ehrenamtlich im Basketball. Als Vorsitzender des Gesamtvereins SC RASTA Vechta e. V. und Geschäftsführer der Profibasketballer von RASTA hat er sich weit über die Grenzen Vechtas hinaus einen Namen gemacht. Vechta stieg 2018 zum dritten Mal in die Basketball-Bundesliga auf und kämpfte in der durch die Corona-Einschränkungen beeinflussten Saison um den Klassenerhalt.

From the region for the region:
Hermann Schüller and Stefan Niemeyer

They run successful business companies in the region and are also committed to top-class basketball: Hermann Schüller and Stefan Niemeyer. Firmly rooted in the North, they are both dedicated not only to driving their companies forward but also to constantly reinforcing Bundesliga basketball in the North West.

Hermann Schüller is a businessman from Westerstede who used to play basketball in the Bundesliga himself. He is a managing partner of the Semcoglas Group which emerged in 1997 following the merge of Schüller Qualitätsglas from Westerstede and the Isoglas Group from Nordhorn. The company focuses on producing and processing flat glass. Headquarters are in Westerstede. The company meanwhile has 19 sites altogether.

Hermann Schüller is also managing partner of the Bundesliga basketball club EWE Baskets Oldenburg. The club was promoted to the top league back in 2000, in those days still as known as Oldenburger Turnerbund, winning the German league championships in 2009 and the German cup competition in 2015. Since 2001, the basketball team from Oldenburg competes in Germany's elite basketball league as EWE Baskets.

Miavit is a business company that is based to the south of Oldenburg. Stefan Niemeyer is the CEO of this firm that specialises in animal nutrition, additives, minerals and vitamins. Founded in 1964, the company meanwhile exports its products to more than 80 countries worldwide.

Just like Hermann Schüller, Stefan Niemeyer is also committed to basketball. As chair of the overall club SC RASTA Vechta e.V. and CEO of RASTA's professional basketball team, he has made a name for himself way beyond Vechta itself. In 2018, Vechta was promoted to the basketball Bundesliga for the third time and has struggled to avoid relegation amidst all the corona restrictions impacting on the last season.

Mr Schüller, Mr Niemeyer, you are both very successful, very busy entrepreneurs. But there's more too: You also each run a basketball team in the German Bundesliga. Why do you do this to yourselves?

Hermann Schüller: (laughs) I'll go first: after all, I've been involved with basketball a bit longer than Stefan, dating back to 1995. I started setting up my business in 1977. Later on, I started thinking about what I could do to take on additional responsibility in society. People usually choose something close to their own hearts, and I have always loved basketball. The foundations were set by merging the basketball departments of the two sports clubs TSG Westerstede and Oldenburger TB. We saw that this offered a good opportunity. I wanted to do something to make the town more attractive and to offer people something.

Stefan Niemeyer: I started as an entrepreneur in 1989. But this is also the 30th year in which I have chaired the sports club RASTA Vechta e. V. I used to play basketball myself, although not on Bundesliga level like Hermann. It's like this: when you're an entrepreneur, you undertake something, you look to see what can be achieved. It's always been like that for me with RASTA, and it still is to this day. I had the great fortune to be a successful entrepreneur and had the necessary resources available to promote basketball in the long term. I'm not saying it was my ambition right from the start to end up in the Bundesliga. Many coincidences have contributed to this achievement, to be honest. The town and the region got right behind us, and the political sector was also involved from the start. You can really say everyone pulled together.

So it's not really an issue: I'm happy to continue doing this!

Similar values in sport and business

After so many years in business and in sport, which aspects of the one help you in the other?

Schüller: It has long been presumed that the basic procedures are similar. For example, when we had to take leave of our coach Sebastian Machowski in 2015, we chose Mladen Drijencic as his successor. Back then, he was an unknown quantity on a professional level. He'd been working with youth teams and generating a lot of enthusiasm. At first people were sceptical, but then he convinced them all. His intuitive approach has resulted in a special, value-oriented team culture. We took this to develop a programme which we have also used in the companies. After all, the foundations of business are the same as in sport: it's a case of how we deal with each other. That is exactly where we find the potential for further development.

Niemeyer: I agree. You have to view a professional team like RASTA Vechta as a company, functioning on the same lines as a proper business. Values are similar, as are the disruptive aspects. It's not always easy to convey this accordingly. There's another thing too: in professional sport, you have to dictate the course quite clearly, something you naturally don't get in the traditional club structure. But in the end, it's all about working as a team. In this context in particular, it's also important that the coach is not the only one to make the decisions.

But what makes sport and business differ is probably the emotional component. In the life of a company, you'll scarcely have an equivalent to a home win against Bayern.

Schüller: Well actually, business also has its special moments. Getting a great project off the ground or bringing it to a successful conclusion is also really special. But winning against FC Bayern does make you live that little bit longer, I must admit. A game like our recent one against Vechta – now that would have put years on me if we'd lost. (laughs)

Was die beiden Bereiche aber unterscheiden dürfte, das ist die emotionale Komponente. Für einen Heimsieg gegen Bayern gibt es im Unternehmen wohl kaum ein Äquivalent.
Schüller: Es gibt auch dort ganz besondere Momente. Wenn man ein tolles Projekt auf den Weg oder zum Abschluss gebracht hat, dann ist das auch etwas ganz Besonderes. Aber ein Sieg gegen den FC Bayern verlängert das Leben, das gebe ich zu. Ein Spiel wie neulich gegen Vechta wiederum – wenn wir das verloren hätten, wäre ich um Jahre gealtert. (lacht)
Niemeyer: Bei dem Spiel hätte uns eine volle Halle vermutlich geholfen. Das ist aus Sicht des Basketballs das größte Problem der Corona-Krise: die fehlenden Zuschauer. Als wir mal gegen Braunschweig im letzten Viertel mit 27 Punkten zurückgelegen und doch noch gewonnen haben, waren die Fans mitentscheidend. Da saß man minutenlang glücklich, aber vollkommen mitgenommen auf der Tribüne.

Weiteres Wachstumspotenzial vorhanden

Ihre persönlichen Gründe für Ihren leidenschaftlichen Einsatz für den Basketball kennen wir nun. Was aber treibt grundsätzlich Unternehmen an, sich als Sponsoringpartner zu engagieren?
Schüller: Das Thema Sponsoring ist sehr anspruchsvoll; nicht zuletzt, weil der Name aus meiner Sicht irritierend ist. Eigentlich ist das für die Unternehmen ein konkretes Instrument für das Marketing. Das wird unterschätzt, und daher gehört der Begriff Sponsoring getilgt. Wenn das ganze Thema in den Unternehmen im Marketing verankert wird, dann verschwindet es auch nicht so schnell von der Bildfläche. Sponsoring steht schnell oben auf der Streichliste, weil es mit Spenden und Mäzenatentum verbunden und oft direkt unter Compliance-Gesichtspunkten behandelt wird. Dabei bietet sich hier die Chance, den Markenkern des Unternehmens zu stärken. Auch der Standort gewinnt durch ein solches Engagement an Attraktivität, und es entsteht ein hohes Maß an Identität. Ich wünsche mir daher auch, dass es weiterhin zwei Bundesliga-Clubs in der Region gibt; auch, um den Clubs im Süden zu zeigen: Hier im Nordwesten passiert viel!

Gibt es eine Wachstumsgrenze für den Basketball in Deutschland? Ist sie möglicherweise schon erreicht?
Niemeyer: Die Grundfrage dahinter ist: Wie wichtig ist das alles für die Unternehmen? Im gehobenen Mittelstand gibt es sehr starke Kräfte in der Region. Und wenn man sich den Landkreis Vechta und den Südkreis Cloppenburg anschaut, muss man konstatieren: Das ist eine reiche Region. Es lässt sich sehr gut leben, zu noch akzeptablen Kosten. Und die Unternehmen müssen sich vor diesem Hintergrund fragen: Was mache ich, um die Region weiterhin attraktiv zu gestalten? Da viele die Chance noch nicht nutzen, sehe ich auch weiterhin Wachstumspotenzial.

Was macht den hiesigen Wirtschaftsraum besonders?
Schüller: Ich bin zwischendurch ja auch mal woanders gewesen und gerne zurückgekommen. Hier herrscht eine besondere Kultur. Die Menschen sind untereinander sehr verlässlich, kommunizieren offen und sind bereit, leidenschaftlich und diszipliniert zu arbeiten. Hinzu kommt eine hohe Innovationskraft, ein gutes Beispiel dafür ist das Unternehmen EWE. Hier finden Menschen zusammen, um gemeinsam etwas zu erreichen. Das war schon 1995 so, als wir im Basketball mit Westerstede und Oldenburg gezeigt haben, dass man aus eins und eins drei machen kann.

Niemeyer: It would have probably helped if we'd had a full crowd behind us. As far as basketball is concerned, that's the biggest problem with the corona crisis: the lack of spectators. When we were 27 points down against Braunschweig in the last quarter and still managed to win, it was all thanks to the fans. We remained in our seats for minutes afterwards, happy but completely exhausted.

Further potential for growth

We now know your personal reasons why you are so passionately committed to basketball. But why do companies generally take on sponsoring commitments?
Schüller: Sponsoring is quite challenging, also because I think the name is misleading. Actually, as far as the company is concerned, sponsoring is a specific marketing instrument. This tends to be underrated, which is why the word sponsoring should be done away with. When this whole aspect is firmly anchored in a company's marketing activities, you're less likely to lose sight of it. Sponsoring is very quickly one of the first things to get crossed off the list because it is associated with donations and patronage and is often treated directly in terms of compliance. And yet it offers an opportunity for reinforcing the brand essence of a company. Commitment of this kind also enhances the appeal of a place in general, giving it a greater sense of identity. And so I hope that we will continue to have two Bundesliga basketball clubs in the region, also to show those in the South that there's plenty going on up here in the North West!

Does basketball in Germany have a growth limit? Has it possibly already been reached?
Niemeyer: The basic question is: how important is all this for the companies? There are many strong forces in the region's upper SME sector. When you look at the districts of Vechta and Cloppenburg, you'll see that this is a rich region. Life is very good here, while the costs of living remain on an acceptable level. In this context, the question for the companies is this: what can I do to keep the region attractive? The fact that many still don't use this opportunity means that I still see further potential for growth.

What makes this economic region so special?
Schüller: I've lived elsewhere in the meantime and was happy to come back again. We have a special culture here. The people know they can rely on each other, they are prepared to say what they think and are willing to work with passion and discipline. It's also a highly innovative region, just look at EWE for example. It's a place where people come and work together to achieve something. It was like that already back in 1995 when we pooled our basketball resources in Westerstede and Oldenburg, showing that one plus one makes three, sometimes at least.

Sport for integration

The future generation is important for both business and sport. How do you deal with this, particularly also in terms of the skills shortage?
Niemeyer: We have five full-time coaches for young basketball players. We feel it's very important to be active on an amateur level as well with the professional teams. Various signs suggest that this is being successful: you can see an increasing number of basketball hoops in people's gardens, we have several national youth players in various age groups, and players that we have promoted such as Philipp Herkenhoff

Sport als Instrument zur Integration

Das Thema Nachwuchs spielt sowohl in der Wirtschaft als auch im Sport eine große Rolle. Wie gehen Sie damit um, speziell auch mit dem Fachkräftemangel?

Niemeyer: Wir beschäftigen fünf Vollzeittrainer für junge Basketballer. Es ist uns wichtig, auch in der Breite aktiv zu sein. Und die Erfolge sind an verschiedenen Stellen sichtbar: Die Anzahl der Basketballkörbe auf den Grundstücken steigt, wir haben mehrere Jugendnationalspieler verschiedener Altersklassen und bei uns geförderte Spieler wie Philipp Herkenhoff oder Luc van Slooten spielen in der Bundesliga. Im Unternehmen sind wir sehr international aufgestellt, haben Mitarbeiter aus 30 Nationen. Und wir brauchen auch in der Produktion gute Kräfte, die zu finden nicht leichter geworden ist.

Schüller: Bei den Baskets haben wir das Engagement im Breitensport schrittweise ausgebaut, nicht zuletzt auch mit der Errichtung von Streetball-Courts. In Zukunft wollen wir auch in die Kitas gehen, um auch die ganz Kleinen zu erreichen. Und im Unternehmen verzeichnen auch wir einen Fachkräftemangel, daher rekrutieren wir international. Wir haben Menschen aus 48 Nationen – auch vor diesem Hintergrund ist der Sport und insbesondere Basketball ein wunderbares Mittel, um Integration voranzubringen.

Und wie lange machen Sie beide noch weiter?

Schüller: (lacht) Eine vollkommen überflüssige Frage! Ich kenne 50-Jährige, die wirken älter als 70. Und es gibt Menschen, die sind in meinem Alter und wollen aufhören. Entscheidend ist doch: Wie ist der Anspruch an sich selbst? Wer sich jung fühlt, Anspruch an Innovation und Kreativität hat, sollte keinen Grund haben, sich zurückzuziehen. Daher mache ich das bei den Baskets gerne weiter. Im Unternehmen ist das etwas anderes; da ist der Verbrauch um ein Vielfaches höher. Auch wenn ich den Werkstoff Glas liebe, so hält die Auseinandersetzung damit nicht ganz so jung wie der Bereich Basketball.

Niemeyer: Ich habe das große Glück, im Unternehmen bereits einen Sohn sitzen zu haben. Und im Basketball haben wir uns als Familie für 20 Jahre verpflichtet. Das fällt umso leichter, wenn wir alle Spaß daran haben. Ob es dann später einmal einer für mich fortführen wird? Das weiß ich nicht, aber aktuell bereitet mir das alles noch große Freude. Ich gebe aber auch zu, um auch noch einmal auf den Beginn unseres Gesprächs zurückzukehren: In der Tat frage ich mich gelegentlich schon, warum ich mir das alles antue. Insbesondere dann, wenn es sportlich mal nicht so läuft, muss man sich doch einiges anhören, gerade in den sozialen Medien. Das muss man ausblenden.

Vielen Dank für das Gespräch.

or Luc van Slooten are now playing in the Bundesliga. In the company, we have a very international workforce with employees from 30 different countries. And on the production lines we really need good workers, and these are no longer so easy to find.

Schüller: We have gradually expanded our commitment to basketball on the grassroots level, including setting up streetball courts, among others. In future we also want to start going into the kindergartens to reach the very young ones. In the company, we too are facing a skills shortage which is why our recruitment activities are geared to the international market. We employ people from 48 countries. In this context too, sport in general and basketball in particular is a wonderful means of promoting integration.

And how long will you both be carrying on?

Schüller: (laughs) What a superfluous question! I know 50-year-olds who seem to be older than 70. And some people want to stop when they reach my age. What really matters is what are your own aspirations? If you feel young and still have aspirations in terms of innovation and creativity, you shouldn't have any reason to stop. That's certainly my intention as far as basketball is concerned. Things are a bit different in the company, where there's a lot more wear-and-tear. Even if I love working with glass, the challenges involved don't keep me quite as young as basketball does.

Niemeyer: I am very lucky in that I already have a son firmly established in the company. And as far as basketball is concerned, we as a family have made a commitment for 20 years. The fact that we all have such fun makes it much easier. Will there be someone there in future to take over from me and carry on? I don't know: at the moment, it all still brings me a lot of pleasure. But I must admit, to return to what we talked about at the beginning: actually, now and then I sometimes wonder why I do this to myself. Particularly when the sporting achievements leave much to be desired and there's such a negative feedback, particularly in the social media. You just have to tune it out.

Many thanks for the interview.

INSERENTENVERZEICHNIS
List of Advertisements

BILDQUELLEN
Picture Sources

Bodo Nussdorfer, Bielefeld: S. 6, 7, 12, 14, 15 u. r., 18, 19, 24, 25, 30–32, 34, 42, 44, 45, 53–55, 62, 63, 69 o., 70, 71 u., 72, 73, 78 u., 82, 83, 89–91, 96 u., 97, 99, 108 u., 112 o., 114 u., 124 u., 125–129, 134–137, 142–147, 152, 153, 159–161, 168 u., 169–171, 176, 177, 182, 184–187, 192, 193, 198, 199.

Titel/title:	PhotoArt/stockAdobe.com
Seite/page 8/9:	Pascal Mühlhausen, Oldenburg
Seite/page 11:	Sebastian Vollmert, Hamburg
Seite/page 13 o.:	Fidenti Personal GmbH, Oldenburg
Seite/page 13 u.:	© ExxonMobil, Dirk Meußling
Seite/page 15 o.:	Christin Linke, Oldenburg
Seite/page 15 u. l.:	Agentur Kehrer, Oldenburg
Seite/page 16:	Mario Dirks, Oldenburg
Seite/page 17:	Steffen Löffler, Fulda
Seite/page 20/21:	Contentley Media, Oldenburg
Seite/page 23:	Hallerstede Lederwaren
Seite/page 26-29:	Strudthoff, Delmenhorst
Seite/page 33:	LemonOne GmbH, Berlin
Seite/page 35 o.:	ray facility management group / Nils Bogdol GmbH
Seite/page 35 u.:	Berno Buff, Bundesinnungsverband der Gebäudedienstleister
Seite/page 36-41:	Big Dutchman AG, Vechta
Seite/page 46-49:	Urban GmbH & Co. KG, Hude
Seite/page 50:	MIAVIT GmbH, Essen (Oldb.)
Seite/page 51 o.:	CAM Energy GmbH, Essen (Oldb.)
Seite/page 51 u.:	Natascha/stockAdobe.com
Seite/page 52:	Thorsten Ritzmann, Oldenburg
Seite/page 56-59:	James Wright (privat)
Seite/page 60:	Moritz Knöringer/unsplash.com
Seite/page 61:	Sound & Picturedesign, Oldenburg
Seite/page 64/65:	Timo Lutz, Werbefotografie
Seite/page 67:	Brand Qualitätsfleisch GmbH & Co. KG, Lohne
Seite/page 68:	Sigrun Strangmann, Hatten
Seite/page 69 u.:	Emsland Food GmbH, Cloppenburg
Seite/page 71 o.:	M FOOD GROUP® GmbH, Steinfeld-Mühlen
Seite/page 74-78 o.:	Abeking & Rasmussen – Schiffs- und Yachtwerft SE, Lemwerder
Seite/page 79:	Fr. Lürssen Werft GmbH & Co. KG, Bremen
Seite/page 80, 81:	MTZW Maritimes Trainingszentrum Wesermarsch GmbH, Elsfleth
Seite/page 84-87:	BOGE Rubber & Plastics, Damme
Seite/page 88:	KRONOS TITAN GmbH, Werk Nordenham
Seite/page 92, 93:	Sealpac GmbH, Oldenburg
Seite/page 94 o.:	Foto Scheiwe, Augustfehn
Seite/page 94 u.:	Stahlwerk Augustfehn Schmiede GmbH & Co. KG, Apen
Seite/page 95 o.:	Michael Helweg

Seite/page 95 u.:	c-Port cargo und Industrie am Küstenkanal, Saterland/Sedelsberg
Seite/page 96 o.:	Nietiedt-Gruppe
Seite/page 98 o.:	W. Produktion/stockAdobe.com
Seite/page 98 u.:	Fritz Spieker GmbH & Co. KG, Oldenburg
Seite/page 100, 101:	DYNAPAC GmbH, Wardenburg
Seite/page 102-107:	Barbara Haskamp (privat)
Seite/page 108 o. u. Mitte:	HASKAMP GmbH & Co. KG, Edewecht
Seite/page 109:	JOWO-Systemtechnik AG, Delmenhorst
Seite/page 110/111:	NKT GmbH, Nordenham
Seite/page 112 u.:	HAWART Sondermaschinenbau GmbH
Seite/page 113:	Hartgen GmbH Maschinen- und Mühlenbau, Hude
Seite/page 114 o.:	Bilfinger Engineering & Maintenance GmbH, Cloppenburg
Seite/page 115 o.:	Erich Stallkamp ESTA GmbH, Dinklage
Seite/page 115 u.:	Foto Hölzen, Bersenbrück
Seite/page 116, 117:	Bilderwerk Oldenburg
Seite/page 118, 119:	Stockwerk2 – Agentur für Kommunikation GmbH, Oldenburg
Seite/page 121:	Vogelsänger Studios
Seite/page 122, 123:	Kalkhoff Bikes / Derby Cycle Werke GmbH, Cloppenburg
Seite/page 124 o.:	Malik Pahlmann, Osnabrück
Seite/page 131:	TGO Technologie- und Gründerzentrum Oldenburg
Seite/page 133:	GO! Start-up Zentrum
Seite/page 134:	Lukas Lehmann/www.lukaslehmann.de
Seite/page 138/139:	fotomek/stockAdobe.com
Seite/page 141:	OmniBot
Seite/page 143 o.:	Bilderwerk Oldenburg
Seite/page 143 u.:	Roland Schiffler, Bremen
Seite/page 144:	Voss Schnitger Steenken Bünger & Partner PartG mbB, Oldenburg
Seite/page 148-151:	Gut Altona, Dötlingen
Seite/page 154-157:	Rehazentrum Oldenburg
Seite/page 158:	Nikolai Wolff, Fotoetage Bremen
Seite/page 162-165:	Die Nordsee GmbH
Seite/page 166 o.:	OOWV Oldenburg-Ostfriesischer Wasserverband, Brake
Seite/page 166 u.:	Tobias/stockAdobe.com
Seite/page 167:	ARGE Jade-Wapeler Siel
Seite/page 168 o.:	Tristan Vankann, Fotoetage Bremen
Seite/page 172-175:	Prof. Dr. Nick Lin-Hi (privat)
Seite/page 178-181:	OFFIS Institut
Seite/page 183:	IBS IT & Business School Oldenburg e. V., Oldenburg
Seite/page 189, 191:	Theater Laboratorium
Seite/page 194-197:	Sportfotos Lafrentz
Seite/page 200/201:	EWE Baskets
Seite/page 203:	RASTA Vechta